AN ECONOMIC HISTORY
OF AFRICA
FROM THE EARLIEST TIMES
TO PARTITION

P. L. WICKINS

1981
OXFORD UNIVERSITY PRESS
CAPE TOWN

Oxford University Press

OXFORD   LONDON   GLASGOW
NEW YORK   TORONTO   MELBOURNE   WELLINGTON
NAIROBI   DAR ES SALAAM   CAPE TOWN
KUALA LUMPUR   SINGAPORE   HONG KONG   TOKYO
DELHI   BOMBAY   CALCUTTA   MADRAS   KARACHI

ISBN 0 19 570192 5

Printed and bound by Citadel Press, Lansdowne, Cape
Published by Oxford University Press, Harrington House,
Barrack Street, Cape Town 8001, South Africa

CONTENTS

PREFACE 1

INTRODUCTION
  i) *Internal developments* 3
  ii) *External influences* 6
  iii) *Arab conquests* 9
  iv) *The coming of the Europeans* 13
  v) *The partition of Africa* 17

I. AGRICULTURE
  1. THE BEGINNINGS
    i) *Egypt* 21
    ii) *Independent domestication in sub-Saharan Africa* 24
    iii) *Exotic crops and animals* 28
  2. THE METHODS
    i) *Nomadism and shifting cultivation* 32
    ii) *Permanent cultivation in northern Africa* 36
    iii) *Permanent cultivation in sub-Saharan Africa* 41
  3. LAND, POPULATION AND LABOUR
    i) *Land laws and customs* 47
    ii) *Population* 51
    iii) *Unfree labour in northern Africa* 56
    iv) *Labour problems in sub-Saharan Africa* 60

II. CRAFT INDUSTRY
  1. SCIENCE AND TECHNOLOGY
    i) *Stone* 67
    ii) *Gold and copper* 70
    iii) *The Iron Age* 74
    iv) *Technological achievements* 79
  2. THE CRAFTS
    i) *Metalware, pottery and glass* 84
    ii) *Building* 89
    iii) *Food and clothing* 94
    iv) *Basketry, leather work and woodwork* 100
  3. THE ORGANIZATION OF INDUSTRY
    i) *The ancient world* 105

ii) *Muslim Africa* 109
iii) *Sub-Saharan Africa* 111

III. TRADE

1. THE CONDITIONS OF TRADE
   i) *Markets and merchants* 116
   ii) *Barter, money and credit* 120
   iii) *Transport and communications* 127
2. MEDITERRANEAN AFRICA
   i) *Pre-Roman trade* 131
   ii) *Roman trade* 135
   iii) *Islam and the Mediterranean* 139
   iv) *Egyptian trade with the east and south* 144
   v) *The trans-Saharan trade* 148
3. WEST AFRICA
   i) *The trade of the interior* 154
   ii) *The Portuguese* 158
   iii) *The slave trade* 162
   iv) *The economic consequences of the slave trade* 166
4. EASTERN AND SOUTHERN AFRICA
   i) *The medieval trade of East Africa* 174
   ii) *The Portuguese* 177
   iii) *The slave trade* 180
   iv) *Southern Africa* 185

IV. ECONOMIC SYSTEMS OF ANCIENT AND PRE-PARTITION AFRICA

1. ANCIENT MEDITERRANEAN AFRICA
   i) *Ancient and Hellenistic Egypt* 189
   ii) *Carthage and Rome* 192
   iii) *The ancient city and capitalism* 197
2. MUSLIM AFRICA
   i) *Muslim feudalism* 204
   ii) *Muslim merchants and states* 210
   iii) *Capitalism in Islam* 213
3. SUB-SAHARAN AFRICA
   i) *The economic basis of sub-Saharan states* 220
   ii) *The African state and the economy* 225
   iii) *The 'African mode of production' and feudalism* 230
   iv) *Class and caste* 235
   v) *The capacity for change* 239

4. EUROPE IN AFRICA
  i)   The Portuguese   248
  ii) Other European nations in West Africa   253
  iii) The Dutch and the British at the Cape   257

V. THE INTEGRATION OF AFRICA INTO THE
INTERNATIONAL ECONOMY
  1. AFRICAN ATTEMPTS AT ADJUSTMENT
    i)   Mediterranean Africa   263
    ii) West Africa   267
    iii) East Africa   277
    iv) South Africa   282
    v)   The consequences of integration   285
  2. EUROPEAN INTRUSION
    i)   The coming of the steamship   290
    ii) Partition   294
    iii) Chartered companies and concessions   300
    iv) The economic consequences of conquest   305

MAPS

(Drawn by Mr. K. A. Behr of the Geography Department,
University of Cape Town)

1. Modern Africa – Political   308

2. Elevations above Sea Level in   Africa   309

3. Rainfall   310

4. The Main Vegetation Belts of Africa   311

5. Northern Africa – Historical   312

6. Central and East Africa – Historical   313

ACKNOWLEDGEMENTS

The author gratefully acknowledges the following extracts used in the book.

Alpers, E. A., *Ivory Slaves in East Central Africa, Changing Patterns of International Trade to the Later Nineteenth Century*, in Eugène de Froberville, *Notes sur les Moeurs, Coutumes et Traditions des Amakoua*, in the Bulletin de la Societé de Géographie, 3e série, 8, 1975, p. 10–11. Societé de Géographie, Paris.

Battūta, I., *Travels in Asia and Africa*, pp. 44–5; 50. Routledge & Kegan Paul Ltd., (1929).

Cipolla, C. M., Vol. 1, *The Middle Ages*, from *The Fontana Economic History of Europe*, extracts from pp. 17–18. Fontana Paperbacks (1972).

Curtin, P. D., *The Atlantic Slave Trade, A Census*, p. 265. Madison: The University of Wisconsin Press; © 1969 by the Board of Regents of the Wisconsin System.

Davies, P. N., *Trading in West Africa 1840–1920*, pp. 37–8. Croom Helm Ltd., (1976).

Gregory, J. W., *The Great Rift Valley* in Richards and Place (eds.), World Classics no. 572, p. 272. John Murray (Publishers) Ltd., (1960).

Hayult, R., *Voyages Vol. III*, from Everyman's Library Edition, pp. 121; 124; 169. Dutton and J. M. Dent, London, (1907).

Herskovits, M. J., and Harwitz, M., (eds.), *Economic Transition in Africa*, pp. 86; 95–6. Northwestern University Press, (1964).

Khaldun, I., from Rodison, M., *Islam and Capitalism*, translated by Brian Pearce, (Pelican Books, 1977, pp. 31; 214); reprinted by permission of Penguin Books Ltd., © 1974, and Pantheon Books, a Division of Random House, Inc.

Levizion, N., *Ancient Ghana and Mali*, pp. 141; 165–6. Methuen & Co. Ltd., (1973).

Loeb, J., (ed.), *Herodotus II Book IV*, p. 399. The Loeb Classical Library (Harvard University Press and William Heinemann), (1921).

Marx, K., *Capital I*, pp. 379; 832. George Allen & Unwin Ltd., (1930).

Nicol, D., (ed.), *Africanus Horton, The Dawn of Nationalism in Modern Africa*, pp. 54–5; 51–2; 56. Longman Inc., New York, (1969).

Park, M., *The Travels*. Dutton and J. M. Dent, London, (1954).

Spaarman, A., *A Voyage to the Cape of Good Hope*, p. 239. Edited by V. S. Forbes, translation from the Swedish, revised by J. I. Rudner. Vol. 1, 2nd Series, No. 6. Van Riebeeck Society Publications, (1975). Also reprinted by Johnson Reprint Corporation.

Wilks, I., *Ashante in the Nineteenth Century: The Structure and Evolution of a Political Order*, p. 651. Cambridge University Press, (1975).

PREFACE

The present book seeks to be a synthesis of expert opinion on the numerous topics which it attempts to cover. Since African economic history does not lend itself to an overall chronological treatment for many reasons, amongst others very often a slowness of change over centuries and, in some respects (for example, in Egyptian flood control), its absence, the approach is more topical and comparative than chronological, though chronology is by no means ignored.

The Introduction is intended to be an orientation survey, a small-scale map, as it were, of the territory traversed in the five chapters of the book. In venturing into so many fields where no one person can be expert in all and where the experts who specialize in a single field are at odds, I run the risk of incurring the wrath and scorn of those scholars. I can only echo, *mutatis mutandis*, Nikolay Gogol's introduction to the second edition of *Dead Souls*, 1846 (Everyman edition, 1915, p. 1).

'. . . for me to learn all that I have wished to do has been impossible, in that human life is not sufficiently long to become aquainted with even a hundreth part of what takes place within the borders of the Russian Empire. Also, carelessness, inexperience, and lack of time have led to my perpetrating numerous errors and inaccuracies of detail; with the result that in every line of the book there is something which calls for correction. For these reasons I beg of you, my reader, to act also as my corrector. Do not despise the task, for, however superior be your education, and however lofty your station, and however insignificant, in your eyes, my book, and however trifling the apparent labour of correcting and commenting upon that book, I implore you do as I have said. And you too, O reader of lowly education and simple status, I beseech you not to look upon yourself as too ignorant to be able in some fashion, however small, to help me.'

I am indebted to several colleagues who have looked at the typescript in part or whole, namely Sean Archer, John Atkinson, James Henry and Christopher Saunders. To Emeritus Professor H. M. Robertson, who with characteristic generosity agreed to make a report on an earlier draft for the Editorial Board of the University of Cape Town and who with characteristic thoroughness made numberless helpful suggestions, I am particularly grateful.

The publication of this book has been made possible by a grant from the University of Cape Town, and a great deal of it was written during study

1

2   AN ECONOMIC HISTORY OF AFRICA

leave. I express my deep appreciation. Another tribute is due to the admirable
libraries of the University.

GENERAL BIBLIOGRAPHY

Ashtor, E.: *A Social and Economic History of the Near East in the Middle Ages* (London,
1976)
Crouchley, A. E.: *The Economic Development of Modern Egypt* (London, 1938)
De Kock, M. H.: *Selected Subjects in the Economic History of South Africa* (Cape Town and
Johannesburg, 1924)
Dickson, K. B.: *A Historical Geography of Ghana* (Cambridge, 1969)
Duignan P. & Gann L. H. (eds.),: *Colonialism in Africa 1870–1960*, Volume 4, *The Econo-
mics of Colonialism* (Cambridge, 1975)
Ekundare, R. O.: *An Economic History of Nigeria: 1860–1960* (London, 1973)
Hopkins, A. G.: *An Economic History of West Africa* (London, 1973)
Issawi, C. (ed.),: *The Economic History of the Middle East 1800–1914, A Book of Readings*
(Chicago and London, 1966)
July, R. W.: *Precolonial Africa, an Economic and Social History* (Blandford, 1976)
Konczacki, Z. A. & J. M. (eds.),: *An Economic History of Tropical Africa*, Volume 1, *The
Pre-colonial Period* (London, 1977)
Munro, J. Forbes: *Africa and the International Economy, 1800–1960; an Introduction to the
Modern Economic History of Africa South of the Sahara* (London, 1976)
Pankhurst, R.: *An Introduction to the Economic History of Ethiopia from Early Times to 1800*
(London, 1961)
Pankhurst, R.: *Economic History of Ethiopia, 1800–1935* (Addis Ababa, 1968)
Pollock, N. C. & Agnew, S.: *An Historical Geography of South Africa* (London, 1963)
Toutain, J.: *The Economic Life of the Ancient World* (London, 1930)
Van Zwanenberg, R. M. A. with King, A.: *An Economic History of Kenya and Uganda
1800–1970* (London, 1975)

INTRODUCTION

i) *Internal developments*
Two thousand years ago, at the beginning of the Christian era, throughout most of the central, eastern and southern parts of the African continent, men lived on what they could collect by way of wild fruit, berries and roots, and on what they could hunt. Since it requires a great deal of space to feed a quite small band on what can be gathered or hunted, even when nature is generous (and over large parts of Africa nature is far from generous), population was sparse. A low density of population and a precarious living based upon an unremitting search for food were not, however, found everywhere on the continent. In northern Africa the situation was very different. Here men lived a settled existence dependent upon farming or animal husbandry. By the birth of Christ, the history of agriculture in the Nile valley was already four or five thousand years old. The annual flood of the river, by depositing a layer of rich alluvial soil which remained after the flood water receded, endowed Egypt with a fertility that could support a dense population to a degree of prosperity that fostered civilization and the development of an advanced state. Towards the end of the 4th millennium B.C. Upper (southern) and Lower (northern) Egypt were united under the Upper Egyptian kings. The capital was fixed at Memphis, just south of the Delta, near the frontier between the two Egypts. Lower Egypt, composed of the Nile Delta and its immediate environs, with its heterogeneous people and cattle cults, had an entirely different character from that of Upper Egypt, with its hunting traditions. There was always the danger of the two parts coming apart again. Ancient Egypt during its long history experienced times of turbulence, but also long periods of stability, known as the archaic or proto-dynastic period and the Old, Middle and New Kingdoms. Between the Old and Middle Kingdoms and before and after the New Kingdom 'intermediate periods' of instability occurred.

EGYPTIAN CHRONOLOGY

Protodynastic Period:	3110–2665 B.C.	– Dynasties I and II
Old Kingdom:	2664–2155 B.C.	– Dynasties III to VIII
First Intermediate Period:	2154–2052 B.C.	– Dynasties IX to XI
Middle Kingdom:	2052–1786 B.C.	– Dynasty XII (from 1991)

3

4 AN ECONOMIC HISTORY OF AFRICA

Second Intermediate
Period: 1785–1554 B.C.   – Dynasties XIII–XVII
New Kingdom: 1554–1075 B.C.   – Dynasties XVIII–XX
Late Period: 1075–664 B.C.   – Dynasties XXI–XXV
Saite Period: 664–525 B.C.   – Dynasty XXVI
First Persian Period: 525–404 B.C.   – Dynasty XXVII
Last Egyptian Kingdom: 404–341 B.C.   – Dynasties XXVIII–XXX
Second Persian Period: 341–332 B.C.   – Dynasty XXXI
Greek Period: 332–30 B.C.
Roman Period: 30 B.C.–A.D. 395
Byzantine or Coptic
Period: A.D. 395–A.D.640

(Source: Harris J. R., edn., *The Legacy of Egypt*, Oxford, 2nd edn. 1971, p. 24–5)

By the beginning of the Christian era both agriculture and the keeping of domestic animals were being practised in the middle Nile valley and in the highlands of Ethiopia. Both areas were subject to the external influences of Egypt to the north and Arabia just across the Red Sea. To the south of Egypt, in Upper Nubia, there developed the Kingdom of Kush, with its centre at Kerma. Conquered by the Egyptians in the 1st millennium B.C., Upper Nubia, after the collapse of the New Kingdom, asserted its independence, giving to Egypt one of its later dynasties, the 25th in the 8th and 7th centuries B.C. The first capital of the revived Kushite state was Napata, its second (from the 8th century B.C.) Meroe, situated near the confluence of the Nile and the Atbara, some one hundred miles north of what is now Khartoum, and celebrated for its iron industry. More or less contemporaneous with Kush, though with little in common and reaching its period of greatest prosperity rather later (3rd and 4th centuries A.D.) and situated to the south of its contemporary and rival in what are now Ethiopia and Eritrea, was Axum, which gave the death blow to a declining Meroe in the 4th century A.D. Links between these regions and the Mediterranean were strengthened by the spread southwards of Christianity, adopted as the official religion of the Roman empire in the 4th century, into Ethiopia not long after its adoption by Rome, and into Nubia, where it became in the 6th century the religion of the states that succeeded Meroe.

In West Africa, too, agriculture was developed, either spontaneously or through the imitation of northern or eastern neighbours. In the sub-Saharan savanna, states of considerable extent and power evolved, enjoying a prosperity based partly on trade (especially in gold) carried on across the Sahara desert with North Africa. The first of these kingdoms, Ghana, founded perhaps as early as the 4th century A.D., had its centre of gravity, as it were, on the watersheds of the upper Niger and Senegal rivers. Succumbing to attack from the north in the late 11th century, it was eclipsed by Mali, its centre of gravity further to the east, which flourished from the 13th to the middle of the 15th century. Another state, one which survived many centuries, was Kanem-Bornu, based on the Lake Chad region.

Further to the south, but north of the forest belt in the so-called middle belt of West Africa, small states whose strength lay in the walled town and mounted warriors, grew up in Hausaland and Yorubaland in modern Nigeria. The forest belt west of the River Volta, the gold-bearing and kola nut region, involved in long-distance trade, also saw the formation of small states, but based on the village rather than the town. Through confederation or conquest, these small states of savanna and forest were on occasion amalgamated into powerful territorial states, such as Oyo and Asante.

Agriculture and pastoralism can support much larger populations than can hunting and gathering. There may have been a population explosion, relatively speaking, in West Africa that forced some of its inhabitants out in search of new land. This migration, taking place from the beginning of or just before the Christian era, was one of the major events in the economic history of Africa. The migrants were the Bantu-speaking people. Their dispersal went on for a thousand years, and it was important not only because they took with them the knowledge of agriculture and animal husbandry, but also because it is quite likely that they spread the knowledge of iron working. They either made this discovery for themselves or they copied it from their neighbours. Iron gave them superior tools – axes for clearing bush, hoes for tilling – and superior weapons – iron-tipped arrows and spears. As they fanned out southwards and eastwards from the Congo Basin, they conquered or absorbed or pushed back the hunters and gatherers, the San (Bushmen), the Pygmies and the Khoikhoi (Hottentots). The Hottentots adopted pastoralism themselves; the Bushmen and Pygmies remained hunters and gatherers.

A change occurred in the culture of the Bantu-speaking peoples from the end of the 1st millennium A.D., which prehistorians see as a transition from an early Iron Age to a later Iron Age. On the western side of the sub-continent there was apparently a continuity between the two ages, but on the eastern side there was a sharp discontinuity and the change to the later Iron Age is associated with a migration of small groups of Bantu-speaking people from the Shaba (Katanga) region of modern Zaïre to as far south as the River Kei in modern South Africa, taking with them new styles of pottery and very often succeeding in establishing political authority over earlier Bantu-speaking settlers. It is suggested that in this way the Lunda and Luba states of the Shaba and Kasai regions of Zaïre and the Mbire (Shona) kingdom that had its seat of government at Great Zimbabwe in modern Zimbabwe, emerged from the first half of the present millennium.

The Bantu dispersion was not the only important movement of African peoples that took place. From the early centuries of the Christian era the Nilotes, too, migrated. These were a pastoral people, divided into western (such as the Lwo), eastern (such as the Masai) and southern (such as the Nandi) groups, which however, interacted with one another. Originating west and south of the Ethiopian Highlands, they migrated into the Rift Valley and the East African plateau, coming into contact with earlier migrants, Cushitic-speaking pastoralists, as well as with the Bantu. Like the Bantu, their migration went on over centuries. In a long process of conflict and accommodation, Cushite, Nilote and Bantu profoundly influenced one another, economically as well as in a broader cultural way. From the 16th century, Bantu-speaking states appeared in the lakes area of East Africa, such as Bunyoro, Buganda and Ankole, which sprang from the interaction of pastoralists, who may have been Cushitic-speaking immigrants in origin (Bahima), Bantu cultivators (Bairu) and Nilotic conquerors (Lwo), who established ruling dynasties.

Another migration, from the 15th century, was that of the Cushitic-speaking Galla, who moved into what are now north-east Kenya and southern Somalia, displacing the Bantu-speakers and coming into conflict with the Somali, also part of the Cushitic family. When the Somali moved into the region at present occupied by them is a matter of dispute. The older view is that they migrated at the end of the 1st millennium A.D. More recently it has been argued that they were in occupation of southen Somalia considerably earlier, before the arrival of the Bantu-speakers in the area.

Finally, with the last great movement of African peoples, there was the scattering of the Nguni people of southern Africa. The rise of the Zulu nation resulted in the *Difaqane*, a dispersal northwards which disturbed the whole of the south-eastern part of the continent as far north as modern Tanzania.

ii) *External influences*
Africa for the most part was not readily accessible to outside influences, nor, over large parts of it, did it offer easy internal communications. Its coast has a length that is short in relation to the land mass, has on the whole comparatively few harbours and is skirted generally by a narrow, sometimes arid, plain. Even the longest rivers have stretches quite near the coast that are not navigable. Most are blocked with sand bars, like the Orange, or obscured by swamps, like the Rufiji and Zambezi. Indeed, only the Congo and the Gambia seem to be free in this respect. To the west and the east lie great oceans, the South Atlantic and the Indian. Even in the north the continent does not invite penetration from the Mediterranean. An inhospitable coast,

with its cliffs and dunes, offers little protection against northerly winds; formidable mountain ranges run parallel to it for a considerable way, and, apart from the Nile, rivers are lacking. Within Africa there are serious obstacles to movement, such as the Sahara desert and the Congo forest.

Africa, however, is not everywhere impenetrable. North Africa has its fertile plains, Cyrenaica, Tripolitania and Tunisia, the last not so far from the Mediterranean islands of Sicily and Sardinia. The Indian Ocean, though vast, at the correct seasons of the year is not difficult to cross. Eastern Africa had relations with the Middle and Far East, facilitated by the monsoons, which vessels approaching and leaving the Persian Gulf and north-west India were able to utilise, and by the South Equatorial Current for ships coming from the Far East. To the south of Kisimayu (or Chisimaio in the modern Somali Republic) near the Equator, there were comparatively numerous natural harbours and offshore islands which offered shelter. Settlers from Indonesia colonized Madagascar (presumably then uninhabited) certainly by the 10th century A.D. and exercised some influence upon the eastern mainland. They may have introduced valuable crops into Africa that had originated in South-East Asia. Later immigrants from Arabia and Persia settled on the coasts of what are now Somalia, Kenya, Tanzania and Mozambique. Their descendants conducted a brisk trade with the Persian Gulf countries and India. Even Chinese junks at one time sailed as far as East Africa. There was, however, little penetration of the interior, except in the Zambezi and Limpopo areas, until the 19th century, when Arab traders sent expeditions from the coast.

On the whole, influences from the north were of greater importance than those from the east, and that is why the Sudan and Ethiopia were more advanced than the other regions of sub-Saharan Africa. Northern Africa was part of the Mediterranean world. Unlike sub-Saharan Africa it passed through a Bronze Age preceding the Iron Age, and was incorporated wholly or partly into great empires that originated in the Middle East or Europe. Over the narrow bridge of land that attaches Africa to Asia at Suez, came foreign immigrants and invaders – the Hyksos in the early part of the 2nd millennium B.C. and the Assyrians and the Persians in the 1st millennium B.C.. Egypt was conquered by Cambyses of Persia in 525 B.C., but its inclusion in his vast empire, stretching from the Indus to the Mediterranean, made little impression on it. Of much greater significance was the influence of the Greeks. In the 7th century B.C. they were permitted to establish a free port there, Naucratis, and in the 4th century B.C. the entire country was brought into the empire of Alexander the Great of Macedonia. On the death of the conqueror his empire was split up among his contending generals, and Egypt fell to the lot of Ptolemy, the son of Lagus, the eponymous founder of a dynasty that ruled over a maritime empire which also included Cyrenaica,

Cyprus, Syria and some of the Aegean islands. The Ptolemaic or Hellenistic régime in Egypt lasted from 305 B.C. to 30 B.C.

In the western Mediterranean the Phoenicians of the Levant settled and conquered. A seafaring people with interests in the minerals of Spain, they established ports of call along the North African coast, beginning with Utica, founded by Tyre towards the end of the 2nd millennium B.C. The much more famous Carthage was founded, according to tradition, as a new capital in 814 B.C. by the Tyrians, then under threat from the Assyrians. Tyre was captured by Nebuchadnezzar in 574 B.C., and the Carthaginians asserted their authority over the other Phoenician colonies of the western Mediterranean and built up their own maritime empire in the islands and on the northern shores of the Mediterranean. They came into conflict with the Greeks, those settled in what is now France – principally Marscilles – Spain and Sicily and those who colonized Cyrenaica in the 7th century B.C. Though repulsed in Sicily in the early part of the 5th century B.C. and excluded from the eastern Mediterranean by the Athenian navy, Carthage forced the Greeks to abandon their settlements on the coast of Africa as far as the eastern end of the Greater Syrtis (Gulf of Sidra), and, with the decline of Athens, was able to reassert her position in Sicily and restore her eastern Mediterranean trade. For all their antipathy, however, the Carthaginians were much influenced by Greek culture, particularly from the 4th century B.C. They established friendly relations with Ptolemaic Egypt and their state was at its most prosperous in the early part of the 3rd century B.C.

In the 3rd century B.C. the Carthaginians became locked in a struggle with the Romans for supremacy in the western Mediterranean. In the First Punic War (263–241 B.C.) they lost Sicily, and its wheat, and in the Second Punic War (218–201 B.C.), Spain and its silver. The final outcome was the Roman annexation of Carthage in 146 B.C. and the spread of Roman rule along the North African coast. At first the province of Africa was confined to the small area around Carthage, but it was gradually extended to incorporate the native kingdoms of Mauretania and Numidia. In the interior the Romans advanced as far as the mountain ranges parallel to the coast in search of a secure frontier. Coming into conflict with pastoralists who tended, when rainfall was inadequate, to be unruly and somewhat predatory, they moved further south and garrisoned the northern oases of the desert, thus establishing a defensive line that stretched from the Syrtes to the Atlantic seaboard.

In 30 B.C. the Romans annexed Egypt where political traditions and economic conditions had been imposed by centuries of flood control which ensured a considerable degree of continuity. The effects of Roman conquest and occupation were more profound in North Africa. Parts are blessed with a fair rainfall, but in those places where the rain was less reliable, the

Romans, extending the work already done by their Greek and Carthaginian predecessors, made skilful use of dams and cisterns and other methods of water conservation to increase agricultural output to the point of supporting a relatively dense population. Cultivation, though not unknown to them, was adopted more widely by the aboriginal inhabitants, the Berbers – or Libyans, as they were called by the Greeks; or Moors, as they were known to the Romans.

Northern Africa, incorporated into the Roman empire, shared its fate. By the 3rd century A.D. the imperial economy weakened and Roman rule became extortionate. There was a temporary recovery under Diocletian at the end of the century, but only at the price of very rigid state controls. When the empire irrevocably split into eastern (Greek) and western (Latin) halves, the latter was submerged under waves of barbarian assaults that reached as far as North Africa. Egypt was part of the inheritance that fell to the Byzantine empire – as the eastern half is known from the name of its capital, Byzantium (Constantinople) – and North Africa was recovered in the 6th century by the Emperor Justinian, who succeeded in establishing a Byzantine presence in the western Mediterranean. Byzantium survived in an increasingly attenuated form for a thousand years, but its African possessions, exposed and of lesser concern in the capital, could not be protected by a state that had been exhausted by Justinian's conquests and, more especially, by a long drawn-out war with Persia in the 6th and 7th centuries. Egypt and North Africa fell easy prey to invaders from Arabia in the 7th century.

iii) *Arab conquests*

The Arab expansion of the early Middle Ages had a profound long-term effect upon North Africa, and important repercussions on sub-Saharan Africa. Not for the first time were the Arabs driven by overpopulation into the lusher territories of their neighbours. After wresting Egypt from Byzantium in A.D. 639–42, they moved into the west, the Maghrib, where they more or less effectively established their rule in the second half of the 7th century. Their newly-adopted religion, Islam, proved popular among the Berbers, and Arabs and Berbers together went on to conquer the Iberian peninsula early in the 8th century. Muslim domination of Sicily, Corsica, Sardinia and the Balearic Islands made the Mediterranean virtually a Muslim lake. The formation of the Arab empire stimulated an international trade that survived subsequent political and doctrinal schisms. These were numerous. The successor of the Prophet Muḥammad, the founder of Islam, who died in 632, was the caliph, both spiritual leader and temporal ruler. The first four caliphs were drawn from the Prophet's closest collaborators, his 'companions', but in 659 a regular dynasty was founded, ruling the empire from Damascus. This was the caliphate of the Umayyads, which gave place in

749 to that of the 'Abbāsids. The new caliphs ruled from Baghdad and their grasp upon the Maghrib was never very firm. In the 10th century their empire started to disintegrate. Soon it had broken up into autonomous regional sovereignties.

The conquering Arab armies had been very small and their initial impact upon the lives of the masses was slight. Among the conquered, however, owing to the poll-tax payable by non-Muslims, an increasing number adopted the religion and the language of the conquerors, and in the course of time a considerable number of pastoral Arab bedouin pitched their tents on the margins of the Nile valley and penetrated Nubia and the Maghrib. Where they settled, they spread Arab customs, being influenced in turn by the culture of the people among whom they took up residence. Their nomadic ways died hard and they were, to say the least, a source of irritation to a succession of Muslim rulers, Arab, Berber and Turkish, in the Maghrib and Egypt. These rulers were able, on the proceeds of agriculture supplemented by the profits of the transit trade of the Middle East or the trans-Saharan trade, to support an administration of some efficiency during the first flush of sectarian or dynastic success. Each administration in turn inevitably became corrupt, bringing renewed misery to its subjects, (especially the long-suffering peasants of Egypt, the fellahin,) but succumbing eventually to palace revolution, religious revivalism, foreign invasion or tribal revolt.

In 909 a descendant of Fātima, a daughter of Muhammad, proclaimed himself caliph in what is now Tunisia, and in 969 the Fātimid dynasty extended its rule to a then famine-stricken and chaotic Egypt. Under its government the country at first enjoyed a period of great prosperity. The state was efficiently run and adequately provided for, and trade flourished. But in the middle of the 11th century the Fātimids, losing control of Tunisia, incited a bedouin invasion of the Maghrib, partly to rid Egypt of an unruly element, partly as revenge. The invasion was the beginning of a great and protracted Arab immigration that arabized the countryside. The devastating effects of its impact, for long accepted by historians, were questioned after the Second World War. There can be little doubt, however, that in the late 11th century the central part of the Maghrib, Ifriqiya, was in a state of decline and that the nomads, whose services were available to any adventurer prepared to pay them in cash or in booty, contributed to it. The coastal towns lost prosperity, partly through European militancy. Pisa sacked al-Mahdia, the old Fātimid capital, in 1087 and in the next century the Normans, who had seized Sicily from Islam, temporarily occupied al-Mahdia and Tripoli.

The Maghrib remained politically independent of Egypt, just as it was separated physically by the Libyan desert. It was ruled by Berber dynasties which displayed as little interest in Egypt as subsequent Egyptian dynasties did in the lands to the west of Cyrenaica. The role of the Berbers in the economic history of the Maghrib, the Sahara and the western Sudan was of great significance. In their espousal of Islam they were wont to embrace puritanical variants that had an egalitarian flavour and were closely related to tribal loyalties. In the 8th century they adhered to the teaching of the Khārijiyya, a protest movement of a political, social and tribal, as well as religious, character. Though unsuccessful in their revolt against Arab rule and Islamic orthodoxy and forced to retreat to the south beyond the mountains, the Khārijites established independent principalities – Tahert (in modern Algeria), Wargala, its successor in importance, and Sijilmāsa (in southern Morocco) – that controlled the northern end of the Saharan trade routes. Khārijite traders were very active in the Saharan trade.

In the 11th century a militant religious sect was given birth by the Sanhaja Tuareg, the sect of the Almoravids. In so far as it had an economic motive, the movement was actuated by a desire to assert control over the trans-Saharan trade. The Almoravids built up a state in Morocco, to which they added Spain. In 1077 they invaded Ghana, breaking it up without advantage to themselves. As their puritanical fervour cooled, the Almoravids were superseded in the 12th century by the Almohads, who drew their support from a different tribal grouping, the Masmuda and Zanata Berbers of the High Atlas. The Almohads unified the Maghrib, expelled the Normans, established themselves in Spain and set up an efficient administration run from Marrākesh. However, owing to factionalism and pressure from insurgent Christianity in Spain and from the bedouin in the east, in the 13th century their caliphate broke up into three sections, roughly corresponding to modern Tunisia, Algeria and Morocco. The Maghrib remained prone to periodic turbulence and disorder.

Egypt, like the Maghrib, was a target for aggressive Christianity. Attacked by the crusaders in the 12th century, Egypt was preserved for Islam by a Kurdish general of the disintegrating Middle Eastern empire of the Seljuk Turks. This was Saladin, who deposed the Fāṭimid caliph in 1171 and founded the Ayyubid dynasty of sultans owing nominal allegiance to the'Abbāsids. This dynasty gave Egypt eighty years of, on the whole, prosperity and stability, repulsing a number of Christian attacks in the first half of the 13th century. It fell victim to its own mercenaries, the Mamluks, a military caste that perpetuated itself by the recruitment of slaves; at the first Kipchak Turks from southern Russia and later Circassians from the Caucasus. The last of the Ayyubid sultans was murdered in 1250 and from then until 1517 Egypt was ruled by this military oligarchy. Like their Ayyubid predecessors, the Mamluks were more interested in the Middle East than in the Maghrib. They successfully withstood the threat posed by the Mongols, who captured Baghdad in 1258 and murdered the 'Abbāsid caliph. A puppet caliph of the same dynasty was installed in Cairo, real power resting with the Mamluk sultan.

Meanwhile, to the south, there grew up over the centuries, Muslim states in Somalia and southern Ethiopia, chiefly through commercial and other influences from the north and from southern Arabia, and these came into conflict with Christian Ethiopia in the 13th century and were prevented from expanding. In Nubia, the Meroitic successor states, the Christian kingdoms of Nobatia and Makurra, which united in the 7th century, with a capital at Old Dongola, survived between the 1st and 5th cataracts at least until the 14th century. South of the 5th cataract, the kingdom of 'Alwa, with its capital at Soba on the Blue Nile, closely situated to where it joins the main river, endured until the beginning of the 16th century. Giving way finally to pressure from the Mamluks of Egypt and from Arab immigrants, particularly bedouin tribesmen from Upper Egypt in conflict with the Egyptian government, Nubia became islamicized and largely arabized. Once the Christian obstacle had been removed, Arabs, mostly from Upper Egypt, but some from Arabia itself, from the 14th century moved southwards and westwards into the pasture land south of the desert, into Kordofan, Darfur and Wadai. Movement across the Sudan was impeded by Lake Chad, which was subject to sudden changes in water level and was surrounded by marshy land. It was here that the nomads from the east were brought to a halt in the neighbourhood of Kanem. They abandoned their sheep and goats for cattle, and, through intermarriage, merged with the native people.

In the 16th century the whole area between the foothills of Ethiopia, the 3rd cataract in the north and the White Nile in the west, across the Gezira, fell under the control of the Funj sultanate, a Muslim, but not an Arab, state, which had its capital at Sennar on the Blue Nile. It was Funj that was responsible for the destruction of Soba early in the 16th century. The state lasted until the early 19th century. To its west the Keira sultanate of Darfur emerged in the 17th century and survived until the late 19th century. Christianity, embattled, but not wholly cut off from the rest of Christendom (for links were retained with the Coptic Church of Egypt and occasional pilgrims reached the Holy Land) survived in the mountain fastnesses of Ethiopia and recovered in the 12th century. Axum, having lost its old trading outlets, declined economically and is reputed to have been destroyed in a revolt. Under the Zagwe dynasty in the 12th century the centre of gravity of the Christian kingdom shifted to the south, to the area east of Lake Tana, in the mountainous region of Lasta; and, under the so-called Solomonic kings in the later 13th century, still further to the south to Shoa, in the plains south of the bend of the Blue Nile. From the middle of the 12th until early in the 16th century it prospered and grew at the expense of neighbouring pagan and Muslim territories.

The Mamluk government in Egypt was vitiated by power struggles within the ruling class, and the sultan became more and more oppressive in his search for money with which to withstand internal threats from the bedouin and external threats from Tamberlane (Timur) and then the Ottoman Turks. Corruption was rife; public security broke down; flood control was neglected; peasants fled from the countryside. By their capture of Constantinople in 1453 the Ottomans were able to prevent the supply of military slaves to Egypt and by adopting firearms they had a decided advantage over the Mamluk cavalry, which scorned their use. Campaigns against Egypt ended in the annexation of the country in 1517. War did not cease, however, as throughout the 16th century the Turks fought with the Spaniards for supremacy in the central Mediterranean. Spain and her allies won the important sea battle of Lepanto in 1571, but were driven from North Africa, where for a short period they held Tunis (1573–1574). Tripolitania, Tunisia and Algeria were incorporated into the Ottoman empire as regencies, each ruled by a pasha. Morocco remained an independent sultanate.

Ottoman administration in practice did not extend beyond Egypt, where, like most new brooms, it swept clean. Order was restored, bedouin incursions contained and peasants protected from the rapacious Mamluks. Even in Egypt, however, effective Ottoman control disappeared before the 18th century, leading to a revival of Mamluk power. When Napoleon Bonaparte invaded Egypt in 1798 he encountered an outmoded army that was battening upon a demoralized people impoverished by its exactions and by the incompetent management of the irrigation system and thinned by repeated attacks of the plague. The population, which at one time stood at five million, was by then little more than three. The situation was scarcely better in the Maghrib. There the rulers of Tunis and Algiers, nominally subject to the Porte, had long asserted hereditary succession, though they, and the sultan of Morocco, exercised little authority beyond the environs of Tunis or Algiers or the Atlantic plains of Morocco. The Berber tribes paid as little heed to the Maghribian rulers as the latter did to the Turkish sultan in Constantinople.

iv) *The coming of the Europeans*
At the western extremity of the Muslim world, during centuries of conflict, the Christian Spaniards and Portuguese, gradually at first, then at an accelerated rate, drove the Muslims out of Europe. Given their age-old confrontation with the Moors of Iberia, it is scarcely surprising that the Portuguese were the harbingers of a new phase of relations between Africa and Europe. From the beginning of the 15th century they pursued the Muslims across the Mediterranean into Morocco. Ceuta fell in 1415, Tangier in 1471 and Safi in 1508, and it was only in 1578, with the disastrous defeat and death

of King Sebastian at the Battle of the Three Kings at Ksar al-Kebir, that their ambitions in Morocco were relinquished. In the meantime, however, they had pressed ahead with exploratory expeditions around and beyond Africa.

In the commercial encounter between Europe and Africa the initiative came from and was retained by the Europeans. Their advances in navigation and naval architecture, which, it is commonly said, owed much to the Arabs and the Chinese in the development of the lateen-rigged vessel and the mariner's compass, ensured their control of the maritime part of the commerce that was opened. In their explorations, the Portuguese were actuated by a variety of motives by no means excluding economic ones and certainly including a desire for West African gold and, subsequently, the intention of diverting the Middle Eastern spice trade around the Cape of Good Hope.

The moving spirit behind the Portuguese explorations was Prince Henry the Navigator. When expeditions started, European seamen were familiar with the African coast only as far as Cape Bojador, stretching out forty kilometres into the ocean and beset with treacherous shallows and currents, frequent fogs and unfavourable winds. In a period of rudimentary navigation, vessels were unwilling to leave the coast behind, as there was great fear of what the Arabs called the 'Green Sea of Darkness'. The rounding of Cape Bojador, in 1434, was the major achievement of the first phase of the discoveries, after which the pace quickened. By Prince Henry's death in 1460 the Cape Verde Islands had been discovered and partly settled and Sierra Leone had been reached. The subsequent discovery of the Congo river was followed by the establishment of Portuguese influence in Angola and the kingdom of the Kongo. In 1438 the Cape of Good Hope was circumnavigated by Bartholomew Diaz. After a ten year delay, in 1497–99, Vasco da Gama made his famous voyage to India via the East African Muslim ports of Mozambique, Mombasa and Malindi.

In the early 16th century Portugal strove to force the trade of the Indian Ocean into a new pattern. Muscat on the Persian Gulf and the island of Socotra at the entrance to the Red Sea were seized as a means of controlling trade along the old-established routes, and an eastern headquarters was set up at Goa on the Malabar coast of India. Forts were built at points along the East African coast. Although these were chiefly designed to serve the interests of the eastern trade and received their orders from Goa, they also served as bases for taking over such local trade as survived. The Portuguese influence upon the interior of East Africa was for a long time only slight, and largely confined to the Zambezi valley. Despite the fact that in 1543 they assisted the Christian emperor of Ethiopia, the fabulous Prester John, in his struggle for survival against the Muslim sultanate of Adal, they did not succeed in establishing a permanent influence there. On the western side of the continent they set up colonies at Luanda and Benguela, but their power in the interior was not very great.

In spite of Portuguese attempts to assert exlusive national rights to Africa, recognized by the papacy in the bull *Romanus Pontifex* of 1455, English and French interlopers were active in West Africa as early as the 1520s. Towards the end of the century, after the outbreak of the revolt of the Netherlands against Spain in 1572 and the closure of Portuguese ports to Dutch ships following the unification of the Spanish and Portuguese crowns in 1580, the Dutch joined in, waging war for more than sixty years. In Senegambia, along the Gold Coast and elsewhere, European traders built forts and trading posts. At first they were chiefly interested in gold, though other African goods, such as wax and pepper were also imported into Europe. However it was the trade in slaves that came to predominate. The growing population of Europe, experiencing a rising standard of living, demanded sugar in ever increasing quantities. The islands of the West Indies were devoted to its cultivation. Labour was required for the plantations, and that labour was sought in Africa. For two centuries and more the external trade of Africa south of the Sahara was dominated by the slave trade. Millions of Africa's inhabitants were transported across the Atlantic, mostly from West Africa, but increasingly from Angola and later Mozambique.

In East Africa another slave trade grew up to satisfy a demand partly in the Middle East and India, partly on the sugar-growing islands of the Indian Ocean. As far as Europe was concerned, however, East Africa was a backwater. The Dutch, who ousted the Portuguese from their dominant position in the East Indian trade, took no more than a passing interest in the East African coast. The Portuguese themselves suffered a severe setback at the end of the 17th century, when African rebellion and the intrusion of the Omani Arabs deprived them of their possessions northwards from Zanzibar. A shift in the balance of power in the region south of the Zambezi lost them their influence between that river and the Limpopo, and though their traders penetrated the interior north of the Zambezi in the 18th century, they had to contend with strong Arab and Indian competition. East Africa reasserted its claim to European interest only towards the end of the 18th century when it became a hunting ground for traders in search of slaves and, somewhat later, anti-slave traders in pursuit of slavers. The Portuguese clung to their settlements, but these were insalubrious and sparsely inhabited.

The heyday of the Atlantic slave trade co-incided with the mercantilist era in the European economy, the era of far-reaching state regulation of commerce. For much of the 17th and 18th centuries, trade was conducted by chartered companies, granted monopolies by their national governments, though there remained plenty of scope for private traders able to gain a profit which the great companies were too cumbrous to pick up. There was an aggressiveness in trade that went beyond the bounds of free competition, and that was particularly so at the international level because of the prevailing belief that the volume of world trade was fixed and one nation's gain was another's loss. Trade frequently erupted into war, or at least a nation's trading position could be a casualty of war. Anglo-French colonial rivalry damaged French trade in Africa in the Seven Years' War (1756–63) and English trade in the American War of Independence (1775–83). In the course of the 18th century it was the British who came to get the biggest share of the slave trade, partly because of gaining, at the end of the War of the Spanish Succession in 1713, the Asiento, the contract to supply the Spanish colonies with slaves; partly because of growing maritime power; and partly because British industry was in an increasingly better position to supply the African market. The fortunes of London, Bristol and, above all, Liverpool were founded at least partly on the profits of slaving. French ports, like Nantes, Bordeaux and St. Malo too, enjoyed a prosperity derived from the trade. The Portuguese were also slave traders on the grand scale, as were the Dutch. Then there were the smaller participants, such as the Danes, the Brandenburgers and the Swedes.

Most European settlements on the African coast were trading posts that recognized the sovereign rights of African rulers and paid for the privilege of trading. African dealers on the coast were able to deliver the slaves that were the chief commercial interest of the Europeans and there was little point in their expending resources in trying to force a way past the middlemen. Here and there, however, on islands and mainland there was an assertion of sovereignty, particularly by the Portuguese, but also by the Dutch. In 1652 the Dutch East India Company founded what was to become Cape Town, primarily for the purpose of protecting the long route to the East and succouring the ships making their protracted voyages there. De Kaap – Cape Town – was sited on Table Bay, the only tolerably good harbour with a fresh water supply south of Angola and already a temporary halting place for east-bound Dutch and English vessels. The settler population, little encouraged by the Dutch East India Company and by the distance from Europe, grew but slowly, and numbered only twenty thousand by the end of the 18th century. Labour shortages found a partial solution in the importation of slaves, though the colony was not given over to plantation agriculture. In the vicinity of Cape Town a return, that was for long only modest, was earned by wheat and wine producers. Despite the restraints imposed by an authoritarian company, the settlement expanded and acquired its own dynamic. The settlers, moving ever onwards in search of fresh land which they carved up into vast farms and scarcely impeded by the indigenous Khoisan – Hottentots and Bushmen – who, indeed, often facilitated white exploitation of wider areas of pasture by becoming cattle-herds, in 1779 came into conflict with the Xhosa in the neighbourhood of the Fish River, thus inaugurating a series of frontier wars which ultimately brought white domination of the sub-continent.

v) *The partition of Africa*
In the closing years of the 18th century the beginnings of a change in the situation outside Africa had repercussions on that continent as important as the growth of the sugar industry had had earlier. European demand for slaves slackened and slowly disappeared. In 1807 it became illegal for British subjects to engage in the slave trade. Denmark had already taken that step for her subjects. Other nations followed and the British government succeeded in having the anti-slave trade principle enshrined in the Vienna Treaty at the end of the Napoleonic wars in 1815. European merchants were compelled to seek new African exports. To regard the substitution of 'legitimate commerce' for slave trading merely as a response to changing economic needs would do less than justice to the growing repugnance in Europe to slaving and slavery. This was one aspect among many of a humanitarian movement that saw the beginnings of factory legislation, curbs upon the consumption of alcohol, mitigation of the savagery of penal codes, and so on. However, it would be naïve to dismiss the influence of economic advantage. The truth is that motives were mixed. The foundation of the African Association in Britain – the Association for Promoting the Discovery of the Interior Parts of Africa – in 1788, illustrated the diversity of interests focussed on Africa. The declared objects of the expeditions it organized were commercial and humanitarian as well as scientific.

Britain's interest in the slave trade diminished partly because the relative contribution of the sugar industry to her economic welfare declined. With the great expansion of British industry there were hopes that Africa might offer more as a potential source of industrial raw materials and as a potential market than as a source of manpower for a sugar industry that was experiencing considerable difficulties as the long-established overworked plantations found their profit margins contracting. However, it must be said that the state of trade between Africa and Europe at the beginning of the 19th century offered very little evidence of the former's capacity to provide either raw materials or a market for European goods. On the contrary, it was not so much a question of the attractive alternatives to slave trading leading to its suppression, as the outlawing of the slave trade requiring the development of a 'legitimate' substitute for slaves. Equally, slavery in the British empire did not die a natural death which compelled thwarted capitalists to look for other means of exploitation. There were still opportunities for profitable slave-grown sugar on the island of Trinidad and in Guiana.

Vested interests put up a strong resistance to the abolition of the slave trade. Although Britain, a poacher turned gamekeeper, changed from slaver to hunter of slavers, the slave trade went on. As long as the demand for slaves was maintained, slave trading inevitably continued. The virgin lands of Cuba and Brazil could afford the high prices demanded by slavers who had to elude British naval patrols.

Attempts were made to stop the supply of slaves at its source, partly through pressure upon African rulers, partly through the encouragement of cash crop production. Such endeavours, together with anti-slave trade measures, entailed a more intrusive European presence in Africa. Although Africa was not partitioned until the last quarter of the 19th century, the establishing of the Sierra Leone settlement in 1787–8 by the British as a home for released slaves was symbolic. It was not, however, the only sign of the times at the end of the 18th century. In the Mediterranean the French began to look covetously at the lands across the sea. In 1798 Napoleon invaded Egypt, and the brief French occupation was followed by a still briefer British one. Yet another portent for the future, was the British annexation of the Cape in 1814. With the growth of her Indian empire, Britain found the Cape of vital strategic importance. Finding British rule little to their taste, many of the Dutch settlers – the Boers – retreated into the interior and founded small republics across the Orange and Vaal rivers.

Awareness of the technological gap between themselves and the importunate Europeans drove some African rulers, particularly in Mediterranean Africa, to try to catch up quickly. Muhammad 'Alī (1769–1849), an Albanian adventurer who was made governor of Egypt in 1805 by the Sultan of Turkey and founded an hereditary dynasty, was such a reformer. Attempts at modernization, however, did not ward off European encroachment and the whole continent succumbed during the great scramble, with the exception of Ethiopia, whose emperor, Menelik, defeated an Italian army at Adowa in 1896.

In 1882 Britain occupied Egypt, and in West Africa the French, moving from their coastal bases, occupied Bamako in 1883, Timbuktu in 1893 and reached Lake Chad in 1900. A net was drawn round the British sphere of interest in Gambia, Sierra Leone, the Gold Coast and the coast of what is now Nigeria; the spheres of Germany in Togo and the Cameroons, where she established herself in the 1880s; Portuguese and Spanish Guinea; and Liberia, an American sponsored settlement for former slaves. The British government was sufficiently sensitive to the interests of British merchants to assert claims in Nigeria and the Gold Coast. Kumasi, the capital of Asante, was captured in 1896. Britain in the end got the best of the bargain in West Africa. French West Africa may have been three times the size of British West Africa, but Nigeria and the Gold Coast were by far the most valuable prizes. Nor was Germany left out. She proclaimed a protectorate over Togo and the Cameroons.

In the Congo King Leopold of the Belgians, taking advantage of great power rivalry, set up a personal empire in the Congo Basin: the Congo Free State, taken over by the Belgian government in 1908 after revelations of brutal exploitation. The French were also active in the Congo and founded a colony there. It was Britain's attempt to exclude France from the mouth of the Congo river by recognizing Portugal's claim to it that brought about the Berlin Conference of 1884, at which Britain and Portugal agreed to discuss the question. The conference was attended by fifteen states, including the United States, and its deliberations were extended from the subject of the Congo to that of the Niger and to conditions that should govern European acquisition of territory. It was decided that in the Congo Basin there should be free trade for all nations and that Britain had clear rights in the Niger valley, founded upon her commercial activity there. With respect to the conditions governing the annexation of territory, the conference defined 'effective occupation' and agreed that any power annexing territory should inform the other powers. One result of the conference was that it stimulated states to stake out their formal claims. The Africans themselves were not consulted except to the extent that they were induced to accept what was somewhat euphemistically called protection, or to sign away concessions that were sometimes extracted by fraud.

Germany, a late-comer to Africa (if the Brandenburger slave traders in West Africa are excepted), did well out of the partition. Apart from her colonies of Togoland and Cameroon, she annexed South-West Africa in 1884 and in 1886 made a partition agreement with Britain, her chief rival, which eventually gave the latter Kenya, Uganda and Zanzibar and herself Tanganyika. To the north an Anglo-Egyptian condominium was set up in the eastern Sudan in 1899. Portugal, despite her long-standing presence in Angola and Mozambique, was lucky to have her extensive claims there recognized, given her lowly status in Europe and the lack of effective occupation in the interior. In North Africa, France, having with great difficulty conquered Algeria between 1830 and 1845, proclaimed a protectorate in Tunisia in 1881. The scramble was largely completed by the Italian annexation of Libya in 1911 and the French annexation of Morocco in 1912. Spain acquired a share of the western Sahara.

South Africa was a special case in that the imperial power was in conflict with European settlers as much as with African states. There the lukewarm interest of the British in the interior was radically altered by the discovery of diamonds to the south of the Orange river in 1867 and the diamond rush of 1871. Brushing aside the claims of the Boer republic of the Orange Free State, Britain annexed the diamond territory in 1871. A similar extension of

British interest followed the discovery of gold on the Witwatersrand, which also led to a huge influx of foreigners and foreign capital (most of it British) into the Transvaal, much to the dismay of the Boer government, which saw it as a threat to its independence. The foreign miners – the *uitlanders* – found plenty to complain about in the Transvaal administration, its alleged inefficiency and obstruction. A Reform Committee was formed in Johannesburg to press the claims of the *uitlanders* in 1895 and Jameson, one of the intimates of C. J. Rhodes, the financier and politician of the Cape, invaded the Transvaal with a small force in December of the same year, forlornly hoping that the Boers would prove no more formidable than recently vanquished Africans in the north, where Britain had already acquired the territories that came to be known as Southern and Northern Rhodesia and Nyasaland. The fiasco of the Jameson raid did not improve Anglo-Boer relations and war broke out in earnest in 1899, leading to the British annexation of both Boer republics.

After the First World War the map was redrawn in some areas. On the grounds of having betrayed her colonial trust, Germany was deprived of her African territories, which were distributed among the Allies as 'mandates' of the League of Nations. Italy, dissatisfied with the sharing of the post-war spoils, overran Abyssinia in 1935–6. But Italian rule lasted only until 1941, when Ethiopia was liberated as a result of the renewal of war. Thus, so soon after the completion of partition, did the process of decolonization begin.

Why European nations thought it worthwhile to carve Africa up and share it out among themselves is, to say the least, a matter of controversy. Clearly economic expectations and motives were part of the explanation. Dispute arises over their nature and their significance. What is certain is that colonization greatly accelerated and exacerbated the inevitable hardship of change in Africa's situation in the world, a change that had begun with the establishment of the slave trade, but which had increased in tempo, rather than slackened off, with the substitution of 'legitimate trade' for slaving.

Further reading

Garlake, Peter: *The Kingdoms of Africa* (Oxford, 1978)
Hallett, Robin: *Africa to 1875* (London, 1974)
Oliver, Roland & Fage, J. D.: *A Short History of Africa* (Harmondsworth, 2nd edn., 1966)
Oliver, Roland & Fagan, Brian M.: *Africa in the Iron Age c. 500 B.C. to A.D. 1400* (Cambridge, 1975)

CHAPTER I

AGRICULTURE

1. THE BEGINNINGS

i) *Egypt*
Such is the significance of the substitution of cultivation and animal husbandry for collecting and hunting that the introduction of farming has been called
the 'neolithic revolution'.

> The first revolution that transformed human economy gave man control over
> his own food supply. Man began to plant, cultivate, and improve by selection
> edible grasses, roots, and trees. And he succeeded in taming and finally attaching
> to his person certain species of animal in return for the fodder he was able to offer,
> the protection he could afford, and the forethought he could exercise.[1]

It was a transformation revolutionary not only in livelihood and way of life,
but also in attitude. The transition from hunting to herding required hunters
to defer consumption in the interests of breeding for future consumption.
Similarly cultivation demanded effort for a future, perhaps uncertain, return.
The outcome was that the supply of food became more dependable and provision against dearth more secure. It became possible to support a larger
population on a given piece of land. Men settled down to a more sedentary
life that encouraged the accumulation of possessions and the development of
the arts of civilization. The surplus of food that the cultivator could produce
over and above his own needs permitted some division of labour and specialization of function. All this is beyond question. But much controversy sur-
rounds the origin of agriculture and stock-farming in Africa and the date and
method of the introduction of those exotic crops and livestock whose importance can scarcely be over-estimated.
   One possible explanation for the spread of farming is diffusion, either
through the migration of peoples or through the flow of ideas from people
to people; another is spontaneous invention in a propitious cultural and geographical environment; and a third is a mixture of diffusion and receptivity.
What seems clear is that Egypt owed its domestication of wild grasses and
beasts to diffusion from south-west Asia, a process, for all its revolutionary implications, slow and fumbling. Cultivation and herding, practised in south-
west Asia by the 9th millennium B.C. or earlier, were adopted by the people
of Egypt late in the 5th millennium B.C. But it was not at first the swampy
valley and delta of the Nile, then overgrown with papyrus and rushes, that
were cultivated. Not until the river had cut its way through a sandstone

21

barrier that impeded it in Upper Egypt, was the swamp gradually filled in with the deposits it brought down. Agriculture began on the shores of the lake that filled the Fayum Depression, now some thirty-two kilometres west of the river (and just south of modern Cairo), at that time connected with it. The edges of the flood plain and the wadis provided the first husbandmen with easily worked land. The earliest farming villages, inhabited by semi-sedentary nomads who bred sheep and goats and grew grain, were, as far as it is known, those of the Fayum and Merimde, the latter situated to the north, on the south-western edge of the Delta. These date from the late 5th and early 4th millennia B.C. It was probably in the 4th millennium that the early cultivators, compelled perhaps by pressure of population or by desiccation, moved down to the floor of the valley and took advantage of its incomparable fertility. Emmer wheat and barley were cultivated for food, and flax for linen, supplemented by the produce of garden (a wide variety of vegetables), vineyard and orchard (date, fig, tamarisk and pomegranate). The olive was never a great success and the oil indispensable for cooking, lighting, cleansing and the preparation of medicines, came mainly from the castor-oil plant. The Delta was brought under cultivation only very slowly as dykes were built and canals dug. It provided pasture for large herds of cattle until well into the New Kingdom. Sheep, goats, pigs and poultry were also raised.

It is difficult to estimate the debt to Egypt of the rest of Africa in the adoption of agriculture and stock-raising. Theories, though dependent too on ethnobotany, are very much tied to the evidence of archaeology and rock paintings, the discovery of which is to some extent fortuitous. New excavations can easily change the known sequence of events. Any consideration of the problem of Egyptian influence must, however, start with the recognition that contact between Egypt and the rest of Africa could not have been easy, hemmed in as it is by geographical obstacles. To the south, between modern Aswan and Khartoum, the course of the Nile is obstructed by six widely spaced cataracts, while to the west and south lie the Libyan, Saharan and Nubian deserts, together comprising a broad belt of arid land that, straddling the Tropic of Cancer, stretches four thousand eight hundred kilometres between the Red Sea and the Atlantic. Certainly this isolation was not always so pronounced. For, between the 6th and 3rd millennia B.C., during the so-called Makalian wet phase, Egypt was not so much cut off from the rest of Africa by desert as united to it by open steppe, and that was so during the crucial period of experimentation in cultivation and animal husbandry. Nevertheless, even during the period of comparatively little physical hindrance to contact, the cultural influence of Egypt south of the 2nd cataract seems to have been slight.

The gradual desiccation of the steppe in the opening centuries of the 3rd millennium B.C. divided the continent into sub- and super-Saharan Africa.

AGRICULTURE 23

Perhaps not even that division, however, presented the major obstacle to the diffusion of husbandry. The barrier was rather an ecological one. The wheat and barley of Egypt, though successfully adopted in the Ethiopian Highlands, were unsuited to the summer rainfall of the Sudan, the Arab name for the narrow belt of savanna that sweeps in a great arc across Africa from the western coast to the Ethiopian Highlands. However, even an ecological obstacle would not have precluded the transmission of the techniques of domesticating plants and animals.

The possibility of the diffusion of agriculture and herding from Egypt can scarcely be in doubt, and it would be surprising if Egypt did not influence North Africa to the west. There is, however, no certainty. The herding of cattle, goats and sheep was carried on in the Sahara, then well-endowed with pasture, as early as the 5th millennium B.C. (possibly even earlier), that is, at a time when Egypt itself was adopting farming. There are, indeed, indications of an autonomous domestication of sheep or goats in Libya as early as the 5th millennium B.C., or before, and of cattle in the Tassili mountain range in the Algerian central Sahara before stock-raising was practised in Egypt. There is also some inconclusive evidence of cultivation in the Sahara in the 5th millennium B.C. or earlier. Although it is clear that pastoralism was typical among the Berbers when the Phoenicians arrived in the 1st millennium B.C., it is equally certain that cultivation was known in North Africa and that a sedentary way of life was not uncommon.

In Upper Egypt and Lower Nubia, rock paintings on both sides of the Nile show that this area must have had south-west Asian cattle, sheep and goats soon after these were introduced to Lower Egypt. Archaeological evidence demonstrates that between the 1st and 2nd cataracts the cultivation of wheat and barley and the herding of sheep and goats, and perhaps cattle, were practised by the so-called A-Group people, whose culture spanned the late 4th and early 3rd millennia. Among these people, physically very similar to the prehistoric people of Egypt, there settled immigrants from the north, perhaps as the result of population pressure or of upheavals preceding the unification of Egypt. Then, in the 3rd millennium B.C., Lower Nubia was conquered and colonized by the pharaohs of the 4th and 5th dynasties.

While it remains conceivable that the practice of agriculture and herding spread westwards from the Nile valley along the southern verge of the desert to the western Sudan, a diffusion in that direction is difficult to reconcile with indications that the first domestic animals of the Nile valley were apparently of a later date than those of the Sahara. The desiccation of the Sahara seems to have been of great importance for the diffusion of pastoralism, providing both a compulsion to move, by destroying old pasture, and at the same time the opportunity of doing so by driving back the frontier of the region where the disease-carrying tsetse fly made animal husbandry impossible. Indeed, it is not impossible that desiccation, though primarily due to climatic changes and the fall in the level of lakes and rivers, was accelerated by the over-grazing of pasture. At all events, from the 3rd or 2nd millennium B.C. herders of cattle, sheep and goats, under pressure possibly from North African enemies as well as deteriorating environmental conditions, were evidently moving southwards into the Sudan, and eastwards into the middle and upper Nile valley. It has been suggested that these immigrants from the west were the founders of the so-called C-Group culture of Lower Nubia, which lasted from the First Intermediate Period of Egyptian history (2258–2052 B.C.), when the northern hold upon the region was relaxed, until the New Kingdom. However, there is considerable controversy about the origin of this pastoral culture, which may perhaps be attributable to influences from the east rather than from the west, or from the south, or even to the revival of the autochthonous culture.

Further to the south there is archaeological evidence of the herding of cattle, sheep and goats and the cultivation of vegetable, and possibly cereal, foods c.4000 B.C. in the region of modern Khartoum, but nothing is known of the provenance of the domestic animals beyond that it was not indigenous to the area. Still further to the south, it is thought, on linguistic and archaeological grounds, that there was, during the 2nd millennium B.C., a dispersal of Cushitic-speakers from what is now southern Ethiopia into the Horn of Africa and the northern parts of Central and East Africa. Such settlers in what are now Kenya and northern Tanzania, who may in fact have been relatively few in number, but assimilated the earlier inhabitants, are known to archaeologists as the Stone Bowl people on account of their artifacts. It is possible that they practised agriculture in the 1st millennium B.C.

ii) *Independent domestication in sub-Saharan Africa*
There is very strong evidence of a development of cultivation in the western Sudan quite independent of events in Egypt, though with a time lag of some three millennia. The desiccation of the Sahara may have provided an incentive as other sources of food became more precarious. In the shallow soil of the desert fringes and the savanna, native strains of millet and, in the river valleys, rice were probably domesticated from the 2nd or 3rd millennium B.C. However, there is no irrefutable evidence to support the view, sometimes advanced, that cotton was domesticated there; and there is some doubt whether the western region of the Sudan has a greater claim to originality in plant domestication than the eastern Sudan or Ethiopia. The first cultivators of the western Sudan were either pastoralists already accustomed to harvesting wild grasses, or people engaged in fishing, which itself encouraged semi-permanent settlement. The level of African lakes was a great deal higher between the 9th and 3rd millennia B.C., especially around 7000 B.C., than it is today. Lake

Chad was considerably bigger than modern Lake Victoria, and settlements have been identified around it and the East African lakes, along the River Nile and by other lakes and rivers that have long since disappeared. There is some archaeological evidence of early cultivation, from the end of the 2nd millennium, at Dar Tichitt in southern Mauritania by people whose dependence upon cultivation of bulrush millet (*Pennisetum*) grew gradually at the expense of fishing, stock-raising and the collecting of the grain of wild plants, and at Daima near Lake Chad, settled in the 1st millennium B.C., probably by pastoralists forced by desiccation to retreat southwards to the floodplain of the lake. Cereals came to be supplemented with various vegetables.

In the tropical forest to the south of the savanna, trypanosomiasis, spread by the tsetse fly, put an effective barrier in the way of the diffusion of the rearing of stock, apart from the West African dwarf shorthorn. Cultivation, too, developed somewhat differently. In the southernmost parts of the savanna and in the forest-savanna mosaic, wherever there was sufficient moisture, the yam became a staple food-crop east of the Bandama river on the Ivory Coast, while west of that boundary the staple was rice, a distribution due to environmental differences and the pattern of diffusion. Both crops could be cultivated in the rain-forest, but were not confined to it, and both were supplemented by other staples of indigenous and exotic provenance. Rice seems to have moved southwards via the internal delta of the River Niger. To the east of the rice region, in the southern savannas, an imperceptible transition apparently occurred from the collection of wild yams and oil-palm fruit to their deliberate cultivation by the 2nd millennium B.C. The innovation was not one of domestication (the improvement of wild plants) but the planting of wild root- and fruit-crops and their protection by clearing and weeding. On the forest edge such cultivation could be combined with the keeping of domestic animals.

The Ethiopian Highlands, where there were no ecological obstacles to animal husbandry and grain cultivation, also saw in all probability independent developments in agriculture. It is possible that the cultivation of emmer wheat was introduced as early as the 3rd millennium B.C., though there is no evidence that it spread further to the south. The early cultivators then probably domesticated some of the indigenous cultigens, *Eleusine* (finger millet) and sorghum, and there was subsequent diffusion into East Africa. The false banana (*Ensete*) was cultivated as well, and it may have been domesticated in this area either before or after the introduction of grain cultivation. Ethiopia and the Horn of Africa, however, were powerfully influenced from outside, from Egypt and by Semitic settlers (Sabeans) from southern Arabia, who made their way from the Red Sea to the fertile highlands of the interior. Whether the Sabeans brought with them agricultural techniques is a matter of conjecture. Teff, a cereal largely confined to Ethiopia, appears to have been cultivated there before their arrival. But the entire question of Semitic origins in Ethiopia is hotly debated. Some authorities go so far as to suggest that Ethiopia itself was the cradle of the Afroasiatic people, Semitic, Cushitic and Omotic in speech, and that the Semitic-speakers moved from there to Asia, not, as is commonly accepted, from Arabia to Ethiopia, though this thesis does not reject influences from Arabia, which are, however, dated to as early as c.5000 B.C. At all events Semitic-speakers predominated in Amhara-land, Harar and Tigre, while in south-central Ethiopia Cushitic speech prevailed.

The reasons for the adoption of agriculture and animal husbandry are not at all obvious. Need rather than imitation may be the explanation. If so, it may have been the outcome of a deterioration of the environment, such as desiccation in the Sahara; or it may have been pressure of population. Thomas Malthus argued that population tends to grow to the limit of its food supply and is stabilized at that level by famine, assuming that other checks do not supervene. There is, however, something to be said for arguing that it is not a question of men multiplying until they outstrip the food available, but rather of their responding to population pressure by changing their production techniques. On the other hand, this sort of argument suggests that primitive men reason in the same way as modern men, that their priorities are our priorities. This is a debatable proposition. Be that as it may, however, whether because they were spared the rod of hunger or because they saw no merit in imitating others, it is evident that hunters could live side by side with farmers for centuries without abandoning a traditional economy that met their needs satisfactorily. Where nature was bountiful and population was small, there was little incentive, it may be supposed, to secure provisions in a more toilsome way. With a hunting economy the productivity of the land is low, but that of labour is high, and the return to the investment of labour is immediate, though aleatory. Agriculture in the long run is more rewarding; in the short term its advantages are not obvious, and it, too, involves much risk.

There is little evidence of an independent development of agriculture or stock-breeding in East Africa south of the Horn or in southern Africa, in spite of the availability of a wide range of cultigens and, more especially, ungulates, such as the zebra and the eland. The arts of farming were apparently introduced into these areas of Africa by migrants, impelled perhaps by a shortage of land, itself the result of the population growth brought about by the very process of cultivation and stock-raising. These migrants were either Bantu (or strictly 'proto-Bantu')-speaking people or both Bantu- and Central Sudanic-speakers. It is agreed that the former acquired farming and iron-working practices from the latter, but there is doubt as to whether the borrowing was made in the Central Sudan itself or in the interlacustrine region of East Africa, to which there had been, in that case, an earlier Central Sudanic migration. There is also considerable controversy about the 'cradle' of the Bantu-speakers – whether it was the Congo forest; the savanna north of the forest; or the savanna south of it – and the extent of their dispersal, if any, south of the forest before they took up farming. There seems, however, to be agreement that they split into eastern and western streams and that, whatever their origins and movements before then, there was a rapid dispersal from the beginning of the present millennium, originating perhaps in what is now south-eastern Zaïre as a result of population pressure. This later migration is associated with the Later Iron Age, distinguished from the Early Iron Age by different pottery styles, the use of stone for building and, possibly, a greater dependence on cattle.

It is apparent that the Bantu-speaking people were established in the interlacustrine region before the opening of the Christian era and by its early centuries in Angola and northern Namibia in the west, and southern Kenya and northern Tanzania in the east. Certainly by the middle of the 1st millennium A.D., and perhaps a good deal earlier, they were settled on the highland plateaux from north of the Zambezi river to south of the Limpopo river as far as Swaziland and southern Mozambique. Settlement south of the Vaal River and east of the Drakensberg occurred early in the first half of the 2nd millennium A.D. The small degree of divergence among the several hundred Bantu languages, coupled with the wide extent of their dispersion, testifies to the relative rapidity of their expansion. South of the rain forest they cultivated root crops, sorghum and bulrush millet and kept cattle.

As for the people amongst whom the Bantu settled, in the Rift Valley and the highlands of East Africa, only a few pockets of the earlier settled Cushitic-speaking pastoralists survived as separate entities. South of the equator the newcomers moved in among the hunters and gatherers to exploit sites most favourable to cultivation. The migration may have been less a mass-movement of population than an infiltration. Although it is unlikely that cultural influences were all one way, most pre-agriculturalists adopted the language of the immigrants or were absorbed or conquered. In some areas, where the Bantu-speakers were relatively few in number, it was a process completed only after centuries, during which some sort of exchange of products and services may have taken place between iron-using cultivators and stone tool-using hunters and pastoralists. Among earlier inhabitants who escaped absorption, though subject to increasing competition for land, were the Pygmies, isolated in the depths of the Congo forest, the San (Bushmen) of the Kalahari desert (perhaps in pockets elsewhere too) and the Khoikhoi (Hottentots) of the remote south-west. The Pygmies and San kept to their old ways. How much the Khoikhoi were influenced by the Bantu-speakers is hard to say. Possibly their debt included the knowledge of stock-raising and the technique of pottery. What does seem certain is that the indigenous hunters and gatherers of South Africa did not domesticate plants and animals themselves. It has, however, been conjectured, though the archaeological evidence is not there to support the thesis, that the Bantu-speakers who migrated southwards on the eastern side of the continent were deprived of their cattle by the tsetse fly, which is endemic in what is now southern Tanzania, and that it was after making contact with the Khoikhoi, who had adopted stock-raising from the western stream of migrants, that they became cattle keepers.

iii) *Exotic crops and animals*
The movement of peoples, like that of the Bantu-speakers, was responsible not only for the spread of the techniques of agriculture and herding, but also for the diffusion of new crops that were introduced into Africa from other lands. Africa, despite its indigenous food crops, owed much to Asia and America. Although the transition from familiar to unfamiliar crops – for example, from millet to maize – was not a difficult step to take, the willingness of its inhabitants to adapt to such changes in their farming and diet in the interests of greater security against hunger, demolishes the once conventional view of a continent trapped in lethargy. Not only exotic crops, but also new types and breeds of domestic animal were adopted.

Apart from the species of cattle and sheep possibly domesticated in what are now Libya and Algeria, and apart from donkeys, ostriches and guinea-fowl, it is unlikely that any breed of domestic animal now found in Africa was indigenous, and it can only be supposed that Africans owed their pastoral farming primarily to introduction from without and diffusion from within and only secondarily to their own trial and error. The first cattle in Africa were of two species, long-horned and short-horned, both depicted in the rock paintings of the Tassili mountains. In the course of time these earlier kinds interbred with or were displaced by humped zebu cattle entering Africa via Egypt from western Asia in the middle of the 2nd millennium B.C. or via the Horn of Africa possibly in association with Semitic migrations in the 1st millennium B.C. In West Africa zebu are particularly associated with the Fulani people, known to have dispersed throughout the savanna from late in the 1st millennium A.D. A great advantage of these cattle was their resistance to drought, though they were more susceptible to trypanosomiasis than were indigenous animals. Horses too were subject to the disease. They appear to have spread throughout the Sudan via the Nile valley, but their distribution was determined by that of the tsetse fly.

Rather more is known about exotic crops than livestock, though even here there is much ignorance, giving rise to much speculation. It appears that just before, and in the opening centuries of, the Christian era, the existing range of crops was widened by the introduction from Asia into East Africa of sugar cane, lintless cotton, citrus, banana and different varieties of yam. Indonesians may have had a hand in bringing in some of these crops, the banana for example and possibly paddy rice, at least to Madagascar, where they settled in considerable numbers, though not until after the middle of the 1st millennium A.D. Paddy rice, the coconut palm, mango and egg plant are said by some to have been introduced between the 9th and 12th centuries by Persian and Arab settlers on the East Africa coast; others date their introduction several centuries earlier. Indisputably, Arabs in particular, and Muslims in general, played an important part in the development of agriculture in Africa. The frequency and size of internal migrations within the vast Arab empire facilitated the diffusion of both unfamiliar crops and the methods appropriate to their cultivation. The Arabs have been credited with the spread of, amongst other crops, rice, cotton, sugar cane and citrus fruit in the Mediterranean world and elsewhere.

In East Africa the Bantu-speakers adopted the cultivation of the banana in the lakes region with much success, at about the beginning of the 2nd millennium A.D. It is possible that they were instrumental in the transmission of the knowledge of Asian crops westwards. This has been disputed on the grounds of the physical obstacles to communication. The East African interior was cut off from the outside world by forests, deserts and mountain scarps and the marshes of the Nile Sudd. Even the coast and its hinterland were rendered remote from each other by a belt of scrubby bushland difficult to get through, though this did not prevent the banana reaching the interlacustrine area. It is not impossible that the Zambezi valley provided a route to Central and West Africa, though there is little evidence that south-east Asian rice, for example, was a regular crop of the Zambezi valley before the end of the 16th century. Perhaps knowledge of these crops reached West Africa by sea. If that is the case, it might conceivably be attributed to Indonesian seafarers. More likely candidates, however, were the Portuguese, who certainly planted sugar cane and citrus trees in West Africa, though it appears possible that some types of citrus and other fruits – as well as cotton – were introduced into the western Sudan by Arabs from North Africa.

Even if it was not they who transferred to West Africa the crops familiar in East Africa, the Portuguese were probably responsible for the importation into Africa of crops of American origin, either directly from Brazil, which fell, like Africa, into their sphere of trade and colonization, or indirectly by way of Portugal, though the possibility exists, too, of a spread by land from the Mediterranean coast, either across the Sahara in the course of trade or up the Nile valley and across the Sudan. The American crops included maize (which some have argued had a pre-Columbian introduction into West Africa), cassava (manioc), groundnuts and sweet potatoes, as well as

vegetables, fruits and tobacco. They may not have been deliberately introduced at all, but have been the chance result of commerce between continents, and the first varieties that spread into the interior were perhaps the
degenerate off-spring of cultivated crops. The evidence, however, seems to
favour the theory of intentional planting by the Portuguese, at least of groundnuts into West Africa as a crop for the feeding of slaves and of cassava into
the Congo, perhaps for the use of their own settlers.

The American crops were of inestimable value to Africa because of their
superiority to many of the existing crops. Maize gave a better yield, especially in high rainfall areas, than did the indigenous cereals and was more
palatable, while cassava (which has a relatively low food value) and sweet
potatoes, besides being immune to locust attack and less vulnerable to the
foraging of wild pigs and other animals, could be stored underground for an
extended period even in the damp tropics, so that they furnished a safeguard
against famine. It is scarcely surprising, then, that the exotic crops to some
extent ousted the indigenous ones.

The pace of diffusion seems to have been irregular and the area of dispersal
somewhat eccentric. Tobacco was adopted decidedly widely and quickly.
Of the food crops, an initially rapid spread of maize cultivation up the Niger
and in the Congo has been established. Cassava, on the other hand, is said
to have spread slowly because of the difficulty encountered in processing
it as a foodstuff. Apparently, it was not until the 19th century that it was
widely adopted in Katanga (Shaba), where it then became very popular.
By the middle of the 19th century, however, its cultivation was widespread
in the central region of the continent. Both Livingstone and Stanley, the
explorers, found it the staple throughout a large part of Angola and the
Congo Basin. In West Africa 19th century population pressure and urbanization favoured its adoption. With all the exotic crops it took several centuries for their cultivation to reach their present limits. In South Africa
maize, though introduced by the Dutch in the 17th century, was unsuited
to the western Cape and therefore little cultivated by Europeans before the
arrival of British settlers in the eastern Cape in 1820 and the movement of
the Dutch across the Orange River from the 1830s. There is evidence, however, of African adoption of this crop in the Ciskei before the effect of European influence was felt. The Dutch were clearly instrumental in the diffusion
of several other exotic plants, such as potatoes and rye, and animals, such as
horses, donkeys, woolled sheep and pigs. Tobacco had already reached the
Cape when they first settled there.

In East Africa manioc and maize were introduced considerably later than
in West Africa, manioc probably during the course of the 18th century by
the Portuguese. Maize appears to have been grown as early as the 16th century, but was not a staple crop before the 18th century, by the end of which

31

cultivation had spread far into the interior. The process of the substitution of maize for millet, sorghum and banana is still continuing, while it was only earlier in this century that the cultivation of cassava became widespread, encouraged by European colonial authorities in order to provide a famine reserve crop.

NOTES

1. Childe, V. Gordon: *Man Makes Himself* (London, 1936), p. 74–5

Further reading

Bender, Barbara: *Farming in Prehistory, from Hunter-Gatherer to Food-Producer* (London 1975)
Bishop, W. W. & Clark, J. D. (eds.): *Background to Evolution in Africa* (Chicago, 1967)
Boserup, Esther: *The Conditions of Agricultural Growth; the Economics of Agrarian Change under Population Pressure* (London, 1965)
Clark, J. Desmond: *The Prehistory of Africa* (London, 1970)
Cohen, Mark Nathan: *The Food Crisis in Prehistory: Overpopulation and the Origins of Agriculture* (New Haven, 1977)
Darby, William J., Ghalioungui, Paul & Grivetti, Louis: *Food: the Gift of Osiris*, 2 volumes (London, 1977)
Davies, O.: *West Africa before the Europeans, Archaeology and Prehistory* (London, 1967)
Emery, Walter B.: *Egypt in Nubia* (London, 1965)
Epstein, H.: *The Origin of the Domestic Animals of Africa*, 2 volumes (New York, 2nd edn. 1971)
Fage, J. D. & Oliver, Roland (eds.): *Papers in African Prehistory* (Cambridge, 1970)
Gabel, Creighton: 'Terminal food-collectors and agricultural initiative in East and Southern Africa' (*International Journal of African Historical Studies*, VII, 1974, p. 56–68)
Gwynne, M. D.: 'The origin and spread of some domestic food plants of eastern Africa' (Chittick, H. N. & Rotberg, R. I. eds.: *East Africa and the Orient, Cultural Syntheses in Pre-colonial Times*, New York and London, 1975)
Harlan, Jack R., De Wet, Jan M. J. & Stremler, Ann B. L. (eds.): *Origins of African Plant Domestication* (The Hague, 1976)
Havinden, M. A.: 'The history of crop cultivation in West Africa: a bibliographical guide' (*Economic History Review*, 2nd ser., XXIII, 1970, p. 532–55)
Inskeep, R. R.: *The Peopling of Southern Africa* (Cape Town and London, 1978)
Jones, William O.: *Manioc in Africa* (Stanford, 1959)
Krzyzaniak, Lech: 'New light on early food-production in the central Sudan' (*Journal of African History*, XIX, 1978, p. 159–72)
Mellaart, James: *The Neolithic of the Near East* (London, 1975)
Miracle, Marvin P.: *Maize in Tropical Africa* (Madison, Wis., 1966)
Murdock, G. D.: *Africa, its Peoples and their Culture History* (New York, 1959)
Phillipson, D. W.: *The Later Prehistory of Eastern and Southern Africa* (London, 1977)

Purseglove, J. W.: *Tropical Crops, Dicotyledons*, 2 volumes (London and Harlow, 1968)

Shaw, Thurstan: 'Early agriculture in Africa' (*Journal of the Historical Society of Nigeria*, VI, 1972, p. 143–91)

Shaw, T.: 'Hunters, gatherers and first farmers in West Africa' (Chapter 5, Magaw, J. V. S. ed.: *Hunters, Gatherers and First Farmers Beyond Europe*, Leicester, 1977)

Trigger, Bruce C.: *Nubia under the Pharaohs* (London, 1976)

Ucko, P. J. & Dimbleby, G. W. (eds.): *The Domestication of Plants and Animals* (London, 1963)

Zeuner, F. E.: *A History of Domesticated Animals* (New York, 1963)

2. THE METHODS

i) Nomadism and shifting cultivation

To this day there are peoples in Africa who live on the proceeds of hunting and gathering (for example, the San of the Kalahari, the Hadza of northern Tanzania) or fishing (for example, the Twa of Zambia). Even when a people adopted agriculture and stock-raising, that did not put an end to their hunting and gathering. In Africa as in medieval Europe, hunting went on as long as there was something to hunt (for sport, clothing and trade goods – above all ivory – as much as for subsistence) and gathering as long as there was something to collect (for medicines and raw materials for manufacturing, as much as for food). The honey of wild bees was particularly prized. The gifts of untamed nature could ensure survival in times of crop failure. Even in a country with as highly developed an agriculture as Egypt, the Fayum remained a hunting ground until it was brought into cultivation under irrigation in Ptolemaic and Roman times. The products of the chase were supplemented by fishing, which, like hunting, was for most men a part-time occupation, for some a full-time one. There is evidence of the exploitation of shell-fish beds along the shore of what is now the Ivory Coast, and in the Cape by people whom the Dutch settlers called strandlopers; and the use of tidal fish-traps throughout the Christian era along the coasts of the Cape. At the other end of the continent the catching and salting of fish was an important North African industry as early as Carthaginian times. West African dried and salted fish was an important item of trade, and dried lake fish was traded in East Africa. Maritime fishing was subject to constraints. The Mediterranean, lacking shallow water, is not well endowed with fish shoals, while a shortage of satisfactory harbours and a lack of ocean-going vessels precluded sea fishing outside of coastal waters along much of Africa's coastline. In southern Africa the ocean fishing industry developed after European settlement and the introduction of European boats, and even there had no great importance before the 19th century.

Pastoralists, like the earlier hunters and gatherers and like some fisher people, maintained a nomadic or semi-nomadic life, driven to fresh pastures by the poor quality of much of the grazing of tropical and sub-tropical Africa, where the rapid growth of grass over a period of a few weeks' rain was followed by an equally rapid loss of 'nutrient status' after maturity. A semi-nomadism was characteristic of the Khoikhoi 'hordes' in southern Africa, who moved regularly with their cattle and sheep from pasture to pasture, each within a territory recognized as their own. Transhumance was the custom of the European settler of the early Cape, who spent the summer in the uplands, the winter in the lower altitudes of the Karoo, and of the Berber nomads of North Africa, who from time immemorial drove their herds and flocks of goats and long-tailed sheep into the more humid Atlas mountain zone during the summer drought of the Sahara fringe. In Egypt, where grazing was poor, from ancient times cattle were pastured for fattening in the marshes of the Delta before the Nile's summer flood. South of the Sahara the pastoralists of West Africa accompanied their animals from the Sahel, the 'shore' of the Sahara, as the Arabs called it, into the savanna during the dry season in search of better grazing, and back again when the southerly rains threatened them with fly-borne diseases. Of these the most deadly was trypanosomiasis, which imposed severe limitations upon animal husbandry over a large part of Africa to the south of the desert. Tick-borne diseases were another hazard, though centuries of natural selection bred beasts that were partially resistant to such diseases, as well as inured to heat.

René Caillié's 1825 description of the Tuaregs in the neighbourhood of Timbuktu illustrates not only their economy, but also their relations with their sedentary neighbours, typical of all such boundaries between cultivation and pastoralism.

> The Tooariks have terrified the negroes of their neighbourhood into subjection, and they inflict upon them the most cruel depredations and exactions. Like the Arabs, they have fine horses which facilitate their marauding expeditions. The people exposed to their attacks stand in such awe of them, that the appearance of three or four Tooariks is sufficient to strike terror into five or six villages . . .
> The Tooariks possess numerous flocks of sheep and herds of oxen and goats. Milk and meat are their only food. Their slaves gather the seed of the nenuphar, which is very common in all the surrounding marshes; they dry it and thrash it. It is so small that it does not require bruising; they boil it with their fish. The Tooariks cultivate no kind of vegetable. Their slaves are employed in tending their flocks and herds. They have no grain for their own use, except what they obtain from the flotillas passing from Jenné to Timbuctoo. During the swell of the waters, the Tooariks retire a little into the interior of the country, where they find good pasture. They have numerous herds of camels, whose milk is always a certain resource for them.[1]

The nomadic way of life was exceedingly tenacious. Some peoples practise an attenuated form of nomadic pastoralism to this day, for example the Cushitic-speaking Somali and Galla of Somalia, Ethiopia and Kenya, the

Nilotic-speaking Nuer and Dinka of the Sudan, the Fulani of West Africa, the Nama of Namibia and the Masai of Tanzania and Kenya, who are alone in not going in for cultivation, even as a subsidiary activity. Milk mixed with blood in most cases forms an important part of the diet of these people. The Dinka supplement their pastoral diet with fish, but Cushitic-speakers and some Nilotes abhor it. The surviving pastoralists inhabit areas suitable for little but very extensive pastoralism. There is no evidence to support the view that pastoralism necessarily precedes agriculture. Agriculture could equally be developed by people dependent upon fishing, and, indeed, nomadism itself could be a response by a sedentary people adjusting to a deteriorating environment, which could no longer support permanent settlement. However, the trend in the better endowed areas has been towards sedentary cultivation owing to increasing pressure upon land. Most herders engaged in some cultivation, even before land began to be a scarce resource, just as most cultivators kept some beasts. Often there was collaboration, taking the form of product exchange, between pastoralists and agriculturalists, though accompanied by suspicion on one side and contempt on the other. Such a relationship was characteristic of the Fulani and the Hausa in West Africa and of the Masai and the Kikuyu in East Africa. A really intimate connection between the two activities, was, however, rare. Mungo Park recorded one instance:

> This town (Kirwani) stands in a valley, and the country, for more than a mile round it, is cleared of wood, and well cultivated. The inhabitants appear to be very active and industrious, and seemed to have carried the system of agriculture to some degree of perfection, for they collect the dung of their cattle into large heaps during the dry season, for the purpose of manuring their land with it at the proper time. I saw nothing like this in any other part of Africa.[2]

As a rule, agriculture tended to be starved of animal manure. Even where it was available, it was seldom used for fertilizer. Cultivation and animal husbandry commonly co-existed without true mixed farming emerging. Shortage or neglect of animal fertilizer enforced an extensive type of cultivation.

Well-watered and fertile soil is rare in Africa. Half or more of the continent can be classified as arid or semi-arid. To be sure, there are places where precipitation is very heavy - the Congo Basin, the West African littoral and the Ethiopian Highlands. In Ethiopia the rain clouds brought in by the Indian Ocean monsoon break on the mountains, leaving Somalia dry and the Eritrean coast in the rain-shadow. For the most part, Africa north of the 15th parallel North, as far as the Mediterranean coast, and south of the 20th parallel South, as far as the Cape coast, together with large areas of East Africa, enjoys meagre rainfall. Most soil is deficient in calcium and phosphorus, as important for stock-raising as for cultivation. Where rainfall is generous, heavy showers leach the soil and harden the surface of the earth.

Shifting cultivation, where land rather than crops was rotated, was widely practised by African farmers because of the poverty of the soil, and it survives over much of Central and East Africa and part of West Africa to the present. This involved the use of the ash of burnt vegetation for fertilizer. Fire and cattle between them had a profound effect upon the physical character of the continent. Burning, not only to clear land, but also to encourage the early regrowth of grasses, together with the grazing and trampling of beasts, turned woodland into grassland and grassland into desert. The destruction of trees exposed the earth to leaching and, by destroying the habitat of the tsetse fly, permitted an extension of cattle farming, which, through overgrazing, brought with it the danger of soil erosion. In Egypt the erosion of the Eastern Desert has been attributed to the destruction of trees and shrubs by charcoal-burners and camels; in Nubia overexploitation of pasture and woodland contributed to the increasing encroachment of desert in the Nile valley in Meroitic times; in North Africa the Sahara desert relentlessly encroached upon the savanna; in South Africa, where European settlers resorted to fire as much as the Nguni did, Karoid scrub steadily spread, to the detriment of the quality of the natural pasture. 'Since the white man has been in South Africa,' reported the Drought Investigation Committee in 1923, 'enormous tracts of country have been entirely, or partially denuded of their original vegetation.'[3] Travelling from the Riet Valley to Mossel Bay in 1775, the Swedish physician and naturalist Anders Sparrman noticed the depredation caused by the overgrazing of Boer cattle.

In direct contradiction to the custom and example of the original inhabitants the Hottentots, the colonists turn their cattle out constantly into the same fields, and that too in a much greater quantity than used to graze there in the time of the Hottentots . . . In consequence of the fields being thus continually grazed off, and the great increase of the cattle feeding on them, the grasses and the herbs which these animals most covet are prevented continually more and more from thriving and taking root; while, on the contrary, the *rhinoceros-bush*, which the cattle always pass by and leave untouched, is suffered to take root free and unmolested, and encroach on the place of others . . . Notwithstanding these inconveniences, the colonists remain immoveable in their stone houses; while, on the contrary, the Hottentots (and this was the case in former times) on the least panic remove their huts and cattle to another place, so that the grass is nowhere eaten off too close.[4]

Shifting cultivation requires a great deal of land. With the *chitemene* system of present-day Zambia the area cultivated requires the collection and burning of the bushes, branches and bark of an area up to five times more extensive than itself. Elsewhere the ratio of area stripped to the garden might be a great deal bigger than that. Fire is not always used. In the *Dinka* system in the Sudan the help of termites is enlisted, and in the *Proka* system of Ghana vegetation is cleared from the land and simply left to rot. But all variants entail an extravagant use of forest or woodland. Therefore in West Africa the increasing pressure upon land compelled the introduction of the more intensive 'rotational bush fallow' method, also practised in parts of East Africa and the Sudan. In the woodland savanna of West Africa, where the soil was comparatively fertile, a cleared patch might be cultivated up to twenty years before declining yields forced the farmer to abandon it. Since it could take half a century to recover fully, as population grew, land in fallow was increasingly recultivated before it had reverted to woodland. With a regular alternation of cultivation and fallow within a defined area, settlement became permanent and fields near larger settlements might be fertilized and kept under continuous cultivation, as Mungo Park observed. In districts of intensive farming all the trees disappeared except for those of economic value – the baobab, the shea butter nut, the tamarind, the locust bean, etc. Among the Yoruba of West Africa an effective rotation of crops was developed, though this was exceptional. Intercropping was a much more common practice, offering, by spreading risks, greater security, which was valued more than higher total output.

ii) *Permanent cultivation in northern Africa*
Permanent cultivation was adopted most readily in those regions, of varying size, whose fertility and water supply afforded the opportunity for intensive agriculture. These included the so-called inland delta of the Niger, watered by the floods brought down each year by the rains that fell on the Fouta Djallon; the flood plain of the upper Zambezi; the interlacustrine region of East Africa, bordering Lakes Victoria, Kyoga and Kivu. The highlands of Ethiopia and Kenya, Mt. Kilimanjaro and the Shire highlands were also blessed with a fertile soil and ample rain. Along the east coast there was the relatively fertile, though narrow, coastal belt. At the southern extremity of the continent there was the Cape of Good Hope region with its Mediterranean-type climate. On the Mediterranean itself there were three enclaves, of varying fertility, in the great North African desert with a regular supply of water – Egypt, the Tell valleys of the Atlas mountains and, rather less favoured, the coastal belt of Tripolitania and Cyrenaica, on the flanks of the Gulf of Sidra.

In Egypt there was little or no rainfall outside the northern part of the Delta, which enjoyed Mediterranean winter rain, but the flood waters of the Nile, though on occasion liable to total failure, normally provided an almost inexhaustible fertility. The inundation usually began at Aswan at the end of May or the beginning of June, reaching its fullest during early September. First came the waters of the more powerful White Nile, which, damming up those of the Blue Nile, released them as their own flood subsided, so that the whole flooding process was happily protracted. In the valley and delta the bounty of nature was husbanded by a comprehensive system of control and irrigation. Flood control and utilization demanded an annual repetition of essential work: dykes and their revetments had to be repaired, irrigation basins, in which the mud was deposited, canals, ditches and runnels excavated and cleared. In the spring and early summer, before the July floods, orchards, fields and gardens had to be watered directly from the river and those which were not reached by the flood at all, from wells. The shaduf was used, a bucket attached to the end of a pole suspended between two vertical pillars and counter-balanced by a weight at the other end, or, from the Hellenistic period, by the sakîye, an ox-driven wheel with pots attached. Such methods were used all along the Nile, even as far as the confluence with the Atbara, where the alluvial plain between the two rivers was able to support the prosperous kingdom of Kush and its successors in the lst millennium B.C. The problem in Nubia, however, was rather different. In Egypt it was a question of exploiting the silt brought down by the river, in Nubia of preventing it from being carried away. Hence substantial retaining walls were constructed in the Middle Ages.

Successive rulers of Egypt maintained with varying devotion and efficiency the irrigation system in working order. Some extended the cultivated area – the Ptolemies, for example, who brought the Fayum into cultivation and encouraged Greek settlement, and the earlier and more energetic Mamluk sultans, who were responsible for the throwing up of new dykes and the excavation of new canals in the Delta – and fostered the raising of new breeds of livestock and the cultivation of new crops and less familiar, but more favoured, plants and trees – winter wheat, which became the chief export crop, the vine and the olive in Hellenistic times, though, in the case of the olive, with only indifferent success, and sugar cane in Muslim times. But Egypt remained above all a producer of cereals.

For preparing the soil for sowing, the plough, attached to the horns of oxen until the invention of the shoulder-yoke and draught pole, was in use in Egypt as early as 3 000 B.C. Originally, and long continuing to be, nothing more complicated than a forked stick, capable of merely scratching the surface with its point, it was used throughout the Mediterranean basin and was all that was necessary where soils were commonly thin and stony. A straight furrow permitted the even sowing of the seed and facilitated weeding, thus increasing productivity and contributing to population growth. The sickle for harvesting was many centuries older than the plough. Threshing was done by the hooves of animals driven round and round a circular threshing floor, though the Carthaginians developed a rudimentary threshing machine, known as a Punic cart.

In north-west Africa the western Mediterranean basin is bounded by the Atlas mountain system, stretching nearly two thousand kilometres from southern Morocco in the west to the Gulf of Gabès in the east. The High Atlas in Morocco, which rises in places to more than 4 000 metres, traps the rain brought in on the westerly winds of winter, thus providing sufficient water for the practice of agriculture in the coastal lowlands, on the hills and in the mountain valleys, in a zone that is seldom wider than 300 kilometres between the coast and the northern edge of the Sahara. At its eastern end there is a tradition of intensive horticulture going back to Carthaginian times. Although at first the Phoenecian colonists, since they were primarily traders, were content to be confined to the promontory on which Carthage was built and to import a substantial part of their foodstuffs, later, from the 5th century B.C., they conquered most of what is now Tunisia and devoted much more attention to agriculture and, by the standards of the time, to scientific cattle breeding. In addition, they bred the native long-tailed sheep and Barbary horse. Among their agronomists was the famous Mago, who evidently wrote in the 3rd century B.C. and whose treatise on husbandry was translated into Latin. A small area (the *chora*), between the foothills of the Algerian mountains and the Gulf of Gabès, was cultivated by Carthaginian nobles and their slaves, producing olives, dates, almonds, grapes, figs and 'Punic apples' – pomegranates. Wine was made, but African wine did not enjoy a high reputation. Outside the *chora*, Berber peasants, compelled by the Carthaginians to restrict their cultivation to cereals, paid a heavy tribute in kind, normally a tenth of their crop, but sometimes rising to a half.

East of the major enclave of north-west Africa lies the coastal plain of Tripolitania and Cyrenaica. Since, however, it is split by the approach of the desert to the sea, the western part, Tripolitania, was in ancient times oriented to Carthage, the eastern part, Cyrenaica, to Egypt. The latter, the more favoured of the two, derived its name from the colony of Cyrene, which the Greeks set up in the 7th century B.C., the first of several colonies along the coast of the Gulf of Sidra. An attempt by the Spartans, however, in the 6th century B.C. to establish a settlement in Tripolitania was thwarted by the Carthaginians, who themselves founded a few colonies along this coast, and these won considerable prosperity, though through trade, not agriculture. In the Greek sphere Cyrene became celebrated for its exports of silphium, a plant which, valued as both food and medicine, grew wild on the slopes of the interior, and for its breeding of sheep and horses, famous for their speed. Silphium was an early victim of man's inhumanity to nature. Uncontrolled grazing stamped it out of existence during the period of Roman rule. Corn was grown on the Barca plateau, where heavy dews compensated for the over-rapid drainage of the rain and its variability. The surplus of good years was exported. The unreliability of rainfall was even more pronounced in Tripolitania, lying as it did at the very edge of the Mediterranean climatic region.

The intensive cultivation begun by the Carthaginians and Greeks was extended with great success under the administration of the Romans. Nomads were encouraged to take up farming, and the Roman armies that moved into the interior were followed to the south by migrants from the more favoured parts of the country, where there was growing pressure upon the available land. The frontier fortification – the *limes* – offered the peace and security conducive to the cultivation of a large part of the steppes (now desolate) of Tunisia and eastern Algeria and, further to the west, where the *limes* ran much nearer to the sea, the coastal plain of western Algeria. In the province of Mauretania Tingitana, modern Morocco, the Rif and the plains of Sébou were farmed.

Wheat was the staple insisted on under Roman, as under Carthaginian, rule, until the Emperor Hadrian in the 2nd century A.D. encouraged the cultivation of olive trees and vines. There was some mixed farming on the larger estates of northern Tunisia, while on the western hills horses, donkeys and mules were bred and sheep kept for wool. Techniques of crop raising made little progress in Roman times. Except in the special conditions of Egypt, a two-year cycle of crops was generally the rule, the land lying fallow every other year, chiefly to permit the soil to recover, but partly also to allow it to store up humidity in a climate where rains tended to be heavy and brief. Although the principle of crop rotation was known, it was little practised. Nevertheless, the Romans were able to raise agricultural output in North Africa by water conservation techniques that had already been used by the Carthaginians and by the Greeks of Cyrenaica. Along the margin of the desert they built on hillsides terraces and walls to prevent water rushing down the slopes and taking the soil with it, while mountain streams were dammed and their water channelled off for distribution to cultivators according to elaborate rules. Deep wells were dug and basins and cisterns made to collect and store rainwater. Along the frontier veterans who were settled as *limitanei* to combine defence with farming derived a modest income from the tending of olive trees. Olives, too, in the Roman period came to be the principal agricultural product of Tripolitania, an area somewhat dry for cereals.

From the 3rd century A.D. North Africa experienced a long history of turbulence. Religious and political disputes and persecution, nomadic incursions and peasant discontent, the Vandal conquest of the 5th century and the Byzantine reconquest of the 6th, all threatened the well-being of the agricultural economy. Exploited peasants took advantage of the Vandal

intrusion to rise against oppressive landlords, and there was a resurgence of
Berber tribalism, even among the sedentary population, which the conquerors found themselves less and less able to control. The Byzantines revived
the neglected *limes* and relied once more on the soldier-peasant *limitanei*, but
their rule was never fully secure. The Arabs, when they overran the Maghrib
in the 7th century, proved to be a pacifying and unifying force, particularly
as Islam spread among the Berbers. Yet, even over the earlier centuries of
violence and upheaval, there were extended periods of quiet and relative
prosperity. The Arabs did not inherit a shattered economy, and indeed,
during the last years of rule from Constantinople, North Africa enjoyed a
period of stability.

Muslim agriculture was efficient and progressive. There was much distinguished writing on agricultural science and patronage of experimentation
was fashionable among the wealthy and great. Soil enrichment, crop rota-
tions and permutations and irrigation received much attention. The underground canal (*qanāt*) for conveying water over long distances and the
current-driven or animal-powered wheel for lifting it from rivers, canals,
cisterns and wells were extensively adopted. The *qanāt*, which linked up a
series of wells, appears to have been invented in Persia and was known in
pre-Islamic Egypt, but its wider adoption, like the diffusion of less familiar
plants, was typical of Muslim innovation.

In the 11th century a new Arab wave struck the Maghrib, the nomadic
Banū Hilāl and Banū Sulaim and others, who, often in alliance with Berber
nomads, crossed the ancient *limes*, destroying the barrages and cisterns or
leaving them to fall into decay. Much more numerous than the first Arab
invaders, the primitive and predatory bedouin devastated the countryside
and began that process of decline that turned the ancient granary of the
Roman empire into a grain importer by the 16th century. That at least is the
conventional view of the effects of the bedouin invasion, one owing much
to the authority of Ibn Khaldūn, the Muslim scholar of Tunisia. It should be
borne in mind, however, that the intensive cultivation of the Romans had
carried with it the risk of soil erosion owing to the deforestation inevitable
with a growing population in need of wood for fuel, timber for building
and land for cultivation. Kept at bay by the conservation policy of the Roman administration, the danger was realized once that policy lapsed. At all
events it is apparent that villages disappeared, cultivation received a set-back
and the coastal plains mostly became grazing lands for the sheep of the
nomadic invaders, except in Tunisia – the Arab Ifriqiya, the old Roman
province of Africa – where the ancient life of the smallholder was preserved
and, in the 17th century, strengthened by the immigration of Muslims deported from Spain, skilled husbandmen. A dichotomy remains to this day,
between the overcrowded cultivators and transhumant herdsmen in the hills,

largely Berber-speaking, and the nomadic herdsmen of the sparsely inhabited steppes and coastal plains.

iii) *Permanent cultivation in sub-Saharan Africa*

Evidence in the form of artificial reservoirs shows that water conservation methods similar to those employed by the Romans in North Africa were copied by the Berbers in Fezzan in Libya and were also used at Meroe in the 1st century A.D. On the southern fringe of the Sahara, too, in the Sahel, wells were dug, cisterns hollowed out and the water lifted up by means of the shaduf. As in North Africa, devastation was wreaked by nomads – Berbers who, after an onslaught upon the ancient Sudanese kingdom of Ghana in the 11th century, neglected the wells with which the sedentary farmers had supported their modest agriculture, and whose herds, by destroying the vegetation, accelerated soil erosion. Irrigation, however, continued to be practised in the West African savanna. At the beginning of 1824 Hugh Clapperton saw irrigated wheat fields near Katagum, in what is now northern Nigeria, though he left no description of methods employed there.

Elsewhere in Africa the water problem was mostly different from that in North Africa and the Sahel, where it was a question of husbanding and distributing limited supplies of water. The trouble was chiefly the irregularity of the water supply. Drought alternated with torrential rain that washed away top soil. High temperatures meant high evaporation rates and this, combined with heavy rain, had a deleterious effect upon the nutrient value of the soil. Effective water control was necessary for efficient agriculture. Africa south of the Sahara, however, did not go far in devising conservation and distribution techniques, at least partly, it may be supposed, because labour was lacking for the construction of extensive damming and irrigation facilities. The waterwheel was unknown outside of the Nile valley and the Saharan oases. Nonetheless, rice was grown under irrigation in Madagascar and terracing and irrigation were practised in the Inyanga highlands of modern Zimbabwe, where extensive terracing and irrigation channels apparently date back to the 16th - 18th centuries. In East Africa, at Engaruka in the Rift Valley on the present Kenya-Tanzanian border, there are the remains dated to some time after the 14th century of an irrigation scheme that watered an area of more than twenty square kilometres. Irrigation channels were stone-lined.

Joseph Thomson, travelling in 1883, described the methods of the Chagga on the slopes of Mt. Kilimanjaro.

The village occupies the top of a narrow ridge formed by a deep glen on either side. From the upper part of the small streams miniature canals, constructed with great

skill, lead off the water and spread it over the entire ridge, thus supplying moisture throughout the entire year. A more rich and varied scene I have nowhere
looked upon in Africa. The rich carpet of grass alternated or intermingled with
banana groves, fields of beans, millet, Indian corn, sweet potatoes, yams, etc. . . .
Lazy cattle lay about the huts, or browsed knee-deep in the succulent grass. Goats,
lively and frisksome, skipped about the banks . . . Sheep loaded with enormous
fat tails wobbling about their legs, looked as if aweary of existence . . .

He saw a similar sight later between Lake Baringo and Lake Victoria.

The soil being the very richest loam, brought down from the mountains and
spread over a comparatively level plain to the south of the lake, it is capable of
producing anything; only the extreme dryness of the air and the very small annual
rainfall, confined to a couple of months, keeps it sterile and barren. To ameliorate
this unhappy condition of things the Wa-kwafi have developed a wonderfully ingenious system of irrigation by artificial canals of (for them) great magnitude.
They construct dams across the deep channel of the Guaso Tigirish and thus raise
the level of the water to that of the plain, and then, by an intricate network of
channels, they spread the precious fluid over a large area, and raise their millet and
melons.[5]

The plough was adopted with various draught beasts by the peoples to the
south and west of Egypt, but no farther south than Ethiopia in the east and
the Sahara in the west. Over large parts of Africa the diseases that prevented
pastoral farming naturally also inhibited the use of draught animals, and the
capital and running costs of plough-cultivation were perhaps higher than
farmers were willing to accept. But the failure to make use of the plough
helped to account for the non-appearance of true mixed farming and, therefore, acted as a restraint upon agricultural productivity.

In those areas where the plough was unknown, or at least unused, the
implements commonly employed for breaking up the ground were merely
digging sticks, hoes (of varying lengths) and machets. Primitive tools were
perhaps more suitable for the shallow soil found in large parts of Africa,
where ploughing, by loosening the ground and increasing the rate of evaporation, would have caused soil erosion. Even if the character of the soil
lent itself to ploughing, the persistence of tree stumps after land had been
cleared by fire would have made it difficult. Furthermore, there was little
incentive to cultivate a great deal more land than was strictly necessary.
'Few people,' observed Mungo Park,

work harder, when occasion requires, than the Mandingoes; but not having many
opportunities of turning to advantage the superfluous produce of their labour,
they are content with cultivating as much ground only as is necessary for their
own support. The labours of the field give them pretty full employment during
the rains. [6]

Although the plough saves labour, and labour was always hard to come by, the clearance of virgin land by slash and burn methods and its preparation with hoe and digging stick undoubtedly gave a higher yield per hectare than plough-cultivation would have done, and therefore the proportion of the crop per hectare that had to be kept for seed was less than it would have been with plough-cultivation. More land could have been planted had the plough been used, and that would have compensated for the lower yield per hectare, but the initial seed-corn requirement might have been difficult to set aside – difficult not only in physical terms, but, above all, psychologically. On the other hand, it can scarcely be argued that traditional agricultural techniques were the ideal adaptation to the environment. The exploitation of some of the best soils – the heavy soils of the alluvial savannas – was beyond the capability of the rudimentary tools available. Backward technology, shortage of labour and capital, social objectives that gave priority to the satisfaction of immediate needs rather than to the maximization of production, and problems of storage, all discouraged better methods of cultivation, whether through more thorough breaking up of the land, more systematic weeding or more intensive fertilization.

During the last days of his life Captain Hugh Clapperton (died 1826), confined to Sokoto, described in some detail the agricultural method employed in the vicinity, showing the enormous application of labour required.

Their agriculture is simple enough. They begin clearing the ground of weeds, and burning them after the first fall of rain, which in Houssa is in the month of May, and when a person wishes to enclose a piece of ground for his own use, he first gets permission from the governor. He then sets his slaves, if he has any, to cut down the smaller trees and brushwood, leaving the micadonia or butter trees, if there be any, standing on the ground: the wood, brushwood, and weeds are then gathered together in heaps and burnt. After the first rains have fallen, the male and female slaves go to work, each male having a hoe with a long handle, and each female a basket, dish, or gourd, filled with the grain intended to be sown: the male goes on in a straight line crossing the field, striking as it were with his hoe on each side, and raising a little earth each blow in the line about two or three feet, or broad enough for a man to walk; the females follow with their baskets of grain, dropping the seeds into the holes made by the hoe, which they then cover over with earth, and give it a slight pressure with the foot. When the doura or other grain has risen above the ground three or four inches, the weeds are hoed off, and the earth loosened around the stalks; when the doura has got to the height of three or four feet, they hoe around it a second time, leaving the weeds in the middle of the rows. This is cleared away, when small millet or calavances are to be sown between the rows of doura, which is frequently the case. The third operation is to draw the weeds and earth towards the roots of the doura a little before it ripens. When ripe, the slaves go into the field or plantation, pull it up by the roots, and lay it in rows between each row of millet which is left to ripen: it lies in this state four or five days, when they cut the heads off, tie them up in bundles, and carry it home; where, after lying upon sheds made of the branches of trees for a few days to dry, what is not wanted for use is stowed away in their granary. As the seeds of the doura begin to ripen, it must be constantly watched by the slaves, who are perched on trees, or on raised platforms, with dried gourds, which they shake to make a noise, at the same time shouting and hallooing to frighten away the flocks of small birds which come to devour the grain, and which at this season fly in myriads, making a whirring noise with their wings when they rise. The doura is very subject to blight, caused by a kind of winged insect, of a black colour ... The millet and calavances remain a month on the ground after the doura.

After describing the cultivation of sweet potatoes, gaza, wheat, and rice, he went on to talk of indigo and cotton:

When they wish to plant indigo, the place chosen is one of a good strong clay or mould, and in a situation where there is moisture through the heat of the summer. After enclosing the ground, they clear it entirely of weeds, and burn them. The ground is well worked up by the hoe (they have no spade or pickaxe), and laid out in furrows, with a flat top, about a foot high, two broad, and six or seven inches between each furrow. The indigo seeds are then planted by the dibble, and just as the rains have begun: they cut it every year during the rainy season. A plantation will last four or five years without renewing the seeds. They crop it about three or four inches above the ground. The leaves are then stripped from the stems, and laid in a heap, exposed to the rains and weather for a month, until they ferment, when they are beaten in wooden troughs of a round form, and about two feet deep, and two feet in diameter; here they remain until dry, and are then consider-ed as fit for use ...

The cotton is here planted in low situations, where the ground is partially cover-ed with water during the rains, or else in a good clay that has moisture in it through the dry season. The ground, or plantation, is generally only surrounded by thorny branches stuck in the ground as a fence, then hoed well, and the clods, if any re-main, broken. A hole is made with the hoe, and the seed is put in and lightly covered. If the season be abundant in rain, the cotton is plenty; if not, the crop is bad. The time of pulling is in the months of December and January. When work-ed, it is done by the women, clearing it of the seeds by two small iron pins, be-tween which the cotton passes over a flat stone lying on the ground; the seeds are thrown behind them, the cotton before. The seeds they give to bullocks and camels, and are considered as very fattening ... They have three different kinds of hoes: one with a handle of about five feet in length, and a small head stuck into the end of the staff; this is used in sowing the grain: one with a handle of about three feet in length, with a small iron head stuck into the end of the staff: the third, call-ed gilma, has a short bent handle, with a large head, and is used in all the heavy work instead of a spade.[7]

Food storage presented a problem in tropical conditions of heat, damp and innumerable pests. Methods varied. René Caillié in 1827 saw among the Bambaras, provisions bundled up in straw and kept out of the damp on stakes or stones. This was a rudimentary method. More common were granaries constructed of matting and raised on poles. Clapperton noted near Sokoto a granary which could store grain for up to three years.

Their granaries are made in the form of a large urn or pitcher, raised from the ground about three feet by stones. They are made of clay and chopped straw, and are raised to the height of eleven or twelve feet. The thickness of the sides is not above four inches, though in any part it will bear a man's weight: the diameter in the widest part may be from seven to eight feet, at the top about three or four feet, and is overlapped at the mouth like a wide-mouthed earthen jar. When the grain is put in, a conical cap of thatch is put over to keep out birds, insects, wet and moisture . . .[8]

In the area of European settlement in southern Africa the agricultural methods of Europe were employed. Although they seem to have little vindicated the reputation their agriculture at home had acquired, the Dutch at the Cape were faced with novel and difficult conditions. It took half a century for the settlement to become fully self-sufficient. Farming was dominated by the needs of the East India Company, which, above all concerned with making a trading profit in the East, regarded the Cape mainly as a source of provisions for its ships calling there. Like the Mande-speaking people noticed by Mungo Park, the farmers of the Cape of Good Hope had little incentive to produce a surplus when the market was so narrow, and into the bargain so unfairly regulated from their point of view. Like the farmers of West Africa again, they suffered from shortage of labour and capital.

Beyond the immediate vicinity of Cape Town subsistence farming predominated. Only a tiny proportion of the immense farms that became characteristic of the interior was cultivated, turned over by a clumsy and ineffective plough. But not all Cape farmers were unprogressive and mistreated their environment.

We returned about noon to the Klavervalley, and in the afternoon visited the brother of our host, Mr Jacob Van Reenen . . . This gentleman lives at a place upon the coast called Ganzekraal, about an hour's distance from the Klavervalley . . . Both this place and the Klavervalley are among the best and most fertile spots, not only of these parts, but of the whole colony. No people deserve more credit for the great pains they have taken in the improvement of agriculture and the treatment of cattle than the numerous family of the Van Reenens . . . As an instance of Mr Jacob Van Reenen's attention to these things, and of his ardour in the pursuit of them, it may be mentioned, that he this year has cultivated two hundred and forty acres of land on which he has bestowed sixteen hundred loads of manure. He told us, moreover, that he could insure excellent crops by only manuring his lands every three years. One of his fields, husbanded in this way, had already produced him crops for twenty-four years successively.

On the other hand:

That such ample returns from the lands is not generally to be expected must not, however, be entirely ascribed to ignorance and want of attention in the owners, but much more to the great distance from the Cape Town, so that they cannot have the same supply of manure, to the want of a sufficient capital to expend upon the culture, and to not having a sufficient number of slaves for tilling the ground. As long as these obstacles continue, and the proprietors depend only on slaves for the culture of their lands, no sanguine hopes are to be entertained of agriculture being greatly improved in the interior of the colony.[9]

As the market widened, methods improved, but serious problems remain to this day, above all soil erosion attributable to the improvident and ill-advised use of resources.

NOTES

1. Howard, C. (ed.): *West African Explorers* (London, 1951), p. 385
2. Park, M.: *The Travels* (London, Everyman edition, n.d.), p. 266
3. Quoted Wilson, Francis: *The Oxford History of South Africa*, Volume II, p. 134
4. Sparrman, Anders: *A Voyage to the Cape of Good Hope* (Cape Town, 1975), p. 239
5. Richards, Charles & Place, James (eds.): *East African Explorers* (London, 1960), p. 201 209–10
6. Park, M.: Op.cit., p. 215
7. Howard, C.: Op. cit., p. 283–4, 287–8
8. Ibid, p. 285
9. Lichtenstein, Henry: *Travels in Southern Africa in the Years 1803, 1804 and 1806* (Cape Town, 1928), p. 30–1, 31–2

Further reading

Abun-Nasr, Jamil M.: *A History of the Maghrib* (Cambridge, 2nd edn. 1975)
Aldred, Cyril: *The Egyptians* (London, 1961)
Aldred, Cyril: *Egypt to the End of the Old Kingdom* (London, 1965)
Allan, William: *The African Husbandman* (London, 1965)
Bovill, E. W.: *The Golden Trade of the Moors* (Oxford, 2nd edn. 1970)
Charles-Picard, Gilbert & Colette: *Daily Life in Carthage at the Time of Hannibal* (London, 1961)
Church, R. J. Harrison, Clarke, John I., Clarke, P. J. H. & Henderson, H. J. R.: *Africa and the Islands* (London and Harlow, 2nd edn. 1967)
Church, R. J Harrison: *West Africa, a Study of the Environment and Man's Use of it* (London, 5th edn. 1966)
De Wilde, John et al.: *Experiences with Agricultural Development in Tropical Africa*, Volume 1 (Baltimore, 1967)
Faulkner, O. T. & Mackie, J. R.: *West African Agriculture* (Cambridge, 1933)
Fisher, H. J.: 'The eastern Maghrib and the central Sudan' (Chapter 4, Oliver, Roland ed.: *The Cambridge History of Africa*, Volume 3, c.1050 to c.1600, Cambridge, 1977)
Forde, Cyril Daryll: *Habitat, Economy, and Society; a Geographical Introduction to Ethnology* (London, 1934)
Forde, Cyril Daryll & Scott, Richenda: *The Native Economies of Nigeria* (London, 1946)

Hailey, Lord: *An African Survey, a Study of Problems Arising in Africa South of the Sahara* (London, 1938, 1945 and 1957)

Hodder, B. W. & Harris, D. R.: *Africa in Transition* (London, 1967)

Johnson, Allan Chester & West, L. C.: *Byzantine Egypt: Economic Studies* (Princeton, 1949)

Johnson, Allan Chester: *Roman Egypt to the Reign of Diocletian* (Volume II, Frank, Tenney ed.: *An Economic Survey of Ancient Rome*) (Patterson, N. J., 1938)

Julien, Charles-André: *Histoire de l'Afrique du Nord*, Volume I, *Des Origines à la Conquête Arabe (647 ap. J.-C.)* (Paris, 1968)

McLoughlin, Peter F. M. ed.: *African Food Production Systems, Cases and Theory* (Baltimore, 1970)

Mair, Lucy: *African Societies* (London, 1974)

Manshard, Walther: *Tropical Agriculture, a Geographical Introduction and Appraisal* (London, 1974)

Mellor, J. W.: *The Economics of Agricultural Development* (Ithaca, 1966)

Morgan, W. B. & Pugh, J. C.: *West Africa* (London, 1969)

Nadel, S. F.: *A Black Byzantium* (London, 1942)

O'Connor, A. M.: *An Economic Geography of East Africa* (London, 2nd edn. 1971)

Pollock, N. C.: *Studies in Emerging Africa* (London, 1971)

Pullan, R. A.: 'Burning impact on African savannas' (*The Geographical Magazine*, XLV11, 1975, p. 432-8)

Raven, Susan: *Rome in Africa* (London, 1969)

Ruffle, John: *Heritage of the Pharaohs, an Introduction to Egyptian Archaeology* (Oxford, 1977)

Semple, Ellen Churchill: *The Geography of the Mediterranean Region; its Relation to Ancient History* (London, 1932)

Watson, Andrew M.: 'The Arab agricultural revolution and its diffusion 700-1100' (*Journal of Economic History*, XXXIV, 1974, p. 8-35, 74-8)

3. LAND, POPULATION AND LABOUR

i) *Land laws and customs*

The extreme complexity, variety and dynamic character of the relationship between group or individual and land in Africa precludes dogmatism. Nonetheless, it would not be an intolerable over-simplification to suggest that, over most of Africa, communal ownership of land was the rule. This did not mean communal cultivation. Pasture was always exploited in common, as, of course, were hunting and collecting grounds, but kinship groups established well-defined claims to particular areas. The economic unit was normally the family or homestead. While membership of a group (tribe, clan, lineage, village, etc.) only conveyed the right to participate in the use of its ancestral land, without giving perpetual right to a specific area, as a rule the individual to whom the land was allocated was left in undisturbed possession of it as long as he put it to proper use and fulfilled the concomitant obligations. Among some peoples periodic redistribution was usual. Elsewhere, with stable settlement, the family allotment became heritable, and when pressure developed upon the land, it was prone to fragmentation into scattered plots through the working of customary inheritance laws. Although the concept of land sale remained an alien one, an analogous procedure did become established in some parts, for example among the Chagga and Kikuyu in East Africa, the Nupe and Tiv of West Africa and the Bemba of Central Africa. This was the admission of strangers to communal land on payment of a gift. It was not the alienation of land so much as the incorporation of outsiders into the community, not unlike the introduction of guests (*hospites*) into the medieval European village community. Perhaps the nearest approach to the sale of land was the practice of pledging land as security for debt (for example, among the Aja and Yoruba of Dahomey), where the creditor had its use until the debt was paid. But the pledge was always redeemable and therefore alienation, at least in theory, was never permanent.

Attitudes to land were influenced by population density and the use to which it was put. Among the Nuer, a pastoral people for whom cultivation was a secondary activity, there was no occasion to quarrel about it among themselves.

> There is enough land for everybody on the Nuer scale of cultivation and consequently questions of tenure do not arise. It is taken for granted that a man has a right to cultivate the ground behind his homestead unless some one is already using it, and a man can choose any spot outside the village which is not occupied by the gardens of others. Newcomers are always in some way related to some of the villagers, and kinsmen do not dispute about gardens.[1]

Yet, any people, however complaisant about one another's access to the land, experienced intense proprietary feelings when it was a question of the land as a whole. The rights of any community were usually upheld with the greatest vigour against encroachment by other persons (though it was not impossible for different groups – such as pastoralists and cultivators – to exercise concurrently different claims to the same land) and were elevated to a religious significance that made alienation sacrilegious. Since migration was not uncommon, the religious awe attached to tribal land was no doubt a sublimation of economic self-interest, such being the intensity of feeling that was aroused where subsistence was precarious because of the primitive character of agriculture. While the community was willing to abandon ancestral land if better became available, it was reluctant to see any curtailment of it when land was in short supply, a situation which made the family and the individual equally averse to putting at risk the ultimate guarantee of their subsistence by relinquishing the land-holding rights that were theirs by virtue of their membership of the community.

In many areas chiefs had rights over the use and disposal of land and sometimes ownership of all land was claimed by a king. This was so in medieval

Nubia. In East Africa the Mwani of Ruanda, where the Hutu cultivators were conquered by Tutsi pastoralists, asserted such a claim though he did not enforce it except to dispossess disobedient subjects. In the same kingdom the renting of pasture by tenants and sub-tenants with rights of inheritance and the distribution of communal land among families as a result of disputes and arbitration became common. In 19th-century Dahomey the ruler claimed ownership of all the land. In Ethiopia monarch and Church were great landowners (holding at the time of the 1974 revolution some 11,8 per cent and 20 per cent of the total arable land respectively). Extensive lands were granted to monasteries from the early Middle Ages and to the bishop of the Ethiopian Church, always an Egyptian. In theory all land was vested in the crown and private occupation was temporary and conditional. 'What chiefly makes the King great,' wrote the Portuguese Jesuit, Manoel de Almeida, in the 17th century,

is that he is lord in *solidum* of all lands that there are in his kingdom, so that he can take and give them when and to whom he sees fit. Private persons, great and small, have nothing except by the King's gift and all that they own is by favour *ad tempus*.[2]

In practice private land ownership, both small- and large-scale, was common, though permanent land-holding, known as *rest* (or *rist*), was subject to limitations. In Amhara, in northern Ethiopia, it did not include the rights of sale and all *rest* was subject to royal confiscation in the event of treason or other serious crime. It was rather hereditary individual righ to the use of certain land on condition that tax and service obligations attatched to it were met.

Private ownership, then, was commonplace in Ethiopia and a method of land-holding very much like it was found in Ruanda. Its development was frequently associated with strong central government and the emergence of classes, separate religious institutions and personnel, intensive agriculture (especially irrigation and plough-cultivation) and a high ratio of people to land. Strong central government and private land ownership were by no means incompatible. Even in Ancient and Macedonian Egypt, where the government was particularly powerful, individual and institutional property in land existed. Theoretically, all land belonged to the crown; practically, although the king was by far the biggest landowner, with estates in every administrative district (nome), private and temple ownership was common. Temple estates, for the maintenance of the priests and the support of religion, and mortuary endowments, for the cult of the dead, were sometimes very large indeed. Ramases III (1198–66 B.C.) gave nearly a thousand square kilometres, inhabited by 86 000 people, to Amun, the god of Thebes. Private estates varied considerably in extent, from a few hectares (granted, for example, to a veteran) to great multiple land-holdings. Some were run as a unit of production, others broken up into plots and cultivated by tenants. In Carthage there was both private and public land. Noble estates, however, were modest in size. In the Roman period, throughout the empire, great emphasis was laid upon private ownership and Roman law accorded to property owners a large measure of immunity from state intervention. In Roman Egypt, however, with its long tradition of intrusive government, most land was retained by the crown until the 4th century A.D., though it was leased to tenants. Because of changes in land classification for tax purposes, crown land then reverted to private ownership, which took the form of both village small-holding and substantial estates. However, the crown kept some land (known during the late Roman and Byzantine periods as the 'divine house') and its holdings grew through fines and confiscations. Such land was either leased or administered by officials. The Church, too, became a large landowner, in some cases leasing land to laymen in perpetuity at nominal rent.

In Muslim Egypt and the Maghrib, the theoretical ownership of all landed property remained vested in the state. Once again, in practice it was alienated through such devices as grants of tax-collecting rights (under the *iqtā'* and *iltizām* systems) and grants of land to religious foundations (*waqfs*), but it was not until the 19th century, after the confiscation of *iltizāms* by Muhammad 'Alī, pasha of Egypt, in 1812–14, that fully legal private land ownership was established in Egypt, a slow process that was completed not before the end of the century. A powerful influence was exercised by the Koran, which recognized private property and laid down rules for inheritance. The equal division of inheritance among sons was normal, tending to promote inequality in ownership. For, whereas the small man inheriting a plot too little to furnish subsistence, disposed of it, the big man could take measures to maintain the integrity of family property. It was not uncommon for a wealthy man to endow a *waqf* with land that passed into the undivided hereditary possession of the founder's direct descendants, who continued to draw the revenues. Islamic law did not, however, forbid undivided family property nor tribal and village ownership of land. Where tribal organization persisted, as in Upper Egypt until the late 18th century, when Arab bedouin immigrants, for centuries a thorn in the flesh of established government, were at last subdued by the Mamluks, and in the Maghrib until French colonial rule, communal ownership was typical.

In areas settled by the Portuguese, landed estates were usual, such as the prazos of Mozambique and plantations of Angola, owned by Europeans or Europeanized Africans or mulattoes. In white South Africa during the period of Dutch East India Company rule, farmers had no interest in the formal ownership of land that was freely available. Although there was some freehold and some attempt at bringing in long leases, with compensation for improvements upon alienation, over-production of grain and wine at the Cape made the Company restrict its grants of freehold land, and a majority of farms fell into the 'loan place' (*leeningsplaats*) category. The loan farm was very large – some 3 000 hectares – and paid a low fixed rent irrespective of its fertility. Nominally requiring quarterly or annual renewal, the lease was in practice held for years on end, often passed on from generation to generation, and sometimes divided like private property. Indeed in 1790, the Company, by imposing a transfer tax on buildings and improvements when such land changed hands, in effect guaranteed permanent holding and implicitly granted ownership. Naturally farmers resisted attempts by the British colonial administration, after the Cape of Good Hope was annexed by Britain in 1814, to convert leases into title deeds on the assumption that this would raise farming standards. It was only gradually that 'loan places' were changed to perpetual quit-rent tenure which in turn gave way to freehold tenure through quitrent redemption. This trend was accompanied by growing land hunger and sub-division of inheritance.

Had this process of subdivision of the land been followed by more skilled and intensive farming, it might have conferred upon the country the boon of a thrifty peasantry of small landholders. But irrational subdivision and the same primitive, wasteful, and unsystematic farming as of old harmed both the land and its owners. Few medieval manors could have been more fantastically subdivided than some South African farms. Only the pitiful holdings discovered in France by Arthur Young, extending only as far as the shade of a single cherry-tree, were comparable with the 1/148,141 share of a farm of 2,527 morgen to which one heir was entitled.[3]

ii) *Population*
Well-defined individual ties to specific pieces of land were exceptional in Africa, at least south of the Sahara, before the present century. Population was generally sparse, particularly where hunting and gathering and nomadic or semi-nomadic pastoralism were practised. It was the adoption of the iron hoe and the introduction of higher-yielding exotic crops that, by raising agricultural production, permitted a greater density of population, though it would be unwise to see too close a correlation between agricultural methods and size of population. Exhaustion of one harvest before the maturation of the next, the failure for one reason or another to store food as an insurance against future shortage, and harvest failure because of drought or locusts, all meant that hunger was commonly experienced. Amongst the Nuer:

Millet is consumed as porridge and beer in large quantities in the months between the first harvest and departure for the dry-season camps. If the harvest has been good people like to eat their daily porridge in camps, and when the camp grain-supply runs short women journey to the villages to replenish it. When camps

break up and people return to their villages millet consumption increases, beer again being brewed, and in a good year there is sufficient to satisfy requirements till the new harvest is ripe. In a normal year Nuer can just tide over these months if they are economical and have been careful not to use much grain in camp. Only in the most favoured parts of the country are they assured of an adequate supply throughout the year. In most parts there is always a very narrow margin between sufficiency and want, and in a bad year starvation is not infrequent. If the crops fail people survive on milk, fish, and wild fruits, and in extremity may kill some of their beasts. Rinderpest is considered the worst calamity. When rinderpest and failure of crops occur in the same year people expect the older age-sets to be wiped out. Much suffering may be caused by excessive drought or flood, which injure both crops and grazing.
There are good and bad fishing years . . . [4]

Africa was no stranger to famine:

I walked gaily up the path to the long narrow gateway, and fired off a couple of shots to announce my arrival. A Native crawled along the passage cut through the otherwise impenetrable hedge of thorns to see who I was. He was a tall Njemp-sian, with a breadth of shoulder that told of former fine physique; but he was terribly emaciated, and stooped from sheer weakness. He looked at me for a moment with his dreamy, hollow, shrunken eyes; then with a sad smile held out his hand and said, 'Yambo, yambo.' His aspect was that of a starving man, and filled me with dismay. I knew from his salute that he must know a little Kisuahili, so I eagerly asked him if there were much food in Njemps. 'Jocula, tele jocula?' he re-peated, and his sickly smile faded into a look of bitter despair. 'Jocula *hapana*' (There is *no* food) he said, with an emphasis that his appearance made superfluous. Yet I assumed, or at least tried to assume, a sceptical aspect, and pointed to the vil-lage, and asked him what the people all lived on if they had no food. In reply he only glanced up at the trees, tore off a few leaves from a branch he carried in his hand, and voraciously munched them. I pointed again to the highlands of Kam-asia, rising like a wall on the western horizon, and asked if there were food there. 'Jocula hapana', he repeated; but after a pause he turned to the north-west, and waving his hand several times in that direction said, 'Mbali, *mbali*, jocula *kidogo*' (Very far, very far away, there is a *little* food).[5]

Egypt was particularly vulnerable because population was so dense and because there was such a high degree of dependence upon a single source of subsistence, the River Nile. It has been plausibly argued that the Intermediate Periods of ancient Egyptian history at the end of the 3rd millennium and again at the end of the 2nd millennium B.C. were at least partly the result of a persistently low level of the Nile inundation, leading to famine. 'All Egypt was dying of hunger, to such a degree that everyone had come to eating his children.'[6] Thus wrote an Egyptian official in the First Intermediate Period. Pharaoh, supposed to be a god with power over the river's flood, was discredited and unable to maintain his authority. Cannibalism was again reported, millennia later, in A.D. 1200. On that occasion hunger was not attended by any serious political disturbances, but a famine thirty years before, during the period of Fāṭimid decline, undoubtedly had had political repercussions. Nonetheless, it is unlikely that capacity to produce was the most important factor governing the size of population, given the opportunities that were offered over a large part of Africa for supplementing regular supplies by hunting and collecting.

> In famine years much greater attention is paid to the wild harvest. 'Wild dates' are then a great stand-by and people eat a wide range of fruits, ripening mainly in the early part of the drought, which they neglect when hunger is not severe, and make use of bush-yams and the seeds of wild sorghum and other grasses.[7]

The limits of population growth must have been set rather by disease, warfare and social custom regarding marriage and sexual relations. Monogamy might have been attractive to nomadic pastoralists, for whom women might be a burden: polygamy to cultivators, who could put their wives and children to work on the land; though other factors, including economic ones such as marginal returns on labour, might have been a great deal more persuasive. Disease, no doubt assisted by malnutrition, itself a cause of deficiency diseases, was a major hazard to life and health, especially among infants. Malaria, smallpox, sleeping sickness, meningitis and plague were common. It is estimated that a third of the population of Egypt was wiped out by the plague epidemic of the 14th century and that Cairo alone lost nearly a million of its inhabitants. And in the 19th century in that same city:

> During all this time the power of the plague was rapidly increasing. When I first arrived, it was said that the daily number of 'accidents' by plague, out of a population of about 200,000 did not exceed four or five hundred; but before I went away the deaths were reckoned at twelve hundred a day. I had no means of knowing whether the numbers (given out, as I believe they were, by officials) were at all correct, but I could not help knowing that from day to day the number of the dead was increasing. My quarters were in one of the chief thoroughfares of the city, and as the funerals in Cairo take place between daybreak and noon (a time during which I generally stayed in my rooms), I could form some opinion as to the briskness of the plague. I don't mean that I got up every morning with the sun. It was not so: but the funerals of most people in decent circumstances at Cairo are attended by singers and howlers, and the performances of these people woke me in the early morning, and prevented me from remaining in ignorance of what was going on in the street below.
> When first I arrived at Cairo the funerals that daily passed under my windows were many, but still there were frequent and long intervals without a single howl. Every day, however (except one, when I fancied that I observed a diminution of funerals), these intervals became less frequent and shorter, and at last the passing of the howlers from morn to noon was almost incessant. I believe that about one half of the whole people was carried off by this visitation.[8]

Then there were the parasitic diseases, which did not kill quickly, but de-bilitated their victims. It was not only a question of human diseases, however. Trypanosomiasis inhibits stock breeding, and rinderpest can have disastrous effects on animal populations. Such diseases had indirect demographic con-sequences. Similarly, for those dependent on crop-raising, warfare and civil unrest were exceedingly destructive because of their indirect effects – such as the ruin of crops and interference with sowing – which were probably more detrimental than death and wounds in battle. There can be little doubt that the population of Egypt and North Africa fluctuated according to the strength and efficiency of the administration. The slave trade in black Africa, often associated with belligerence, was a significant cause of population loss.

In Africa south of the Sahara there appears to have been until the 19th century, subject to local vicissitudes, a slow but continual growth in popula-tion and an extension of settlement over the whole habitable portion of the continent. Estimates of population have varied widely and have been largely dependent upon the opinion of European observers of the 18th and 19th centuries who were guided by the population density they encountered themselves: 18th-century guesses that put the population at as much as 150 million were drastically revised in the mid-19th century to less than 50 million, only to rise steeply once again in the later 19th century to anything up to, or even beyond, 200 million. More sober estimates of the early part of this century were at rather less than 150 million. It is now commonly accepted that population has grown very rapidly this century, roughly doubling between 1900 and 1950. Estimates of present population trends, though less obviously wild guesses, are still far from being more than ap-proximations. What is apparent is that there are as yet few signs of a stabiliza-tion. Despite this, however, except in places such as the Nile valley, where population density is well over 1 000 per square kilometre, and Rwanda and Burundi, where it is verging on that, Africa even to-day is comparatively sparsely inhabited. Though accounting for one-fifth of the land surface of the world, it has only one-tenth of the world's population. The savanna and the Central African plateau are thinly populated, the arid areas still more so.

Most of the inhabitants of the continent in the past lived in rural settle-ments, either the nucleated village or the dispersed hamlet. There was a wide variation in the degree of nucleation or dispersal. In many parts of East Africa the individual farmer lived on his holding and not in a village at all. In South Africa the trekboers 'lost the gregarious habit of their fore-fathers in Europe. They built few villages. On the great farms each man fled the tyranny of his neighbour's smoke.'[9] The degree of permanence also varied. Naturally the temporary dwelling is characteristic of the nomad, but even with the agriculturalist, shifting cultivation required the periodic removal of houses. Villages have sometimes been very large 'agro-towns', found in ancient Egypt and North Africa, as well as in sub-Saharan Africa at all periods. The Bantu-speaking Sotho and Tswana had settlements comprising as many as 3 000 houses and 15 000 inhabitants, each the capital of a chief; while the capital of Buganda probably had a good deal more. Few such towns could have been wholly dependent upon agriculture. Trade and tribute also counted. The fairly large pre-industrial towns of North and West Africa certainly owed their size to trade and craft manufacturing as much as to, or even more than, agriculture. West Africa had many more towns of consequence than did the other regions of sub-Saharan Africa because of the greater volume of trade. Apart from isolated instances like Mbanza, the capital of the Kongo kingdom, which is estimated to have had a population of 30 000 in the late 16th century, the interior of Central, East and South Africa had little urban life before the 19th century, when towns like Ujiji and Tabora sprang up in East Africa in response to the needs of coastal traders for supplies, and white towns were established in the interior of South Africa.

Town size was influenced by a number of factors, cultural and environmental. Political structure – the growth of territorial chieftaincies – and religious practice could be important. Sokoto and Kano in Hausaland, Ife in Yorubaland and Great Zimbabwe near the Zambezi are all thought to have had at least partly a religious origin. Kumasi was of religious significance as the depository of the Golden Stool, but also had commercial and other claims to importance. Availability of water, which dictated the concentration of the population if access to it was restricted, could be decisive. Fertility and intensive agriculture could bring a large number of farmers together in one place, though no town dependent on agriculture or pastoralism could be so large as to make the journey to and from fields or pastures insupportably far. Defence, especially in areas preyed on by slavers, or the desire to dominate, provided the *raison d'être* for substantial stockaded towns and villages like the 'war towns' of Sierra Leone in the 18th and 19th centuries, and, on waterways, for villages constructed on platforms.

Richard Jobson, an English merchant trading on the Gambia in the early 17th century, describes the town of Cassan:

> This Towne is the Kings seate, and by the name of the towne hee holds his title, King of *Cassan;* It is seated upon the Rivers side, and inclosed round, neare to the houses, with hurdles, such as our shepheards use, but they are above ten foot high, and fastened to strong and able poles, the toppes whereof remaine above the hurdle; on the inside in divers places, they have rooms, and buildings, made up like Turrets, from whence they within may shoot their arrows, and throw their darts over the wall, against their approaching enemies; on the out-side likewise, round the wall, they have cast a ditch or trench, of great breadth, & beyond that againe a pretty distance, the whole Towne is circled with posts and peeces of trees, set close and fast into the ground, some five foot high, so thicke, that except in stiles,

or places made of purpose, a single man cannot get through, and in the like manner, a small distance off againe, the like defence, and this is as they do signifie unto
us, to keep off the force of horse, to which purpose, it seemes to be very strong
and availeable.[10]

Such fortifications were by no means unusual in West Africa throughout its
history. Benin in the 17th century had a double stockade filled with clay,
while late 19th-century Kano in Hausaland had walls thirty feet high and
twenty feet wide at the bottom. The town was nineteen kilometres in
circumference. Hausa town walls had iron-plated wooden swing gates.

iii) *Unfree labour in northern Africa*
Throughout the whole ancient Mediterranean world forced and servile
labour was commonplace. In Egypt, slaves were found from the Middle
Kingdom onwards, sometimes responsible for some of the cultivation on
royal and other estates, but most often engaged in household service. They
could be bought or emancipated, bequeathed or hired out, even by people
of low social standing. Frequently they were branded like cattle for identification purposes, but they were otherwise not badly treated, nor were they
without rights, which could be very extensive. They were either purchased
from Nubia and Syria, or, more likely, were captured in war, for example
in the successful wars waged during the New Kingdom; or possibly they
were immigrants from Asia who were subsequently enslaved. Some were
native Egyptians enslaved for crime or debt. Though at times numerous,
they formed a small minority, both in ancient and classical times, in a society
where the overwhelmingly large proportion of the people suffered from a
marked degree of unfreedom, and they were not vital to the functioning of
the economy. The typical Egyptian cultivator, in ancient times and after,
was the village-dwelling, over-taxed tenant farmer, mostly on state land and,
if not, either on temple or private land, enjoying a degree of freedom that
varied from age to age. Though always liable to the corvée, imposed by
the state on all citizens, with rare exceptions, for the maintenance of flood
control (to say nothing of quarrying, brick making, the transporting of stone
and the construction of tombs and temples when farm work was slack),
he could expect in pharaonic times to be fed from the state granaries when
famine raged. In addition, landless labourers, paid in kind, were found
in all periods, and at times of labour shortage – perhaps caused by particularly harsh state exactions – might be compelled to take up tenancies,
especially on land to be reclaimed.

On its estates, the Carthaginian nobility used slave labour and slave over-
seers, but also wage labour, including migrant Berbers from outside Punic
territory. For slaves Mago the agronomist recommended humane treatment – family life and the right to save – but in fact slave discontent was

always stirring. However, slave-cultivated estates were to be found only in the area directly exploited by the Carthaginians themselves. Beyond the *chora* there were Berber smallholders and village communities. In the Berber kingdoms such communities were subject to chiefs who could demand labour services and payments in kind.

The conquering Romans enslaved on a massive scale. The slave-cultivated estates, the latifundia, however, seem to have been largely confined to parts of Italy and to a specific period, the late Republic and early Empire, when slaves were plentiful and comparatively cheap. There is some evidence of the use of farm slaves in Tripolitania, but little of their use elsewhere in Roman Africa. Given the abundance of cheap native labour available, slavery was scarcely necessary. In any case, the slave ranch or plantation was not typical of Roman agriculture, though no doubt it was efficient and productive. Agricultural slaves were often highly skilled, e.g. in viticulture, and their use was more appropriate in a small undertaking. The agronomists of the Roman world regarded the medium-sized estate as the optimum and praised the peasant proprietor as the pillar of the republic. Although doubtless the modest estate was an ideal that appealed but little to the rich Roman who busied himself with adding to his estates, and the sturdy independent yeoman was something of a myth, Roman Africa was very much a land of small or medium cultivators, using family labour, supplemented in the case of the more affluent farmers with some slaves and hired hands, especially itinerant and seasonal workers. Wage labour was provided by nomads, urban unemployed, landless country dwellers and farmers unable to extract an adequate living from their own holdings. There were labour contractors who organized migrant labour. Smallholders comprised both native proprietors' and tenants and Roman settlers, the latter farming more substantial properties. No doubt the smaller men could make ends meet only by casual labour on the land of their more prosperous neighbours or by engaging in trade or craft manufacture. Prosperity was not necessarily related to ownership. There were poor proprietors and well-to-do tenants.

There can be little doubt that the situation of native cultivators did not improve as a result of the imposition of Roman rule. However, in time the status of all peasant proprietors (*coloni*) deteriorated, becoming subject to galling restrictions. There was a tendency for dependent cultivation to increase. It has been suggested that the development of a depressed colonate enabled landowners to dispense with slaves, and that it was this that led to a decline in slavery rather than any dwindling of supply. The condition of the remaining slaves tended to appreciate as that of the *coloni* depreciated, the two classes in practice becoming indistinguishable in a quasi-servile situation.

A trend towards concentration of land ownership and growth of tenant farming was apparent from the very beginning of the Roman occupation of North Africa. Some landlords who had acquired confiscated estates preferred to break them up into holdings let to small farmers. Similarly, small men, native as well as Roman, prosperous townsmen as well as country-men, built up modest estates and divided them into plots. Estates of this sort increased in number as the province was extended and village communities became incorporated into imperial or private estates. As pressure of popula-tion upon the land grew and holdings fragmented, pieces of land too small for subsistence were bought up by the more successful. The political dis-turbances of the later Empire, when unsuccessful contenders for the imperial throne and their supporters were deprived of their property, concentrated landownership to an increasing degree into the hands of the emperor. The big estate, the *saltus*, frequently, but not always, owned by the emperor and frequently leased by an entrepreneur (*conductor*) using slave and hired labour, developed as early as the 1st century A.D. into a proto-manor, with its demesne or home farm and its tenants compelled to devote a few days' annual labour to help with the cultivation of the home farm and to part with a proportion of their crops (a third on imperial estates). The tenants did not cultivate for the market and part of the reason for their worsening position was their proneness to chronic debt to the estate owner. Like the Egyptian peasant when he found rural life insupportable, the North African *colonus* sometimes fled or at least threatened to.

During the final period of the Roman empire and during the Byzantine period the growth of the big (though not necessarily consolidated or com-pact) private estate quickened and spread to Egypt. Characteristic was the absorption of land at the expense of both the state and the small landowner, a development accompanied by the tying of the peasant proprietor to his home village or district and, in most cases, of the *colonus* to the soil by an hereditary bond. Although it viewed this situation with some misgiving, the state had to accept it – indeed encouraged it – to ensure that the land was tilled and yielded a tax revenue, and it was only by enlarging the power and respon-sibility of the big landowners that it could ensure that the smallholder paid his tax and was available for military service. A law of A.D. 332 ran:

> Any person, with whom a *colonus* belonging to some other person is found shall not only restore him to his place of origin but be liable for his poll tax for the period. It will furthermore be proper that *coloni* themselves who plan flight should be put in irons like slaves, so that they may be compelled by a servile penalty to perform the duties appropriate to them as free men.[11]

The power and influence of the landowners, enhanced in that way, was increased still further by the growing practice of *patrocinium*, where the free peasant, in return for the protection of a patron, surrendered his land and his own freedom, another tendency that the state helplessly deplored. In Egypt it was the practice (known as *epibole*) – and this spread elsewhere in the empire from the end of the 3rd century – to compel villages and private landowners to lease and pay the tax on untilled crown land and, later, derelict private land. Such land in the long-run as a rule merged into the estates of the big, successful owners with the means to cultivate it.

The Arab conquerors of Mediterranean Africa in the 7th century were not at first allowed to acquire land there. This was to set them apart from the conquered. Existing landowners were left in possession of their estates unless they had resisted the invaders. It was not long, however, before the caliphs were rewarding notable followers with state or forfeited land in virtually full ownership, though without the public rights that had been characteristic of large-scale land owning under Byzantine rule. If the apparent behaviour of the Muslim conquerors of Spain is a guide, one can assume that there was some forcible seizure of property in the Maghrib. From Egypt comes evidence of the existence of substantial landowners, Muslim and Coptic, renting out land in return for a share of the crop. Doubtless, under Muslim rule the situation of the rural population remained what it had always been, sometimes better, sometimes worse, as régimes changed and as nature was cruel or kind. Of crucial importance was the strength and efficiency of the central government. Strong governments provided the conditions necessary for cultivation and protected the cultivators from ill treatment at the hands of the rich and powerful. Weak and threatened governments taxed heavily and were unable to ensure security. The typical cultivator was still a small farmer, tenant or owner, subject, as in the past, to a varying degree of exploitation by state or private person. Wage and slave labour was not extensively used. Slaves were imported primarily for military and domestic service, not for agricultural work.

Between the free cultivator and the state there was as a rule, interposed the tax-farmer or the holder of the *iqtāʿ* (the right to collect taxes from a particular area) or the religious foundation (*waqf*). While in theory the intermediary was not the landowner, but merely enjoyed the usufruct, in practice the distinction tended to become entirely formal. Neither the tax farm nor the *iqtāʿ* was run as an estate, as a unit of production like the ancient *saltus* or medieval manor in Europe. Nevertheless, the fellah, like the manorial serf, could well find himself burdened with labour dues beyond the traditional corvées required to maintain the irrigation system; and virtually tied to the soil.

Waning régimes were generally worse than waxing ones. The fiscal burdens imposed by the ʿAbbāsids in the 9th century were relieved by the Fāṭimids in the 10th. Their enfeebled and oppressive dynasty in turn gave way to the more just rule of the Ayyubids. The peasant who paid his tax to the *iqtāʾ* holder under the rule of Saladin and his successors in the late 12th and early 13th century, was protected from extortionate demands, but this protection was subsequently eroded under Mamluk government. When the power of the Mamluks was broken by the Ottomans, the peasant's situation improved. Owing to the previous neglect of cultivation peasants were wooed by lower taxes and release from forced labour on both public works and private land. They were allowed to buy extra land and build up small estates. Provided they cultivated their land and paid their taxes promptly, they were secure in their holdings and able to bequeath them to their heirs. They were not shackled to them and were free to leave as they wished. As Ottoman authority declined and the Mamluks reasserted themselves, building up estates that were nominally only tax farms, their position once more deteriorated. In bad times taxes in kind, either to the state or to the private individual who had lawfully or unlawfully appropriated them, might amount in extreme cases to four-fifths of the harvest, besides taxes on animals and fruit trees. Deprived of his freedom and burdened with such taxes and with corvées, the peasant resorted to the desperate remedy everywhere adopted by serfs cruelly exploited, flight from the land or rebellion. The revolt of dissatisfied tenants and, in times of population pressure, land-hungry peasants, a perennial feature of the Egyptian countryside, was still occurring as late as the middle of the present century.

In the Maghrib the big estate in the immediate post-Roman period was confined to the comparatively small areas that were most Romanized and frequently did not survive the political turbulence of the early Middle Ages. In theory the land belonged to the state, in practice to the tribe, and was either cultivated by the village community or grazed by the livestock of the Berber nomads. Tribal chiefs, Arab as well as Berber after the arrival of the Banū Hilāl and the Banū Sulaim, were granted *iqṭāʿ* privileges that included usufruct in some cases, but there was no question of serfdom. In Upper Egypt, too, the Arab bedouin escaped the worsening fate of the Lower Egyptian fellahin until the late 18th century.

iv) *Labour problems in sub-Saharan Africa*
Except in areas of particular fertility and of dense population, land was not a scarce resource in the past. Labour, on the other hand, frequently was, especially in tropical Africa, where physical effort was more than usually exhausting and likely to be sapped by disease and malnutrition. The tasks of cultivation, from land preparation to threshing, were all exceedingly laborious owing to the primitive technology in use. The extended family, which was the normal unit of production in the 'traditional' or 'pre-capitalist' economy, would usually have met its labour needs from among its own members, all of whom, male and female, worked from early childhood to old age. Toil was apportioned between the sexes in different ways throughout

Africa, but the tendency in black Africa was for men to concern themselves with hunting and fishing and the care of animals and for women to busy themselves with cultivation and food processing. Men, however, did the heavy work of land clearing, and it frequently happened that both men and women performed the same tasks. When the resources of the family were inadequate, it might be possible under the prevailing system of reciprocal obligations amongst kinsmen to call upon the services of a 'work party' for especially onerous work, such as clearing new land or house construction.

> In a narrow sense the simple family might be called the economic unit, but . . . it is not self-sufficient and the active participation of a wider group is often necessary, e.g. in building, fishing, and hunting. It is also clear that a single family cannot herd its cattle in distant pastures and, at the same time, herd the calves elsewhere, attend to the tiny calves in the kraal, milk, churn, clean the kraal, prepare dung for fuel, cook the food, and so on, by itself. Co-operation is found among neighbours who are also kinsmen. There is also much mutual assistance when co-operation is essential to the performance of a task, e.g. in weeding and harvesting, for it is not conventional to ask people for help, the obligation to assist being part of a general kinship relationship.[12]

People in authority could make use of age-regiments, both for public works and for their own private purposes. Among the Ngwato, in what is now Botswana, men's regiments might be called upon to build huts or cattle-kraals for the chief; women's regiments to thatch or weed. The widespread institution of clientship, too, was to some extent a solution to a labour problem, though by no means exclusively so. Wage labour was rare before the introduction of cash crop production for overseas export and land became scarce. For both the noble and the commoner the usual source of additional labour was slavery. Where everyone had access to the means of subsistence, some sort of compulsion was the only way to secure labour other than that made available by the family or through community co-operation.

While there can be no doubt that slavery expanded in volume under the influence of the external slave trade, the institution predated the export of slaves across the Atlantic, though it was not, it is true, universal throughout sub-Saharan Africa; for the Bantu-speaking Nguni neither dealt in slaves nor enslaved their own people for debt. Elsewhere war captives or those guilty of some offence against king or custom were habitually enslaved. Some relinquished their own freedom to avoid starvation. A proportion of the slaves did agricultural work, either integrated into households where they were functionally indistinguishable from the free members, or producing a surplus for consumption or sale by a class of proprietors, such as the Fulani, who conquered the Fouta Djallon plateau in West Africa in the 17th and 18th centuries and settled slaves there to cultivate on their behalf. In the western Sudan, before the end of the 1st millennium A.D., there existed such villages, enslaved by conquering horsemen.

In Muslim East Africa coconut and, in the 19th century, clove plantations were run with slave labour. Slaves, protected to some extent by religious law, were comparatively well-treated there. They were allowed their own plots of land and cattle, and some did skilled work or were even in positions of authority. However, slave escapes and revolts were common, especially in the latter part of the 19th century, when unrest was fomented by the anti-slavery campaign in Europe. Clearly, the treatment of slaves and their economic and legal status could vary widely. Not all had economic value. Ostentation was one motive for slave-owning. 'The chief aim,' reported a British Colonial Office official in 1891,

> and greatest desire of man and woman too amongst the Mande tribes is to possess slaves; it is at once the gauge to Native respectability and position, and the owner of such property rises in local importance in proportion to the number of slaves which he or she may have acquired.[13]

Ostentatious prodigality entered into the ritual sacrifice of slaves practised in Dahomey and other places.

Mungo Park estimated in 1795 that three-quarters of the inhabitants of the Gambia region were

> in a state of hopeless and hereditary slavery . . . employed in cultivating the land, in the care of cattle, and servile offices of all kinds.[14]

Slavery, however, was clearly not always as harsh as is here implied, even in the slave villages. Writing a quarter of a century later, of Sokoto, Captain Clapperton described agricultural slaves who bore a closer resemblance to villeins than to chattel slaves.

> The domestic slaves are generally well treated. The males who have arrived at the age of eighteen or nineteen are given a wife, and sent to live at their villages and farms in the country, where they build a hut, and until the harvest are fed by their owners. When the time for cultivating the ground and sowing the seed comes on, the owner points out what he requires, and what is to be sown on it. The slave is then allowed to enclose a part for himself and family. The hours of labour, for his master, are from daylight till mid-day; the remainder of the day is employed on his own, or in any other way he may think proper. At the time of harvest, when they cut and tie up the grain, each slave gets a bundle of the different sorts of grain, about a bushel of our measure, for himself. The grain on his own ground is entirely left for his own use, and he may dispose of it as he thinks proper. At the vacant seasons of the year he must attend to the calls of his master, whether to accompany him on a journey, or go to war, if so ordered..[15]

Serfdom of the sort described above originates in a situation where relatively intensive cultivation has become the practice, labour is scarce and the security of tenure for small farmers under threat. Short of labour, more powerful men tie weaker ones to the soil or, in search of security, poor men are willing to submit themselves to dependent cultivation in order to survive. Wage labour may not be available and unmitigated slavery may for one reason or another be undesirable. There may be, for example, some compunction derived from religious or humanitarian scruples about the use of slaves. From the point of view of the master, serfdom, which involves a sharing, however unequal, of rights in land, and imposes obligations, however slight, upon him, may well be a degree of unfreedom sufficient for his purpose, viz. feeding himself and his household. Normally, moreover, the relationship between him and his dependants involves other non-economic elements, such as protection and, perhaps, the provision of law in unquiet times. The advantage of serfs is that they can be left to fend for themselves, raising their own subsistence from land that is not in short supply. There is no question of maximizing production for the market. Slave production, with its attendant management problems, is feasible only when there are commodity and slave markets. Chattel slavery has, of course, existed in Africa's history, and the slave owners have been European, Arab and African, but on the whole serfdom, under a variety of names and in a variety of forms, has seemed the most satisfactory solution to labour problems. The individual slaves of the African household, the slaves grouped in villages in the West African savanna, the tenants of Ethiopian estates until quite recently (bearing a strong likeness to medieval European feudal serfs) and labour tenants of European settlers in East and South Africa are all comparable, and do not resemble the slaves of the European-owned sugar plantations of Fernando Po and São Thomé or the Arab-owned clove plantations of Zanzibar.

In Ethiopia the big estate, owned by state, Church or noble, with its 'demesne' cultivated by forced labour, was found in the southern provinces conquered in the 19th century. But it was rare for those with landholding rights to cultivate land themselves on a big scale. The value of an estate, like a pre-1861 Russian one, was measured less by its size than by the number of peasants settled on it. These were depressed into a share-cropping class, receiving seed from the landlord and giving in return at least half the crop, or even three-quarters. The big estate in Ethiopia, like the *iqtā'* of the Islamic world, could more justifiably be described as a fief rather than an estate. Ownership or use meant an hereditary or temporary right, granted by the government in exchange for services rendered to the state, to collect certain revenues and demand certain services, including labour services. The organization of production remained unaffected by the allocation of cultivators (or even nomads) to title-holders who very often resided in town.

In white South Africa, forced labour of one sort or another was fairly widespread from the 17th century onwards. The degree of force employed ranged from enslavement to virtual serfdom and the degree of formality, from casual compulsion to labour taxes and contractual ties. From the early years of the settlement of the Cape, slaves were imported from Madagascar, Mozambique, India and Indonesia. In 1795, when the Dutch East India Company's rule came to an end, the 18 000 slaves outnumbered the free settlers. Not all of them were imported: natural increase also played a part in the growth of the slave population. Most were engaged in agriculture, but many were occupied in domestic service and some were retained by the Company for its own needs. The Khoikhoi were also drawn into white employment once the loss of their stock and land had rendered them more amenable to its discipline.

In 1828, the British colonial authorities under missionary and imperial government pressure, promulgated the 50th Ordinance, which was intended to make it more difficult to coerce the Khoikhoi into service. Article II enacted that,

> no Hottentot or other free person of colour, lawfully residing in this colony, shall be subject to any compulsory service to which other of His Majesty's subjects therein are not liable, nor to any hindrance, fine, imprisonment or punishment of any kind whatsoever, under the pretence that such person has been guilty of vagrancy or any other offence, unless after trial in due course of law, any custom or usage to the contrary is anywise notwithstanding.[16]

Article IV protected 'ignorant and unwary Hottentots and other free persons of colour as aforesaid from the effects of improvident contracts for service' by making the normal period of employment one month in duration.

The 50th Ordinance, although the evidence seems to indicate that it was not conspicuously effective, is commonly thought to have exacerbated the labour problem, more particularly among the cattle farmers of the Eastern Cape, dependent upon Hottentot herdsmen. One might expect the labour problem of the wheat and wine farmers of the Western Cape to have been likewise adversely affected by the abolition of slavery in the British Empire in 1833 and the emancipation of the slaves in 1838 after a transitional period of so-called apprenticeship, but once again there is no certain evidence to demonstrate this. No doubt such legislation was an added inducement to disaffected farmers to move further into the interior. Labour difficulties there were eased in a variety of ways. North of the Orange River, wherever the indigenous population was dense, white farmers took to leasing out arable land, or, more often, grazing land to African families in return for labour services, either on demand or for a certain number of days a year. Such labour tenancies were remarkably like serfdom.

NOTES

1. Evans-Pritchard, E. E.: *The Nuer: a Description of the Modes of Livelihood and Political Institutions of a Nilotic People* (Oxford, 1940), p. 77
2. Pankhurst, Richard: *An Introduction to the Economic History of Ethiopia from Early Times to 1800* (London, 1961), p. 189
3. De Kiewiet, C. W.: *A History of South Africa, Social and Economic* (London, 1941), p. 191
4. Evans-Pritchard, E. E.: Op. cit., p. 82
5. Gregory, J. W., (1893) in Richards, Charles & Place, James (eds.): *East African Explorers* (London, 1960), p. 272
6. Quoted Bell, Barbara: 'The dark ages in ancient history' (Sabloff, Jeremy A. & Lamberg-Karlovsky, C. C. eds.: *The Rise and Fall of Civilizations, Modern Archaeological Cultures, Selected Readings*, Menlo Park, California, 1974), p. 367
7. Evans-Pritchard, E. E.: Op. cit., p. 75
8. Kinglake, Alexander: *Eothen* (Icon edition, London, 1963, first published in 1844)
9. De Kiewiet, C. W.: Op. cit., p. 18–19
10. Howard, C. (ed.): *West African Explorers* (London, 1951), p. 30
11. Quoted Jones, A. H. M.: *The Roman Economy; Studies in Ancient Economic and Administrative History* (Oxford, 1974), p. 294
12. Evans-Pritchard, E. E.: Op. cit., p. 91
13. Quoted Abraham, A.: 'The institution of "slavery" in Sierra Leone' (*Genève-Afrique, Acta Africana*, XIV, 1975, p. 46–57), p. 54
14. Park, M.: *The Travels* (London, 2nd Everyman edition, 1954), p. 16
15. Howard, C.: Op. cit., p. 281–2

Further reading

Akinola, G. A.: 'Slavery and slave revolts in the sultanate of Zanzibar in the nineteenth century' (*Journal of the Historical Society of Nigeria*, VI, 1972, p. 215–28)
Baer, Gabriel: *Studies in the Social History of Modern Egypt* (Chicago and London, 1969)
Biebuyck, Daniel (ed.): *African Agrarian Systems: Studies Presented and Discussed at the Second International African Seminar, Louvanium University, Leopoldville, January, 1960* (London, 1963)
Biebuyck, Daniel: 'Land holding and social organisation' (Chapter 5, Herskovits, Melville J. & Harwitz, Mitchell, eds.: *Economic Transition in Africa*, Chicago, 1964)
Bohannan, Paul: 'Land use, land tenure and land reform' (Chapter 7, Herskovits M. J. & Harwitz, M.: Op. cit.)
Charles-Picard, G. & C.: Op. cit. (see p. 46)
Cohen, John M. & Weintraub, Dov: *Land and Peasants in Imperial Ethiopia, the Social Background to a Revolution* (Assen, 1975)
Duly, Leslie C.: *British Land Policy at the Cape 1795–1844* (Durham, N. Carolina, 1968)
Fisher, A. G. B. & H. J.: *Slavery and Muslim Society in Africa, the Institution in Saharan and Sudanic Africa and the Trans-Saharan Trade* (London, 1970)
Grace, John: *Domestic Slavery in West Africa* (London, 1975)
Hailey, Lord: Op. cit. (see p. 47)
Hattersley, A. F.: 'Slavery at the Cape, 1652–1838' (Chapter XI, *The Cambridge History of the British Empire*, Volume 8, Cambridge, 1936)

Haywood, R. M.: *Roman Africa* (Volume IV, Frank, Tenney ed.: *An Economic Survey of Ancient Rome*, Baltimore, 1938)

Hoben, Allan: *Land Tenure among the Amhara of Ethiopia, the Dynamics of Cognatic Descent* (Chicago and London, 1973)

Hull, Richard W.: *African Cities and Towns before the European Conquest* (New York, 1976)

Johnson, A. C. & West, L. C.: Op. cit. (see p. 47)

Lloyd, P. C.: *Yoruba Land Law* (Oxford, 1962)

Maini, Krishan M.: *Land Law in East Africa* (Nairobi, 1967)

Meillassoux, Claude, ed.: *L'esclavage en Afrique précoloniale* (Paris, 1975)

Montet, Pierre: *Eternal Egypt* (London, 1964)

Shaw, Stanford J.: 'Landholding and land-tax revenues in Ottoman Egypt' (Holt, P. M. ed.: *Political and Social Change in Modern Egypt, Historical Studies from the Ottoman Conquest to the United Arab Republic* (London, 1968), p. 91–103)

Tamrat, Taddesse: 'Ethiopia, the Red Sea and the Horn' (Chapter 2, Oliver, Roland, ed.: *The Cambridge History of Africa*, Volume 3, c.1050 to c.1600 Cambridge, 1977)

Van der Horst, Sheila: *Native Labour in South Africa* (Cape Town, 1942)

Van Seters, John: *The Hyksos, a New Investigation* (New Haven, 1966)

Westerman, William L.: *The Slave Systems of Greek and Roman Antiquity* (Philadelphia, 1955)

Wilson, Monica & Thompson, Leonard (eds.): *The Oxford History of South Africa Volume I, South Africa to 1870* (Oxford, 1969)

CHAPTER II

CRAFT INDUSTRY

1. SCIENCE AND TECHNOLOGY

i) *Stone*

For millennia, men used mostly stone for their tools, beginning with pebbles and proceeding to roughly shaped lumps of rock, mostly choppers – so-called, but multi-functional in purpose and of no well-defined design. They are known in Africa as Oldowan-type tools after Olduvai Gorge in Tanzania. These were used by early ancestors of man, the australopithecines (southern apes), as early as two million years ago, and have been discovered at various sites throughout Africa. More refined than pebble-tools were the so-called Chellean-Acheulian tools recovered in large numbers at Olduvai and also, among many other sites in different regions, at Olorgesailie in Kenya. They are named after a site in Europe that may in fact have been on the fringe of a culture having its centre in East Africa, and they are associated with the pithecanthropines (apemen). They include handaxes or, more correctly, bifaces – because there is no certainty of their use as axes – cleavers and picks, made by striking small flakes from pieces of basalt, granite, chalcedony or some other rock, until the desired shape was obtained. Together with small flake-tools, they were used for preparing food – skinning carcasses, cutting up meat, pounding the vegetable foods that were collected, and breaking open bones. They were made with only slight changes in technique and design over a period of 300 000 years, though the incidence of different tools, e.g. cleavers, varies greatly from one site to another, the result possibly of different cultures, possibly of different activities. In all probability wood and bone too were used for making crude spears, clubs and hammers.

Acheulian tools were succeeded in sub-Saharan Africa by Sangoan, named after Sango Bay on Lake Victoria, going back some 50 000 years. Cleavers disappeared, and bifaces became relatively less common and picks relatively more common. Heavy scrapers and choppers came into use in forest zones. This development in tool making has been associated with a fall in temperature coinciding with the last glaciation in Europe, changes in vegetation and the widespread adoption of fire. Man's ancestors moved into parts of the continent previously unoccupied and to more settled homes in caves and rock shelters.

The development of lithic technology in Africa has been divided into periods, the Early (equivalent to Lower Paleolithic in Europe), Middle (equivalent to Middle and Upper Paleolithic) and Late (European Mesolithic and Neolithic) Stone Ages, though more recently, to give greater precision, a classification based on successive tool modes has been adopted by some archaeologists. Acheulian and Sangoan tools fall into the Early Stone Age. The Middle Stone Age covers a period from perhaps as far back as 50 000 B.C. up to about 15 000 B.C. Its industries show greater local variations than those of the Early Stone Age, possibly a response to different regional environments, themselves possibly affected by human activity, such as bush-burning, to assist hunting. The characteristic tool of the Middle Stone Age was lighter than earlier tools and was commonly produced by the Levallois technique. A core was prepared by the removal of flakes from a piece of stone and then given a blow that would separate a flat oval- or triangular-shaped flake of predetermined size, which could be used as a spearhead, for example. A number of different Middle Stone Age industries have been identified, such as the Mousterian and the later Aterian of northern and north-eastern Africa, Fauresmith in South Africa, the Stillbay of eastern and southern Africa and the Lupemban of the Congo basin.

The technology of the Late Stone Age is associated with *Homo sapiens*, the fully developed human being. Increasing population required still more varied adaptation to different environments, so that a wide range of lithic industries developed. Materials other than stone were exploited in new and more subtle ways. Wood was used for spear handles and tool shafts and handles; wood and bone for hammers; bone and horn for needles and arrowheads; sinew and fibre for string and skin for clothing. Through his invention of spear and harpoon, bow and arrow, trap and snare for hunting and fishing, and of pottery and baskets for utensils, man's ability to master his environment was enlarged.

The important development was the invention of the composite tool, that is the hafted flake or 'blade', and the microlith. Blades and, later, microliths were slotted into sticks and held in place with binding or with mastic or resin to make arrows or sickles for cutting wild or cultivated grasses. Such microliths were only one or two centimetres long and were made from flakes of stone detached from a core by means of a blow with a punch. They were of various shapes – blades, lunates, triangles, trapezoids – and used for a variety of purposes – skinning, cutting bark from trees, digging up wild roots and tubers and working wood and bone. In addition the Late Stone Age toolkit sometimes included ground stone axes, which were fitted with handles, and bored stones, the former facilitating occupation of forest, the latter used, for example, for weighting a fishing net. Pottery was also made from at least the 6th millennium B.C. onwards.

These technological improvements, as in the past, may have been connected with climatic changes that brought about innovations in hunting methods. With a rise in temperatures and an increase in precipitation, a change completed by about 12 000 B.C., open plains became covered with denser vegetation, forcing bigger game to migrate. Hunting smaller game in wooded conditions, men developed the microlith-tipped arrow. Microliths which have been dated as early as 16 000 B.C. have been discovered at various points, for example Nachikufu in northern Zambia, the region of the earliest known microlithic industries in sub-Saharan Africa. Such industries emerged at different times at different places. Districts separated by a few hundred kilometres practised technologies separated by thousands of years, perhaps because of differences in environmental conditions which dictated the way in which a livelihood was obtained.

In southern Africa microlithic industries, notably Wilton, are of considerably later date, appearing some time in the 8th millennium B.C. The description 'Wilton' has been applied to similar artifacts produced at various places from the Horn of Africa southwards. Another lithic tradition was called 'Kenya Capsian' because of its similarity to the Capsian of Tunisia, though archaeologists now reject any affinity between the two. 'Upper Kenya Capsian' obsidian microliths have been dated to the 7th millennium B.C. 'Typical Tunisian Capsian' was apparently confined to the southern slopes of the eastern end of the Atlas Mountains, but sites of a later stage of the same tradition (Upper Capsian), in which microliths were dominant among artifacts, have been excavated in the higher ground further to the north. More widespread than Capsian was Ibero-Maurusian, which at one time was thought to extend over both the Maghrib and Spain. Egypt was the home of a number of industries, including Sebilian.

It is not known whether the various traditions influenced one another, whether microlithic technology spread from one region to another or whether, more probably, there was spontaneous development at different places in response to local conditions. Differences between one stone working tradition and another may be due to differences in the kind of local stone used. Technology did not necessarily always advance. In some areas, for example parts of the Cape of Good Hope, the production of microliths was abandoned in favour of crude scrapers, with the co-existence of both over a long period however. It is possible that different tools were used for different activities and their presence side by side indicates a degree of economic specialisation, for example between hunting and fishing. In the Orange Free State microlithic Wilton gave way to 'Smithfield' scrapers, apparently from the 17th century, each perhaps the technology of a different people. The people of the Smithfield technology were evidently in conflict with iron-using Bantu-speakers and, later, with Europeans.

For the manufacture of implements and weapons, stone and bone were in time displaced by metal, though even in areas that became familiar with metal-working techniques it was centuries before those earlier materials were discarded. In technologically advanced Egypt stone tools remained common till the 2nd millennium B.C. Stone hoes were still being used in central Nigeria at the end of the 19th century and obsidian scrapers and knives to this day by the Gurage in Ethiopia. Bone, however, and, more particularly, ivory were increasingly confined to the manufacture of jewellery and fine furniture and other objets d'art, industries that flourished in Egypt from the 4th millennium B.C. Ancient materials, then, even if their uses changed somewhat, persisted. But conservatism was also displayed in styles and techniques, even when new materials were adopted. The early Egyptian potters imitated stone vessels. Even in modern industrial society new materials are used in old ways or to imitate traditional materials.

ii) *Gold and copper*
The first metal that was extensively worked in Africa (though not the first to be worked at all) was gold, devoted almost exclusively to the manufacture of objects of luxury. Of all the metallurgical techniques, that of gold is the least difficult to grasp, which is no doubt why it was the first to be extensively used. Alluvial gold is readily recoverable by the simple, though laborious, process of panning, while to obtain the metal from ore is merely a question of hammering the rock into pieces and pounding or grinding it into powder, from which the gold is then washed. Such methods were being used in Egypt from the beginning of the 3rd millennium B.C. A quern was used for grinding, and gold refining reached a high level of skill. Base metals were extracted through oxidization by a process known as cupellation. Later the Romans introduced the use of mercury to separate the gold. Cupellation was also applied for the separation of silver from lead sulphide. Small pockets were mined at various places, e.g. southern Morocco in the Middle Ages, but Africa was more richly endowed with gold.

The chief gold-producing centres before the 18th century A.D. were Nubia, which gave the ancient Egyptians their word for the metal, the western Sudan, the West African forest, the empire of the Mwene-Mutapa (Monomotapa), in what is now Zimbabwe and the province of Damot in Ethiopia. In Nubia, alluvial gold was panned, between the 2nd and 3rd cataracts of the Nile, and ore was mined in the hills and desert to the east and south-east of Aswan, at least as early as the 4th millennium B.C. During the Middle and New Kingdoms, when Nubia was Egyptian-ruled, the chief source was Wawat, between the 1st and 2nd cataracts, and in particular what is now called the Wādī al-'Allāqī in the Eastern Desert. Veins of quartz were broken by fire, then ground to powder. Donkey caravans plied between the mines and Qubbān, a fort situated on the Nile, taking food and drinking water, fetching the gold for, in all probability, final processing at the river. It is evident that Nubian gold was still being obtained in the Ptolemaic period and during the heyday of Kush, but in the decline that overtook the region after the fall of Meroe in the 4th century A.D., exploitation was neglected until the rediscovery of the mines (and of emerald mines) by the Arabs in the 9th century led to a veritable gold rush. It was from the Wādī al-'Allāqī mines that Egypt obtained most of its gold until their exhaustion at the end of the 13th century.

In West Africa the principal goldfields were Bambuk, between the Senegal and Faleme rivers, Bure on the upper Niger, Lobi in the valley of the Black Volta and the Akan goldfields in what is now Ghana and the Ivory Coast. Gold was being produced as early as the 1st millennium B.C., but it was not until about the 8th century A.D., with the development of commercial contacts with the Arab world, that output underwent a marked expansion. The goldfields of Bambuk were exploited during the early Middle Ages, when ancient Ghana was the leading power in the western Sudan. Enclosed as it was by two rivers, Bambuk may have been the 'island of gold', or Wangara, referred to by the Arabs as a place where alluvial gold was collected. In order to satisfy an increasing demand in the Maghrib, Sudanese traders in the 11th and 12th centuries made contact with the evidently more productive goldfields of Bure. In the 14th and 15th centuries they went on to open routes to the still richer goldfields on the fringes of the Akan forest, primarily to meet European demand. At Bure and in the forest, mining was carried out to considerable depths, of thirty metres or more, and the gold was extracted from the ore either by crushing and washing or by smelting. It was exported in the form of dust or twisted wire or bars.

The exploitation of gold deposits in the empire of the Mwene Mutapa was also apparently in response to external demand, coming from the Indian Ocean coast. Alluvial gold was obtained, but mining too was practised. According to a 17th century Portuguese observer a well-like pit (*marondo*) was dug.

The mouth is so narrow that a man may stand with his legs extended from one side to the other. They make steps to go up and down within the circumference of the well, and on these the Kafirs station themselves, passing the *mataca*, or earth, which is dug away, from hand to hand, which the diggers pass to them in *pandes*, or wooden bowls. The first *mataca* does not contain any considerable quantity of gold, the *mataca* which contains it is well known, and when they come upon it, or upon gold in stone, as sometimes happens, they do not desist until it is exhausted, following the vein under the earth in every direction.

Sometimes it happens that such a rush of water bursts into the mine that it is flooded, and it is impossible to extract the *mataca*, and still less the quartz, which has to be broken with great labour. Some of these *marondos*, containing infinite quantities of gold, are abandoned for want of skill to pump out the water.[1]

Once again pounding and washing or smelting were employed to recover
the metal. Over a thousand prehistoric gold mines have been recorded in
modern Zimbabwe.
Ethiopian gold was apparently largely alluvial.

> Upon the confines of the *Negus* dominions, near the Kingdom of Damut (Damot)
> are Mines of Gold about the lake (Tana) out of which the River Niger (Blue Nile)
> proceeds, so that this river carries away some of the sandy part, and rowls it with
> the stream that is extreme fierce (for it falls from high Mountains) and runs with a
> great impetuosity to the main Ocean; upon the sand the *Negers* do pick up much
> gold which crumbles from the Rocks and proceeds out of the Mines that are dis-
> persed all over the Country.[2]

Although gold production is much better documented than iron production,
it is not easy to determine quantities. The annual output of the Nubian mines
during the New Kingdom has been put at rather less than a quarter of a
metric ton and the annual output of the West African mines at peak production in the 18th century at some eight tons. According to information
obtained by the Portuguese in the 15th century, the mines of the Mwene
Mutapa were exporting before their arrival at least a million mithqals (some
four and a half tons) a year, sometimes more. That is almost certainly an
exaggeration. They themselves were getting in the early 16th century only
some fifty kilograms. For purposes of comparison one might notice that
Southern Rhodesia, as it then was, produced over fifteen metric tons in
1950, a small fraction of the output of South Africa.

Gold was too soft and plastic to have much practical use in primitive
technology, and consequently it was used only for coining, gold plate and
ornaments. The introduction of the harder metals, copper and iron, had important implications for agriculture, industry and warfare, since they could
be used for the manufacture of superior hoes, axes, adzes, hammers, knives,
spearheads and arrowheads, as well as scythes, plough-shares, swords and
scissors. Although, like gold, and, for that matter, meteoric iron, it does
occur naturally in an uncombined state, copper, the first of the more useful
metals to be employed, is found like that only rarely in quantity, and therefore it was extensively mined in ancient times. But references to early copper
mining in Africa are sparse. Pliny, writing in the first century A.D., made no
mention of mining in North Africa, though Strabo in the first century B.C.
had referred to a copper mine in the country of the Berber Masaesyles.
Egypt, on the other hand, had a number of deposits at its disposal. Some of
them were in the Eastern Desert and Nubia, but by far the most important –
indeed virtually the only – source for most of the pharaonic period was the
Sinai peninsula. In Sinai proper the sites included Wādī Maghara, and on the
borders of Sinai there was the Timna valley, some thirty kilometres north of

the modern port of Eilat. At the latter place the Egyptians, employing local Midianite and Amalekite labour, were quarrying and smelting copper from the middle of the 2nd millennium B.C. though they were not the first to do so. The Romans too subsequently mined in that area. Using metal chisels instead of stone hammers, they cut galleries into the mountain sides on several levels, the deepest being more than a hundred metres below the surface. The different levels were connected by vertical shafts up to fifteen metres in depth, with foot and hand holes cut in them.

The Timna ore was ground in the immediate vicinity of the mines, but smelted some distance away in the valley, at sites determined by considerations of defence, owing to the Egyptian's insecure hold on the area, and of the supply of water, fuel and food. The Egyptians constructed a bowl furnace in the ground, lining it with calcareous mortar, with a stone-lined pit underneath to catch the fluid slag tapped from the furnace, leaving behind a copper ingot. The necessary temperatures were achieved through the use of bellows. Such furnaces could be continuously recharged, thus conserving fuel (charcoal from local acacia trees and brushwood), which was scarce. The Roman furnace was constructed on much the same principle, and it continued to be used after the Roman period. A variety of materials was employed as a flux for separating the metal from the ore. Iron ore, in the form of fossilized wood converted to haematite, and lime, were used very early on, even before the Egyptian period, and the Egyptians themselves made use of manganese.

Copper was used in the Mediterranean world for the manufacture of tools, weapons and utensils. For shaping the metal, hammering hot and cold – which had the effect of hardening – and casting were practised, together with the technique of wire drawing. But copper is relatively soft and from the 2nd millennium, or perhaps earlier, in Egypt and Libya it was being mixed with tin, imported from Europe, to make bronze, which had the additional advantage of a lower melting point than copper. Copper and bronze tools and weapons were not necessarily sharper than stone, but they lasted longer, were mostly less brittle and permitted a much wider range of shapes. Bronze could be used to make implements with sockets – axes and spearheads – and found useful employment in the manufacture of the heavy sledgehammer, the carpenter's rasp and the sword.

In the southern parts of the Sahara the copper deposits of Akjoujt in Mauritania were mined in the first half of the 1st millenium B.C., probably by the Berbers, though the mines were situated at the point where Berber and Negro met. In the Middle Ages Takedda near Aïr was a celebrated copper mining and smelting town. South of the desert tin was mined in Hausaland, modern Nigeria, and on the Transvaal Highveld. Copper was produced along the Copperbelt of Katanga (Shaba) and Zambia and south of the Limpo-

po in the Messina area and in the Transvaal Lowveld, in some instances before
A.D. 1 000, but on a much greater scale from the 14th and 15th centuries.
Pits were commonly dug and at Phalaborwa in the Transvaal Lowveld
passages were driven through the ground. On the Copperbelt the ore was
brought to the surface by means of bark buckets and ropes, and rocks were
split by the alternate application of fire and cold water. The ore was charcoal-
smelted in furnaces made of clay or hollowed out ant-hills, and the copper
thus obtained was refined by a second heating before being cast as ingots or
drawn into wire. At the southern extremity of the continent copper was
mined and processed in Namaqualand and it appears from the accounts of
early European travellers that it was relatively common in the Cape. The
'Diary of Vasco da Gama's Voyage to India' records at the end of 1497:

> In this land there seemed to us to be much copper, for they wore it on their legs
> and on their arms and in their much curled hair. In this land there is also tin, which
> they use on the hilts of daggers; the sheaths of them are of ivory. The people of
> this land greatly prize linen cloth, and they gave us much of this copper for as
> many shirts as we cared to give.[3]

iii) *The Iron Age*
Iron tools and other artifacts dating from the beginning of the 2nd millennium B.C. have been found in Egypt, but it is apparent that they did not
become common until towards the end of the 2nd millennium, and there is
no evidence of iron smelting in Egypt before about the 7th century B.C.
Perhaps because of the inadequacy of local sources the Egyptians were slow
in adopting it on a large scale for weapons and tools. It is generally accepted
that the first iron-using people were the Hittites of Syria and Asia Minor
in the 2nd millennium B.C., whose techniques became known in Egypt
possibly after the collapse of their empire and the dispersal of their smiths.
It has also been argued that iron working was introduced into Egypt by
Assyrian conquerors in the 7th century B.C. or by Greek mercenaries and
traders settled at Defennen, a fort in the Eastern Desert, and Naucratis in the
Nile Delta in the 7th and 6th centuries B.C. or by Persian conquerors in the
6th. The Phoenicians seem to have been responsible for the spread of the
technology to the western Mediterranean.
    Although it presented fewer mining problems, at least at first, since the ore
is commonly found at or near the surface of the earth, iron was more difficult than copper to prepare and use. Its high melting point meant that, until
the invention of the blast furnace (dependent upon water-powered bellows)
in medieval Europe, casting was beyond the skill of the smiths. However,
iron-ore reduces before the iron itself melts, that is, oxygen is drawn off
and the non-iron solids (the gangue) melt. The slag runs off, leaving a
'bloom' of iron crystals, mixed with bits of charcoal and other impurities

from the furnace, which can be repeatedly hammered at red heat to produce wrought iron. Alternatively, it can be broken up and pounded to reduce the charcoal and impurities to a dust that can be blown away. Such iron does not take a very sharp edge, but is a good deal tougher than other metals and, without any admixture, makes a much more satisfactory sword than bronze does.

The smelting of iron both required and made possible the manufacture of new tools – hinged tongs, anvils, frame-saws and files. For fuel, although coal and peat were known, charcoal was almost universally employed in smelting in ancient times. The earliest type of furnace was the bowl furnace, as in the case of copper-smelting. Its use continued into the Roman period. Charcoal was laid at the bottom and, after being lit, covered with alternate layers of ore and charcoal. Since no natural draught was possible, hand or foot-operated bellows had to be used to get the necessary temperature to melt the gangue. It was not an efficient furnace because the forced draught of the bellows introduced more oxygen, instead of drawing it off. A more advanced type was the shaft furnace, built above ground. This could be made of clay, but had to be lined with stone if it was to be used more than once. Ore and charcoal were mixed together and either a natural or a forced draught was used.

In the latter part of the 2nd millennium B.C. the quality of iron was improved by the invention of cementation, which steeled the wrought iron by means of repeated hammerings and heating in direct contact with charcoal, and of tempering. It was possible, by luck or judgment, to retain sufficient carbon in the smelting process to produce steel, though this was rare. It was the Arabs who transmitted to the Mediterranean area the methods of steel-making devised in India and the Far East. The Romans imported small cakes of crucible steel from south India, and being under the impression that it came from China, they called it 'Seric iron'. They, like the Greeks, made relatively few contributions to the technology of metallurgy, but made extensive use of iron, particularly for the manufacture of swords, spears and armour and the invaluable entrenching tools of the legionaries. Ore was mined throughout the Roman empire and drainage was improved by the introduction of the Archimedean screw or cochlea, and the scoop-wheel. The former possibly originated in Egypt, where it was used for irrigation. In the last period of the empire iron production fell off as all the surface deposits were exhausted, labour for deep mining became expensive and charcoal grew scarce owing to deforestation. In Egypt in particular most of the available metalliferous ores were situated in the desert, where shortages of fuel and water made costs prohibitive.

The Romans used lead for their aqueduct pipes and pewter (tin and lead) and brass (copper and zinc) for utensils. The technology of brass casting spread to West Africa in the Middle Ages, but the first metal with which

most of sub-Saharan Africa became familiar was iron. Iron working techniques were probably diffused from the Mediterranean, though neither
spontaneous invention nor importation into Ethiopia from southern Arabia
can be ruled out. The fact that sub-Saharan Africa passed straight from the
Stone Age to the Iron Age suggests the adoption of a relatively advanced
metallurgy from outside rather than an indigenous prior development
through the easier metallurgy of copper, which in fact became known at
the same time as iron metallurgy.

Nubia may have become acquainted with the use of iron through conflict
with the Assyrians in the 7th century, when Egypt had a Kushite dynasty,
or from Greek mercenaries advancing as far as the 2nd cataract in the 6th
century B.C. At all events, Meroe, the second capital of the successor to the
ancient kingdom of Kush, whose iron industry may have originated about the
middle of the 1st millennium B.C., but was at its height between the 1st
century B.C. and the 4th A.D., may have been the centre of diffusion for
both East Africa and, along routes between the middle Nile and Lake Chad,
West Africa. On the other hand, the techniques of iron-smelting in West
Africa may have been derived either from Carthaginian or Roman North
Africa via the Atlantic coastal region or the Sahara, which the Berbers, who
could have learnt iron working from the Carthaginians, were crossing in the
1st millennium B.C. There is, however, little evidence of iron smelting in
the desert, where it would have been difficult to find enough wood for charcoal. Pot-bellows (a pair of vessels, of pottery or wood, inflated and deflated
by pressure of hand or foot on a leather cap), which were used in Egypt,
were also employed in West and Equatorial Africa. The shaft furnace was
found in both Meroe and West Africa, but some of the West African furnaces betray North African influence. It is quite likely that West Africa learnt
from both Nubia and North Africa.

The earliest known iron-mining community in West Africa, flourishing
during at least the last three centuries B.C. and the first two centuries A.D.,
was in the Nok valley in central Nigeria, north-east of the confluence of the
Niger and the Benue rivers and south-west of the Jos plateau. PossiblyNok
was the cradle of the culture of the Bantu-speaking peoples; and they,
in their migration eastwards and southwards, propagated knowledge of
metallurgy to other African peoples ignorant of it, just as they had been responsible for the spread of agricultural techniques. On the other hand, the
proto-Bantu may in fact have been a stone-tool using people that acquired
their knowledge of iron after they left their homeland. It is possible that iron
working was introduced into the western highlands of Kenya by Nilotic-
speaking people.

Iron seems to have been introduced into the Lake Victoria area from the
central Sudan not long after the middle of the 1st millennium B.C. and sub-

sequently, just before the birth of Christ, into Angola and northern Namibia. In the early centuries of the Christian era it spread from the interlacustrine region into an area stretching from south-east Kenya, through Tanzania, north-east Zambia and Malawi, into Zimbabwe and the Transvaal. In western Zambia and Shaba (Katanga) it appears to have been introduced from the west, about the middle of the 1st millennium A.D. or just before. South of the Vaal River, in the Orange Free State, there is no evidence of Iron Age settlement before the 14th or 15th century. The chronological discrepancies can be explained in terms of the two interacting southward migrations of Bantu-speaking people, the western stream deriving its knowledge of iron working from contact with the eastern stream south of the equatorial forest. The arrival of European settlers in South Africa in the 17th century found the Khoikhoi and San still in ignorance of metal working, with the possible exception of the Nama, who worked copper rather than iron, for decoration rather than for utility.

The type of furnace excavated at Taruga in the Nok culture area is the shaft furnace. More efficient was the dome furnace, used in West Africa between the Niger and the Gulf of Guinea and capable of generating high temperatures, with or without the use of bellows. It incorporated an underground pit into which the slag was run off during the smelting process. This type of furnace probably originated in the upper Niger area, where it may have been introduced by the Berbers, and can perhaps be traced back to the Carthaginians or, more likely, to the Romans. Another type of furnace, used on the lower Niger, by the Nupe among others, and composed of a wall, with a vent at its base for introducing a blast of air from bag bellows into a reduction chamber below ground level, resembles the so-called Catalan furnace, said to have been brought into Africa by the Arabs.

Iron mining was mostly a question of excavating shallow pits. In West Africa, however, it was sometimes a complicated operation, involving shafts and underground tunnels.

African smiths could turn out a good implement, which was preferred to the shoddier article sometimes traded by Europeans. The traditional manufacture of iron goods (such as hoes, knives and axes) still flourishes at least in West Africa, though nowadays mostly using imported iron. Imported iron has always been in great demand, as have been weapons in the past. On the whole, in sub-Saharan Africa the supply of iron implements was never adequate and a cultivator was more likely to use a wooden digging stick than an iron hoe. Some areas, however, were well supplied, as Mungo Park noted at the end of the 18th century.

The Negroes on the coast being cheaply supplied with iron from the European traders, never attempt the manufacturing of this article themselves; but in the inland parts, the natives smelt this useful metal in such quantities, as not only to supply themselves from it with all necessary weapons and instruments, but even to make it an article of commerce with some of the neighbouring states.

He went on to describe the iron-working process as he saw it.

During my stay at Kamalia, there was a smelting furnace at a short distance from the hut where I lodged, and the owner and his workmen made no secret about the manner of conducting the operations and readily allowed me to examine the furnace, and assist them in breaking the ironstone. The furnace was a circular tower of clay, about ten feet high and three in diameter, surrounded in two places with withes, to prevent the clay from cracking and falling to pieces by the violence of the heat. Round the lower part, on a level with the ground (but not so low as the bottom of the furnace, which was somewhat concave), were made seven openings, into every one of which were placed three tubes of clay, and the openings again plastered up in such a manner that no air could enter the furnace but through the tubes, by the opening and shutting of which they regulated the fire. These tubes were formed by plastering a mixture of clay and grass round a smooth roller of wood, which, as soon as the clay began to harden, was withdrawn, and the tube left to dry in the sun. The ironstone which I saw was very heavy, and of a dull red colour, with greyish specks; it was broken into pieces about the size of a hen's egg. A bundle of dry wood was first put into the furnace, and covered with a considerable quantity of charcoal, which was brought ready burnt from the woods. Over this was laid a stratum of ironstone, and then another of charcoal, and so on, until the furnace was quite full. The fire was applied through one of the tubes, and blown for some time with bellows made of goats' skins. The operations went on very slowly at first, and it was some hours before the flame appeared above the furnace; but after this it burnt with great violence all the first night, and the people who attended put in at times more charcoal. On the day following the fire was not so fierce, and on the second night some of the tubes were withdrawn, and the air allowed to have freer access to the furnace; but the heat was still very great, and a bluish flame rose some feet above the top of the furnace. On the third day from the commencement of the operation, all the tubes were taken out, the ends of many of them being vitrified with the heat; but the metal was not removed until some days afterwards, when the whole was perfectly cool. Part of the furnace was then taken down, and the iron appeared in the form of a large irregular mass, with pieces of charcoal adhering to it. It was sonorous; and when any portion was broken off, the fracture exhibited a granulated appearance, like broken steel. The owner informed me that many parts of this cake were useless, but still there was good iron enough to repay him for his trouble. This iron, or rather steel, is formed into various instruments, by being repeatedly heated in a forge, the heat of which is urged by a pair of double bellows, of a very simple construction, being made of two goats' skins, the tubes from which unite before they enter the forge, and supply a constant and very regular blast. The hammer, forceps, and anvil, are all very simple, and the workmanship (particularly in the formation of knives and spears), is not destitute of merit. The iron, indeed, is hard and brittle, and requires much labour before it can be made to answer the purpose.[4]

iv) *Technological achievements*

The progress of tropical Africa in technology was meagre after the introduction of agriculture and the invention of metal working. Over most of the sub-Saharan part of the continent the wheel and the harnessing of animal, water, wind and steam power were unknown; tools were rudimentary; and the division of labour in production unpractised beyond a degree of specialization in craft or function. The tsetse fly and the failure to adopt plough and cart (possibly because their economic advantages were not obvious) are part of the explanation for technological backwardness. Change was perhaps also inhibited by the existence of social pressures upon the innovator to share the benefits of his enterprise and by the isolation that deprived small communities of the stimulus of the exchange of ideas. The slow pace of change, which discouraged readiness to discard long-established hypotheses, and the lack of a cultivated, literate and leisured class, able to take an interest in the observation and explanation of natural phenomena, did not provide the conditions necessary for the development of scientific thought. Scientific analysis depends upon the identification of the impersonal observable and predictable forces of nature. Furthermore, inquiry demands accurate measurements, written records and calculation. In sub-Saharan Africa standardized measures of weight and volume were largely lacking. David Livingstone in his Journal of 1853, wrote of the Makololo people of northern Botswana,

> It is extremely difficult to explain to the people of this country the use of money or machinery, or of any of the sciences as sources of pure intellectual pleasure. If they can count as many as serve in all their simple transactions, which can always be effected on the fingers, what need is there for the rules of proportion &c? The art of writing is very curious, but of what use is it to those who can send all their messages viva voce and who have all their family and connections within five minutes walk of their own residence, and who have so little news to communicate that they begin their narration invariably with the formula, 'There are no news, We heard a few lies'?[5]

Mungo Park, too, noticed in West Africa how people were contented with simple measurement and incurious about natural phenomena.

> The Mandingoes, and, I believe, the Negroes in general, have no artificial method of dividing time. They calculate the years by the number of *rainy seasons*. They portion the year into *moons*, and reckon the days by so many *suns*. The day they divide into morning, mid-day, and evening; and further sub-divide it, when necessary, by pointing to the sun's place in the heavens. I frequently inquired of some of them what became of the sun during the night, and whether we should see the same sun or a different one in the morning; but I found that they considered the question as very childish. The subject appeared to them as placed beyond the reach of human investigation; they had never indulged a conjecture, nor formed any hypothesis about the matter.[6]

European and African conceptions of what was significant simply did not coincide. African concerns were essentially pragmatic, the common hazards of life such as disease and crop failure.

Given the premises that were accepted, the traditional African way of reasoning was in no way illogical. Livingstone, recording a discussion he had with a 'rain-doctor', goes on to say: 'The above is only a specimen of their way of reasoning, in which, when the language is well understood, they are perceived to be remarkably acute.'[7] Mary Kingsley makes a similar point.

> The more you know the African, the more you study his laws and institutions, the more you must recognise that the main characteristic of his intellect is logical, and you see how in all things he uses this absolutely sound but narrow thought-form. He is not a dreamer, nor a doubter; everything is real, very real, horribly real to him.[8]

It is commonly said that explanations in sub-Saharan Africa tended to be religious rather than scientific, to be couched in terms of the intervention of men and of spirits thought to permeate the whole of nature. The mysterious forces of men and nature had to be enlisted or averted. Misfortune was attributable to personal wrong-doing or to the malice of others. This is not to say, however, that all occurrences and phenomena received that sort of explanation. The usual explanation and remedy for misfortune were derived from common sense. It was when the usual explanation and remedy did not match the exceptional nature of the event that there was recourse to supernatural explanation. Human life in Africa, where the environment was particularly harsh, was more than usually hazardous, and so fatalism and fear of malignant forces were perhaps understandable. What other explanations were open to people whose experience was so restricted by physical and, in the absence of writing, intellectual isolation? The scientific method requires the postulating and testing of hypotheses, discarding those which prove to have no practical value. Although even modern scientists are unwilling to abandon pet theories, their reluctance is as nothing compared with the tenacity with which traditional African society clung to its postulates. Rather than abandon their assumptions, traditional cultures preferred, by what has been called 'secondary elaboration', to explain away predictive failure. Indeed, there was no choice but to adhere to traditional beliefs. The alternative was chaos. Among the Azande people:

> All their beliefs hang together . . . In this web of belief every strand depends upon every other strand, and a Zande cannot get out of its meshes because it is the only world he knows. The web is not an external structure in which he is enclosed. It is the texture of his thought and he cannot think that his thought is wrong.[9]

In the Mediterranean lands of Africa the progress of science and technology was more rapid. Ancient Egypt achieved much that excites admiration and astonishment, not least the development of calculation, astronomical observation and craft tools and, more particularly, its spectacular building feats. Nonetheless, the technology of the Egyptians remained stunted and unenterprising. For their building they had nothing beyond ropes, levers and rollers, together with an extravagant use of labour and a total indifference to time. Egyptian science was limited by a preoccupation with practical problems and a lack of interest in knowledge for its own sake, in analysis and in abstract thought, and by an incapacity for generalization and synthesis. Reverence for dogma, ritual and tradition frustrated inquiry and innovation, in technology as well as science. The science of Phoenicia, too, imported into Carthage, proved an intellectual cul-de-sac. Although they had a calendar and a system of weights and measures, the Carthaginians had no conception of ascertainable, immutable natural laws. Natural forces were regarded as capricious, but susceptible to the power of magic and the persuasion of sacrifice, including human sacrifice. Carthaginian technology was dependent upon foreign craftsmen and initiative and was resistant to change. Nonetheless, it was superior to that of their Berber neighbours. Berber kings in Numidia employed Carthaginian architects and craftsmen.

In contrast, the science of Greece, introduced into Egypt by the Macedonians and furthered by the great Museum of Alexandria, and fostered by Rome, attained a high level of abstract reasoning. Scientific discovery was, with the exception of engineering and architecture, largely divorced from practical application. Even Greek and Roman engineers were not much concerned with replacing human labour and did not go beyond devising machinery, such as the derrick and winch, which rendered labour more effective without providing a substitute. Though aware, for example, of the power of water, they did not make much use of it, at least not until towards the end of the Roman empire. This indifference undoubtedly stemmed to some extent from the institution of slavery and the contempt of the intellectual for manual labour. There was no incentive to conserve labour as long as slaves were plentiful. Nevertheless, in the field of military engineering the Romans did excel, because of the practical problems which they were compelled to solve, though there was little transfer to other branches of technology. Their contributions were not large even to the technology of the honourable profession of agriculture, including farm management, the chief interest of agronomists like Cato, and certainly to that of mining and metallurgy and other industries. The same may be said of industrial organization. Division of labour was not carried far and mass production was largely confined – with the exception of textiles – to production for the middle class, of pottery, jewellery and bronze ornaments in imitation of the individually-made and artistically-designed products purchased by the very rich. In Egypt, despite a tradition of state control of industry, there is little evidence of mass production or, for that matter, of standardization, even in the manufacture of armaments.

The Arabs took over Graeco-Roman science and technology, at the same time drawing upon the knowledge accumulated in the Middle and Far East, which they were brought into contact with through their conquests. Indeed, as Ibn Khaldūn pointed out, Islamic science to begin with owed more to Persians, Christians and Jews than to Arabs, and even after its arabization it remained indebted to Christian and Jewish contributions. Arabic proved to be a suitable language for scientific writing. In the early Middle Ages Islam was far in advance of barbarised western Europe, which, in the event, acquired a good deal of its knowledge of its classical past through Arab intermediaries. Although Arab science tended to be derivative, obsequious to ancient authorities, especially Plato and Aristotle, and not free of preoccupations with astrology and magic, its discoveries in mathematics, chemistry and optics were far from negligible. The adoption of the Hindu system of numbers had profound implications for the conduct, and therefore for the efficiency of, government and business.

> This technical device had almost the same effect on arithmetic as the discovery of the alphabet on writing. Before then, arithmetic, other than what can be done on the fingers or the abacus, was a mystery which only the most learned understood. With arabic numbers it was within reach of any warehouse clerk; they democratised mathematics.[10]

Progress in chemistry was advanced by the improvement of the still, which was used for distilling perfume. One of the strengths of Arab science, not least shown in chemistry, was that it was not separated from technology and advances in each reinforced the other.

Like Hellenistic science, Arab science received the patronage not only of rich merchants and officials, but also of caliphs and other princes, including Saladin. By the 12th century, however, it was past the peak of its achievement, and by the 15th it had virtually come to an end. Various reasons have been put forward to explain its decline: the advent of 'feudalism'; the increasingly exclusive character of all Muslim learning, leading to an excessive deference to acknowledged authorities; and a conflict between science and religion. Unlike medieval European science, which was not divorced from theology, Arab science had been wholly secular and Arab scientists unaware of, or indifferent to, any conflict between the science they investigated and the Islam they mostly professed. The Fātimid academy founded in Egypt in 1005 combined the teaching of Shi'a doctrines, which was its primary purpose, with a study of science and philosophy. Conflict, however, had always threatened because of orthodoxy's distrust of knowledge not derived from revelation and tradition. Increasingly the scepticism of early medieval scholars, such as Abū Bakr Muḥammad b. Zakariyyā al-Rāzī (865-925), could find no place in Muslim intellectual life. As the West recovered and its science freed itself from the dominance of astrology, the intellectual vigour of the Islamic world, its science and technology, declined. By the time the culture of Islam spread to the western Sudan, where Timbuktu and Jenne became notable centres of Muslim learning, Arab science had atrophied. When, after a lapse of centuries, Africa renewed its acquaintance with up-to-date technology, its experience was traumatic, the outcome of European colonization or settlement.

NOTES

1. Quoted Axelson, E.: *Portuguese in South-East Africa 1488-1600* (Cape Town, 1973), p. 50
2. Baratti, G.: author of a 17th-century travel book, quoted Pankhurst, Richard: *An Introduction to the Economic History of Ethiopia from Early Times to 1800* (London, 1961), p. 226
3. Axelson, E.: *South African Explorers* (London, 1954), p. 11
4. Park, M.: *The Travels* (London, Everyman 2nd edition, 1954), p. 217-19
5. Schapera, I. (ed.): *Livingstone's Private Journals 1851-1853* (London, 1960), p. 157
6. Park, M.: Op. cit., p. 208
7. Perham, Margery & Simmons, Jack (eds.): *African Discovery, an Anthology of Exploration* (Harmondsworth, 1948), p. 149
8. Kingsley, M.: *West African Studies* (London, 2nd edn. 1901), p. 105
9. Evans-Pritchard, E. E., quoted Horton, R.: 'African traditional thought and western science Part 2 – The closed and open predicament' (*Africa*, XXXVII, 1967, p. 155-87), p. 155
10. Bernal, J. D.: *Science in History* (Harmondsworth, 3rd edn. 1965), Volume I, p. 276

Further reading

Bernal, J. D.: Op. cit. (see above, note 10)
Charles-Picard, G. & C.: Op. cit. (see p. 46)
Clark, J. D.: Op. cit. (see p. 31)
Cole, Sonia: *The Prehistory of East Africa* (New York, 1965)
De Gregori, Thomas R.: *Technology and the Economic Development of the Tropical African Frontier* (Cleveland and London, 1969)
Derry, T. K. & Williams, T. I.: *A Short History of Technology, from the Earliest Times to A.D. 1700* (Oxford, 1960)
Forbes, R. J. & Dijksterhuis, E. J.: *A History of Science and Technology*, Volume I, *Ancient Times to the Seventeenth Century* (Harmondsworth, 1963)
Forbes, R. J.: *Metallurgy in Antiquity, a Notebook for Archaeologists and Technologists* (Leiden, 1950)
Harris, J. R. (ed.): *The Legacy of Egypt* (Oxford, 2nd edn. 1971)

Hodges, Henry: *Technology in the Ancient World* (Harmondsworth, 1971)
Holt, P. M., Lambton, Ann K. S. & Lewis, Bernard (eds.): *The Cambridge History of Islam*, Volume II, *The Further Islamic Lands, Islamic Society and Civilization* (Cambridge, 1970)
Horton, Robin: Op. cit. (see above, note 9); 'Part 1 – From tradition to science' (*Africa* XXXVII, 1967, p. 50–71)
MacBurney, C. B. M.: *The Stone Age in Northern Africa* (Harmondsworth, 1960)
Phillipson, D. W.: Op. cit. (see p. 31)
Rothenberg, Beno: *Timna, Valley of the Biblical Copper Mines* (London and New York, 1972)
Schacht, Joseph (ed.): *The Legacy of Islam* (Oxford, 2nd edn., 1974)
Shinnie, P. L. (ed.): *The African Iron Age* (Oxford, 1971)
Singer, Charles, Holmyard, E. J. & Hall, A. R.: *A History of Technology*, Volume I (Oxford, 1954)
Stigler, Robert et al.,: *Varieties of Culture in the Old World* (New York, 1975)
Westermann, Diedrich: *The African Today and Tomorrow* (London, 2nd edn. 1939)

2. THE CRAFTS

i) *Metalware, pottery and glass*
Although metals had their severely practical uses, they were equally valued for their decorative and religious purposes. This was true most obviously of gold and silver, but even iron was used for jewellery before it was used for tools and weapons. Jewellery was an ancient and widespread craft, reaching thousands of years ago a very high standard of artistic achievement, employing not only metals, but also ivory, shell, precious and semi-precious stones and leather. Ostrich shell beads some nine thousand years old have been dug up at archaeological sites in Kenya and elsewhere in sub-Saharan Africa. The gold- and silversmiths of Egypt, even in the archaic period of the 3rd millennium B.C., were extremely dextrous in making jewellery and coverings for weapon handles, furniture and panels, by hammering, casting and soldering. In Hellenistic Egypt fine metalwork was executed in the Greek style, though with a detectable Egyptian influence. Memphis was an important centre, giving way to Alexandria. Egypt and Greece exercised much influence upon the metalworkers of Carthage, where both men and women had a lively taste for jewellery and other finery. Later, in the medieval Maghrib, there were colonies of Jewish goldsmiths and jewellers with a high reputation.

In sub-Saharan Africa Khoikhoi men and women wore rings on arms and legs.

Most of these rings are made of thick leather straps, generally cut in a circular shape, which by being beat and held over the fire, are rendered tough enough to retain the curvature that is given them. . . . Rings of iron or copper, but especially of brass, of the size of a goose-quill, are considered as genteeler and more valuable than those made of leather. They are, however, sometimes worn along with these latter, to the number of six or eight at a time, particularly on the arms.[1]

To the north the Katanga- Zambian Copperbelt produced copper and iron bracelets and anklets, beads, bells (part of rulers' insignia), copper crosses, needles and razors, as well as weapons, hoes and axes. Necklaces, were manufactured with particular skill, of copper wire interwoven or wound into spirals. In what is now Zimbabwe, gold and silver orna- ments were made and in some areas wooden objects covered with gold foil. In the gold-bearing and trading areas of West Africa, especially at the courts of the great medieval kingdoms of the western Sudan, gold was lavishly used for personal adornment and for decorating shields and weapons. Ibn Baṭṭūṭa speaks of the ceremonial weapons and musical instruments made of silver to be seen at the court of the emperor of Mali, and silver jewellery has been recovered by archaeologists in Senegal. Examples of superior work- manship in sub-Saharan Africa can easily be multiplied.

Sculpture was an art responsible for considerable advances in the skills of metalwork, particularly in welding and casting. There survive fragments of a life-size statue of an Egyptian pharaoh, dating from late in the 3rd millen- nium B.C., made of copper sheets nailed to a wooden core. At Meroe wrought-iron armatures were used as a skeleton for plaster statues. The *cire- perdue* – waste wax – process was used for casting in the Middle East as early as the 4th millennium B.C. In West Africa the method was in use by the early Middle Ages (possibly in imitation of super-Saharan practice learnt through the Saharan trade) for casting masks, heads and statuettes from cop- per, bronze and brass. The most notable centres were Igbo-Ukwu, Ife and Benin, all in modern Nigeria. The archaeological findings at Igbo-Ukwu have not been given a date that is generally accepted. Since the artifacts were probably made of imported metal and were associated with imported beads, the likelihood is that they date to a period after the development of the Saharan trade, probably from after the 11th century A.D. Ife, too, almost certainly obtained the necessary copper and copper alloys by way of trade. Dating the two dozen or so surviving brass heads has presented a problem because they have not been found in the context of archaeological excava- tions, and another difficulty is that they are so alike in style and technique that they give the appearance of having been cast within a short period. However, on the evidence of other excavated material, the flowering of Ife culture has been assigned a period running from the 12th to the mid-15th century.

Rather more is known about Benin brasses and bronzes, but even here there are areas of doubt and controversy. It is only comparatively recently that the assumption of Benin's debt to Ife for the art of brass casting has been questioned. Opinion is divided on this question as also on the question of the dating of the castings, which include plaques as well as heads and statuettes. They have been classified by characteristics of style, but there is no consensus among the experts. The only firm scientific evidence is that manillas (pieces of copper and brass in horseshoe shape used as money) and bracelets were being made in the 13th century and that the casting traditions persisted until the 19th. Some would argue that the art was at its finest in the last quarter of the 16th century and the first half of the 17th, thereafter declining rapidly in quality as quantity rather than quality became the aim. In Asante the famous copper, bronze and brass weights used for measuring out gold were cast by the *cire-perdue* method.

These West African centres also produced very fine copper, bronze and brass vessels, which probably, like their other artifacts, had a religious significance. Metals, sometimes even iron, were too precious to be used for mundane purposes except by the wealthy. The rich in Egypt and North Africa used gold plate and bronze vases in ancient and classical times, either made by local craftsmen or imported, especially from Greece. The not-so rich made do with local imitations of the best. The earliest manufactured receptacles were of stone, but they too were in a sense a luxury product because of the labour required. Early Egyptian craftsmen lavished enormous skill and toil on stone vessels. Working with flint and copper tools, they were able to cut rock crystal tubular jars with walls that were only a millimetre thick. It was the invention of pottery that provided a comparatively cheap and easy way of making containers. The first Egyptian pots were a utilitarian imitation of the stone ones. Stone went, more or less, out of use, though, where it was available, soapstone continued to be used for special purposes. For example bowls for salt manufacture were carved in the later Iron Age in the Transvaal Lowveld.

The everyday utensils indispensable to the household were mostly made at home. A variety of materials was pressed into service, but probably the commonest was mud or clay, made into pots. Clay was widely found and the skills involved in pottery were rudimentary. The potter's wheel, introduced into Egypt from western Asia as early as the 3rd millennium B.C., and the kiln were never widely diffused. Outside North Africa and perhaps some of the East African coastal settlements of the Middle Ages, pots were either moulded or constructed with clay strips, then sun dried or fired in an open fire. Despite their fragility, weight and awkward shape, which posed transport difficulties, pots were mass produced. From ancient and classical North Africa and Egypt they were carried by sea over far-flung trade routes, often not so much for their own sake as for their contents, wine or oil. Over fairly short distances, in sub-Saharan Africa, they were taken to market by the women who made them.

Egyptian 'coarse ware' was mostly made of Nile mud, less often of local clay. It was coloured and sometimes slightly burnished, with little variation in style before the middle of the 1st millenium B.C. In addition to vessels, pottery figures were made. In North Africa, in the first centuries of Carthaginian history, pots were imported from Tyre as ballast for ships voyaging to the western Mediterranean to pick up minerals. As the link with the mother city weakened, however, pottery did become an important industry, mass producing jars (including very large ones for household storage in sparsely furnished Carthaginian houses), phials, statues and statuettes of gods, ritual masks, braziers and, particularly for export, lamps – as well as the oil they burnt. Wheel and kiln were used, but Punic products tended to be imitative and of rather inferior quality. The pots were heavy and clumsy, usually uncoloured, and wealthier people preferred the imported article.

Pottery was widely practised in sub-Saharan Africa and was a very ancient craft. As in super-Saharan Africa pots were used for transporting commodities in trade – notably salt – but mostly, of course, for domestic purposes. Whether pottery was a spontaneous development in sub-Saharan Africa or spread from Egypt and North Africa is open to question. Certainly the pottery of the western Sudan displayed, hardly surprisingly in view of the trade links, the strong influence of the Maghrib; that of Kerma and Meroe and other places in the middle and upper Nile valley, the influence of Egypt; that of Kilwa on the East African coast, the influence of the ware imported from the Middle and Far East.

'Wavy line' pottery, which was first excavated near modern Khartoum, may have developed quite spontaneously. Going back to the 6th millennium B.C., it has been found over a wide belt of Africa, from the Nile valley westwards to the southern Sahara and southwards as far as Lake Rudolf in modern Kenya, very often in association with fishing harpoons. The first pottery was made by people with a Stone Age technology. Other types, varying in shape and decoration, were associated with communities acquainted with iron making. These include the so-called dimple-based ware, a distinctive feature of settlements in the vicinity of Lake Victoria known to archaeologists as the Urewe group; Kwale ware from Kenya; Kalembo ware from Zambia; Gokomere ware from Zimbabwe; Kisalian ware from Sanga in Shaba; and Nok ware from Nigeria. The later Iron Age of sub-Saharan Africa, beginning just before the end of the 1st millennium A.D., brought new styles, such as the Kalomo and Luangwa of Zambia, Leopard's Kopje and Great Zimbabwe of Zimbabwe, and so on, some of which have persisted to this day.

Baked clay and terracotta were not only used for cooking and water pots, but also for braziers and statues, statuettes and figurines. From the Nok culture area and from Ife and Benin, very fine heads and fragments of limbs have been recovered, as well as hundreds of figurines or fragments of them depicting human beings and animals. (The likelihood is that they too had a religious significance.) Fragments of terracotta heads, probably made in the middle of the 1st millennium A.D., have been found near Lydenburg in the Transvaal.

An important advance in pottery was glazing. In Egypt, where the necessary materials for glass – soda, lime and sand – were plentiful, and fuel was supplied by papyrus roots, the glazing of pots was introduced in the 7th century B.C. by Greek potters who settled at Naucratis. Before this the Egyptians produced a faïence, an unfired ware, made of a friable core of quartz covered with a fired coloured glass. From as early as the 1st dynasty, figures, vases, tiles, beads and amulets were manufactured. Glass objects, for example jars and vases, date from the 2nd millennium B.C., and were made either in clay moulds, or by grinding or carving a lump of glass, or by dipping a bag of sand into molten glass and shaping a vessel by rolling. In the Hellenistic period Alexandria was an important centre for the manufacture of variegated coloured glass (an effect achieved by fusing different types of coloured glass, the result of the presence of mineral impurities in the sand used), which was made up into jewellery, fancy jars and bottles for ointments and perfumes and glass burial urns. Egypt probably enjoyed a monopoly of the manufacture of glass cubes for mosaics. The very important advance of glass blowing probably originated in Syria at the beginning of the Christian era, but spread rapidly across the whole Roman world. Alexandria remained important for glass after the Arab conquest, and a new centre grew up at al-Fustāt.

Egyptian glassware was imitated by Phoenician craftsmen, whose products have been found throughout the western Mediterranean. In sub-Saharan Africa there is evidence of the manufacture of glass, or at least of beads from imported glass. Crucibles for that purpose have been unearthed at Ife and dated to the 14th and 15th centuries A.D. Bida in Nupe became, and remains, famous for its glass bracelets and beads. The technique, like that of casting, was presumably introduced from North Africa in the course of trade.

Muslim ceramics, glassware and other artifacts pose for the experts immense difficulties in distinguishing regional differences. Whatever their precise place of origin, however, important technical innovations clearly originated in Islam, in particular the introduction of lustre painting, in the 9th century. Tin glazing was first used during the 'Abbāsid caliphate by potters trying to imitate Chinese porcelain. Aesthetically, Islamic pottery is highly esteemed, especially that produced in the Near and Middle East between the 9th and 13th centuries, and amongst the principal centres of luxury ware was al-Fustāt. Egyptian pottery is considered to have been at its best during the Fātimid dynasty.

ii) *Building*

The distinction between the artist and the artisan (becoming obvious in the manufacture of late Benin bronzes) and that between the functional and the aesthetic has never been rigid. It is of some significance that in the ancient world of the Mediterranean the tools and methods of th eartisan were not markedly different from those of the artist. This was true even of the stone-mason's implements. The building made of stone was intended to be a work of art, for the fitting performance of public functions or for the delectation of the wealthy, a work of art in which the contributions of architect, sculptor and artisan were fused. It was in the Mediterranean area and that part of Africa most influenced by the Mediterranean, such as Kush and its successors, that the most advanced building techniques practised in Africa were to be found. While over the whole of the continent people lived for the most part, as they do today, in simple houses built of mud and thatch, in Egypt sun-dried bricks were in use before the end of the pre-dynastic period (4th millen-nium B.C.), and they continued to be the standard materials for building until classical times, when brick-kilns were introduced. Stone, however, the quarrying and use of which were subject to royal prerogative, was also used from as early as the 2nd dynasty.

Stone was the material for the construction of the pyramids. Egypt was endowed with ample supplies of high quality stone that could be quarried from the tall cliffs separating the Nile valley from the desert on both sides of the river – limestone, sandstone, granite and alabaster. The pyramids were a development from the mastaba of the early pharaohs, a tomb with an elabo-rate system of compartments. The first of the great pyramids was the step pyramid of Zoser (the first king of the 3rd dynasty, early in the 3rd milen-nium B.C.) which was constructed at Sakkara, the necropolis of Memphis, on the Nile just south of Cairo. It was built of small blocks, which could be handled without mechanical devices, and made use of no new technology, departing from previous tombs only in size. The second of the great pyra-mids, at Meidum, south of Sakkara, partially collapsed, during an attempt, it has been suggested, to add an outer mantle to convert what was basically a step pyramid into a smooth-sided true pyramid. If there was in fact a disaster at Meidum, the curious shape of the so-called Bent Pyramid is at-tributable to a modification of an originally more ambitious plan, and the lower elevation of Senefru's pyramid at Dahshur (the Red Pyramid), the first of the true pyramids, is to be explained by the greater caution of the builders. The technical problem was overcome in the three pyramids at Geza, just outside Cairo, which were built with megaliths, in the 'cyclopean' style, which necessitated the mastery of techniques of handling such enor-mous blocks. The third of this group was on a much more modest scale than the first two (the pyramids of Cheops and Chephren) and was in fact the

last of the great pyramids, all built within a period of just over a century.
After the 4th dynasty, pyramids were not on the same grand scale although
they continued to be built until the middle of the 2nd millennium.

The building techniques of Egypt spread to Nubia during the Egyptian
colonization of the region. The construction of forts was followed by that
of temples designed to propagate the cult of Egyptian gods, as part of a
policy aimed at entrenching Egyptian influence. The first temples were
small, either free-standing stone buildings or hewn from the rock cliffs
flanking the Nile. Later, in the New Kingdom, there were larger temples,
such as the Great Temple cut out of the cliffs at Abu Simbel, completed in the
reign of Ramases II (1290–1224 B.C.). Egyptian buildings were imitated
(e.g. in the brick and stone temple of Amun at Meroe, which was 140 metres
long) by the kings of Kush, who, like the pharaohs, were interred in pyramids. Similarly, South Arabian building techniques were introduced into
northern Ethiopia by immigrants. A stone, double-storey, temple survives at
Yeha, dating from the 1st millennium B.C. It is not known whether the
giant monolithic stelae of Axum (only 50 kilometres from Yeha) are pre-
Christian or not. They seem to be associated with tombs.

In North Africa the massive mausoleums known as the Medrassen and the
Tomb of the Christian Women appear to have been an indigenous development, though influenced by Phoenician practice. It was the Greeks and the
Phoenicians, themselves much under Greek and Egyptian influence, who
introduced the construction of stone buildings. Carthage was a splendid
sight from the sea. It had two harbours, one for merchant ships, the other
for warships.

> The harbours had communication with each other, and a common entrance from
> the sea seventy feet wide, which could be closed with iron chains. The first port
> was for merchant vessels, and here was collected all kinds of ships' tackle. Within
> the second port was an island which, together with the port itself, was enclosed
> by high embankments. These embankments were full of shipyards which had
> capacity for two hundred and twenty vessels. Above them were magazines for
> their tackle and furniture. Two Ionic columns stood in front of each dock, giving
> the appearance of a continuous portico to both the harbour and the island.[2]

In the city itself were an acropolis, on which was situated the great temple of
Eshmun; lines of defence, along which four-storied towers were stationed
at regular intervals; and streets of houses and blocks of flats four or more
storeys high. Sandstone and limestone, which were plentiful, reinforced
during construction by lead clamps, were the usual materials for larger
public buildings. Floors were cemented in imitation of Greek practice with a
cement made from crushed bricks. In most houses unfired bricks were used.
In Roman times bricks were put as ballast into the holds of grain ships re-

turning to North Africa from Italy. Many Carthaginian buildings did without, their walls made of rubble-filled stone casing, often faced with stucco in imitation of marble. The Romans introduced the use of concrete for the casing. Such methods survived into the Middle Ages and later. Most country-dwellers, however, were housed in crude huts.

Hellenistic Egypt saw an astonishing flurry of public construction, not least the building of Alexandria, on which architects by the hundred and artisans by the thousand were engaged. The light-house of the port was one of the wonders of the ancient world. The Romans, too, made important advances in the theory and practice of engineering and architecture, one of the few spheres in which theoretical speculation and technology met and interacted. Dispersed throughout the Maghrib are the ruins of splendid Roman temples, markets, baths, forums, amphitheatres and town and country houses. Water was supplied by aqueducts from sources sometimes many kilometres distant, remarkable examples, like the military roads, of Roman engineering. To what extent Roman domestic architecture in North Africa was influenced by Phoenician and Hellenistic styles is a matter of dispute.

Christianity and Islam exercised a powerful influence on building. Christian architecture of varying accomplishment produced churches in the Mediterranean lands, in Nubia and in Ethiopia. Every Nubian village had one church or more, and at least three cathedrals have been excavated. They were built of stone or of stone and brick and, from the 10th century, with brick vaults. At Faras, now under Lake Nasser, a basilica, its interior decorated with more than a hundred paintings, was excavated in the early 1960s. Ecclesiastical architecture from the 7th century seems to have been less influenced by Egypt than by the Holy Land, where Nubian pilgrimages were evidently frequent. A number of mud brick villages have also been investigated by archaeologists, such as Meinarti and Debeira West, which though architecturally undistinguished were equipped with a sanitation system.

In Ethiopia in the 13th century the Zagwe dynasty was responsible for the carving out of a number of underground churches in Adefa (near modern Lalibela), to which the capital, originally at Axum, was shifted. These were evidently in imitation of various holy places in Jerusalem, though a long tradition of rock-hewn churches at Axum seems to indicate indigenous inspiration.

Although in its religious buildings it evolved a unique style, Islam borrowed freely from the architectural and engineering skills of the Greeks and Romans. In the Maghrib, Roman buildings were rifled by the Arabs to build their mosques, such as the great mosque of Kairwan. But the Arabs and Berbers of North Africa were no mean builders. Kairwan, the capital of Ifriqiya, was a new city, like Cairo. Al-Mahdia and Cairo, the successive capitals of the Fāṭimid dynasty in Tunisia and Egypt, were graced with fine public and private buildings. The mosque of Ibn Ṭūlūn, of brick and timber, was the first of a series of mosques constructed in Cairo before the Ottoman Turks overran Egypt in the 16th century. Saladin's citadel at Cairo, begun in 1176, is a celebrated example of Muslim military architecture. The Mamluk successors of the Ayyubids were responsible for a great deal of very impressive building, such as the Qalā-'ūn, a theological college-cum-hospital built in the later 13th century. Their public works included mosques, colleges, roads, bridges, markets, inns and baths. By contrast, the Ottomans were not builders on a grand scale.

The great mosque of Kairwan and the Moroccan mosques were clearly imitated in the western and central Sudan, and religious architecture also influenced secular building, such as royal palaces. From the north the art of building in stone and of making burnt bricks was introduced into the West African kingdoms of Ghana and Mali in the 13th and 14th centuries. In the Sahelian towns northern merchants had their two-storey houses. Where stone and timber were not available, as in Timbuktu, Jenne and Gao, bricks were employed. The style of this region was propagated further south by traders and political refugees from the Sudan or even North Africa. The use of bricks permitted the construction of two-storied buildings, though they were not common. In Hausaland craftsmen – without plans and ignorant of accurate measuring and of the use of level and plumb – constructed perfectly symmetrical domes on clay roofs. Clay had the advantage of being fire-proof.

In East Africa the trading towns of the coast boasted palaces and mosques of considerable size, built of coral stone, such as the Husuni palace-cum-emporium and the multi-domed great mosque of Kilwa. In Kilwa, too, some of the private houses were very large, sometimes three storeys. It has been suggested that architecturally these towns came under Indian influence, the result of commercial relations. It is apparent also, however, that Swahili building was influenced by South Arabia. Swahili styles in turn influenced the interior, especially after the growth of trade in the 19th century. The East African interior was also affected by Nubian influence from the north.

Kilwa was described by Ibn Baṭṭūta in the 14th century as 'one of the finest and most substantially built towns', though 'all the buildings are of wood, and the houses are reeds'.[3] The Portuguese were impressed in the 16th century by these solid, well-laid out towns. They were themselves great builders, particularly of massive forts, such as São Jorge da Mina and Axim in West Africa, Fort Jesus at Mombasa and the fort at Mozambique in East Africa, the latter built by Indian stone-masons brought over from Diu in Gujerat. Their buildings and those of other Europeans on the West African coast influenced African building. Further south, from the 17th century,

European-style towns and farms were found in South Africa, though many a Boer lived out his existence in a tented wagon or in a house built of mud bricks and thatch.

Elsewhere in Africa building in stone was comparatively rare. Stone walls however, were built for huts, fences, terrace-retaining walls and town protection at various periods in East, Central and South Africa. The most remarkable surviving are those of Engaruka on the western side of the Rift Valley towards its southern end on the present Tanzanian-Kenyan border, a settlement of either Cushitic-speaking people of the 1st millennium A.D. or Nilotic-speakers of some centuries later, and Great Zimbabwe, each of which had a population of perhaps two or three thousand or more. The wall of the great enclosure at Zimbabwe is more than two hundred metres long and there is a solid conical tower some ten metres high. Granite slabs, either picked up as they were or made from rock broken up by heating and rapid cooling with water, were used without mortar. There are three styles of masonry, of varying quality, the finest executed in the 14th and 15th centuries, though, even at its best, the building technique was rudimentary. The building of stone walls and terraces spread from the 15th century throughout the area between the Zambezi and Limpopo rivers and further south to the Transvaal, where stone-walled sites were still occupied before the Difaqane of the 1830s, and to the Highveld south of the Vaal River. In the northern Transvaal, indeed, the technique of stone building has survived to the present day.

Some splendid edifices were constructed from wood, such as the great palace of the king of Benin with its spacious galleries and copper-encased pillars, and the large reed palaces of Buganda and Bunyoro in modern Uganda. Sun-dried bricks, mud plastered on a framework of twigs, mud alone or poles or saplings bent into a beehive shape, together with grass, leaves or reeds for thatching met most people's needs for shelter – often just grass or leaves alone. Nomads in particular had dwellings which were easily assembled and dismantled. The functional simplicity of African dwellings and their furnishings was observed by European travellers, such as John Barrow in early 19th-century South Africa.

The ground plan of every house was a complete circle, from twelve to fifteen feet in diameter; the floor of hard beaten clay, raised about four inches above the general surface of the enclosure. About one fourth part of the circle, which was the front of the house and observed generally to face the east, was entirely open; the other three fourths were walled up with clay and stones, to the height of about five feet. By an inner circular wall passing through the centre, and described with the same radius as that of the first circle, and consequently cutting off one third of the circumference, an apartment is formed for the depositing of their valuables, as skin clothing, ivory ornaments, hassagais, knives and other articles which to them

are of essential use. In this apartment, also, the elder part of the family takes its
nightly rest . . .
   The whole is covered with a tent-shaped roof, supported on poles built into the
wall, and forming in front an open colonnade. The roof is carefully and compact-
ly thatched with reeds, or the straw of the *holcus*, and bound together with leath-
ern thongs. All the houses were enclosed by a fence made of strong reeds, of the
straw of *holcus*, or twigs of wood . . .
   The dwelling of a *Booshuana* is not ill calculated for the climate. In elegance and
solidity it may probably be as good as the *Casae* or first houses that were built in
imperial Rome, and may be considered in every respect superior in their construction and in comfort to most of the Irish cabins, into which the miserable peasantry
are oft-times obliged to crawl through puddles of water. The hut of a *Booshuana*
is not only raised upon an elevated clay flooring, but the ground of the whole enclosure is so prepared that the water may run off through the gateway; and the
whole of their cookery being carried on in this open area, the inside of the dwelling is free from smoke and soot. So well is he acquainted with the comfort and
convenience of shade, that his hut is usually built under the branches of a spreading mimosa, every twig of which is preserved with a religious care, and not a
bough suffered to be broken off on any emergency, though the article of fuel must
sometimes be sought at a very considerable distance.[4]

There were several different common indigenous styles of mud-walled
house, not all of them circular with conical roofs, though the cone on the
cylinder was the most prevalent. Flat roofed rectangular buildings were
constructed in areas where rainfall was light and thatch scarce, for example,
in East Africa. In what is now Ghana, oblong buildings were built with clay
with a stone-paved courtyard in the middle. Similar buildings were found,
too, in modern Cameroun and Zaïre.

iii) *Food and clothing*
Much manufacturing was associated with the processing of food and drink.
Although it varied with the type of economy practised – pastoral or agricultural – meat probably formed only a relatively minor part of the diet of
most people. Only the wealthy could freely indulge a taste for such a luxury.
Yet in good times even the less affluent ate well. According to Herodotus the
average Egyptian in an cient times lived on,

   bread made of spelt which they form into loaves . . . Many kinds of fish they eat
   raw, either salted, or dried in the sun. Quails also, and ducks, and small birds, they
   eat uncooked, merely firstly salting them. All other birds, excepting those which
   are set apart as sacred, are eaten either roasted or broiled.[5]

By contrast, a royal menu of the 3rd millennium B.C. lists,

   milk, three kinds of beer, five kinds of wine, ten kinds of loaves, four of bread,
   ten of cakes, fruit cakes, four meats, different cuts, joints, roast, spleen, limb,
   breast, tail, goose, pigeon, figs, ten other fruit, three kinds of corn, barley, spelt,
   five kinds of oil, and fresh plants . . .[6]

A great deal of work and ingenuity went into the dinner of a rich 19th-century Egyptian:

It generally consists, for the most part, of 'yakhnee', or stewed meat, with chopped onions, or with a quantity of 'bámiyehs', or other vegetables; 'káwurmeh', or a richer stew, with onions; 'warak mahshee', or vine-leaves, or bits of lettuce-leaf or cabbage-leaf, with a mixture of rice and minced meat (delicately seasoned with salt, pepper, and onions, and often with garlic, parsley, etc.) wrapped up in them, and boiled; cucumbers ('khiyár'), or black, white, or red 'bádingáns', or a kind of gourd (called 'kara kooseh') of the size and shape of a small cucumber, which are all 'mahshee', or stuffed, with the same composition as the leaves above mentioned; and 'kebáb', or small morsels of mutton or lamb, roasted on skewers. Many dishes consist wholly, or for the most part, of vegetables, such as cabbage, purslane, spinach, beans, lupins, chick-peas, gourd cut into small pieces, colocasia, lentils, etc. Fish, dressed with oil, is also a common dish. Most of the meats are cooked with clarified butter, on account of the deficiency of fat, and are made very rich: the butter in the hot season is perfectly liquid.[7]

The fellahin fared a good deal less well, but not badly.

Their food chiefly consists of bread (made of millet or of maize), milk, new cheese, eggs, small salted fish, cucumbers and melons and gourds of a great variety of kinds, onions and leeks, beans, chick-peas, lupins, the fruit of the black egg-plant, lentils, etc., dates (both fresh and dried), and pickles. Most of the vegetables they eat in a crude state. When the maize (or Indian corn) is nearly ripe, many ears of it are plucked, and toasted or baked, and eaten thus by the peasants. Rice is too dear to be an article of common food for the felláheen, and flesh-meat they very seldom taste. There is one luxury, however, which most of them enjoy, and that is smoking the cheap tobacco of their country, merely dried and broken up.[8]

Bread and porridge featured prominently in sub-Saharan diet.

The bread ordinarily in Sofala is of their Wheate and Rice mixt together, whereof they make Cakes which they call Mocates: tollerable whiles they are hot, but cold, insufferable.[9]

Among the Tswana

different kinds of grain and pulse appear to be sown promiscuously and, when reaped, to be thrown indiscriminately into their earthern granaries; from whence they are taken and used without selection, sometimes by broiling, but more generally boiling in milk.[10]

In Kano:

Wheaten flour is baked into bread of three different kinds; one like muffins, another like our twists, and the third a light puffy cake, with honey and melted butter poured over it. Rice is also made into little cakes.[11]

Ancient Egypt was a wine producer from the early 3rd millennium B.C., evidently mostly on royal, private and temple estates for the consumption of kings, nobles and priests. The taste was for sweet wine and sometimes honey or the juice of dates or pomegranates was added. Red wine predominated in the Old Kingdom, white becoming popular from the Middle Kingdom. Wine jars with individual clay sealings survive from as early as the 1st dynasty, and the wealthy were in the habit of laying down cellars of wine kept in tall amphorae. The more common drink, however, was beer, made by fermenting wheat and barley loaves in vats of water, and this continued to be the case until the Arab conquest. To Muslims fermented liquor was forbidden, and for them coffee was the most popular beverage, though it was always something of a luxury. In sub-Saharan Africa palm wine, mead and beer were made in the west, banana wine in the east and grape wine in the European south. A beverage made from millet or maize was common:

> They steepe two dayes in water a pecke or thereabouts, which in that space growes forth: and then the water being put out, they let it drie two or three houres, and being well dried they stampe it till it settle into a masse: which they doe in a great Morter as high as a mans middle, called Cuni, by them, by the Portugals, Pilano. After this they set a great earthen vessell on the fire halfe full of water, whereon when it seeths, they put in about halfe the pecke of Mais-meale by little and little, still stirring it, as when men make pottage: and after it seeths a little, they take the vessell off the fire, and put in the rest of the said masse, stirring them together till their Pombe be made; which is let stand two dayes, and then they drink it, many of them neither eating nor drinking ought else, but living onely hereof. If it stand foure or five dayes it becomes Vinegar; and the sowrer, the more tipsie; they say that it makes them strong.[12]

Apart from the manufacture of cooking oil and the baking done by public bakeries and pastry-cooks in ancient and Muslim times in Egypt and North Africa, there was naturally little processing of food for the market, especially south of the Sahara. Most was produced at home by the women of the family. There was, however, one commodity for which even the most self-sufficient household was normally dependent upon outside supplies – salt. There was an insatiable demand for it over large tracts of a continent where the climate required a high intake for health and where readily accessible sources were all too few. Of the total area of sub-Saharan Africa ninety-one per cent lies within the tropics and few of its people dwell near the sea. Along the coast seawater was evaporated in pits or boiled in copper or earthenware pots, while in the less fortunate areas salt was laboriously extracted by burning straw or other vegetable matter. In the western Sudan, at Awlil and Bilma, it was obtained from saline soil by leaching, and in Egypt from saline springs. Natural salt pans were found in the more arid parts of Central and South

Africa and some of them played an important part in stimulating early trade, the Ivuna salt pans, for example, some fifteen kilometres south-east of Lake Rukwa. Mineral salt was mined in regions as far apart as Egypt, Kisama in modern Angola and the Sahara. The Saharan deposits were at Idjil, mined from the 11th to the 15th century, Teghaza, from the 8th century, a place so rich in salt that it was put to use as a building material, and Taoudeni, captured by the Moroccans in 1585. The availability of transport was the key to the exploitation of such deposits. In the Sahara and the western Sudan huge camel caravans distributed the product over a wide area.

In Ptolemaic Egypt both common salt (sodium chloride) and natron (a natural mixture of sodium bicarbonate and sodium carbonate) were a state monopoly. Natron was preferred to common salt, partly because a certain religious significance was attached to it. Apart from being used for preserving and seasoning, it had an industrial use, for instance, in making glazes. It was an ingredient of certain medicines, the manufacture of which, together with that of perfumes and cosmetics, was an ancient art that continued into Arab times. One of the few Carthaginian manufactures that could compete in foreign markets was perfume. However, it was Alexandria, famous for its school of medicine, that was the best-known centre for the production of all those things, using both local and imported raw materials. It was an industry that required considerable capital resources and tended to be carried on in fairly large workshops.

Clothing for most people, exposed as they were to the hot sun, was of a very simple kind. At some places it was a matter of a loin cloth; at others a more substantial garment, for example, according to a Portuguese castaway in southern Africa,

> a mantle of ox-hide, with the hair outwards, which they rub with grease to make it soft. They are shod with two or three soles of raw leather fastened together in a round shape, and secured to the feet with straps.[13]

A variety of other local materials was utilised. Many different fibres were used for textiles – flax, cotton, wool, camel hair, silk, papyrus, tree bark, coconut coir, raffia and palm fibre. Egypt had a linen industry of great antiquity, dating from the 5th millennium B.C. or even earlier. It was only a simple loom that was used to begin with, a narrow ground loom that could be set up easily even by nomadic people, and methods of spinning gave only a coarse and uneven yarn. By the 1st dynasty, however, very fine linen cloths were being woven from yarn made with suspended spindlewhorls. Rugs were made from the 3rd millennium B.C. and tapestries from the 2nd. By the second half of the 2nd millennium, during the New Kingdom, a vertical loom in a rectangular wooden frame was in use. The manufacture of woollen cloth came in during the Ptolemaic period, and there is some evidence of cotton weaving then. Woollen cloth was woven in Carthage, as well as linen, and Carthaginian cushions and embroidered carpets were of a high enough quality to export. From Carthage carpet weaving spread to the Berbers.

In Hellenistic and Roman times, as a rule, manufacturing for the market catered for two very different categories of customer, the rich, who wanted the best, and the poor, who did not have the facilities at home for making their own cloth and clothes. The middling affluent could get things done by their households. There is, however, some evidence of experimentation in dyeing in Hellenistic times, with the aim of producing dyed cloth in imitation of the finest types, for sale to people who aspired to the best, but had to make do with the second best. The common dyes in Egyptian textile manufacturing were indigo (also cultivated in the western Sudan), madder, henna and sunflower. To the west, Carthage – like Tyre – was renowned for its production of a highly regarded purple dye from the shell-fish murex. Alum was used as a mordant. In the Roman age, Egypt produced large quantities from the oases west of the Nile valley. It found other uses as well, medical and industrial (for example, in leather work).

After the Arab conquest the manufacture of textiles remained the most widespread industry, producing a wide range of fabrics apart from clothing. High grade linen (which predominated, as in the past), cotton and silk were produced at Damietta and other places in the Nile Delta. A textile woven at al-Fustāṭ from cotton and wool was familiar to Europe as fustian. In Roman times silk imported from China had been worked up at Alexandria and the complete process of manufacture undertaken in the Byzantine period. It was the Arabs, however, who greatly extended its manufacture, despite the anathema of Muḥammad against the wearing of silken garments. Raw silk became more readily obtainable from the 6th century as its production shifted first to Persia, subsequently to the Mediterranean, especially Spain and Sicily.

The manufacture of textiles on a considerable scale was by no means limited to Egypt: Tlemcen in Morocco had, for example according to Ibn Khaldun, four thousand handlooms in the 14th century. Towns in the central Maghrib – Gabès, Sfax, Sousse, Kairwan – were producing silks and brocades in the late 10th and 11th centuries. In nearly all the countries of the Arab empire fine hard-wearing broadcloth was made. High quality clothing was made for the wealthy, but most people made do with cheap, coarse cotton, linen and woollen cloth, while many country people wore homespun.

Cotton weaving was carried on extensively throughout sub-Saharan Africa. Possibly the introduction, certainly the expansion, of cotton growing, spinning and weaving and other branches of the textile industry in the western Sudan is attributable to the influence of the Arabs. Timbuktu and Jenne, in the Middle Ages and later, were important centres for the weaving and dyeing of linen and cotton fabrics, as was Kano, probably before, as well as during, the 19th century. Skilled tailors made the cloth up into garments. As in medieval Flanders and Italy, there were innumerable smaller centres, each producing its distinctive type of cloth and using locally grown cotton and indigo. According to Ibn Baṭṭūṭa, Bornu was an exporter of saffron-dyed cloth. In the West African forest Benin was producing its own cloth for export in the late Middle Ages and the habit of wearing locally-made clothes had spread to Senegal by the middle of the 15th century. At the end of the 18th century Mungo Park saw cotton and indigo growing in the neighbourhood of villages on the Gambia, to provide materials for local weaving and dyeing. In the Zambezi-Limpopo area machira cloth was woven from locally grown cotton and on the coast of East Africa, at Mogadishu, a superior cloth was made from local cotton. Cloth for local consumption was made at Kilwa and Sofala. At Sofala, according to Duarte Barbosa (c.1517–18),

> they make great store of cotton and weave it, and from it they make much white cloth, and as they know not how to dye it, or have not the needful dyes, they take the Cambaya cloths, blue or otherwise coloured, and unravel them and make them up again, so that it becomes a new thing. With this thread and their own white they make much coloured cloth, and from it they gain much gold.[14]

Similarly, in Asante, silk cloth was unravelled and the threads used in a mixture with cotton yarn for the production of kente cloth, which had designs on it conforming to local taste and custom, and from the same part of the country there was adinkira cloth, a plain cotton fabric on which black designs were stamped.

The technology of cotton textile manufacture south of the Sahara was not advanced. For spinning a distaff was used with a spindle and whorl suspended from the hand, and for weaving, a simple wooden frame which produced a narrow fabric, perhaps only eight or nine centimetres wide. Pieces of web were sewn together to make a complete cloth.

Various fine raffia fabrics were woven in the Kongo kingdom from threads taken from palm leaves. 'They are truly beautiful,' wrote an 18th-century missionary,

> and curiously wrought. Some of them closely resemble velvet, others are so richly adorned with various decorations and arabesques that it is a wonder that anyone working with leaves from the palm and other trees could make such fine and beautiful fabrics, which are every bit as good as silk.[15]

Bark cloth was the common material for clothing in Asante, and it continued to be manufactured into modern times. The bark was stripped off the tree in long pieces about thirty centimetres wide and, after being softened in water, beaten out with a wooden mallet, a process that almost trebled the width of each strip.

iv) Basketry, leather work and woodwork

Industries related to textiles were those of rope and mat making, and basketry. In ancient Egypt rope and string were made from flax, while reed and grass were used for mats, which were employed extensively in architecture and furnishing and were probably made on a horizontal loom in much the same way as they are to-day. Everywhere the mat was the poor man's carpet. In West Africa it served as a bed. Everywhere baskets, frequently of considerable artistic merit, as well as of utility, were produced, in all shapes and sizes, from a variety of fibres and for a variety of purposes. Storage and carriage were obvious functions, but they were also used for fishing, for serving food and for decoration and furnishing. Loosely woven, they served as sieves; tightly woven and made watertight, they were often a light-weight substitute for pots and were, for example, used for draining the silver mines of the Carthaginians in Spain. Basketwork hats were made, and so were straw hats. Throughout much of Africa, and among Cushitic- and some Nilotic-speakers in East Africa, putting milk in any container not made of vegetable material was forbidden, calabashes and gourds were used as storage and drinking vessels, and these were also put to use in the manufacture of musical instruments. They were frequently artistically decorated, just as patterns were woven into baskets.

One of the most famous ancient industries was the manufacture of writing paper (of which Egypt had the monopoly) from papyrus, a plant that was common in the marshes of the Nile Delta. Several other grades of paper were produced as well, the coarsest being used for packing. Making paper from rags – cheaper and more practical than papyrus – was introduced into Egypt by the Arabs, who derived it indirectly from China in the middle of the 8th century.

Tanning and leather work were industries found throughout Egypt, North Africa and the western Sudan. Moroccan leather, a reddish leather made from the skins of sheep and goats, was probably being made in North Africa before the foundation of Carthage. All kinds of leather were used in the manufacture of buckets, bags and wallets, shields, scabards, arrow quivers, cushions, clothing, footwear, tents and furniture. To some extent it was a substitute for scarce wood and metals. An Arab writer of the 12th century spoke admiringly of the sandals and shields made from tough but supple oryx leather in the western Sudan, and his admiration was echoed by later European visitors. Only the wealthy could afford shoes. The poor were acquainted with leather chiefly in the form of a scanty and simple garment. In North Africa and the Sudan there was a big market for harnesses and saddles for horses, camels, mules and asses. Those for wealthy customers were very ornate, embroidered with silk or adorned with metal plates studded with pearls and semi-precious stones. Leo Africanus in the 16th century admired the gold-plated harness of the sultan's horses in Bornu.

Woodwork was another common craft. In Egypt all the principles of joinery were known as early as the 1st dynasty, and a craftsman was capable of elaborate carving and inlaying of wood with ivory and faïence. Precious woods were specially imported for fine work. The tools remained the same throughout the entire dynastic period. The plane was introduced in Roman times. In Carthage a speciality was the cedar wood chest, used for storing the possessions of this life, and as a coffin after death. In sub-Saharan Africa wood was made into many objects – vessels, dishes, bottles, jars and lids, trays, spoons, bins, funnels, weapons, quivers, sheathes, shields, spades, and hoes, combs and hairpins, sandals, furnishings and musical instruments. Such things were often made with the simplest of tools. William Burchell saw Khoikhoi craftsmen at work early in the 19th century.

In another quarter, sitting by the side of their waggons, the wooden-bowl makers displayed their workmanship and industry, busily intent on carving out bowls and jugs, from the green wood of the willow; while at a distance a large willow tree was just falling to the ground, hacked through by hatchets, so weak and small, that nothing but perseverance and much time could enable them with such tools, to sever trunks above a foot or eighteen inches in diameter. These were cut into convenient lengths, according to the utensil intended to be made; and the soft, tough nature of the wood, rendered it peculiarly fit for the purpose. After the rough log had been chopped with the hatchet or adze, nearly to the required shape, a common knife was the only tool employed to smooth and complete the outside; and another knife, having its top bent laterally into a semi-circular hook, was used with great dexterity and neatness to hollow out the inside. As soon as this was done, the whole was thoroughly smeared with fat, to prevent it splitting from the heat and dryness of the weather. The bowls are of various sizes, but most frequently from twelve to eighteen inches across, shallow and mostly oval. The jug, or jar, which they call a bambus, is made in the form of a short cylinder, having the mouth or neck contracted generally to about two-thirds. Their most usual capacity is about a gallon, but they are made of all sizes, from a pint to five gallons.[16]

Wood carving was often devoted to the production of religious or ceremonial objects, such as masks, umbrellas, stools (in Asante, for example), figurines and drums. A rather similar art was ivory carving. Portuguese travellers on the West Coast admired the ivory necklaces and bracelets, as well as spoons, salt-cellars and dagger handles manufactured there. Benin was an important centre for fine work in ivory, and ivory and bone were carved in Kilwa in East Africa. The art of inlaying – with mother-of-pearl or ivory – was well-known in some areas.

Naturally, wood was used in the important coastal and river industry of boatbuilding. Reeds and bark, however, were also employed for this purpose. Although not much is known about early boatbuilding, there can be little doubt that river boats were constructed of reeds in Egypt and Nubia even in prehistoric times. Reed rafts and canoes of different sizes were used for a variety of purposes, but particularly for fowling and fishing. Some were sea-going and propelled by sail. Those for river use were commonly paddled or poled. On the upper Nile reed rafts and canoes are still in use, as well as on the marshes and lakes of other parts of Africa – Lake Albert in East Africa, Lake Tana in Ethiopia, Lake Chad, the Okavango swamp in Botswana and the lagoons of north-west Morocco.

Egyptian wooden vessels, similar to those made to this day along the upper Nile, were conspicuous for their shallow draught and wide beam. There is evidence of craft in ancient times that were 100 cubits (52 metres) long, as early as the 3rd dynasty; and by the 18th dynasty some were capable of carrying weights of more than 650 tons. They were propelled by oars and trapezoidal sail. Herodotus described the construction of cargo-vessels in Egypt in the 5th century B.C. Planks each two cubits (1 metre) long were fastened together edge to edge with tenon and mortice joints, which were reinforced with cords passed through holes in the planks. There were no ribs, but a frame was added. A rudder oar was used for steering. There is a close resemblance between Herodotus's description and the appearance of a surviving Egyptian vessel, the Cheops ship of 2600 B.C., which is almost flat-bottomed.

Nowadays, craftsmen, with saw, adze and compass, build similar boats of acacia planks on stocks set up on flat stretches of sand left dry by the falling river. They are sometimes over 18 metres long and more than 7 metres in the beam, carrying a crew of six and a cargo of 45 tons. As in ancient times, there are no pre-formed ribs, though on the Nile north of the 2nd cataract, transverse frames are inserted after the completion of the hull, and further north still, between Luxor and the Delta, a framework is set up on the stocks and the planks nailed on to it. It seems, however, that this latter method was unknown in the ancient world. The Graeco-Roman contribution to shipbuilding technology lay rather in the use of very superior joinery, making a closely fitting shell, and in their ability to insert, after the completion of the hull, a framework that was as snug as a pre-erected skeleton.

The Arabs who overran Egypt and the Maghrib were much indebted to their Graeco-Roman predecessors for their shipbuilding techniques. Employing Syrian and Greek shipwrights, they were able to create a fleet strong enough to capture Cyprus as early as 649. Alexandria, just as it had been in Byzantine times, and Damietta were the chief centres for shipbuilding, dependent upon timber imported from Lebanon and Europe. According to al-Idrisi, writing in the 12th century, Bougie in Ifriqiya had a shipyard, with access to local supplies of timber, resin and tar. The difficulty facing Muslim shipbuilders, however, was mostly a shortage of local timber. This had been a perennial problem for Egypt, where, by Muslim times, the reserves of acacia wood were so depleted that their exploitation was a state monopoly. In the Maghrib itself, forests open to the coast, adequate in Carthaginian and Roman times and during the early centuries of Islam, were, with the inroads of later centuries for building and charcoal-burning, scarcely able to support a shipbuilding industry. By the 16th century Algiers was an importer of shipbuilding materials.

On the East African coast the planks that made up the boat were sewn together with twine, coconut coir or palm fibre, a feature of shipbuilding all along the coasts of the Persian Gulf, the Red Sea and the Indian Ocean. Boats of up to 50 tons, their sails of palm matting, were constructed in the East African trading settlements, mostly for the coastal trade. The use of nails was copied from the European intruders of the 16th century, but did not wholly replace the old sewing method. The sambuk of the Red Sea and the jehazi of East Africa borrowed features from the Portuguese caravel. The later swift and shallow-draught zaruks were used for transporting slaves. From the 19th century such vessels sailed lakes as well as oceans.

Elsewhere in sub-Saharan Africa canoes of various types were made, such as the bark canoes found widely dispersed throughout Central and East Africa. Dugout canoes were not generally of a high standard of design or workmanship, but there were exceptions, such as the small and delicate canoes built by the Kru of West Africa, who achieved in them remarkable feats of ocean fishing. Some dugouts in West Africa were very large indeed, 20 metres or more in length, capable of taking on as many as a hundred men or more than twenty tons of cargo and sometimes rigged with small sails. Mungo Park encountered on the Niger in 1796 'very roomy' canoes used as ferries, made out of two hollowed-out tree trunks joined together end ways.

I observed in one of them four horses, and several people crossing over the river.[17]

Also on the Niger, Richard Lander was pursued in 1830 by

war-canoes, of prodigious dimensions; immense flags of various colours were displayed in them, a six-pounder was lashed to the bow of each; and they were filled with women and children, and armed men, whose weapons were in their hands. Such was their size, that each of them was paddled by nearly forty people.[18]

NOTES

1. Axelson, Eric (ed.): *South African Explorers* (London, 1954), p. 78–9
2. Appion, quoted Moscati, Sabatino: *The World of the Phoenicians* (London, 1958), p. 149
3. Battuta, Ibn: *Travels in Asia and Africa 1325–1354* (London, 1929), p. 379
4. Axelson, E.: Op. cit., p. 94–5
5. Quoted Darby, William J., Ghalioungui, Paul & Grivelli, Louis: *Food: the Gift of Osiris* (London, 1977), Volume 1, p. 55
6. Ibid
7. Lane, Edward William: *An Account of the Manners and Customs of Modern Egyptians, Written in Egypt during the Years 1833–1835* (Paisley and London, 1895), p. 162
8. Ibid, p. 204
9. Axelson, E.: Op. cit., p. 21
10. Ibid, p. 96
11. Howard, C. (ed.): *West African Explorers* (London, 1951), p. 249
12. Axelson, E.: Op. cit., p. 30–1
13. Quoted Wilson, Monica & Thompson, Leonard (eds.): *The Oxford History of South Africa*, Volume I, *South Africa to 1870* (Oxford, 1969), p. 80
14. Freeman-Grenville, G. S. P. (ed.): *The East African Coast, Select Documents from the First to the Earlier Nineteenth Century* (Oxford, 1962), p. 128
15. De Lucques, Laurent, quoted Balandier, Georges: *Daily Life in the Kingdom of the Kongo, from the Sixteenth to the Eighteenth Century* (New York, 1968), p. 115
16. Axelson, E.: Op. cit., p. 130–1
17. Howard, C.: Op. cit., p. 123
18. Ibid, p. 321–2

Further reading

Adams, William Y.: *Nubia, Corridor to Africa* (London, 1977)
Balandier, Georges: Op. cit. (see above, note 15)
Casson, Lionel: *Ships and Seamanship in the Ancient World* (Princeton, N. J.: 1971)
Charles-Picard, Gilbert & Colette: Op. cit. (see p. 46)
Dark, Philip J. C.: *An Introduction to Benin Art and Technology* (Oxford, 1973)
Edwards, I. E. S.: *The Pyramids of Egypt* (Harmondsworth, 1947)
Emery, W. B.: *Archaic Egypt* (Harmondsworth, 1961)
Engelbach, R.: 'Mechanical and technical processes. Materials' (Glanville, S. R. K.: *The Legacy of Egypt*, Oxford, 1942)
Forbes, R. J.: *Studies in Ancient Technology*, Volumes III, IV, V, VIII & IX (Leiden, 1964)
Greenhill, Basil: *Archaeology of the Boat, a New Introductory Study* (London, 1976)
Harris, J. R.: Op. cit. (see p. 83)
Holt, P. M., Lambton, Ann K. S. & Lewis, Bernard: Op. cit. (see p. 84)
Hornell, James: *Water Transport, Origins and Early Evolution* (Cambridge, 1946)
Lawal, Babatunde: 'The present state of art historical research in Nigeria: problems and possibilities' (*Journal of African History*, XVIII, 1977, p. 193–216)
Lewicki, Tradeusz: *West African Food in the Middle Ages: According to Arabic Sources* (Cambridge, 1974)
Lucas, A.: *Ancient Egyptian Materials and Industries* (London, 2nd edn. 1934)

Mauny, Raymond: *Tableau géographique de l'Ouest africain au moyen âge, d'après les sources écrites, la tradition et l'archéologie* (Dakar, 1961)
Mendelssohn, K.: 'A scientist looks at the pyramids' (Lamberg-Karlovsky, C. C. and Sabloff, Jeremy A., eds.: *The Rise and Fall of Civilizations, Modern Archaeological Approaches to Ancient Cultures, Selected Readings*, Menlo Park, California, 1974, p. 390–402)
Oliver, Paul: *Shelter in Africa* (London, 1971)
Phillipson, D. W.: Op. cit. (see p. 31)
Posnansky, M.: 'Brass casting and its antecedents in West Africa' (*Journal of African History*, XVIII, 1977, p. 287–300)
Schacht, Joseph: Op. cit. (see p. 84)
Shaw, Thurstan: *Discovering Nigeria's Past* (Oxford, 1976)
Sundström, Lars: *The Exchange Economy of Pre-Colonial Tropical Africa* (London, 1974)
Trowell, Margaret & Wachsmann, K. P.: *Tribal Crafts in Uganda* (London, 1953)

3. The Organization of Industry

i) *The ancient world*

Full-time practice of a craft, involving the division of labour essential for economic growth, was not widespread. To this day it has been common for farmers to engage in craft production as a part-time or seasonal activity. In many crafts, where the skill was a simple one and the materials freely available, it was impossible for the specialist to compete with the household producer. Transport costs frequently precluded mass production for a wide market. The poverty of most villagers was such that they were unable to afford the services of a professional weaver or a professional potter, which helps to explain the neglect of the potter's wheel. Nevertheless, there were exceptions to this general rule of absence of specialization.

A far-reaching division of labour was found in Egypt, even in ancient times. There it took two forms, the fragmentation of particular processes among a team of workmen, and specialization in particular crafts. During the New Kingdom companies of miners, gold washers and smelters were attached more or less permanently to the goldmines of Nubia and Upper Egypt, and pitmen, shorers and porters to the turquoise mines of Sinai. In the stone quarries there were gangs of stone cutters and handlers engaged in meeting a demand for stone that was almost unceasing during periods of peace and stability, when, in all probability, thousands of masons, bricklayers and plasterers were employed in the construction of temples and royal and private tombs. Then there was the relatively well-to-do and respectable class of textile workers, carpenters, cabinet makers, leather workers, sculptors, painters, jewellers, lapidaries, glass workers, potters, smiths and perfumers, together with their unskilled and semi-skilled assistants, who sharpened tools, ground glue and paint, pumped forges, fetched and carried.

Few craftsmen were independent. Most worked in royal, state or temple workshops or for great officials. All the big estates had their millers, bakers, butchers, brewers, treaders of wine, pressers of oil, basket and rope makers and spinners and weavers, besides innumerable domestic servants. Some industries – the preparation of papyrus and goldmining, for example – were state monopolies or quasi-monopolies, and even when this was not so, state production was of far greater importance than private or temple industry. This rôle of the state in manufacturing and mining continued to be significant after pharaonic times. In the Ptolemaic age the system of monopolies was very comprehensive indeed, and it will be discussed below, together with the modifications introduced by the Romans.

In Carthage the most important industries, those supplying the needs of the army and navy, were state-run, and some manufacturing was carried on in temple and estate workshops, sometimes with slave labour. There were, however, many independent workers, particularly in copper and iron, as well as professional spinners, though spinning and weaving were for the most part household tasks. Industrial production for the market, especially for overseas customers, greatly expanded after the spread of the Macedonian empire, though North Africa was never of great consequence as a manufacturing region in Carthaginian, Roman or Muslim times. Even in Egypt, where production was sometimes highly concentrated geographically (such as glass in Alexandria), the typical unit of production was the small or medium-size workshop, run by the state or a private entrepreneur, who might be a lessee of a government workshop, or independent craftsman assisted by a few slaves.

Slave labour does not appear to have been widespread, and only in mining and metallurgy was the work force composed almost entirely of slaves, supplemented (for example, in the Egyptian goldmines and the stone quarries of Carthage) by prisoners of war and criminals. There is a well-known description by Agathachides, writing in the 3rd century B.C., of the conditions under which gold was mined and processed by state prisoners, possibly political prisoners.

The metal rocks which are called gold-bearing are intensely black, but among them is produced a stone than which nothing is whiter. Of these mountains those which are rugged and have an altogether hard nature they burn with wood; and when they are softened by fire they experiment on them and cut the loosened stone into small pieces with an iron chisel. But the principal work is that of the artificer who is skilled in stones. This man shows to the diggers the track of the metal, and apportions the whole work to the needs of the wretched men in the following manner: those whole in strength and age break the places where shines the white stone with iron cutting hammers. They use not skill but brute force, and then they drive in the rock many galleries, not straight but branching in all directions, like the roots of a tree, wherever the rock pregnant of gold may diverge. These men thus, with candles bound to their fore-heads, cut the rock, the white stone showing the direction of their labours. Placing their bodies in every conceivable position, they throw the fragments to the ground – not each one according to his strength, but under the eye of the overseer, who never ceases from blows. Then boys, creeping into the galleries dug by the men, collect with great labour the stones, which have been broken off, and carry them out to the mouth of the mine. Next, from these a crowd of old and sickly men take the stone and lay it before the pounders. These are strong men of some thirty years of age, and they strenuously pound the rock with an iron pestle in mortars cut out of stone, and reduce it until the largest piece is no bigger than a pea. Then they measure out to others the pounded stone in the same quantity as they have received it. The next task is performed by women, who, alone, or with their husbands and relations, are placed in enclosures. Several mills are placed together in a line, and standing three together at one handle, filthy and almost naked, the women lay to at the mills until the measure handed to them is completely reduced. And to every one of those who bear this lot death is preferable to life.[1]

Although there is some evidence that larger industrial establishments under direct or indirect state control and using slave labour – female slaves in textile workshops – emerged in the Hellenistic world from the 2nd century B.C. in response to a growing market, a development apparent also in the later Roman empire in the west, it appears that Ptolemaic Egypt did not follow this trend. The pharaonic tradition of cheap free labour was stronger than the predisposition of Greek immigrants to make use of industrial slaves, even in the Greek cities, and slave artisans were evidently largely confined to the households of the wealthy. For the numerous state industries the government was able to conscript whatever labour it required.

The big workshop was likely to have a systematic division of labour that in the small workshop, though each might have its own speciality within the broader field of the manufacture in which it was engaged, was either not feasible or not bothered with, even when the opportunity existed. The building site always had an exceptional degree of specialization. In the construction industry the Romans distinguished lime burners, masons, makers of arches, builders of interior walls, plasterers, and carpenters, and other craftsmen as well. In textiles, processes were highly differentiated – carding, spinning, weaving, fulling, dyeing – within each branch of an industry that embraced work in wool, linen and cotton, but, although some establishments might be relatively large, especially for fulling and dyeing, it was typically, in the classical period, a division of labour among separate small workshops, not one on factory lines within a single large workshop. Textile production for the market was comparatively rare in the ancient world and was usually part of a woman's domestic duties. It remained largely a female occupation even when carried on commercially. Though broken down into a variety of processes, its techniques were elementary and only fulling and, more particularly, dyeing required more complex equipment or more advanced skills. The most numerous classes of male artisans in ancient times were potters, smiths, carpenters and masons.

Although industry in Hellenistic and Roman Egypt was dominated by Alexandria, turning out both luxury goods and cheap mass-produced articles, manufacture (particularly of textiles, carpets and vegetable oil) continued elsewhere, in small towns and villages and in temple workshops. When Christianity replaced the worship of the old gods, some manufacturing (for example, wine making and especially weaving, which could be accompanied by prayer) was often carried on in the monasteries of Egypt and Nubia. Great landowners too continued to employ their own craftsmen, though rather for the production of more commonplace goods, such as pots for everyday use. In the late Roman empire, particularly in the west, the estate workshop developed *pari passu* with the *saltus* and was especially common on the imperial estate which had a mine or quarry. These estate enterprises, using wage labour and sometimes producing for the market, were in the van in the development of technology – the water-mill notably – and the systematic division of labour.

In the big cities, such as Alexandria and Thebes, independent craftsmen congregated in particular suburbs according to their speciality, but in the countryside there were individual craftsmen who, sometimes combining their craft with agriculture, offered a specialized service to the local market. One Egyptian village of the Roman period about which a good deal happens to be known, supported the following specialists – dyers, fullers, weavers, goldsmiths, a salt seller, an oil worker, a merchant, a wool carder, a wool seller, a broker, a brewer, a tailor, a tavern-keeper, a gardener, a stonemason, a vegetable seller, scribes, donkey drivers, tenders of flocks, a grain merchant, a cobbler, a bronze worker, a goose tender, a fisherman, a teacher, a physician, a maker of heavy garments, a miller, a baker, a tinsmith, a potter, a brickmaker, a garment maker, a strigil (i.e. flesh-scraper) maker, a lead worker, a carpenter, a curer of fish (or perhaps an embalmer), a wood worker and a maker of arms and breastplates. There is no reason to doubt that a similar situation existed before and after the Roman occupation of Egypt and was found elsewhere in Roman Africa. Not all villages, of course, served a local market exclusively. Some were engaged in production for long-distance markets, especially in the production of textiles. Different districts catered for the tastes of particular foreign markets.

The status of the craftsman in Carthaginian, Hellenistic and Roman Africa was not high. Carthaginian industry was not of much account before the 5th century B.C. and the first artisans were slaves imported from Sicily. Consequently craftsmen tended to be looked down on, though workers in wood seem to have enjoyed a better position in society. The use of slaves, especially among the Romans and Greeks, reflected – or rather was the cause of – the contempt in which the practice of a craft was commonly held. It was not that servile labour competed with free labour, so that the legal or economic status of the free man was depressed. Wherever there were slaves, free men, however far down the social scale, endeavoured to push on to them the most arduous work. Nonetheless, the very performance of a particular type of work by slaves brought it into disrepute and therefore degraded the free men who also carried it out. Even those merchants and entrepreneurs whose affluence was derived from the work of slaves were considered to an extent to be contemptible themselves. In the eyes of the Greek and Roman intellectual, the craftsman was despicable, a dependant, at the behest of others, performing tasks that were often done by slaves. Only the practice of politics, law and war, and income drawn from landowning, even farm work itself, were truly honourable. To the pagan Roman or Greek, unlike the Christian or socialist, labour 'appeared as a sentence to which no redeeming value was attached . . . Idleness was not a vice, but an ideal to which every gentleman aspired, and which was praised by wise men too.'[2] Wealth was nothing to inspire shame, rather the prerequisite for the good life.

Yet, if they were despised by the scholar and the gentleman, artisans neither lacked opportunities for earning a comfortable living, nor pride in their skill and vocation. They were organized in *collegia*, often translated as 'gilds', somewhat misleadingly because their functions, though in some respects co-inciding with those of medieval gilds, were in others significantly different, particularly in the matter of controlling production and entry into the craft. Augustus and his successors permitted them more willingly in Egypt than elsewhere in the empire. Such associations were subject to the control of the state, which could require them to undertake government work. In some cases, for example among the linen workers of Egypt, the bond that united the craftsmen was much stronger than professional association. They constituted an hereditary caste sharing a common sub-culture. In the later Roman empire a caste-system was virtually imposed by the state in the interests of ensuring the performance of particular trades that would otherwise have been neglected. The free artisan and the slave artisan drew closer together in their *de facto* condition.

ii) *Muslim Africa*
In Muslim Africa most industrial production was carried on by craftsmen in workshops run by families or partnerships, and these sometimes employed in addition to slaves, wage labourers who might or might not themselves become independent craftsmen in time. Partnerships covered a wide range of industries and varied in length between six months or so (possibly a trial period) and almost a lifetime. The economic circumstances of the partners were very varied. Where they contributed equal shares of work, capital and

implements, they shared equally in the profit and loss, but if one partner contributed no capital, then he was virtually a wage labourer, since he had to put in twice as much work as the other partner, though the profit was still equally divided. Some partnerships were composed of several partners.

Egypt was the most advanced area industrially and within that country manufacturing was concentrated in the Cairo-Alexandria-Damietta triangle, where there were more than two thousand towns and villages. The bigger enterprises, such as paper mills, sugar refineries, textile workshops and glass factories, were owned by the state or by individual entrepreneurs, including nobles, or by partnerships in which nobles might participate. These enterprises involved relatively large investments and might employ a dozen or so men, independent craftsmen who worked for piece-rates and wage labour, ill-paid, though protected up to a point by the state, which exercised a close supervision of many branches of industry. In some industries big workshops co-existed with small ones, and there is some evidence of a putting out system. Slave craftsmen were found both in urban enterprises and in the workshops of landed estates. Independent craftsmen were more likely to use unpaid apprentices or wage labour. There were some fifteen thousand day labourers in Cairo at the end of the 18th century. The situation of the employers varied widely, as is only to be expected. Some superior craftsmen, such as goldsmiths, invested in trade, and they often moved up into the merchant class (at least in the Middle Ages).

Far-reaching specialization and division of labour were practised among craftsmen. Specialization sometimes fostered a high degree of skill, for example among dyers, who specialized in certain materials and in certain dyes, but it could result in reducing the amount of skill required, for example in shoemaking, where the craft was divided into a number of different processes. In the early Middle Ages no restrictions were placed on either Christians or Jews with regard to economic occupations or activities, but certain groups tended to gravitate towards particular occupations and to live in separate quarters of the towns. Jews specialized in the manufacture of silk, drugs, metalware and glassware and in tailoring (besides money lending), while Christians went in for the spinning of flax. Muslim refugees from Spain resident in Tunisia were not absorbed into the general population. Their industrial speciality was the manufacture of the red fez, or *shashiya*. Generally non-Muslims operated new industries, such as silk, and did work which was hard and hot, for instance dyeing and metal work. But Muslims also engaged in these trades. It was only in periods of intolerance that minority groups were confined to unpleasant and menial occupations.

Craftsmen exercising the same trade tended to congregate in the same streets – the peripheral streets in the case of those whose work involved noise or stench (for example blacksmithing, carpentry, leather work and butchery) – and they sold their products in their shops to local customers. There seems to be little evidence of formal co-operation among these craftsmen in the Middle Ages. Religious brotherhoods apparently had no craft basis. Quality of production was maintained through the supervision of state police assisted by experts. Parents were expected to see to the training of their sons and normally, as elsewhere, crafts were taught by father to son. There does appear, however, to have been a system of apprenticeship and the execution of a masterpiece as qualification to practise as an independent craftsman was evidently required. Independent artisans, each working with one unpaid apprentice or more, usually earned well above a bare subsistence livelihood, but they were far from an homogeneous class. A stigma was attached to those crafts that were dirty or worked on base materials.

True gilds certainly emerged in the Ottoman period. In the late 17th century there were nearly three hundred in Cairo, and virtually all the citizens, including beggars and pickpockets, were members, but not important government servants, soldiers, and *ulama*. Gilds of similar professions were grouped together, each group controlled by a government official. Indeed, the major purpose of these associations was to facilitate government control and tax collection. Gild heads were respected members of society, consulted on occasion by the government. Since the value of the gilds to the government was dependent upon their monopoly of the crafts they practised, they controlled entry into the profession, and they also fulfilled certain purposes of social value (for example, maintenance of quality of production), though apparently not welfare functions. The sharp contrast which appeared in European gilds between masters who controlled entry to the trade and journeymen unable to set up as independent masters did not manifest itself in the Ottoman empire.

The gilds survived well into the 19th century as government agencies, even supplying labour and services to the government and private employers. What killed them off was the influx of European manufactures, which undermined the indigenous crafts; the change in the character of Egyptian trade, which opened the way for foreign penetration; the movement of non-gild labour into the expanding towns from the countryside; and the great increase in the burden of taxation. The government lost interest in their survival as it found other means of meeting its administrative and fiscal requirements.

iii) *Sub-Saharan Africa*
In West Africa, where there was considerable urban development, crafts were practised by full-time specialist artisans. Elsewhere in sub-Saharan Africa the practice of a craft was usually a sparetime or seasonal occupation of individuals or families, and sometimes a communal undertaking. The

following description of iron making in East Africa, among the Makua people of Mozambique, was composed by a Frenchman in the 19th century.

> The first step is to erect a vast enclosure of clay earth, in which the chief assigns a space to each man, woman, and child, where they will come to deposit the ore which they collect in the vicinity. Meanwhile, others cut wood and make charcoal. Each person stacks his ore in the enclosure, which he then fills with charcoal. The entire lot is covered over with iron bars and earth, arranging openings from place to place to serve as chimneys; finally the hide bellows are prepared, the bellow pipes are connected to the interior of the furnace, and the fire is lighted . . . The greatest activity then reigns among the smiths. The bellows operators, who have no respite either day or night, work in shifts, while others renew the charcoal and still others ascertain that the melting is operating properly. After a fortnight of incessant work, the chief announces that the iron is smelted. The furnace is extinguished by throwing water on it . . . Finally the furnace is uncovered and each person comes to collect the produce of his ore. The blocks of cast-iron are broken into medium-sized lengths of iron and carried to individual forges where local smiths manufacture axes, knives, bill-hooks, spearheads, musket balls, rings, etc. . . .[3]

Building was mostly a communal, occasional activity, though, if the dwelling was largely a matter of weaving and plaiting grass, this might be a traditional female task. In those parts of sub-Saharan Africa where more complicated stone and brick structures were erected, masons and other craftsmen were needed. It was potters, not masons, who made the Musgu clay huts in the Lake Chad area. Gold production in the Zambezi region was a part-time activity of the agricultural slack season. In the production of textiles, pottery, salt and metal and wooden objects and utensils specialization was widespread.

In West Africa specialist craftsmen were very often associated in brotherhoods or gilds that had a hand in the organization of production or marketing and sometimes (in Benin, for example) the power (concentrated perhaps in the person of the gild head) to enforce regulations. In Dahomey the members of the craft gild (so) worked on one another's raw material, but the marketing of the finished product was left to the individual. They helped one another in sickness and one another's families in the event of death. In some of the West African states (for example, Benin and Nupe) gilds were subject to the authority of the ruler, from whom they might receive monopoly or other privileges. Membership tended to be hereditary and in practice confined to particular families, though admission of outsiders was known.

The status of craftsmen varied. Some, for instance the goldsmiths of Asante and the blacksmiths of the kingdom of the Kongo and among the Yao, had an honoured place in society. Others encountered contempt, especially if they were the descendants of conquered peoples, perhaps the sedentary subjects of pastoralists, forbidden to marry into the ruling class. The Wolof of West Africa and the Masai of East Africa looked down upon iron workers.

Sometimes fear was mixed with contempt because of the esoteric nature of the skill. As a rule craftsmen were concentrated in certain quarters or suburbs and in some cases there were industrial villages devoted to the making of pots or the smelting of iron and its manufacture into implements and utensils for trade. Itinerant smiths were also found.

The practice of crafts and religious beliefs were much more intimately connected in sub-Saharan Africa than they were in ancient, classical or Muslim Africa. In the latter, gilds served a religious as well as a worldly purpose, but in the former, the actual success of the work was attributed to spiritual forces and its failure to a disregard of religious proprieties. In some areas iron workers were credited with mastery of magic and divination. There was a tendency for women to be wholly or partially excluded from some manufacturing processes.

> While weaving in Ashanti is an art entirely confined to the male sex, cotton may be picked and spun into thread by the women – especially old women – who have reached the menopause. The woman's share in the work begins with the planting of the seed, and ends with the spinning of the cotton into thread . . . Bonwere, a village not far from Coomassie, was the great centre of weaving for the Kings of Ashanti in olden times, and it was to this place that I went for a final inquiry into what I had learned elsewhere about this craft. 'Women could never be weavers owing to the fact that they have menstrual periods,' said the chief of the village. No piece of weaving may ever be commenced or completed on a Friday, 'because Friday was the day when Ota Kraban set up the first loom.' Looms and weavers are subject to certain taboos. A woman during her periods may not touch a loom . . . An old loom must on no account be burned or broken up; if it is broken accidentally, a fowl must be sacrificed upon it. A weaver who is going trading or on a journey will take up the parts of his loom and throw them into the river to prevent their ever being broken up for firewood.
>
> Should the wife of a weaver be unfaithful to her husband, and the co-respondent be another weaver, a sheep must be sacrificed to the loom . . .[4]

On the other hand, pottery was largely a female craft in Asante, except for the making of pipes in human or animal form, which was reserved to men.

> Religion and taboos are not absent from the potter's art. At Tuffo, neither water nor clay must be taken from the Santan river on a Friday. An unbaked pot may not on any account be taken away from the village; pots before being baked may not be counted; pots might not be made when the Ashanti army was away on a campaign. To break a pot intentionally is a serious offence, and entails the sacrifice of a sheep upon the spot where the pot was broken.[5]

Skills were passed on from generation to generation, for example, weaving from father to son, pottery from mother to daughter. Craftsmen were often set aside in occupational groups united by ties of blood. Many craftsmen were in the service of the great, especially kings, who sometimes kept the craft exclusively for their own use, for example, brass casting and glass-bead making in Ife, or exercised some other sort of privilege, such as the allocation of textile designs either to themselves or to important personages.

As in agriculture, amongst craftsmen the entire household was often drawn into the productive process, its labour resources being frequently supplemented with slaves. Servile artisans were very common in most places at most times, though in some societies – Asante, for example – slaves, perhaps because they were aliens, were deliberately excluded from crafts that had a religious significance. In the Arab-Swahili towns on the East African coast they were employed in boatbuilding, construction and woodwork. Domestic slaves in 19th-century Zanzibar were sometimes taught a trade and were allowed to keep part of their earnings after the completion of their training. In the Cape of Good Hope slaves brought in from Indonesia were trained in a variety of crafts. After the emancipation of the slaves such artisans remained entrenched in some of the old crafts despite the anomaly of such a situation in a society where whites came to demand a monopoly of skills.

NOTES

1. Quoted Forbes, R. J.: *Studies in Ancient Technology*, Volume VII (Leiden, 1966), p. 147–8
2. Mossé, Claude: *The Ancient World at Work* (London, 1969), p. 1
3. De Froberville, Eugene: quoted Alpers, Edward A.: *Ivory and Slaves in East Central Africa, Changing Patterns of International Trade to the Later 19th Century* (London, 1975), p. 10–11
4. Rattray, Captain R. S.: *Religion and Art in Ashanti* (London, 1927), p. 221, 234
5. Ibid, p. 305

Further reading

Adams, William Y.: Op. cit. (see p. 104)
Akinola, G. A.: Loc. cit. (see p. 65)
Aldred, Cyril: *The Egyptians* (London, 1961)
Baer, Gabriel: 'Guilds in Middle Eastern history' (Cook, M. A., ed.: *Studies in the Economic History of the Middle East, from the Rise of Islam to the Present Day*, London, 1970, p. 11–30)
Burford, Alison: *Craftsmen in Greek and Roman Society* (London, 1972)
Charles-Picard, Gilbert & Colette: Op. cit. (see p. 46)
Dieterlen, G.: 'A contribution to the study of blacksmiths in West Africa' (Alexandre, Pierre, ed.: *French Perspectives in African Studies, a Collection of Translated Essays*, London, 1973, p. 40–61)
Goitein, S. D.: *A Mediterranean Society, the Jewish Communities of the Arab World as Portrayed in the Documents of the Cairo Geniza*, Volume 1, *Economic Foundations* (Berkeley and Los Angeles, 1967)

Goitein, S. D.: *Studies in Islamic History and Society* (Leiden, 1966)

Harris, J. R.: Op. cit. (see p. 83)

Herskovits, M. J. & Harwitz, M. (eds.): *Economic Transition in Africa* (London, 1964)

Hodgson, Marshall G. S.: *The Venture of Islam, Conscience and History in a World Civilization*, Volume 2, *The Expansion of Islam in the Middle Periods* (Chicago and London, 1974)

Holt, P. M., Lambton, Ann K. S. & Lewis, Bernard: Op. cit., (see p. 84)

Hrbek, Ivan: 'Egypt, Nubia and the Eastern Deserts' (Chapter 1, Oliver, Roland ed.: *The Cambridge History of Africa*, Volume 3, *From c.1050 to c.1600*, Cambridge, 1977)

Johnson, Allan Chester & West, L. C.: Op. cit. (see p. 47)

Johnson, Allan Chester: Op. cit. (see p. 47)

Jones, A. H. M.: *The Decline of the Ancient World* (New York, 1966)

Kjekshus, Helge: *Ecology Control and Economic Development in East African History, the Case of Tanganyika 1850–1950* (London, 1977)

Krapf-Askari, Eva: *Yoruba Towns and Cities* (Oxford, 1969)

Lloyd, P.: 'Craft organisation in Yoruba towns' (Wallerstein, I. M. ed.: *Social Change; the Colonial Situation*, New York, 1966, p. 383–401)

Mossé, Claude: Op. cit. (see note 2)

Polanyi, Karl (in collaboration with Rotstein, Abraham): *Dahomey and the Slave Trade, an Analysis of an Archaic Economy* (Seattle and London, 1966)

Rodinson, M.: *Islam and Capitalism* (London, 1974)

Ruffle, J.: Op. cit. (see p. 47)

Sundström, Lars: Op. cit. (see p. 105)

Van der Horst, Sheila: Op. cit. (see p. 66)

Warmington, B. H.: *Carthage* (London, 2nd edn., 1969)

Westerman, William L.: Op. cit. (see p. 66)

CHAPTER III

TRADE

1. THE CONDITIONS OF TRADE

i) *Markets and merchants*

Trade within Africa and between Africa and the outside world was necessarily limited. Internally, given the agricultural methods in use, the agricultural surplus available for exchange was small and the inelasticity of demand did not provide much incentive for increased production. Moreover, trade in foodstuffs posed grave problems of storage in hot and humid climates and (except in the case of cattle) of bulk transport. There were likewise technical difficulties hindering the production of non-agricultural goods. Local self-sufficiency predominated in the production of food, clothing, tools and utensils. Villages in the same locality produced much the same sort of commodity and the monopoly enjoyed by local producers could not be breached owing to the high costs of transport. Externally it was only in the north and north-east that Africa was sufficiently close to other continents for a trade of much volume to take place. Even in the Mediterranean, however, trade was discouraged by the essential physical and climatic homogeneity of the lands bordering upon it, with the exception of the Libyan desert. Most Mediterranean countries had a capacity to produce much the same sort of things.

Household self-sufficiency was the rule in Africa, exchange the exception, carried out for the benefit of the rich or privileged, a class that would include the hungry plebeians of ancient Rome, fed on African grain exacted as tribute. Such commerce as there was frequently took the form of gift-exchange or tribute and largess rather than genuine trade. Yet, trade there was. Despite pronounced obstacles to it, there was still room for exchange even within an area comparatively homogeneous from the point of view of natural endowment, exchange due perhaps to the co-existence of peoples of different culture – iron-using and stone-using people, pastoralists and agriculturalists, pastoralists and hunters. There can be little doubt that local trade, vigorous, though small in volume, was carried on in most places at most periods, even between bands of hunters and gatherers. Stone suitable for making implements might have to be brought in from sources many kilometres distant from the site of manufacture. There is plenty of evidence of regular and multifarious exchanges over very long distances and even the shipment of substantial quantities of goods, such as grain from northern Africa to Italy. The key to much Mediterranean trade lay in Egypt, capable of producing a relatively predictable surplus of grain and of assembling it for export by means of river transport, but poorly endowed in certain essential resources, particularly timber and readily accessible metals. Opportunities that existed for exchange could be seized because of the comparative cheapness of maritime transport. Another factor of importance was the favourable situation of Egypt as a point of contact between Europe on the one hand and the Middle and Far East on the other. The Mediterranean represented a frontier between the north, supplier of minerals and furs, and the south, source of spices and gold. Two important items of intra-African trade were salt and iron, deposits of which, at least easily worked ones, were relatively sparse and iron working skills were rather scarce.

A good deal of trade in Egypt and along the coast of East Africa was carried on, at least from Muslim times, at annual fairs. More important in sub-Saharan Africa, particularly in West Africa and the lacustrine region of East Africa, were markets, both wholesale and retail and varying in frequency and significance. Vendors were mostly segregated according to the product they sold, and all markets had their customs and rules respecting price fixing, the settlement of disputes and the quality of the things offered for sale. Craft gilds or associations of vendors or local merchants sometimes had a hand in the running of the market. Village markets opened at intervals determined by the proximity of others and the nature and scale of the transactions. Some markets engaged in long distance trade of great diversity and considerable volume, though all, big or small, forming as they did part of a wider network, were the recipients of goods coming from a distance and the source of other goods that entered into regional or even international trade. Most had a speciality, such as salt or kola nuts or gold, which might indeed account for the development of the market in the first place. However, although the existence of markets is an obvious indication of commercial activity, it is equally true that they are typical of a relatively low level of economic activity, operating in an environment characterized by inelastic demand. Even those urban markets which were open daily, as some were in West Africa, still conducted their business from stalls.

In Egypt there occurred that connection between religion and commerce which was to recur in other lands where there were regular places and times of worship and fixed festivals, and which provided the traders with both a trading site in the temple precincts and customers from among the worshippers. Centuries later, in South Africa, fairs, which tended to develop into permanent villages, were held at places where the quarterly communion service of the Dutch Reformed Church was celebrated. In the Islamic world fairs coincided with annual religious feasts. The greatest one of all was held at Mecca, but others of regional or local significance took place at various places in Muslim Africa on the occasion of the commemoration of holy men. The latter fairs normally went on for a week or so, but at Alexandria, a centre of international trade, there was a recognized trading season that lasted up to two months. Of importance was the Arab *funduq* (familiar to Europeans as the Italian *fondaco*), a combination of merchant quarter, warehouse and market, where freedom of religion and a degree of autonomy were permitted. Cairo and its river port, Fusṭāṭ, had many such *funduqs*.

Markets tended to be situated on the border between different geographical zones – forest and savanna, coastal belt and interior – or between different ethnic groups – Kikuyu (cultivators) and Masai (pastoralists), Europeans and Africans, Arabs and Africans – and on interregional trade routes, providing travelling merchants with food and shelter, as well as facilities for exchange. Karl Polanyi suggested that the international market, or 'port of trade', where different, perhaps mutually hostile, economies met to conduct mutually beneficial exchange, depended for its existence upon the fulfilment of three conditions: authorities capable of administering the trade, political neutrality and ease of access combined with security. Greek Naucratis and Alexandria and Phoenician Carthage, ancient cities of Mediterranean Africa, protected by their peninsular sites; Timbuktu, surrounded by desert, but accessible by canoe; and Goree and Fernando Po, West African islands, are all cited as examples. It is evident that, in the absence of long-distance trade, markets are unlikely to spring up, and such was the case over a large part of Southern Africa. On the other hand, trade, including long-distance trade, did not necessarily require markets. It depended very much on the stage of development of the society engaging in the trade. A dispersed population employing a backward technology and not organized in territorial states able to regulate and protect markets, was unlikely to have them. Sometimes markets were set up and regulated by private individuals for their own profit, but these tended to be impermanent. Towns did not necessarily attract significant markets, though important markets tended to attract new residents, and an administrative centre was less likely to attract trade than was a trading town to attract political importance. State capitals tended to be mobile, changing with the succession to the chiefship or kingship. This was true of Buganda, early Kanem and Mali. In the western Sudan, capitals became fixed when permanent market centres grew up.

The big market or port of trade, where the products of different regions were exchanged, set up, as it were, a magnetic field conducive to the development of smaller satellite markets. Traders, who frequently formed large caravans, had to be fed by local produce and might be supplied with locally made or procured trade goods. Local producers were themselves customers for imported commodities. It seems therefore inappropriate to distinguish sharply between the port of foreign trade, often subjected to strict state regulation, and the local market, arising in response to a quickening of economic activity.

In Egypt and North Africa international and interregional commerce was highly organized and capitalized from ancient times. At the other end of the scale, local markets, particularly in sub-Saharan Africa, might have no professional merchants at all, perhaps only women engaged in trade as a part-time occupation and visiting pedlars. A good deal of trade, petty and not so petty, local and long-distance, was conducted by peripatetic traders. The residents of 17th-century Cape Town, in the absence of shops, bought many of the things they needed from slaves employed as pedlars and in the 19th century the country districts – the *platteland* – were travelled by the *smous* (often a Jew), whose services, it has been suggested, facilitated the advance of the European frontier of settlement. Sometimes trade had a decided ethnic aspect. Merchants sharing a common culture, religion or language traded with one another, frequently lived in commercial communities and travelled in groups. The Jews provided a conspicuous example in Muslim lands, where, neutral in the conflict between Islam and Christianity and enjoying a linguistic affinity with the Arabs, they were very active in trade and industry. The medieval Jewish community in Cairo had its own officials, courts and social services. In the Middle Ages Jewish merchants were found in all parts of the Arab empire and beyond its boundaries from Spain to China. They represented and acted on behalf of one another. The advantages of the mutual assistance of co-religionists, however, were offset by the hostility they sometimes experienced from their hosts, especially in the form of European anti-semitism, which eventually greatly limited the Jewish share of Mediterranean trade.

Apart from its Jews, North Africa had its Mozabites, Djerbans, Soussi and Fassi, while West Africa had its Dyula, Kede and Hausa merchants. Although they varied in the scope and value of their trade, which could indeed be substantial, these merchants had one thing in common: they were set apart from the people with whom they dealt. The Kede, a section of the Nupe people, with settlements along the Niger and Kaduna rivers, were renowned as traders and canoemen; and the Dyula were the best-known of the Mande-speaking (or Mandingo) traders, converts to Islam, known to the Arabs as the Wangara, who included also the Diakhane. Originating in the Mande towns of the Niger, such as Tiraqqa and Jenne, and operating at first within the Mali empire between the Senegal and upper Niger rivers, they extended their activities all over West Africa and became very prosperous from their dealings in gold, salt, slaves and kola nuts. Although they were responsible for the settlement of a number of towns along the main West African trade routes, such as Bobo-Dioulasso and Begho, their trade never lost its itinerant character. In some areas they met competition from Hausa merchants – in Timbuktu, for example – but the latter for the most part operated further to the east. The Dyula were not entirely homogeneous, and it is doubtful whether all so-called Hausa traders were really Hausa. A rather similar group was that of the Djellaba, orginally emigrants from Egypt and active in the central Sudan, from Bornu across Wadai and Bahr el Ghazal as far as Khartoum.

In many parts of Africa long-distance trade was carried on not by specialists engaging in it alone, to the exclusion of all else, but rather by chiefs who adapted their traditional functions to the needs of commerce, or by merchants who set themselves up as rulers. Some trade, by no means all of merely local importance, was not conducted either by specialists or by political authorities, but was combined with the production of the goods that entered trade, for example ivory. In Central and East Africa there were many hunting and trading tribes, such as the Imbangela, the Nyamwezi and the Chokwe.

ii) *Barter, money and credit*

The free circulation of money in Africa until late in the 19th century was the exception rather than the rule. This was not only because the market in commodities was restricted, but also because markets in land and labour were even more limited, and services often renumerated, and taxes usually paid, in kind. Currencies were developed long before they were in widespread use. Very often they were introduced, not in response to market needs, but for political reasons – for the payment of mercenaries or for prestige. Their use was related to the growth of market exchanges, particularly to the extent that internal markets formed part of complex interregional or international trading networks. Barter was extensively found throughout Africa, sometimes exclusively, sometimes in combination with some form of currency. The most celebrated example of this method of trading, the 'silent trade', practised according to Herodotus and Philostratus in the gold trade of both the western and eastern Sudan and according to Cosmas Indicopleustes in that of Ethiopia, may have been mythical, but seems plausible.

> Another story too is told by the Carchedonians. There is a place in Libya, they say, where men dwell beyond the Pillars of Heracles; to this they come and unload their cargo; then having laid it orderly along the beach they go aboard their ships and light a smoking fire. The people of the country see the smoke, and coming to the sea they lay down gold to pay for the cargo and withdraw away from the wares. Then the Carchedonians disembark and examine the gold; if it seems to them a fair price for their cargo, they take it and go their ways; but if not, they go aboard again and wait, and the people come back and add more gold till the shipmen are satisfied. Herein neither party (it is said) defrauds the other; the Carchedonians do not lay hands on the gold till it matches the value of their cargo, nor do the people touch the cargo till the shipmen have taken the gold.[1]

There was a tendency, which persisted until the 19th century, for the most commonly traded commodities to be used as a standard of value. Trading on the River Gambia in the 17th century, Richard Jobson 'asked which should be the Staple commodities, to pitch the price upon, to value other things by'.[2] At various times and places, apart from cloths of different types and sizes, cattle; salt; copper, iron and gold in a variety of forms; beads; shells; firearms and ammunition; and mats served this purpose. To some extent these so-called transitional currencies also served as a medium of exchange, though this was a less important function.

In ancient Egypt no proper money ever developed, though commodities were often valued in terms of gold, silver or copper weights. Most payments and exchanges were transacted in kind, understandably in a society where the market was of little importance compared with the state in the allocation of resources. Apart from the bronze and silver coinage struck at Naucratis, the Greek trading settlement in the Delta, the nearest ancient Egyptian approach to money was the silver ingots stamped by temple treasuries from the 8th century B.C. onwards. The first coins in the Mediterranean area originated in the Greek states of Asia Minor and the Aegean in the 7th century B.C. or earlier, minted first of all from an alloy of gold and silver (electrum), later from gold and silver separately and later still, from the 5th century B.C., from bronze as well. These coins circulated very widely, especially the Athenian silver drachma and the more common two-drachma piece (the stater), which were the international currency of their day. They were followed in that role by the silver coinage introduced by Alexander the Great throughout his dominions, including Egypt, and copied from the Athenian currency.

The Ptolemaic successors of Alexander abandoned the Alexandrian monetary system and adopted the Phoenician standard for their coinage. Their silver coins did not penetrate the Hellenistic kingdom of the Seleucids in the Near and Middle East, but did circulate throughout the Mediterranean, and Carthage, (which had hitherto little use for money in the course of trade, but which was now drawn into a closer economic relationship with the eastern Mediterranean), felt impelled in the 4th century B.C. to mint its own gold and bronze coins, also based on the Phoenician standard. The use of silver depended upon access to the mines of Spain, which changed hands from time to time. In the 3rd century B.C. shortage of metal compelled the Carthaginians to put into circulation a token money composed of sealed leather bags, each said to contain an object worth a stater. Bronze and silver coinages were also issued in North Africa by the Berber kingdoms of Numidia and Mauretania (roughly equivalent to modern Morocco and Algeria), in imitation of Carthaginian coinage.

Carthaginian coins, needless to say, ceased to be minted after the Roman annexation of the city in 146 B.C. The Romans themselves coined a silver denarius. Gold coins were struck as early as the middle of the 2nd century B.C., but they became widely current only after the Republic had given way to the Empire shortly before the beginning of the Christian era. The gold coin of Rome was the solidus (4,4 grams in weight), which continued to be struck – as the nomisma – by the Byzantine emperors after the collapse of the empire in the west. Silver coins were rare in the later Roman empire and Byzantium.

The advantage of a uniform coinage – Alexandrian, Roman, Byzantine – circulating over a wide area, was that it ended the inconvenience of a variety of coins of uncertain exchange rates and discouraged currency speculation. But there are always problems with money. One was associated with the use of more than one metal for coining. The ratio of one to another inevitably became disturbed as one or the other became more or less abundant. The decline in the value of copper in terms of silver in the 2nd century B.C. in Egypt is said to have added to existing social tensions. Another perennial problem was the abuse of the monetary system by rulers. Egypt and North Africa, after incorporation into the Roman empire, suffered from the recurrent debasements made by the emperors, beginning with Nero in the 1st century A.D., to relieve their financial embarrassments. In the political and economic troubles that beset the empire in the 3rd century the coinage was so distrusted that it was in danger of falling into disuse. The reform introduced by the Emperor Diocletian in 296 gave the empire its last period of stable currency before its collapse.

Gold coins were struck from the 3rd century A.D. in the kingdom of Axum, an ally of Rome, but more influenced by the Greeks of the eastern Mediterranean. Nubia, on the other hand, except the small part that constituted the Roman province of Dodekaschoenos, did not have a monetary economy until the Middle Ages and then only in the north. The introduction of money was due to the activities of Muslim merchants. Gold coins were the standard currency of North Africa and Egypt after the Arab invasion. The Muslim coin, first modelled on the Byzantine nomisma, was the dīnār and its equivalent in bullion was the mithqal. In the days of the united Arab empire the dīnārs minted by the 'Abbāsid dynasty circulated throughout Egypt, the Maghrib and beyond. After the division of the empire the various successor states of northern Africa struck their own, which circulated as far as the Horn of Africa. As elsewhere, currency debasement was a common response to the financial straits of government. The dīnār tended to disappear from circulation and become merely a money of account. In Egypt debasement occurred under the Mamluks and later under the Ottomans. Ottoman Egypt issued the gold sequin and the silver para in the 16th century and the gold findikli in the 18th century. There was no uniform currency in the Ottoman empire. According to an English source of the late 16th century,

The money that is coined in Alger is a piece of gold called Asiano, & Doublaes, and two Doublaes make an Asiano, but the Doubla is most used, for all things be sold by Doublaes, which Doubla is fiftie of their Aspers there. The Asper there is not so good by halfe & more, as that in Constantinople, for the Chekin of gold of the Turkes made at Constantinople is at Alger worth an 150. Aspers, and at Constantinople it is but 66. Aspers.

The pistolet and roials of plate are most currant there.

The said pistolet goeth for 130. Aspers there: & the piece of 4. roials goeth for 40. Aspers, but often times is sold for more, as men need them to carry up into Turkie.

Their Asianos and Doublaes are pieces of course gold, worth here but 40s. the ounce, so the same is currant in no place of Turkie out of the kingdom of Alger, neither the Aspers, for that they be lesse then others be, for they coine them in Alger.[3]

And in Egypt:

Roials of Spaine are currant money there, and are the best money you can carry. And 4. roials are woorth 13. Medins, and 2. Medins are 3. Aspers. Pistolets and crownes of France and Dollars will goe, but of all Roials are best.[4]

Such was the confusion faced by traders in the Mediterranean. Weights and measures were equally varied.

Gold was also current in the commercial centres of the southern Sahara and the Sahel in the Middle Ages and later, either as gold dust or as unstamped dinārs. Gold dust could be used in very small quantities.

The currency of the Gold Coast is gold dust, an ounce of which is sold for 31.12s. The smallest quantity recognised in trade or for general use is a pessua, or 1½d., which is regarded by a Fantee man in the same light as we regard a farthing. Thus, when a thing is considered worthless, a Fantee man will say that it is not worth a pessua.[5]

In North Africa silver coins – dirhems (originally ten to the dīnar) and qirats, round and square, were used for purchases of lesser value, while some of the Muslim trading settlements – Mogadishu, Kilwa and Zanzibar – of the East African coast were minting silver and copper coins from at least the 13th century. European and American coins circulated in West Africa in areas under European control, or subject to European influence. Angola, under Portuguese rule, was granted its own copper coinage, minted in Portugal, at the end of the 17th century.

A common currency, especially for small purchases, was shells, above all, cowrie shells. These came from the Indian Ocean, from the Maldive Islands, supplemented in the course of time by additional supplies from Zanzibar; and they were introduced into the western Sudan by Arabs and Italians as early as the 11th century and used as currency from the heyday of the Mali empire. Their advantage was that they could not be counterfeited and were not easily damaged. In addition to cowrie shells, there were nzimbu shells, which were collected at what is now Luanda and were in use in the Congo before the arrival of the Portuguese. Like other media of exchange the shells fluctuated in value according to the vagaries of their supply, which bore little relation to the balance of external trade. Yet over long periods their value was very stable, partly because their use over a wider and wider area offset the increasing supply and partly because prices were not very sensitive to the supply and demand of either shells or consumer goods. Political authorities and gilds of craftsmen and merchants frequently administered prices, and sellers were reluctant to close a sale by accepting an offer below the customary price.

Shells were supplemented by a variety of other currencies, including copper crosses, in Katanga, and, in West Africa, manillas, iron bars, copper rods and what William Bosman called *fetiches*, cast from gold mixed with silver or copper,

> These *Fetiches* are cut into small bits by the *Negroes*, about the worth of one, two or three Farthings. 'Tis a common Proverb, *That you cannot buy much Gold for a Farthing*, yet even with that value in Gold you may here go to Market and buy Bread or Fruit for your Necessities. The *Negroe* Women know the exact value of these bits so well at sight, that they never are mistaken; and accordingly they tell them to each other without weighing, as we do coined Money. They are here called *Kakeraas*, the Word expressing something of very little value; and the Gold it self is indeed worth very little: For we connot sell it in *Europe* for above forty Shillings the Ounce; and yet it passes currant all over the Coast; and our Garrisons are paid their Subsistence Money in it. And for this they may buy all sorts of Edibles of the Negroes.[6]

West African currencies were generally convertible one into another, and those of smaller value, such as cowries, were sometimes lumped together in standardized multiples, each with its distinctive name. One of the West African currencies, the iron bar, developed into a unit of account, as Mungo Park explains,

> In their early intercourse with Europeans, the article that attracted most notice was iron. Its utility, in forming the instruments of war and husbandry, made it preferable to all others, and iron soon became the measure by which the value of all other commodities was ascertained. Thus, a certain quantity of goods, of whatever denomination, appearing to be equal in value to a bar of iron, constituted, in the trader's phraseology, a bar of that particular merchandise.[7]

Entirely artificial units of account were the 'sorting' and the 'ounce'. The bar and the sorting (a package of assorted goods valued at eight gold ounces) were in use as early as the 17th century, the ounce (originally a package of goods exchanged for an ounce of gold) in the 18th. The advantage of the system for the African importer was that he got a variety of locally popular goods. The European merchant on the other hand was able to keep his books more easily. The existence of such standard units of value greatly facilitated trade. In their absence – over large parts of East and South Africa – disputes were much more likely to arise.

More abstract forms of money were not essential for the accumulation of capital. Investment in cattle, itself a form of money, and slaves, was common. With money, however, accumulation became easier, and, in some parts of Africa, institutions evolved to facilitate its accumulation. Banks operated in Egypt certainly from Hellenistic times. In Ptolemaic and Roman Egypt there were both public and private banks. The Ptolemies instituted 'the first banking system in the world',[8] with a head office in Alexandria and branches throughout the country. The branches were administered, whether they liked it or not, by wealthy citizens, as was the case with so many other public institutions in the Hellenistic and Roman world, where the 'liturgy', or enforced performance of official functions by private citizens, was common. Each bank received payments on behalf of the state, which probably included revenue from the tax farmers and taxes payable on the registration of property transfers, and made necessary disbursements, transferring the balance to head office, probably as a rule by means of rudimentary bills of exchange from merchants purchasing wheat and other goods in the nome where the branch was situated. Individual accounts were kept, transfers effected and short- and medium-term loans made. However, the evidence seems to suggest that the typical loan was for non-productive purposes, for example, for the purchase of land or political support, and that even the prototype bills of exchange were not negotiable instruments.

During the period of Roman domination of the Mediterranean, Rome itself was the banking capital, where business was largely concentrated. Nonetheless, in Egypt and North Africa private banks, subject to a varying degree of state control, were of growing importance. They included notarial banks, which were banks-cum-record offices, exchange banks, dealing in currency, and deposit banks, which transferred funds if necessary to other cities on behalf of clients and were used by the government to collect taxes and make payments. Prospective borrowers could also apply to the temples or lending clubs for loans. A rather quaint banking service was that offered by the officials in charge of the state granaries (the sitologi), who dealt in accounts composed, not of money, but of grain, receiving deposits, transferring to other accounts and authorising payments from granaries in other cities. The existence of such a system shows that the use of money remained restricted. Indeed, loss of confidence in money and a partial return to barter as a result of the inflation of the 3rd century A.D. killed off banking in most of the Roman empire. It survived in Egypt – free from invasion and with a separate administration – but even there it was adversely affected.

In the Arab world as early as the 10th century, the *Jahbadh* accepted deposits, tranferred funds by cheque and bill, discounted money orders and made investments on behalf of his clients. In Egypt banking was one of the activities of the Kārīmī merchants, who had very extensive interests, reaching as far as China. There were other financial specialists as well, such as money lenders and exchange brokers. Jews were prominent in finance. Speculation in currency and commodities was not unknown. Needless to say, the risks of the trade of the Sudan and the Sahara, where distances were great, transport effected in conditions of great difficulty and population sparse, together with a general shortage of capital, forced up interest rates, despite Muslim disapproval of usury. Borrowers frequently had recourse to colleagues or kinsmen, furnishing security in the form of either bonds surrendered by a guarantor or property, landed or otherwise. There were occasions when traders pledged their own persons, as in the following instance in Tripoli in the later 16th century.

> There was a man in the said towne a pledge, whose name was Patrone Norado, who . . . was indebted unto a Turke of that towne, in the summe of foure hundred and fiftie crownes, for certain goods sent by him into Christendome in a ship of his owne, and by his owne brother, and himselfe remained in Tripolis as pledge untill his said brothers returne: and, as the report went there, after his brothers arrivall into Christendome, he came among lewde companie, and lost his brothers ship and goods at dice, and never returned unto his againe.[9]

In East Africa, Arabs and Indians furnished credit as did Europeans in West Africa, chiefly in the form of trade goods. Elsewhere credit was difficult to obtain outside the family, given the absence of freehold property in land to secure a loan. Although the pawning of future labour was one possibility, where the defaulting debtor worked off his debt, such an arrangement was normally the consequence of a crisis of subsistence, not of commercial opportunities, and frequently the lender was performing a social service rather than consciously making an investment. Sub-Saharan Africa was innocent of banks and other financial institutions until, towards the end of the Dutch East India Company's administration at the Cape, a Loan Bank, called the Lombard Bank, was set up at a time of severe money shortage (due at least partly to difficulties of communication with the Netherlands as a result of war with Britain during the American Revolution) and high interest rates. It made loans, nominally only on relatively short term, at 5 per cent. on fixed and movable property and even perishable goods. Its entire capital was in paper money, rixdollars, first issued by the governor in 1782. The result of a lavish printing was inflation, a recurring wartime disease, with deflation a recurring peacetime remedy. After it became a British colony, the settlement switched to sterling at the beginning of 1825.

iii) *Transport and communications*
Shortage of capital placed one limitation upon trade, and poverty of transport and communications another. Poor transport facilities hampered the movement of goods, poor communications raised the costs of information. Water transport was used where possible, since it was the cheapest means of transporting bulky commodities over long distances. Sea-going vessels plied the Mediterranean and the Indian Ocean, though at the mercy of rudimentary techniques of navigation. In ancient and medieval times, until the invention of the mariner's compass in the 13th or 14th century, the Mediterranean was closed to shipping in the winter, while expansion of the Indian Ocean trade waited upon the discovery of how to take advantage of the monsoons. In the Mediterranean in ancient times boats were of two types: the long and narrow oar-propelled warship – the galley – and the broad cargo boat powered by a rectangular sail at right-angles to the mast. A rudder-oar was used for steering. The distinction between galley for war and sailing ship for trade persisted into Muslim times. It was the Italians in the Middle Ages who used the galley both for peaceful and for warlike purposes. Their ability to convert their ships from one function to the other at a moment's notice gave them a great advantage over their Muslim competitors and enemies, though there was, of course, an attendant disadvantage in using the galley for trade with its high-cost power and its more restricted cargo space.

Of the rivers, the Nile was a much frequented thoroughfare. It was easily accessible and the traffic passing along it was assisted downstream by the current and upstream by the prevailing northerly wind. The middle reaches of the river were impeded by the cataracts. Many other African rivers, too – the Congo, Zambezi and Niger among them – had rapids where they commenced their descent to the sea after meandering through flat, sometimes marshy, land. Rivers tended to be too full in the rainy season and too low in the dry. Canoes did make use, however, of the Niger, the Zambezi, the Shire, the Senegal and parts of the Volta, as well as many smaller rivers, the lakes and coastal lagoons. Coastal traffic by canoe was not unknown, but the unbroken and steeply-rising coastline frequently discouraged it.

For transport overland the horse-drawn two-wheeled cart was used in Egypt from the 2nd millennium B.C. There was, however, no comprehensive system of roads until the Romans built theirs, mainly for their soldiers and administrators, in North Africa and Egypt. The donkey was the normal means of overland transport in Ancient Egypt. The Roman roads were not much used by wagons, and they fell into disuse after the Arab invasions. The vast Arab empire was largely dependent upon roughly marked tracks, impeded by bridgeless rivers. Religious foundations provided travellers with hospitality, but inns were rare before the later Middle Ages. South of the Sahara wheeled transport was not used until comparatively recently, though it must have been known in the savanna south of the desert or at least known of. A possible explanation for its absence is that the cost of acquiring carts and keeping them in a state of repair where there were no proper roads and of buying and keeping the necessary beasts was prohibitive. The tsetse fly and beasts of prey were limiting factors, and widespread ignorance or neglect of the plough meant that the possibility of using horses or oxen for the double purpose of farm-work and transport did not exist. There can be little doubt, too, that if the inadequacy of transport limited trade, the shortage of trade, due in some measure to the sparseness of the population, did not justify either the introduction of superior methods of transport or the construction and maintenance of roads.

Horse-drawn chariots or carts were crossing the Sahara as early as the 2nd millennium B.C., but the camel proved to be more effective, and wheeled transport fell into disuse. The camel was of immense significance. Already employed in the eastern Sahara as early as the end of the 4th century B.C. and certainly present in the western Sahara in the 1st century B.C., it spread throughout the desert during the early centuries of the Christian era, but came into general use only after the Arab invasions. In the savanna donkeys and oxen were the chief pack animals and were found as far as the coast of Senegambia. In the forest, where trypanosomiasis was rife and pasture rare, porters took over. Porterage was the typical means of transport in East Africa and in the West Africa forest. In West Africa, goods passing through desert, savanna and forest became ever more expensive as they had to be packed and repacked in ever smaller loads, except where they could take advantage of river transport, on the Niger for example. Porterage was a particularly costly form of transport, and that is why porters were often slaves who were sold off at the end of the journey. The right to requisition porters was an important prerogative claimed by chiefs in areas where there was no other form of transport. In Southern Africa, in pre-European times and after, the Khoikhoi rode upon oxen, while the Dutch introduced heavy ox-wagons, pulled by twenty yoke, which struggled over indifferent roads or made their own.

The movement of trade was hindered by the proliferation and greed of political authorities and foreign and domestic warfare. Mediterranean commerce was disrupted by the struggle between Carthaginians and Greeks and between Carthaginians and Romans. The struggle between Christian and Muslim had a similar effect over a much longer period. Merchants and

complaisant rulers could be embarrassed by the denunciation of Catholic
clerics and Muslim marabouts. Rulers themselves intermittently forbade
the export of goods likely to be of value to a potential enemy. Christian
kings were sometimes reluctant to provide Muslims with timber for ships;
and Muslim rulers to provide Christians with grain. Frequently, jihad or
crusade degenerated into piracy and privateering, often followed by reprisals,
and they bedevilled trade for centuries. Commercial rivalry was exacerbated
by religious differences, and in general a good deal of fighting that went on
was simply for control of trade routes, those of the Sahara, for example,
those of Ethiopia in the Middle Ages and those of East Africa in the 19th
century. The rapacity of nomadic peoples was another source of disturbance.
Somali nomads proved a constant threat to trade routes from the Gulf of
Aden to Ethiopia. Camel-borne nomads in the Sahara were formidable
antagonists to merchants from the early centuries of the Christian era. There
is some evidence that the Romans encouraged camel-breeding in Tripolitania with the object of furnishing camel patrols on caravan routes. It remained a perennial problem. The activities of the Hilal and Sulaim tribes
were as harmful to trade as to agriculture. Three centuries after their incursions Ibn Baṭṭūṭa, journeying through Ifriqiya on a pilgrimage to Mecca,
made all too clear the hazards of 14th-century travel.

From Qusantínah (Constantine) we reached Bona (Bône) where, after staying
in the town for several days, we left the merchants of our party on account of
the dangers of the road, while we pursued our journey with the utmost speed.
I was again attacked by fever, so I tied myself in the saddle with a turban-cloth
in case I should fall by reason of my weakness. So great was my fear that I could
not dismount until we arrived at Tunis.[10]

He had only recently witnessed an example of arbitary official intervention.

The commander of Bijáya at this time was the chamberlain Ibn Sayyid an-Nás.
Now one of the Tunisian merchants of our party had died leaving three thousand
dinars of gold, which he had entrusted to a certain man of Algiers to deliver to
his heirs at Tunis. Ibn Sayyid an-Nás came to hear of this and forcibly seized the
money. This was the first instance I witnessed of the tyranny of the agents of the
Tunisian government.[11]

At the end of the 18th century Frederick Horneman crossed by caravan
from Cairo to Fezzan.

It was but a few days after our leaving Cairo, that the appearance of an horde
of Bedouins gave alarm to our caravan; indeed it was extraordinary that we
should reach Siwah without attack, as the Arabs had of late been so bold, as even
to pass the French posts, and rob near to the very capital. Whilst at Siwah, we
were apprised of the movements of different hordes of Bengasi and other Arabian

tribes; and not far from our road between Augila and the frontiers of Fezzan, we descried numerous vestiges of their depredation, viewing some hundreds of dead camels and beasts of burthen which they had plundered and left, probably from deficiency of water for their support. They had robbed in the neighbourhood, and even made an attack on Temissa.[12]

South of the Sahara the traffic in slaves, though a form of trade itself, was destructive of other forms. This was especially true of Central and East Africa in the 19th century, when cheap firearms became more freely available. The population shifts of the 19th century, too, particularly the migrations of the Ngoni, threw great areas into turmoil.

NOTES

1. Herodotus IV, 196 (Loeb edition, 1950, Volume II, p. 399)
2. Howard, C. (ed.): *West African Explorers* (London, 1951), p. 42
3. Hakluyt, Richard: *Voyages* (Everyman edition, 1907), Volume III, p. 121
4. Ibid, p. 123
5. Nicol, Davidson (ed.): *Africanus Horton, the Dawn of Nationalism in Modern Africa; Extracts from the Political, Educational and Scientific Writings of J. A. B. Horton M.D. 1835–1885* (London and Harlow, 1969), p. 109
6. Howard, C.: Op. cit., p. 64
7. Park, Mungo: *Travels* (London, 2nd Everyman edn./, 1954), p. 19
8. Bogaert, Raymond: *Banques et Banquiers dans les Cités Grecques* (Leiden, 1968), p. 30
9. Hakluyt, R.: Op. cit., Volume III, p. 141
10. Baṭṭūṭa, Ibn: *Travels in Asia and Africa 1325–1354* (London, 1929), p. 44–5
11. Ibid, p. 44
12. Howard, C.: Op. cit., p. 163

Further reading

Adams, William Y.: Op. cit. (see p. 104)
Arndt, E. H. D.: *Banking and Currency Development in South Africa (1652–1927)* (Cape Town and Johannesburg, 1928)
Bohannan, P. & Dalton, George: *Markets in Africa* (Chicago, 1962)
Bulliet, Richard W.: *The Camel and the Wheel* (Cambridge, Mass., 1975)
Carson, R. A. G.: *Coins, Ancient, Medieval and Modern* (London, 1962)
Charles-Picard, Gilbert & Colette: Op. cit. (see p. 46)
Ehrenkreutz, Andrew S.: 'Monetary aspects of medieval Near Eastern economic history' (Cook, M. A. ed.: *Studies in the Economic History of the Middle East, from the Rise of Islam to the Present Day* (London, 1970), p. 37–50)
Finley, Moses I.: *The Ancient Economy* (London, 1973)
Fisher, Humphrey J.: 'The eastern Maghrib and the central Sudan' (see p. 46)
Forbes, R. J.: *Studies in Ancient Technology*, Volume II (Leiden, 1955)
Fraser, P. M.: *Ptolemaic Alexandria*, 3 volumes (Oxford, 1972)

Goitein, S. D.: *A Mediterranean Society* (see p. 114)

Gray, Richard & Birmingham, David (eds.): *Pre-Colonial African Trade, Essays on Trade in Central and Eastern Africa before 1900* (London, 1970)

Hill, Polly: 'Notes on traditional market authority and market periodicity in West Africa' (*Journal of African History*, VII, 1966, p. 295–311)

Hodder, B. W. & Ukwu, U. I.: *Markets in West Africa, Studies of Markets and Trade among the Yoruba and Ibo* (Ibadan, 1969)

Indicopleustes, Cosmas: *The Christian Topography of Cosmas, an Egyptian Monk* (London, 1897)

Johnson, Allan Chester: Op. cit. (see p. 47)

Johnson, Marion: 'The cowrie currencies of West Africa' (*Journal of African History*, XI 1970, p. 17–49)

Johnson, Marion: 'The ounce in eighteenth-century West African trade' (Ibid, VII, 1966, p. 197–214)

Johnson, Marion: 'The nineteenth-century gold "mithqal" in West and North Africa' (Ibid, IX, 1968, p. 547–69)

Levtzion, Nehemia: *Ancient Ghana and Mali* (London, 1973)

Lombard, Maurice: *Espaces et réseaux du haut moyen âge* (Paris, 1972)

Lombard, Maurice: *Monnaie et histoire d'Alexandre à Mahomet* (Paris, 1971)

Lopez, Robert S.: 'The trade of medieval Europe: the south' (Chapter V, Postan, M. & Rich, E. E. (eds.): *The Cambridge Economic History of Europe*, Volume II, *Trade and Industry in the Middle Ages*, Cambridge, 1952)

Meillassoux, Claude (ed.): *The Development of Indigenous Trade and Markets in West Africa* (London, 1971)

Neumark, D. S.: *Economic Influences on the South African Frontier 1652–1836* (Stanford, California, 1957)

Orsingher, Roger: *Banks of the World* (London, 1967)

Polanyi, K., Arensberg, C. M. & Pearson, H. W. (eds.): *Trade and Market in the Early Empires; Economics in History and Theory* (New York, 1957)

Polanyi, Karl: Op. cit. (see p. 115)

Semple, Ellen Churchill: Op. cit. (see p. 47)

Herskovits, M. J. & Harwitz, M.: Op. cit. (see p. 115)

Sundström, Lars: Op. cit. (see p. 105)

Tarn, Sir William: *Hellenistic Civilisation* (London, 3rd edn. 1952)

2. MEDITERRANEAN AFRICA

i) *Pre-Roman trade*

Medium- and long-distance trade was the product of differences in geographical, economic and cultural conditions, which resulted in variations, not only in agricultural produce, but also in craft production. The goods of Egypt, economically the most advanced region of Africa in ancient and medieval times, were much in demand, even in the archaic period. Ancient Egypt exported both manufactures in the form of unblown glass, textiles, stone vessels and papyrus and primary products – decorative stone (especially alabaster), agricultural produce, dried fruit and cattle. However, having few natural resources apart from the mud of the Nile, she had to import many of her own needs – timber for shipbuilding, the construction of temples and houses, and for the manufacture of furniture; certain metals that were completely lacking or in short supply, particularly gold, silver and tin and probably also copper, iron, lead and manganese; incense for ritual purposes; oil for culinary, medicinal and religious purposes; spices (myrrh, cassia and resin) for mummification; and certain precious and semi-precious stones.

Egypt traded chiefly with the eastern Mediterranean countries and islands, the Middle East and Arabia and beyond, both by sea and by land across Sinai. The Amorite city of Byblos on the shores of the Levant is recorded as early as the 3rd millennium B.C. as a source of cedar wood for shipbuilding. In the heyday of the Minoan empire, in the 2nd millennium B.C., Crete was the principal entrepôt of trade between Egypt and the Aegean, but after the destruction of Knossos in 1400 B.C. Mycene on the Greek mainland dealt directly with Egypt. Numerous Minoan and Myceneaen vases, which may have been used as containers for other exports, have been recovered along the Nile. Greek and other foreign merchants – Canaanites and Syrians particularly – were attracted to Egypt. The Greeks, who went to serve as mercenaries as well as to trade, participated in the foundation of the 26th dynasty in the 7th century B.C. and were permitted to establish in the Nile Delta the city of Naucratis, governed by *prostatai* representing various Greek communities. It retained its importance as the only free Greek port until the establishment of Alexandria, and like Alexandria was a manufacturing centre as well as a port, making china scarabs for example. Merchants from Asia Minor and the Aegean frequented it most, but some came from Greece proper in search of grain in exchange for vases and silver. From the 5th century, Athens, until its decline after the Peloponnesian War, was predominant in the trade.

A certain amount of trade was conducted with Nubia and the 'Land of Punt' from the pre-dynastic period. The latter is commonly identified as the area at the southern end of the Red Sea, perhaps including Yemen as well as Somalia, and inhabited by people physically alike to the Egyptians. Much of this trade was conducted overland across the southern boundaries of Egypt and was to begin with, of a casual nature. Goods were brought in by Sudanese merchants or wandering tribesmen or perhaps simply passed from hand to hand. With the unification of Egypt steps were taken to safeguard the southern border against Sudanese raiders and to control the trade. The obvious centre for controls was upstream of the 1st cataract of the Nile, where the barren desert closed in on the rocky ravine of the river and forced all traffic to take one and the same route. The control point was Elephantine at the 1st cataract, where a customs house and a collecting centre were set up. From time to time the Egyptians supplemented these more regular exchanges with military raids that had the object, not only of buying, but also of loot-

TRADE   133

ing and maintaining Egyptian prestige. Under the 6th dynasty, in the 3rd
millennium, a new fortress and customs house was built at Kerma at the head
of the 3rd cataract, as an advanced trading post to which the Sudanese could
bring their goods, but the Egyptian hold upon this southerly region was not
consistently maintained, tightening and relaxing as dynasties waxed and
waned. During the expansionist New Kingdom of the 2nd millennium the
pharaohs extended their rule beyond the 4th cataract, and Nubians and
Sudanese began to enter Egypt, either as slaves or free immigrants, in some
numbers, being employed as workers, domestic servants and, above all,
soldiers and police.

The principal Egyptian imports from the south, often in the form of
tribute, were gold, semi-precious stones and timber from Nubia, which was
wooded in ancient times, and, from further afield precious woods, ivory,
myrrh, frankincense, gold, panther skins, ostrich feathers, cattle and wild
animals. Difficulties of transport meant, of course, that only very small
quantities of heavier and bulkier goods could be shifted, and increasing use
was made of the sea route. This was done with some reluctance at first because the reef-infested Red Sea was dangerous and its largely harbourless
shores were uninviting, with their mountain ranges and arid coastal plains.
The early expeditions were embarked on only occasionally, when needs
were more than usually urgent. The first recorded expedition took place
in the 5th dynasty and was a great success. The vessels, specially built on the
Red Sea coast, brought back myrrh, electrum and ebony. Expeditions continued to be sent from time to time, but the trade was subject to long lapses
for political reasons. Foreign trade was a state monopoly and the ships
engaged in it were the pharaoh's, so that the collapse of a dynasty meant a
severance of commercial ties. The fact that a celebrated expedition of five
vessels sent to the Somali coast by Queen Hatshepsut in the middle of the
2nd millennium was hailed as the first of its kind, indicates the intermittent
nature of the relationship. Aromatic gum, ivory, precious woods, gold,
leopard skins, apes and slaves were exchanged for weapons and jewellery.

Another ancient trade was conducted in the western Mediterranean during
the Bronze Age, linking North Africa with Spain, where copper was worked.
It was chiefly the copper, silver and tin of Spain that attracted the Phoenicians to the west. Carthage at her most prosperous maintained a monopoly
of trade in the western Mediterranean, sinking all foreign ships found in
those waters. Indeed, she relied upon force and unequal exchange rather
than upon superior manufactures and advanced business methods. Until the
3rd century B.C. her most profitable trade was with the backward tribes of
western Europe, as far north as Cornwall and Brittany. From these she
obtained gold, silver, tin, lead and probably iron, supplying in return manu-

factured articles, probably mostly Carthaginian and foreign wine, cloth and trumpery ware. The Carthaginians were not much dependent upon their African neighbours for trade, as the Berber tribes were too primitive and the Maghrib too poor. Some wool, skins, timber, purple dye, ivory and ostrich feathers were obtained. In Cathaginian and Roman times North Africa was still rich in its fauna and was a source of wild beasts for menageries and games.

According to Herodotus there was an overland trade route between Egypt and Fezzan. Certainly, trade took place between the Punic colonies of North Africa and the peoples of the desert and beyond. For access to the interior from Tripolitania there were three important settlements, known as the Emporia – Sabratha, Oea (Tripoli) and Leptis. Carbuncles (Cathaginian stones) were obtained from the Garamantes, a people partly sedentary, settled in the oases of Fezzan, partly nomadic, roaming between Fezzan and the coast. It is possible that slaves and gold were also purchased. The Carthaginians used slaves for agriculture and traded in them – mainly prisoners of war and victims of piracy – exporting them, for example, to the Balearics, a valuable market. Rock paintings of chariots and carts suggest two principal early trans-Saharan routes from the Mediterranean to the Niger, an easterly one from Tripolitania via the Hoggar, a westerly one from modern Algeria. It is possible that the Cathaginians founded their colony at Lixus, near Larache in Morocco, at the beginning of the 1st millennium B.C. for the purpose of participating in the West African trade. They are believed to have sailed along the coast lying beyond the Straits of Gibraltar. Hanno, on a celebrated voyage in the mid-5th century B.C., is said to have coasted present-day Morocco. The places he is supposed to have touched at have been variously identified. There is no archaeological evidence to support claims of Carthaginian contacts with West Africa by sea.

Carthage was largely dependent on the carrying trade and much that was imported was re-exported. Her own industries were not highly developed and her manufactures, decidedly inferior to Greek and Egyptian products, were mainly for internal consumption, though they could be disposed of to the primitive people with whom Carthage traded. From the 5th century, however, an effort was made to reduce dependence upon imported luxuries after defeat at the hands of the Greeks at Himera in Sicily in 480 B.C. Skilled workmen were brought in and a market for Cathaginian manufactures was found, especially after the establishment of Hellenistic rule in Egypt, to whom Carthage allied herself. Carthaginian purple cloth was admired, and from the latter part of the 4th century B.C. the city exported substantial quantities of corn and other foodstuffs to the growing towns of the eastern Mediterranean.

The trade of the ancient Mediterranean world was transformed by the conquests of Alexander the Great. Egypt under the Ptolemies was drawn into an eastern Mediterranean world that enjoyed a common Hellenistic culture and brought for her products an enlarged market. The Ptolemies displayed much interest in foreign trade, being especially eager to secure a greater share of the Indian trade which passed partly through the Persian Gulf via Seleuceia on the Tigris to the Mediterranean and partly through south Arabia and then, mostly by land, to Alexandria via Petra between Gaza and Aqaba. The covetousness that led them to strive hard to expand their territories, stimulated their concern with the Red Sea route as an alternative to the overland routes from the Persian Gulf and south Arabia. Exploratory expeditions led to the foundation of a number of settlements on the west coast of the Red Sea, known as the Trogodyte or Troglodyte Coast, in particular Berenice the Golden, which can perhaps be identified with Adulis, near modern Massawa, the only good natural port between Suez and Cape Guardafui. These fortified trading posts that later developed into towns were chiefly collecting points for ivory and elephants (used in war), which were taken overland to a point on the Nile for shipment downstream. Nubia continued to provide Egypt with timber. The prosperity of Meroe more or less coincided with Ptolemaic rule in Egypt and can no doubt be attributed to some extent to an expansion of a trade which had wide contacts in Central Africa, reaching perhaps as far westwards as the Niger, and with the Red Sea and Indian Ocean, though no doubt excluded from the south by the Sudd marshes.

To facilitate trade with the south and east the Ptolemies maintained an armed fleet in the Red Sea as a protection against piracy, and one of them, Philadelphus, restored once again the ancient canal from the Red Sea to the Nile that had first been built by the pharaoh Necho and then cleared by the Persian Darius. By the 2nd century B.C. or earlier, Egyptian ships reached the Horn of Africa at Cape Guardafui and also opened direct coastal trade with India. A settlement, Berenice Epidires, was made at the entrance to the Red Sea and trade with India became regular. Indian traders began to visit the Red Sea ports and even found their way to Egypt.

ii) *Roman trade*
The enlarged trading area of the Hellenistic world was still further extended by Rome, whose empire embraced the entire Mediterranean basin. Under her rule Egypt and Cyrenaica became major exporters of grain (and of other foodstuffs, such as dates and cured fish, to a smaller degree) to Italy and other parts of Europe, and Egypt became an important exporter of flax to the west. The manufactures of Egypt – textiles, papyrus, glassware, drugs, ointments, perfumes and objets d'art – continued to feature prominently among exports to the countries of the Mediterranean, though some, especially

glassware, encountered stiff competition from Italy, Gaul and Germany in the later Roman period, in their export markets and even in their domestic market. But Egyptian production costs were low in both agriculture and industry owing to the fertility of the soil and the cheapness of labour. As in the past, Egypt was an importer of certain metals (antimony, cobalt, silver and tin), timber, wine and olive oil, but depended very little upon western European exports.

The incorporation of Egypt into the Roman empire did not disturb the economic relationship between Egypt and the African interior. Augustus made a raid upon Napata in Nubia and attempted to annex territory as far south as the 2nd cataract, but the frontier was stabilized at Hiera Sycaminos. It is known that Egyptian pottery, glass and bronzeware were exported to Nubia, while Central African goods continued to reach Egypt via Nubia – ebony, ivory, gold and other metals and wild beasts. The trade may have faltered somewhat with the internal troubles of the empire in the 3rd century, as well as the subsequent decline of Meroe, associated with the rise of Axum, which prospered to the extent that it was able to challenge and then wrest away Meroe's dominant position on the trade routes between Egypt and the African interior. Axum acquired the Red Sea port of Adulis and merchants from Egypt preferred sailing along the Red Sea to making the long and tedious journey up the Nile. Adulis was both an entrepôt and an importer of goods locally used – luxury goods, such as glass and metalware, but also knives and axes for hunting elephants. Ivory was the most important of the Axumite exports, which included as well tortoise shell and rhinoceros horn. Gold was obtained from the Cushitic-speaking Agaw.

The Romans took over whatever trade there was with the Garamantes. Relations between the two were uneasy and towards the end of the 1st century B.C. the Romans made a punitive expedition into Fezzan. In A.D. 200 a garrison was put into the capital, Garama (now the oasis of Djerma). Evidently trade continued until the 4th century A.D. and the chief commodity taken by the Romans was carbuncles. Possibly some gold and ivory were obtained, but if so they could not have been of much importance. The Emporia grew in importance, especially Leptis, which the Emperor Septimius Severus (A.D. 193–211) particularly favoured because it was his birthplace. However, the economic significance of these towns was less attributable to trade than to agriculture, fishing and the manufacture of purple dye. Grain was exported mostly as tribute, but some was left over for sale. After the building of Constantinople and the diversion of Egyptian grain exports there, Rome was fed chiefly by North Africa. There was the advantage of the short sea route. One of the most important exports from Africa was wild animals for shows. Thousands were slaughtered but exports continued right up until the end of the 4th century. By then elephants, which were wanted for their ivory as well, were apparently extinct. Many other species of animal disappeared, though no doubt pressure of population was partly responsible.

North Africa was primarily agricultural and it had no great industrial centre like Alexandria. Towns, even large ones, were essentially administrative and religious centres, inhabited by landowners. However, there was some industry, including a pottery industry. Lamps were made and some of these were exported to the northern shores of the Mediterranean. Mosaics were also manufactured, using local stone. Woven products were exported and, indeed, clothing was the only manufactured product of North Africa that enjoyed an international reputation. Many agricultural products were processed before export – olives, grapes, wool, leather and fish. Oil was exported in large quantities to the rest of the empire. Imports were probably chiefly manufactured goods from Europe and Egypt. People mostly made their own things and local industry must have supplied the majority of other common articles required except when undersold by foreign competitors. The most prosperous Africans could easily import articles of luxury not obtainable in Africa.

The Roman occupation of Egypt also resulted in a further expansion of the trade with Arabia and India. In the 1st century A.D., Strabo wrote,

> Previously not even twenty ships dared to cross the Arabian Gulf and put their nose outside the straits. But now large merchant fleets are despatched to India, and the eastern parts of Ethiopia, by means of which the most valuable cargoes are brought to Egypt, whence they are exported to other regions.[1]

Augustus enlarged commerce by building a fleet based on the Red Sea ports, and by the middle of the 1st century A.D., Egyptian Greeks had learnt how to make use of the south-west monsoon for a direct sea passage to India in summer and the north-east monsoon back in the winter, so that there was very considerable exchange of goods with Arabia, India and even China. Goods coming from the east up the Red Sea were landed at Myos Hormos or Berenice and taken by caravan to Coptos, but some must have been transported by the Red Sea-Nile canal, restored yet again by Trajan. Alexandria was the chief entrepôt of this inter-continental trade and the major industrial consumer of exotic spices, a large proportion of which were re-exported, especially to Rome, after having been processed as drugs, perfumes or ointments: pepper from India; the highly prized cinnamon, which the Greeks believed came from Arabia and Somalia, so tight was the Arab control of the supply, but which in fact came from Malaya, Ceylon and the Indonesian islands; and frankincense, which really did come from south Arabia.

Foreign trade was in the hands of private merchants, some operating on a big enough scale to have their agents abroad, and including both native

Alexandrians and foreigners, among them Italians, who had been active in the eastern Mediterranean ever since the 3rd century B.C. It is said that as many as a hundred and twenty vessels, based at Alexandria, were engaged at any one time in the Red Sea and eastern trade was at its greatest in the Roman period. To Arabia, India and her nearer Asian and African neighbours Egypt exported her glass, metalware, papyrus, textiles (above all linen), drugs and jewellery, and re-exported wine and olive oil, in return receiving – apart from spices – rare woods, such as ebony, fine textiles (silk and muslin), raw cotton and silk, silk yarn, precious stones, horses, slaves and a variety of rare and fantastic commodities. Some foodstuffs were imported by the Roman empire, including butter, rice, sugar-cane, palm oil and sesame oil, as well as birds and animals, such as peacocks and parrots. In terms of value, it is thought that silk and spices predominated. They were normally paid for with specie. In the 3rd century A.D. silk was exchanged for an equal weight of gold.

The most valuable Roman export to India was the red coral of the western Mediterranean, exported as a rule after being cut. Glassware, bronzeware and pottery made their way eventually to China via India. On the whole, it was a luxury trade over long distances and through many entrepôts. Pliny tells us that the Roman trade with India and Arabia was worth 50 million sesterces a year. How much of it passed through the Red Sea and Egypt can only be guessed, anything between half and four-fifths. Overland trade, then, through Petra and Palmyra in the Syrian desert, must also have been substantial.

A trade was regularly carried on from the 1st century B.C. with the ports along the Red Sea, the Horn of Africa and the East African coast, where there have been found Ptolemaic, Roman and Persian coins. An account of that trade survives in a Greek commercial handbook of about A.D. 100, *The Periplus of the Erythrean Sea* (the Indian Ocean). Based upon first-hand experience, it is a description of trade with the ports along the coasts of what are now Somalia, Kenya and Tanzania. There were two great markets (emporia), at Opone (Ras Hafun, just south of Cape Guardafui) and Rhapta (though not positively identified, evidently on the mainland near Zanzibar). Opone had commercial ties with India, as well as Egypt. Ships from western India brought cotton cloth, grain, oil, sugar and ghee. Graeco-Roman ships took in manufactures and semi-manufactures, such as dyed cloaks and tunics, copper and tin, wine, and metal utensils, and took away ivory, tortoise shell, slaves (highly prized in Rome), and spices. Rhapta, ignorant perhaps of the art of smelting, imported iron weapons and implements and exported ivory and re-exported cinnamon, perhaps brought from Indonesia, seven thousand kilometres away, in double out-rigger canoes. The trade of Rhapta was controlled by Arab merchants based at Muza – near modern Mocha – at the entrance to the Red Sea. Its population was evidently a racial mixture, possibly including an Indonesian element, but certainly with Arab blood.

A later account of the trade is to be found in the *Geography* attributed to Ptolemy (A.D. 90–160), but containing additions made in the 4th or 5th century. In the interval between the *Periplus* and Ptolemy's *Geography* the economic activity on the East Coast had increased. Rhapta had become more important, the centre of a network of trade that stretched to the south and into the interior. Yet the external trade must have been only modest even at its greatest, if the meagre size of the coin hoards discovered in East Africa is any guide.

The direct trade between the Mediterranean and the Indian Ocean began to decline about A.D. 400. Downturns in the trade were not new, but this time it disappeared. Two explanations have been offered for this, firstly the rise of Persian seapower in the western Indian Ocean in the 4th century, and secondly the economic development of the empire of Axum from the late 3rd century. Axum, as it eclipsed Meroe, became an intermediary in the Roman trade with Africa and India. While neither Axum nor Persia appears to have exerted any control over the East Africa markets, it is evident that both carried on a direct trade with them, by sea from the Persian Gulf, overland by routes that ran parallel to the coast from Adulis and Axum. This redistribution of trade advantage in favour of Persia and Axum may, however, be attributed less to their growing self-assertion than to the economic enfeeblement of the Roman empire. Commerce suffered from growing insecurity and currency depreciation. Rising prices and lagging wages led to industrial unrest and unemployment. The burden of taxes became heavier. Imports from India and the Far East fell off. The imperial reorganization of Diocletian meant an all-embracing state control, with shipowners and artisans tied to their occupations. After the transfer of the capital from Rome followed by the collapse of the empire in the west, Constantinople overtook Alexandria in commercial significance and by the 6th century was the chief entrepôt for eastern goods.

iii) *Islam and the Mediterranean*
It was the argument of the distinguished Belgian historian, Henri Pirenne, that the Arab conquest of the southern shores of the Mediterranean destroyed its unity, bringing down an iron curtain between Europe and Africa and putting to an end the classical Mediterranean civilization that had succeeded in surviving the incursions of Teutonic barbarians. An urban, commercial economy was replaced by the closed agrarian, moneyless economy of the revived Roman empire of Charlemagne. Christian commerce survived only in the eastern Mediterranean under the protection of Byzantium. The barrier between Islam and Christendom only Jewish merchants could surmount.

How far the changes wrought in Christendom were the effect of the conflict with Islam is not a matter that can be discussed here, but the catastrophic consequences of the Arab expansion for the unity of the Mediterranean basin may be questioned. Trade went on, though it should be noted that the Arabs in the 7th century did not burst into and destroy a conspicously prosperous economic relationship. For commercial contacts between Europe and Africa had already been adversely affected before the rise of Islam by, for example, the piracy of the Vandals. It is doubtful if commerce properly recovered even after the Byzantine reconquests of the 6th century. Western Europe was insecure, barbarised and impoverished and in no position to import large quantities of North African and Egyptian products. Nevertheless, in the 8th century and early 9th, Byzantium was still powerful enough to exclude Muslim shipping from the western Mediterranean and although she imported her eastern goods through the Black Sea ports of Trebizond and Cherson rather than from Syria and Egypt, some direct trade, even during this period of pronounced religious enmity, appears to have been carried on between Byzantium and Egypt and between North Africa and Byzantine-ruled Sicily. Thus the commercial effects of the rise of Islam should not be exaggerated. On the other hand, the process of Arab conquest did nothing to promote trade, especially when Saracen brigands devastated the northern coasts of the Mediterranean, even terrorising travellers crossing the Alps.

There was, naturally, a good deal of trade carried on within Islamic Africa, and that survived political differences. As in earlier times Egypt exported to the Maghrib manufactures of glass and metal, textiles of silk, linen and cotton, spices and wheat, receiving in return oil, woollen cloth, coral, hides, salted fish and slaves. This exchange was largely land-borne despite the difficulties of transport through the Libyan desert. Sea-borne commerce, however, though subject to severe disturbance, did not come to an end. There were close commercial ties between Spain and North Africa, which often shared a common government. Sea-borne trade revived as greater political stability was achieved.

Tunisia under the Fātimids became extremely prosperous. Their capital of al-Mahdia on the coast developed into an important trading centre, distributing eastern goods to the countries of the western Mediterranean. Such goods were in growing demand as the economy of Europe expanded. Commercial contact between Christian and Muslim was strengthened and the hostility between them, although periodically renewed, abated. They were mutually attracted as well as repelled. For both absorbed a significant measure of Greek culture and a certain cultural affinity was reinforced by commercial interests common to them both. As the expansion of Islam was checked, the holy war, the *jihād*, gave way to the safe-conduct, the *amān*, which permitted non-Muslims to visit and even take up residence in a Muslim land. After the Byzantine loss of Crete and Sicily in the 9th century a brisk trade developed between Africa and the nominally Byzantine cities of Italy, especially Amalfi and Venice, even though trade between Christians and Muslims was frowned on by the pope in Rome and the emperor in Constantinople. Before the First Crusade of 1095 Amalfitans were holding an annual fair at Jerusalem and probably had a *fondaco* at Antioch.

Christian-Muslim trade was composed of the exchange of luxuries from Egypt, Arabia and the Far East for the iron and wood that Egypt, in particular, acutely needed. Slaves, furs and grain, too, were imported. Slaves were in great demand in the Muslim world. During the early period of Arab expansion there was an abundant supply from the conquered territories, but once the conquest ceased it was necessary to obtain them from outside the boundaries of Islam. (It was contrary to Muslim law to enslave the faithful and manumission of slaves was common.) The relationship between Islam and Christendom was that of a comparatively advanced economy dealing with an underdeveloped one. There had, even in Roman times, been an unfavourable balance of trade between, what may loosely be called, east and west, and when the Arab invasions placed the principal sources of gold in Muslim hands, western Europe lacked the wherewithal to pay for eastern imports. The imbalance was redressed when Islam began to import European slaves and commodities. Gold began to enter Europe again, thus contributing to commercial recovery there.

The export of slaves from western and central Europe ceased with the spread of Christianity to the Slavs (the chief source of slaves) and the development of state organization among them. Egypt therefore looked to the Black Sea for her supplies. South Russia became the region from which military slaves were drawn. In the mid-15th century two thousand a year were entering from the Black Sea ports. The trade of western Europe, by contrast, developed in a markedly different way from the end of the 11th century. The growth of its woollen industry and of cloth exports to North Africa and the Levant put the trading relationship between Islam and Christendom on a more equal footing. At the same time western merchants assumed a greater and greater significance and began to displace Muslim and Jewish ones. There was a growing demand in Europe for the spices and other luxuries of the Far East which passed through Muslim territory. Of importance, too, was the demand for African gold and ivory.

Africa, especially West Africa, was the chief source of Europe's gold supply during the Middle Ages. European merchants, however, did not make direct contact with the gold-bearing area, and were discouraged from doing so, though there were instances of individuals travelling and even residing in Morocco as far south as the desert. In the eastern Maghrib during the

Hafsid period of rule, from the 13th to the 16th century, European merchants were not permitted in the interior at all, though Jews, particularly locally born ones, were not subject to the same restrictions. The Saharan trade and the North African trade with Europe tended to be conducted separately. Gold entering Europe from Africa in the Middle Ages did so because of North Africa's unfavourable balance of trade with Europe. This trade took the form of an exchange of North African raw and semi-processed materials, especially hides, leather, wool, wax, indigo, alum, coral, figs, dates and olive oil (though the supply of oil tended to fall off with the decline of the North African rural economy) for European manufactures, particularly weapons and cloth. There was a movement of grain in both directions. Normally North Africa was an exporter in the earlier Middle Ages, supplying Andalusia with its needs in the 10th century. Later it was a net importer, exporting only during good years. The North African trade was less lucrative and less sought after by European merchants than the Syrian and Egyptian trade and therefore tended to be left in the hands of the smaller trading towns and the smaller men of the big ones. Gold was important, to be sure, but access to that was barred.

European policy was a mixture of commerce and religious aggression, itself not untinged with commercial violence. Intermittent crusades, partly directed at the Mediterranean coast of Africa, no doubt sought economic as well as religious advantages. Muslim motives were equally mixed. Attacks on Christian coasts and shipping were often mere banditry and piracy. The Christian counter-attack began with the Pisan and Genoese raid on al-Mahdia in 1087, itself a reprisal for Muslim piratical exploits, and ended with St. Louis' unsuccessful attempt on Damietta in 1249–1250 and Tunis in 1270. European states did not have the resources to maintain distant territorial enclaves amidst hostile populations, as the weakness and ultimate collapse of the crusading kingdoms of the Levant showed. The Italians, however, though wrangling constantly among themselves, retained command of the sea, challenged only sporadically by the Fāṭimid, Ayyubid and Mamluk rulers of Egypt, and they were able to extort concessions, such as customs privileges and access to ports, from the weaker rulers of the Maghrib. *Funduqs* for example were made available for Christians and Jews trading in Tunis during the Hafsid period. North African trade on the whole prospered and involved not only various Italian city states – Venice, Pisa, Genoa – but also Aragon and Marseilles, as well as the islands and the eastern Mediterranean mainland. Such was the Italian dominance that in the 12th and 13th centuries even North African imports of eastern spices were handled by Christian middlemen who purchased them in the eastern Mediterranean.

Periodic outbreaks of piracy continued to cause disruption. In the 14th century there was a resurgence of Tunisian piracy under the Hafsids. This led to abortive French and Genoese expeditions in 1390 against the centre of piracy, Bougie. Thereafter piracy became inextricably mixed up with the general religious conflict that arose from the reconquest of the Iberian peninsula by the Christian kings, who then carried the war into North Africa.

The commercial hegemony of the Italians, dependent upon a maritime empire in the Aegean and Black Seas and the eastern Mediterranean, was wrested from them by the Ottomans in the 15th century. The trade pattern changed, especially after the conquest of Egypt. Exports of Egyptian grain which had hitherto gone to the central and western Mediterranean, especially to Venice, now required the permission of the Porte, and that was sometimes withheld, particularly in times of open hostilities. From the latter years of the 16th century Constantinople itself, previously dependent upon supplies from the Black Sea, found it necessary to supplement that source with supplies from Egypt. Another change was the diminishing trade rôle of the Venetians, so often at war with the Turks, and the growing importance of the French. The latter made a treaty with the Ottomans in 1535, giving them a privileged position that was later extended to Tunis and Tripoli when these became Turkish. In 1580 England also obtained a charter of privileges from the 'great Turke', which, among other things, protected English traders from enslavement, exempted them from poll-tax and permitted them to elect for themselves in each of the Egyptian and North African ports a consul with power to settle intra-communal disputes. This charter, however, was not able to protect English merchants from the interference of the French representatives or English vessels from the depredations of the sultan's vassels. In 1584 the mayor of London pleaded with the viceroy at Algiers to 'give orders to the captaines, masters and people of your gallies, that from hencefoorthe they would suffer us to use our traffique with six ships yerely into Turkie unto the dominions of the Grand Signor in peace and safetie'.[2]

Shipping in the western Mediterranean was constantly harassed by corsairs and privateers. Booty became an important source of income and ransoming of Christian prisoners an important source of gold for the North African (Barbary) states. However, many ships that were molested fell victim, not to the Barbary states themselves, but to European pirates and privateers, based mostly on the Atlantic coast of Morocco, taking advantage both of the political unrest there in the early 17th century and of the sandbanks, creeks and shallow lagoons characteristic of the coast. Indeed, pirates operated in the Mediterranean from as far afield as Ireland, that 'Nursery and Storehouse of Pirates'.[3] It was only in the late 17th century that the power of the corsairs began to weaken as European powers took preventive measures, including the repeated bombardment of the North African towns.

Corsairing did not kill off trade. The French (especially the Marseillais), the Italians, the Spaniards, the English and the Dutch, were all active. In the 17th century the French had consuls in Algiers, Tunis and Tripoli, a *funduq* in Tunis and – though these changed hands from time to time – factories at Bastion and Cap Nègre. They engaged in coral-fishing as well as trade, chiefly in cereals. At the beginning of the 18th century separate French companies trading in eastern Algeria and Tunisia merged as the Compagnie d'Afrique. The English, who at the end of the 17th century tried unsuccessfully to displace the French in Tunis, were from the end of the 16th the most important European traders in the Moroccan ports, exchanging chiefly cloth and firearms for sugar and saltpetre.

iv) *Egyptian trade with the east and south*
In the early centuries of the Arab empire the centre of gravity of Muslim trade lay in the Middle East, and it was an overland, rather than a sea-borne commerce. The sea-routes of the Mediterranean were comparatively neglected and Egypt and, still more, North Africa, were relatively peripheral. With the decline of Baghdad from the 10th century and the establishment of the independent Fāṭimid dynasty, which made a determined effort to acquire a bigger share of the trade, Egypt assumed a great importance and the route to India shifted from the Persian Gulf to the Red Sea, partly because of the disturbance to trade caused by the wars of the Seljuk Turks in the Middle East. The Fāṭimids and their successors maintained a fleet in the Red Sea for the protection of commerce. Foreign merchants, Christian as well as Muslim, took up residence in Cairo and Alexandria, each national group assigned a *funduq*, where it carried on its business, stored goods and resided. While Alexandria was the centre for the Mediterranean trade, it was Cairo that predominated in the trade with the Near, Middle and Far East.

From the south-east Egypt imported spices and drugs, precious stones, pearls, ivory, porcelain, dyestuffs, rare woods, and muslin and other cottons. Payment was made in re-exports and native products such as textiles, alum and, after the development of the industry there, paper. The Egyptians jealously maintained their position as middlemen. The trade was usually conducted through the Yemenite ports, especially Aden, which were sometimes subordinate to the rulers of Egypt, but sometimes at odds with them. In the late 12th century Christian crusaders, perhaps hoping to force their way into the eastern trade, were thwarted by Saladin in an attempt to establish themselves on the Red Sea. Christian merchants were no longer permitted to enter Egypt except for Alexandria. The Cairo *funduqs* were closed. The crusaders were, however, able to build a fortress between the Mediterranean and the Gulf of Aqaba, cutting the trade route from Egypt to Syria and the pilgrim route to Mecca. Pilgrims had to make their way to Upper

Egypt and cross the Red Sea from the port of 'Aydhab. This was also the landing place for eastern goods, which, after being brought up the Red Sea, were taken overland to Aswan or Qus on the Nile and then by river northwards. After the expulsion of the crusaders in the 13th century 'Aydhab lost some of its importance. When, in the 15th century, it was destroyed, it was succeeded by Suakin as the port for pilgrims coming from the Nile valley, while Jedda, on the other shore, replaced it as the chief Red Sea terminus for the eastern trade route. In the closing years of the Mamluk régime Upper Egypt was in a state of economic decline owing to the depredations of Arab bedouin and Beja.

To the south of Egypt, in Christian Nubia, stiffer opposition to the spread of Arab power was offered than had been the case with Christian Egypt. Nonetheless, the Nubians were compelled to pay a tribute of slaves under the terms of a treaty (Baqt) concluded in the 7th century. Although there is some doubt about the precise nature of the agreement, it appears that Nubia undertook to furnish some four hundred slaves each year, receiving in return foodstuffs, cloth and horses. The Baqt was renewed in the 10th century and continued in operation until the 13th. In the 9th century the nomadic Beja between Aswan and Dahlak were compelled to pay a tribute of camels or money. Lower Nubia was penetrated by Arab merchants and infiltrated by thousands of bedouin, often at odds with the Egyptian government, who settled in the Red Sea hills and intermarried with the Beja, eventually bringing about its incorporation into the Islamic world. The camels bred there found active employment conveying pilgrims and goods between the Nile and the Red Sea ports. The chief attraction, however, was gold. The mines were acquired by Muslim merchants and by the Fāṭimid government, and they were worked partly with local wage labour, but also, as in ancient times, by slaves.

Trade was carried on with the Nubian kingdoms, which imported, at least during the early period, wine, mass-produced Aswan pots (particularly in the 11th and 12th centuries), glassware, luxury goods of bronze, ivory, and ebony, and textiles. In return Nubia exported cattle, ivory, ostrich feathers and, above all, slaves. For these there was a growing demand for use as labourers and domestic servants and, particularly, as soldiers. There is evidence of Muslim merchants trading for slaves, not only in Nubia, but also across its southern boundaries. Egyptian rulers made punitive raids from time to time in reprisal for Nubian raids upon Egypt and gradually extended their rule and obliterated Christianity. The importation of black slaves into Egypt for military service reached a peak under the Fāṭimids. In the 11th century they were turbulent and in continual conflict with Turkish and Berber mercenaries. The Ayyubids expelled them in the 12th century, though there remained a market for slaves for other purposes.

Nubian trade was largely in the hands of Muslim merchants, except perhaps the slave trade, which may have been a state enterprise during the
Christian period, but by the end of the Middle Ages was in the hands
of private entrepreneurs. As long as the Christian kingdoms of Nubia
were strong – and even later, when unruly Arab nomads moved southwards – contact between Egypt and the further interior was restricted,
and it was the foundation of the Muslim state of Funj that facilitated commercial intercourse. A mostly indirect trade, however, did exist between Egypt
and Christian Ethiopia despite conflict between the latter and the Muslim
states of the Horn. Until the 13th century there were two routes into Ethiopia. One, entirely overland, ran to 'Aydhab – or Suakin – thence to the Nile
and was used by pilgrims going to the Holy Land and further afield. There is
some evidence of Ethiopians visiting European countries in the first half of
the 15th century and of the presence of Europeans in Ethiopia. The other,
more important, route terminated at the Red Sea coast opposite the Dahlak
islands, which were Muslim controlled and which had ties with the Yemen.
Muslim merchants frequented and even resided in Ethiopia. In the 13th
century Dahlak lost importance to the Somali towns of Zeila (Awdal) and,
to a smaller extent, Berbera on the Gulf of Aden, partly because the centre
of the Christian kingdom under the rule of the Zagwe dynasty moved to the
south, partly because vigorous but highly competitive sultanates and sheikdoms emerged in Somalia. Christians and Muslims struggled for control of
this route. Like Dahlak, Zeila was much under Yemeni influence. The
Ethiopian trade was chiefly in slaves, but also in ivory, spices, skins and amber, which were exchanged for manufactures, including Egyptian textiles
and weapons.

In the 15th and early 16th centuries Egyptian trade was overtaken by a
series of disturbances, the result of external pressures and administrative oppression, corruption and incompetence. The external threats came first
from the Turco-Mongol forces of Timur, subsequently from the expansion
of the Ottoman Turks. Short of bullion for coinage, the Mamluk sultans
resorted to currency depreciation, and in their desire to maintain their revenues for defence, they extended their monopoly control from alum to
sugar, then (in 1429) to pepper. Restrictions on private trade led to the departure of the Kārīmī merchants and their capital and to conflict with
European governments. The higher prices that the Mamluks attempted to
extort for eastern produce provided an additional incentive, if one were needed, to the Portuguese search for an alternative route to the east, the opening
of which disrupted for a time the established pattern of trade.

The opening of the route to the orient via the Cape of Good Hope had an
adverse effect upon Egypt's trade with India and the Far East. After Vasco
da Gama landed in India, the Portuguese proceeded to seize ships, bombard

the Malabar coast and establish themselves in strategic positions. The Mamluks, thoroughly alarmed, unsuccessfully endeavoured to drive them off. In 1509 their fleet was destroyed at Diu. In the first years of the 16th century few shipments of spices travelled by the traditional routes. But although throughout the century Portugal was a match for any enemy on the high seas, her monopoly was short-lived. A permanent exclusion of others or even a requirement that other ships obtain a licence and pay customs duties was beyond her powers. She failed to capture Aden, and Socotra, tried as a substitute, was not adequate for an effective blockade of the Red Sea. The Mediterranean spice trade revived, partly because the old routes had decided advantages over the new. The Ottoman Turks overthrew the decadent Mamluks, and were much more effective in ensuring control of the eastern trade. They captured Aden in 1538, and with it the command of the Red Sea. Very large quantities of pepper were reaching Cairo in the middle of the 16th century. The Egyptian transit trade remained subject to fluctuations because of political events, such as the war between the Ottomans and the Venetians, but it was generally prosperous until the 17th century. The Venetians continued to be very active in the spice business. They and France had consuls at Alexandria. Richard Hakluyt's 'Notes concerning the trade in Alexandria', describes the position at the end of the 16th century.

> Commonly the Caravans come thither in October from Mecca to Cairo, and from thence to Alexandria, where the merchants be that buy the spices, and therefore the spices are brought most to Alexandria, where each Christian nation remaineth at the Consuls houses. Yet oftentimes the christians go up to Cairo to buy drugs & other commodities there, as they see cause. And the commodities there vendible are all sorts of kersies, but the most part blewes, and of clothes all colours except mingled colours and blacks. Pepper is usually sold for 24 ducats the quintal, Ginger for 14 ducats. You must take canvas to make bags to put your commodities in from Alexandria, for there is none.[4]

It was when the Dutch destroyed Portuguese dominance in the eastern trade early in the 17th century, gained control of the spice-producing areas in the East Indies and diverted trade round the Cape, that Egypt ceased to be an important entrepôt for oriental products. At the same time the power of the Ottomans in the Red Sea declined. They lost Aden in the 17th century. The population of Alexandria, believed to have been almost a third of a million in the Roman era, sank to some four thousand by 1800.

During this same period, in the 16th, 17th and 18th centuries, the local trade of north-east Africa also experienced a number of vicissitudes. Political instability in Ethiopia and the Muslim principalities and the depredations of the Portuguese and Turks interfered with its exercise. There was something of a commercial revival in the late 17th century, chiefly associated with the export of Yemeni coffee, which attracted Indian and European merchants.

Zeila and Berbera, where a fair was held every year, retained their medieval importance, providing an outlet for the trade of the sultanate of Harar, which emerged in the 17th century. However, because of the decline of Egypt and the turbulence of the Ethiopian hinterland of the Red Sea, trade was stagnating by the end of the 18th century.

v) *The trans-Saharan trade*
The trade of the 'Great Desert' was a very ancient one, carried out under conditions of great risk and hardship. For the Sahara covers an area more extensive than Europe, is only sparsely endowed with springs and is intersected by mountain ranges, such as the Tibesti Air and the Hoggar. In classical times the trade was comparatively modest and casual, subject to warlike interruptions as Carthaginians or Romans clashed with nomads and as nomads fought the settlers of the savanna. Since Carthage and Rome were able to draw upon other sources of gold and slaves, their interest was limited. The trade quickened after the introduction of the camel, helping to bring an Indian summer of commercial prosperity to Tripolitania during the reign of the Emperor Septimius Severus in the late 2nd and 3rd century A.D., and more particularly after the expansion of the power of the Arabs, who displayed a keen interest in the gold trade. Camel-borne Berber tribesmen roamed the Sahara and forged a link between the north and the south, a link that was greatly strengthened when Islam became the religion common to them, to the traders of the Maghrib and to the traders and rulers of the Sudan. The growth of the empires of the Sudan – Ghana, Mali and Songhai – was both a consequence of and an impetus to the trade. From the 13th century the important states of the western Sudan had Muslim rulers.

The variety of commodities traded across the Sahara was limited partly by the length of the journey – the desert part alone taking over six weeks – which meant that highly perishable goods could not be taken, and partly by the high transport charges, which are said to have at least doubled the cost of most goods carried and meant that it was worth while to carry only things of small bulk and high intrinsic value. It was a trade that met the limits of growth much more quickly than ocean trade, with which it has so appositely been compared. While even wooden ships constantly grew in size and there was virtually no physical limit to the size of fleets, desert traffic could expand only to the extent of the availability of food and water for the vast number of traders, guides, drivers and slaves that made up the caravans, as well as fodder and water for the camels. It had to be a very large caravan that could bear as great a volume of goods as a single vessel.

The main northward-bound goods were gold, slaves, cotton cloth, pepper, ivory, kola nuts, hides, skins and leather goods and, in the 19th century, ostrich feathers. René Caillé speaks of the two portions into which the products of West Africa destined for the north were divided in the early 19th century. The first

> consisted principally of matters of alimentation, such as millet, rice, karite butter, manioc, peanuts, honey, kola nuts, neta, baobab flour, monkey bread, tamarinds, onions and tobacco (cheaper and inferior to that of Tuat), dried fish, and in addition, soap, iron, antimony, cotton, straw hats, potteries, and calabashes. The other portion was specially allotted to Morocco, Tuat, and Ghadames, and comprised gold, ivory, ostrich plumes, raw leather, wax, incense, civet musk, indigo, gum, etc., and a few slaves.[5]

A 12th-century description of one section of the trade, from Aghmat in Morocco, shows the sort of commodity that went southwards.

> The people of Aghmat are wealthy merchants. They go to Bilad al-Sudan with many camels loaded with rich merchandise of copper, red and other colours, garments, woollen clothes, turbans, aprons, all kinds of beads of glass, shell or stone, varieties of spices and perfumes, as well as manufactured iron tools. Their slaves and agents go in caravans of seventy to a hundred camels, all loaded.[6]

To this list should be added a certain amount of foodstuffs (dates, wheat, even dried grapes and nuts), swords and horses, and, probably, before the 16th century, centres of Muslim learning, such as Timbuktu, were importing books too. Many of the goods were imported from Europe, which in turn was the final purchaser of many of the north-moving goods. To the products of Europe and North Africa were added the salt of the Saharan mines of Teghaza and Idjil.

Gold was the most valued West African export and the Muslim world was heavily dependent upon it for its monetary needs from the 10th century and even earlier. It dominated the trade of the western Sahara. Slaves were the staple in the eastern and central Sahara. Fezzan was an important staging post for slaves from the central Sudan. The size of the trade, which continued until late in the 19th century and even after, has been variously estimated – at 20 000 a year in the later Middle Ages, more than 100 000 a year in the 16th century and 10 000 a year in the early 19th century. There is evidence at widely different dates of caravans composed of several hundred slaves, and Kano alone in the mid-19th century was thought by a contemporary visitor to be exporting five thousand a year. Some writers claim that a large proportion of the slaves remained within the Sudan, where they were employed mostly in agricultural production, and that therefore the interior slave trade was less damaging economically than the Atlantic trade, which entailed a total loss of productive labour. Certainly the ordeal of the Sahara crossing was no less hideous than the so-called middle passage of the ocean, with a mortality rate estimated by some to have been in the order of 20 per cent in the 19th-century caravans. Others have put losses very much higher, exceeding survivals.

The Sahara was criss-crossed with trade routes that, starting from the trading towns of the Maghrib on or near the Mediterranean coast (for example, Fez, Tlemcen), passed through towns on the northern edges of the desert (such as Sijilmasa, Ghadames and Zawila in Fezzan) and the southern edges (such as Walata and Agades), where the camel caravans were assembled and disbanded at start and finish, and through desert oases (such as those of Touat and Kufra), where refreshment was available, and ended at the various trading towns of the western Sudan. In the early centuries of the trade, before the spread of Islam among the Sudanese peoples, the Muslim Berber towns on the southern edge of the desert provided a useful base where Arab and Berber traders from the Maghrib felt at home in their trade with the Sudan. Such were Audaghost and Tadmekka, which were respectively in close relationship with Kumbi Saleh, the capital of Ghana, and with Gao, at one time part of the empire of Mali and then capital of the Songhai empire that succeeded it. Walata, on the other hand, which became an important trading town at the beginning of the 13th century, had a mixed population of Berbers and Sudanese, accustomed to each other through centuries of contact and united by a religion that had become common to them both. Similarly, Timbuktu, originally a Tuareg settlement and eventually incorporated into the empire of Songhai, second only to Gao in importance, had a cosmopolitan population, though the most prominent citizens in trade and religion were Berber. Only five or six kilometres from the Niger, Timbuktu had an advantage denied to Walata and Audaghost, that of carrying on a vigorous trade by river with both Jenne (like Timbuktu a Muslim town, but Sudanese, not Berber) upstream and with Gao downstream.

Some of the Saharan routes were more important than others and their importance varied over the years as the fortunes of the termini rose and fell in conformity with political changes both in the desert and north and south of it. A tug-of-war was fought between the Maghribian and Sudanese states for control of the trade. There existed too a struggle among the states of the Maghrib to get hold of the northern termini, and the ability of the state, for the moment in the ascendant, to police the trade routes, varied. The Almoravids were able to exercise sufficient authority in the desert to promote trade, and, indeed, they restored peace to Morocco after a long period of dynastic and tribal strife and interference with trade. The Almohads, on the other hand, seem to have been unable to ensure security along the western routes. South of the desert, Mali reached its zenith in the 13th and 14th centuries and extended its authority over the Sahel, gaining the upper hand in the battle for control of the routes. In the 15th century its authority over its northern provinces weakened and its control was disputed in the 16th century by both Songhai, its successor in the Sudan, and the Sa'did rulers of Morocco. In the central Sudan, Kanem in the 13th century was able to impose its rule on Fezzan, its outlet to the north, but could not maintain its position at such a distance. Distance was the enemy of every attempt by any political power to assert authority on the far side of the desert.

In the long run, though with many ups and downs, the eastern routes proved more enduring than the less formidable western ones. The prosperity of the routes depended partly upon that of the Sudanese kingdoms particularly associated with them. As Ghana, Mali and Songhai developed and then declined, the routes terminating at Audaghost, Walata and Timbuktu prospered in turn. The fact that Mali, or at least its centre of power, lay further to the east than Ghana, and Songhai and the long enduring and resilient Kanem-Bornu still more easterly, helps to explain the tendency for the eastern routes to displace the western ones in significance. Another influence at work was the activities of Arab nomads, the Banu Hilal and the Banu Maaqil, the latter overrunning southern Morocco in the 13th century and attacking caravans on the western routes. Additional factors were the attraction of the desert salt mines and the prosperity of the trading towns of the Maghrib, such as Tahert (which declined in the 10th century), Sijilmasa at the foot of the High Atlas (much fought over until its eventual disappearance to all intents and purposes in the 17th century), Tlemcen (very well-off in the 13th and 14th centuries, not least because of its connection with Europe as well as the Sudan), Aghmat and Fez (established in the 8th century as the capital of the Berber Idrisids), all of which went through many vicissitudes that had mostly a political origin. The route to Tunisia was enhanced in importance in the 13th century during the rule of the Hafsids, who maintained a stable government at a time when the central and western Maghrib were in a turmoil with the dissolution of the Almohad caliphate, and who conducted a brisk trade with Europe as well. The stability of Tunisia at that period coincided with the flourishing of the kingdom of Kanem, which also commanded routes to Tripoli and Egypt.

Gold and other West African exports made their way from the northern Saharan termini along the edge of the Tell across the Libyan desert via Awjila to Egypt. A more direct route to Egypt, an extension of those which had been used by caravans to Kufra and other oases in the western desert at least as early as Roman times, had some importance in the earlier Middle Ages until it fell into disuse, evidently in the later 9th century, because of its hazards – sandstorms and attacks by desert nomads. Few Egyptian merchants made their way to the central and western Sudan, and there was little direct exchange of products. Egyptian interest in the Sudan revived in the 14th century, perhaps as a result of the visit to Cairo by the king of Mali, Mansa Musa, on his way to Mecca. As sources of gold hitherto open to them, notably Nubia, became exhausted, the Egyptians were attracted by West African gold. In exchange they exported textiles. Although Egyptian slavers were active in the western Sudan, slaves did not feature prominently amongst Egyptian imports, presumably because the Mamluks were uninterested in black servile troops, and Nubia and Ethiopia were a more convenient source of slaves for domestic work. No doubt slaves were imported from the Sudan, though that region was itself a slave importer, buying Turkish and Ethiopian boys and girls. Such was the extent of, principally, the gold and fabric exchange, that in the 14th-century caravans with up to 12 000 camels are reported to have travelled between Egypt and Mali. The route from Egypt, after passing through Awjila, split in Fezzan, one branch going to Kanem-Bornu via Bilma (a source of alum), the other to the Niger via Ghat and Touat (after the 15th century, Air). The European demand for gold, the chief Egyptian interest, diverted it increasingly away from Egypt, but trade between Egypt and Fezzan continued at least until the 18th century.

In the 16th century the trans-Saharan trade encountered a certain amount of competition from Portuguese trading posts established on the West African coast, and it suffered some disruption with the overthrow of the Songhai empire by a Moroccan army sent by El Mansour in 1591. There is not much evidence to suggest that the opening of overseas trade in West Africa had an immediate or catastrophic effect upon the economy of the interior. It had little impact at first outside the forest and the river basins, and even there it was often subordinate to the trade of the interior. Trans-Saharan trade, including the trade in gold, survived even the Moroccan on-slaught. Although by the 18th century the routes from Morocco were less frequented, those to Tunisia, Fezzan and Egypt from Kanem-Bornu re-mained profitable after the Ottoman empire asserted its hegemony over the eastern Maghrib in the 16th century, and they grew in importance from the 17th. Even Morocco continued to import black slaves as soldiers in the 17th and 18th centuries.

The Bornu-Fezzan route retained its importance until the 1830s, when the whole Chad region was racked by warfare and Tripoli, the Mediterranean terminus, by internal dissension. The Turks were no longer able to protect the trade route, which at times was impassable owing to the mutual hostility of the Tuareg and Tibu of the Sahara. During the course of the century a route from Ghadames to Kano via Air attained importance, largely because of the establishment of the powerful Fulani empire of Sokoto. Another development was the emergence of the Cyrenaica-Kufra-Wadai route, discovered early in the 19th century, but of importance in the second half of the century, when the Sanūsīya brotherhood brought peace to the warring bedouin tribesmen along the route. It was this one that survived all the others, even-tually brought to an end by the spread of French and Italian rule in the early years of the 20th century. The more westerly routes were adversely affected by the construction of railways in West Africa, which directed trade rather to the coast than to the desert, and by the gathering momentum of the campaign against slavery. Slaves predominated amongst the commodities moving north, with ostrich feathers, then very fashionable in Europe, and ivory next in importance. Arms and ammunition and textiles, particularly cotton goods, were the chief southward-moving commodities.

NOTES

1. Strabo: *Geography*, II, 5, 12, quoted Fraser, P. M.: *Ptolemaic Alexandria* (Oxford, 1972), Volume I, p. 184
2. Hakluyt, Richard: *Voyages* (London, Everyman edition 1907), Volume III, p. 121
3. Quoted Fisher, Sir Godfrey: *Barbary Legend: War, Trade and Piracy in North Africa 1415–1830* (Oxford, 1957), p. 142
4. Op. cit., Volume III, p. 124
5. Quoted Skinner, Elliott P.: 'West African economic systems' Herskovits, M. J. and Harwitz, M. (eds.): *Economic Transition in Africa*, (Chicago, 1964), p. 96
6. Al-Idrisi, quoted Levtzion, N.: *Ancient Ghana and Mali* (London, 1973), p. 141

Further reading

Adams, William Y.: Op. cit., (see p. 104)
Arkell, A. J.: *A History of the Sudan, from the Earliest Times to 1821* (London, 1955)
Bovill, E. W.: Op. cit. (see p. 46)
Braudel, Fernand: *The Mediterranean and the Mediterranean World in the Age of Philip II*, Volume II (London, 1972)
Charles-Picard, Gilbert & Colette: Op. cit. (see p. 46)
Collins, Robert O. (ed.): *Problems in African History* (Englewood Cliffs, New Jersey, 1968)
Cook, M. A. (ed.): *Studies in the Economic History of the Middle East from the Rise of Islam to the Present Day* (Oxford, 1970)
Cordell, Dennis D.: 'Eastern Libya, Wadai and the Sanūsīya: a ṭarīqa and a trade route' (*Journal of African History*, XVIII, 1977, p. 21–36)
Culican, William: *The First Merchant Venturers, the Ancient Levant in History and Commerce* (New York, 1966)
Fisher, A. G. B. & Fisher, H. J.: Op. cit. (see p. 65)
Fraser, P. M.: Op. cit. (see note 1)
Goitein, S. D.: *A Mediterranean Society* (see p. 114)
Gray, Richard (ed.): *The Cambridge History of Africa*, Volume 4, *From c.1600 to c. 1790* (Cambridge, 1975)
Hasan, Y. F.: *The Arabs and the Sudan, from the Seventh to the Early Sixteenth Century* (Edinburgh, 1967)
Heyd, W.: *Histoire du commerce du Levant au moyen âge* (Leipzig, 1936)
Hintze, Fritz & Ursula: *Civilizations of the Old Sudan, Kerma, Kush, Christian Nubia* (Leipzig, 1968)

154   AN ECONOMIC HISTORY OF AFRICA

Holt, P. M., Lambton, Ann K. S. & Lewis, Bernard: Op. cit. (see p. 84)
Johnson, Allan Chester: Op. cit. (see p. 47)
Levtzion, Nehemia: Op. cit. (see note 6)
Lewis, A. R.: *Naval Power and Trade in the Mediterranean A.D. 500–1100* (Princeton, 1951)
Mathew, Gervase: 'The East African coast until the coming of the Portuguese' (Chapter IV, Oliver, Roland and Mathew, Gervase eds.: *History of East Africa*, Volume I, Oxford, 1963)
Miller, J. Innes: *The Spice Trade of the Roman Empire 29 B.C. to A.D. 641* (Oxford, 1969)
Mollat, Michel (ed.): *Sociétés et compagnies de commerce en orient et dans l'Océan indien* (Paris, 1970)
Pirenne, Henri: *Mohammed and Charlemagne* (London, 1939)
Warmington, B. H.: *The Commerce between the Roman Empire and India* (London, 1974)

3. WEST AFRICA

i) *The trade of the interior*

The trade of West Africa was of great significance, but because of its ramifications throughout the whole north-western part of the continent it is difficult to distinguish the intra-regional trade from the trans-Saharan trade and the coastal trade with European merchants that developed from the 15th century. The most valuable staples were gold, slaves and ivory, and these were destined largely, though certainly not exclusively, for North African or European purchasers. There were, however, other products exchanged over limited distances, not drawn into what might loosely be called international trade, or at least lacking the same importance as gold, slaves and ivory in international commerce; and there were trading centres which were not direct participants in international trade, or at least in which international trade was not dominant.

To some extent the interchange of products among desert, desert margin, savanna, forest and coast was a trade in foodstuffs – rice, yams, cattle, sheep, goats, dried fish, palm oil and palm wine. The desert oases could not meet their own food requirements, and some of the great trading towns in the western Sudan, like Timbuktu and Walata, were substantial food importers. Jenne, on the other hand, at the south-eastern end of the fertile and densely populated inner delta of the Niger, exported agricultural produce as far as the salt-producing centres of the Sahara. At the end of the 17th century William Bosman commented on the production of and trade in foodstuffs along the coast. He found the inhabitants of Axim on the Gold Coast

industriously employ'd either in Trade, Fishing, or Agriculture, and that is chiefly exercised in the Culture of *Rice*, which grows here above all places in an incredible abundance, and is Transported hence all the Gold-Coast over. The Inhabitants in lieu returning full Fraught with *Millet, Jammes, Potatoes*, and *Palm*

Oyl; all which are very rare here, for the Soil is naturally moist, and tho' fit to produce *Rice*, and Fruit-Trees, doth not kindly yield other Fruits.[1]

An important forest product was the kola nut, exchanged for, among other things, shea butter, a savanna product. A mild stimulant not forbidden to Muslims, it came chiefly from the north of what is now Ghana. Its use spread to Hausaland, in the north of modern Nigeria, from Nupe, in the region of the confluence of the Niger and Benue rivers, evidently in the first half of the 15th century. By the middle of that century Dyula merchants were engaged in the trade. The route between the state of Gonja, which controlled the supply not only of kola nuts but also of gold from the Akan forest, and Hausaland, along which the nuts were brought, was of increasing importance as their popularity was extended to the Sudan, the Sahara and North Africa. In Hausaland, Kano became a major distribution centre. The trade statistics of that city compiled by Henry Barth in the middle of the 19th century are instructive.

Volume, Value, Type, Source and Destination of Goods in Kano Market, 1851

Product	Volume (per year)	Value (Millions of cowries)	Source and Destination
Cloth	300 camel loads	60	Kano area to Timbuktu
Kola nuts	500 ass loads	80–100	From forest zone for shipment north to Sudan zone
Natron	20 000 loads		From Bornu to Nupe and Nyffi
Salt	1 000 camel loads	50–80	Salt merchants from Sahara bought Kano merchandise
Ivory	100 'Kantars'	Not an important item – less than 100 000 cowries	
Coarse silk	300–400 camel loads	70	From Tripoli by way of Ghadames
Woollen cloth		15	
Calicoes & prints		40	Bleached and unbleached from Manchester via Ghadames. Some dyed and re-exported

Product	Volume (per year)	Value (Millions of cowries)	Source and Destination
Sugar	100 camel loads	12	
Wrapping paper		5	Probably from France
Needles & mirrors		8	Formerly from Nuremberg, lately from Leghorn
Sword blades	50 000	50	Most blades sold out of the country to neighbouring groups
French silks		20	Imported and re-exported to Yoruba country and Gonja
Arab clothes		60	From Tunis and Egypt, but some from Leghorn
Beads		50	
Frankincense, rose oil, spices & cloves		55	Many of these luxury items for princes
Copper & zinc	70 loads	15–20	From Tripoli and Darfur
Leather products, e.g. sandals		15	
Slaves	5 000	150–200	Sold mainly to American slave dealers. American produce found in Nupe market.

(Source: Elliott P. Skinner, 'West African economic systems', Chapter 4 Melville J. Herskovits and Mitchell Harwitz, eds., *Economic Transition in Africa*, Chicago, 1964, p. 90–1)

Copper, supplies of which were supplemented from beyond the desert and beyond the ocean, was highly prized. Its main source was Takedda in the neighbourhood of Agades, south-west of the Air massif. It was visited by Ibn Baṭṭūta in 1352.

There are no grain crops there except a little wheat, which is consumed by merchants and strangers. The inhabitants of Tagaddá have no occupation except
trade. They travel to Egypt every year, and import quantities of all the fine fabrics to be had there and of other Egyptian wares . . . The copper is exported
from Tagaddá to the town of Kúbar, in the regions of the heathen, to Zagháy,
and to the country of Bornú, which is forty days' journey from Tagaddá.[2]

When Takedda went out of production, it was succeeded by a mine lying
to the south of Darfur, Hofrat en Nahas.

Salt was produced at Bilma in Kawar, which supplied the Lake Chad
area, perhaps from early in the Middle Ages, and Hausaland evidently from
the middle of the 15th century; Teghaza, north-west of Timbuktu; Idjil in
the Adrar, which became important in the 15th century; and Taoudeni, said
to have furnished Timbuktu with fifty or sixty thousand camel loads a year
in the late 19th century. Timbuktu was, of course, an important terminus
of the trans-Saharan trade long before the 19th century and even in the Middle Ages enjoyed an important commercial intercourse by river with Jenne.
The latter was a distribution point for salt to the gold mining areas. Marine
salt came from the Niger delta, among other places.

Perfumes, such as civet, from Hausaland and Bornu; ambergris from the
coast; and ostrich feathers (incorporated into the regalia of many African
monarchs) from the Sahara and the Sudan were all used within West Africa,
as well as being exported further afield.

In the forest area, as in the savanna, trading centres of some importance
developed. Dyula merchants had a settlement by the later 15th century in
Begho, a source of gold, just north of the Akan forest. Two other centres that
had similar communities were Bobo-Dioulasso and Kong, both situated between Jenne and Begho and both of importance in the gold and kola nut
trade. In a later period the development of Kumasi, the capital of the 18th-
century Asante empire, owed much to its position as a junction of trade
routes coming from the interior and from the coast. Ife, it seems likely, paid
with slaves in the later Middle Ages for the metal it imported for its celebrated bronzes and brasses, as well as for the salt and other commodities it
required. Benin, further to the south than Ife, was better placed for participation in the trade of the coast, but clearly had some trading relations with
the north by the time Europeans arrived. There is evidence of an export of
locally manufactured cotton goods to the western Sudan in exchange for
copper and horses. A late 16th-century description left by an observer from
Europe gives some idea of the variety of goods exchanged at one of the two
big Benin markets.

Pepper and elephant teeth, oyle of palms, cloth made of cotton woll very
curiously woven, and cloth made of the barke of palm trees were procured in

exchange for cloth both linen and wollen, iron works of sundry sorts, Manillos or bracelets of copper, glass beades and corrall . . . They have good store of soap and it smelleth like beaten vilets – Also many pretie fine mats and baskets that they make, and spoones of elephants' teeth very curiously wrought with divers proportions of foules and beasts made upon them.[3]

South of the Gulf of Guinea, in west Central Africa, trade and urbanization were much less developed. The reason for this was chiefly the sparseness of the population and the long distances between communities. Nowhere was this more so than in the southern savanna, where, however, it is likely that some sort of trade took place between Stone Age hunters and Iron Age farmers, an exchange of the products of the hunt for pots, food and iron tools. A partial exception to a situation of little or no trade was in the area immediately to the south of the tropical forest belt. Here there were states at least partly dependent upon trade. In the kingdoms of Kongo, Ndongo and Loango a brisk trade was carried on, not only in salt, iron and copper, the staples of sub-Saharan trade, but also in textiles, pottery and basketry. A currency of nzimbu shells, blocks of salt and standardized lengths of palm cloth was in use. Further south, across the Kwanza river, the Ovimbundu kingdoms emerged possibly in the 17th century, certainly in the 18th. Bihé, the most easterly of these, seems to have had a local exchange in iron products and pots. Most of the trade of the western region of Central Africa was, however, rudimentary, indirect rather than direct, seasonal, and without markets, currency, full-time merchants or manufacturing for exchange. It grew in volume and complexity when it became linked to overseas trade.

ii) *The Portuguese*
The Portuguese, who broke into West African trade in the 15th century, were attracted principally by the hope of obtaining gold. At the beginning of the century they were desperately short of it. Unable to mint gold coins, they had to make do with a coinage struck from an alloy composed of copper with a little silver. Muslim coins, struck in Morocco from West African gold, circulated in their country (continuing to do so until well into the 16th century), and the Portuguese, aware possibly before, certainly after, the capture of Ceuta in 1415, of the trade in the precious metal carried on in the Moroccan markets, wanted direct access to it. The exploratory voyages along the west coast of Africa were aimed at by-passing the trans-Saharan routes. The first gold dust, obtained from nomads, was brought back in 1442, and in 1445 a 'factory', or trading depot, was established on Arguin Island, south of Cape Blanco and close to the flourishing trading towns of the Mauritanian Adrar, north of the River Senegal. It was the terminus of an existing trading route along which merchants came in search of coastal salt. After a brief period of indiscriminate enslavement of the fishermen who inhabited

the coast, the Portuguese settled down to trade. For a short time they tried to set up an entrepôt in Wadan in the Mauritanian Adrar, but because of the hardships of the desert and the hostility of the population they abandoned it, maintaining instead a modest trade from Arguin, chiefly in gold, ivory and slaves.

At its peak Arguin exported on average some twenty to twenty-five kilograms of gold to Portugal each year, but it was of declining importance as the Portuguese made their way further along the coast nearer the sources of gold. In 1444–1445 the Senegal river was reached and Cape Verde rounded. The Senegal, though abundant in slaves, was a disappointment as far as gold was concerned. It was on the Gambia, navigable for small trading vessels further inland than the Senegal, that the Portuguese made contact, at Cantor, with Mandingo (Mandinka) merchants bringing gold from the interior. They were able to purchase a further twenty to twenty-five kilograms of gold a year, maintaining that level of export for more than a century. In Sierra Leone, on the River Scarcies, an additional, though small, amount of very fine, locally produced gold was obtained by way of trade. But gold, though the most valued, was not the only commodity sought. Apart from slaves and ivory, there were hides and skins, wax, gum, dye woods and pepper. In return the Portuguese exported horses, cloth (European, North African and local), metal utensils, manillas, tin and beads.

The administrative centre and commercial entrepôt of Senegambia and the coast stretching as far as modern Liberia (an area known as Upper Guinea) was Santiago, the capital of the Cape Verde Islands, which the Portuguese had colonised early in their process of exploration. The islanders themselves went in for trade, cattle raising and the manufacture of cloth. Dyes and cotton were grown on the spot; silk and wool, for mixing with the locally produced cotton, imported from Europe. This cloth was exported to the mainland – in return for slaves for re-export – where it was preferred to European-made textiles. Cloth and dyes, as well as hides and livestock, were exported to Europe and the New World.

To encourage settlement on the Cape Verde Islands the government at first permitted the colonists to trade freely with the mainland. In time many of them settled there, as well as other Portuguese, including exiled convicts. They lived dispersed throughout the villages of the region, dealing with the ruling class of kings, chiefs and noblemen and placing themselves under the protection of the local ruler, with whom they enjoyed a host-guest relationship regulated by customs with reciprocal rights and obligations. Intermarriage was common, and those who merged with local society and adopted local customs were called lançados. Associated with them were Africans, frequently slaves originally, known as grumetes. The lançados were required to make 'gifts' to their patrons, but, on the other hand, enjoyed their protection. The relationship was not always harmonious, and as time went by hosts were more and more exacting in their demands.

The Portuguese authorities disliked and discouraged the tax-evading lançado, preferring to keep settlement to the off-shore islands, where it was easier to maintain control. Stern measures were taken against the private traders on the mainland and restrictions were placed on the trade of the Cape Verde Islands, where most of the lançados came from. Eventually they were forbidden altogether to trade on the Upper Guinea coast. These restrictions, however, were not effective. The Cape Verdeans continued to trade and the number of lançados increased. In time the attitude of the authorities softened, partly because the lançados, however much mistrusted, performed a useful function even for Portuguese trading enterprise.

The nature of the trade on the Upper Guinea coast favoured the lançados. There was no government fortress further south than Arguin and only a royal factor at Cacheu in modern Guinea-Bissau. Trade was carried on by ships calling at various, widely separated, places along the coast. Upper Guinea had a network of rivers and, although their upper reaches were too swift and shallow to be navigable, in the flat coastal plain tributaries were close together and formed a complex system facilitating communications north-west to south-west by canoe and short portages. The function of the lançados was to scour the rivers and creeks in small boats and assemble slaves and goods at the coast. They had little capital of their own and took trade goods on credit from European ships. Their willingness to deal with ships of all nationalities, since Portuguese prices were high and their range of goods limited, was one reason for the hostility of the authorities towards them.

After reaching the Ankobra and Volta rivers in 1471, the Portuguese obtained from this region (El Mina or the Gold Coast) a much greater supply of gold. There they persuaded a reluctant ruler to permit the construction of São Jorge da Mina in 1482 and thither they aimed to send a ship monthly. An annual rate of twelve vessels was maintained, or nearly so, in the latter part of the 15th century and the early part of the 16th. Thereafter the number of vessels making the voyage tended to fall off, but nonetheless large, though fluctuating, amounts of gold continued to reach Portugal.

GOLD FROM THE GOLD COAST ENTERING THE LISBON MINT

Year	Number of Ships	Weight of Gold (22, 125 carats)
1517	8 caravels	423, 492 kilograms
1518	12 caravels	483, 700 kilograms

Year	Number of Ships		Weight of Gold (22,125 carats)
1520	9 caravels		464,755 kilograms
1521	9 caravels		428,644 kilograms
1523	6 caravels		300,326 kilograms
1524	5 caravels		283,967 kilograms
1525	3 caravels		205,861 kilograms
1526	7 caravels		247,673 kilograms
1528	5 caravels		222,934 kilograms
1529	5 caravels		211,484 kilograms
1530	2 caravels		150,113 kilograms
1531	4 caravels		212,492 kilograms
1532	11 caravels	1 carrack	679,545 kilograms
1534	2 galleons	4 caravels	271,796 kilograms
1540	1 galleon	7 caravels	392,399 kilograms
1543	2 galleons	7 caravels	349,037 kilograms
1544	4 caravels		141,594 kilograms
1549	2 galleons	4 caravels	167,653 kilograms
1550	1 galleon	2 caravels	154,866 kilograms
1551	3 galleons	1 caravel	211,624 kilograms
1553	1 galleon	1 caravel	94,182 kilograms
1555	4 galleons	1 caravel	377,581 kilograms
1556	1 galleon	1 caravel	242,435 kilograms
1560	2 galleons	1 caravel	143,640 kilograms
1561	1 galleon	2 caravels	144,622 kilograms

(Source: Vitorino Magalhães-Godinho, *L'économie de l'empire portugais aux XVe et XVIe siècles*, Paris, 1969, p. 216)

There was a marked difference between Portuguese activity in Lower Guinea (the region between Cape Palmas and the Niger delta) and that in Upper Guinea. Imports and exports were much the same, but the organization of the trade was different. In Lower Guinea there was no dispersal of lançados and only a limited penetration of the interior, partly because the area was beyond the influence of the Cape Verde Islands, where most of the lançados originated. Trade was carried on very much on African terms. A few trading posts were established on the coast, but they were there on sufferance. São Jorge da Mina was fortified more for the purpose of restricting illicit trade by other Europeans than as a threat to the African peoples. These were organized in powerful states, particularly Benin and, in the interior, those of Yorubaland and the Akan, which were capable of with-standing Portuguese intervention. Not only were they powerful in political terms, but they also had economies sufficiently robust and adaptable to meet the relatively modest additional demands made upon them by overseas trade. When the Portuguese arrived there were already well-established commercial links with the interior as far as the middle Niger in the western Sudan, and the Portuguese were content to make use of existing trade ar-rangements, confining themselves to their trading posts, round which how-ever, considerable black and mulatto communities developed.

Lower Guinea was divided into four sections, each named after its prin-cipal export; the Grain Coast (named after malagueta pepper, 'grains of paradise') (modern Liberia), the Ivory Coast, the Gold Coast and the Slave Coast (from the River Volta to the Niger delta). The Portuguese had little contact with the Grain and Ivory Coasts, where there were no natural har-bours, but strong off-shore currents and frequent storms. They also had little to do with the stretch of coast between the River Volta and Lagos (modern Togo and Benin). They were attracted chiefly to the Gold Coast because of its nearness to the sources of gold, though they were also active on the coast between Lagos and the Niger delta (the western part of modern Nigeria), especially, at first, the kingdom of Benin. This coast offered safe anchorages, and access to the interior was offered by rivers and creeks. It supplied pepper and ivory.

Benin had certain political and religious attractions. The Portuguese hoped that the king would be susceptible to Christianity and prove an ally against Islam. They established a trading post there at Ughoto (Gwato) in 1486, thirty kilometres from Benin city. In addition to pepper and ivory, slaves were obtained for re-export to the Gold Coast for work as porters and goldminers. Beads and cloth were bought for the local trade. But Benin proved to be something of a disappointment. Ughoto was given up after some years, partly, perhaps, because it was unhealthy. It also ceased to be worthwhile. The king was not very co-operative, and withdrew his per-mission to export male slaves. With the opening of the trade with the east the pepper of West Africa ceased to be thought worth buying.

iii) *The slave trade*
The first consignments of slaves from Africa were destined for agricultural work in Portugal, where there was a shortage of labour, and slaves con-tinued to be imported into the metropolitan country until 1761. There was, moreover, always a market for domestic slaves among settlers throughout the Portuguese empire, who owned them by the dozen or even by the hundred for reasons of ostentation. Sometimes slaves were used by the Por-tuguese as irregular soldiers. It was, however, the demand for plantation

labour that kept the slave trade going on the scale that it attained. From the early years of the 16th century there was a growing demand for labour in the sugar plantations established by the Portuguese on islands off the coast of Africa, particularly Fernando Po, São Thomé and Principe in the Gulf of Guinea. More important, however, was the eventually almost insatiable demand from the plantations and mines of the Caribbean and South America.

The Portuguese soon learnt to get their slaves by regular commercial dealing, as the kidnapping methods employed at first proved to be self-defeating. As early as the 1460s there was a regular supply acquired from Senegambia and the Upper Guinea coast. Santiago on the Cape Verde Islands was the entrepôt. Subsequently, slaving was extended to Lower Guinea and to the Congo and Angola, with São Thomé as the entrepôt. The early, relatively small, slave trade stayed largely in Portuguese hands until in the 1630s the Dutch West India Company launched a vigorous attack upon the Portuguese position with the primary aim of supplying slaves to the sugar plantations of Brazil, which the Company was trying to wrest from the Portuguese. After serious setbacks, Portugal managed to expel the Dutch from Brazil by 1654. She did not, however, succeed in re-establishing herself on the Gold Coast, nor did she ever again enjoy predominance in Upper Guinea.

Despite their reverses, the Portuguese continued to be very considerable slave traders, and they kept the trade up longer than any other European nation. Their Brazilian tobacco was very popular with African dealers. But they were supplanted as the chief slavers by the Dutch, who became the biggest purveyors of slaves to the Spanish Indies and the newly-settled English and French planters in the Caribbean. From the middle of the 17th century their leading position was in turn challenged by English, French, Danish, Swedish and Brandenburger companies, and individual merchants. Planters in America and the West Indies, expanding production to meet growing demand in Europe, always had difficulty in compensating adequately for the constant wastage of their slave populations. Of the major slaving countries, Britain, France, Holland and Portugal, it was the French and British who came to be chief rivals. In 1713 Britain won the right to supply the Spanish colonies in Central and South America with slaves, the asiento, and during the course of the 18th century their share of the Gold Coast slave trade enlarged progressively, while that of the Dutch correspondingly diminished as their general commercial position deteriorated.

In 1618, in Upper Guinea the English established a fort on James Island, near the mouth of the Gambia, and by the early 18th century their Royal African Company maintained several factories on the river, with factors, clerks, artisans and soldiers. Mungo Park described the English Gambian trade at the end of the 18th century, when it was at a low ebb.

The commodities exported to the Gambia from Europe consist chiefly of fire-arms and ammunition, iron ware, spirituous liquors, tobacco, cotton caps, a small quantity of broad cloth, and a few articles of the manufacture of Manchester; a small assortment of Indian goods, with some glass beads, amber and other trifles: for which are taken in exchange slaves, gold dust, ivory, bees' wax, and hides. Slaves are the chief article . . .[4]

This had not always been so. Richard Jobson, on the Upper Gambia early in the 17th century, on being offered slaves by an African merchant, had

made answer, We were a people, who did not deale in any such commodities, neither did wee buy or sell one another, or any that had our owne shapes; he seemed to marvell much at it, and told us, it was only merchandize, they carried downe into the countrey, where they fetcht all their salt, and that they were solde there to white men, who earnestly desired them, especially such young women, as hee had brought for us: we answered, They were another kinde of people different from us.[5]

Jobson, though chiefly interested in gold, took ivory, cotton yarn, and locally produced cloth and gave in exchange salt and iron. Slaves, however, did come to predominate later.

The French were well-established on the Senegal and also had interests on the Gambia. Their chief post was St. Louis, founded in 1659, and they ran a number of outstations, some of them formerly Portuguese, then Dutch. Profits were disappointing, seldom covering the costs of exploration and administration, mainly because of the relative paucity of slaves available. The population between the Senegal and the Gambia was sparse and there was competition in the interior from African slave traders, Fulani and Mande. The Senegal region was exploited as a rule by a nationally chartered company. Beyond its limits, however, trade was left to private traders who operated along the formidable Ivory and Grain Coasts, where they dispensed with the facilities of forts and factories required by the companies, and further afield, along the Gold Coast, and east as far as the Gabon.

Trade on the Gold Coast was intensely competitive. Some two dozen or so European forts and factories (not counting smaller trading posts) were crammed into the area. To begin with gold was as big an attraction as slaves, but in the 18th century traders were finding it necessary to use gold for the purchase of slaves. The Portuguese were doing so with Brazilian gold at Whydah on the Slave Coast early in the century. As they had done during the period of Portuguese predominance, African middlemen controlled the landward side of the trade.

As the demand for slaves continued to grow, increasing attention was paid to the Slave Coast, which had been largely neglected by the Portuguese after they had lost interest in Benin. Slavers were also attracted to the area still further to the east, the Niger delta, then known as the Oil Rivers. The coast between Benin and the Cameroons was the most important source of slaves in West Africa by the end of the 18th century. When Britain withdrew from the business and began to campaign against it, the intricate waterways of the Niger delta provided a useful means of evading naval patrols. The trade all along this coast, as on the Grain and Ivory Coasts, was mostly in the hands, not of large monopolistic companies, but of individuals and small companies. European forts were supplemented by ports run by African rulers, who provided facilities that had to be paid for in the form either of taxes or of higher prices. The busiest ones were Whydah and Bonny and Old Calabar on the Niger delta. Whydah, a slaving port from the latter part of the 17th century until the middle of the 19th, was annexed in 1727 by the king of Dahomey, who went in for both the capture of slaves and their sale. Old Calabar, on the other hand, remained an independent port during its two centuries of slaving. It was under the direction of the Efik people, who obtained most of their slaves from suppliers in the interior. Its government and the supervision of its trade became concentrated in the hands of an oligarchy of merchants, the elected heads of the so-called canoe houses, the trading houses specializing in slaving.

From the 16th century the Congo and Angola were important sources of slaves, which were however, considered inferior to the Sudanese captives sold on the Slave Coast. Those coming from further south were destined at first for the Portuguese-settled African islands, subsequently for the Caribbean and, more particularly, for Brazil, where there was a steady demand from the sugar plantations of Bahia and Pernambuco throughout the 17th century. At the end of that century the discovery of gold in Brazil, in the area given the name of Minas Gerais, greatly increased the demand, though a smallpox epidemic in Angola in 1685–1687 made it somewhat difficult to meet. The trade was in the hands partly of Europeans and partly of Africans. After they had established an effective presence on the coast, the Portuguese authorities sold slave export licences to slaving firms. Contractors and subcontractors employed local agents, who normally commissioned African or mulatto *pombieros* to scour the country for slaves. Accompanied by their domestic slaves carrying trade goods, they were absent for more than a year at a time, trading with local chiefs. Another source was the land granted to Portuguese settlers. Chiefs living on Portuguese estates were required to pay taxes, and these often took the form of slaves. The Portuguese were not above slave raiding themselves, but for the most part they had to rely on African intermediaries.

A trade route was established from the mouth of the River Congo at Mpinda, which was, until 1571, the official Portuguese embarkation port, where export taxes were levied, to the Kongo capital, Mbanza, renamed São

Salvador, and extended after 1530 to Stanley Pool. This was the chief route until the end of the century, when direct communication was opened between Luanda and Stanley Pool and between Loango and Stanley Pool. The latter route was controlled by a coastal people, the Vili, who provided the Portuguese and later the Dutch with the ivory which was their chief early interest. As the elephant herds near the coast were exterminated, the Vili extended their trading into the interior. Copper was another of their interests. Slaves, however, came to take first place. By the mid-18th century the Vili were travelling in search of them hundreds of kilometres into the interior, up the Congo, north-eastwards and southwards. As the supply increased, other European trading posts were set up on the coast, such as Cabinda and Malemba to the south of Loango.

The Portuguese also dealt with the Imbangela, who provided slaves and ivory, obtained by trade and tribute, in exchange for firearms, palm cloth from Loango and salt from mines situated at Kisama. The Imbangela kingdom of Kasanje and the Mbundu kingdom of Mutamba controlled the area between the Kwanza and the Kwango rivers and long prevented Portuguese attempts to penetrate beyond the Kwanza. By the middle of the 17th century Kasanje was in contact with the Lunda kingdom of the Mwata Yamvo, situated in the area of the Kasai and Lulua tributaries of the Congo. The Mwata Yamvo himself engaged in trade. Katanga copper, as well as slaves, passed along the trade routes to the west coast.

Another people that engaged in the slave trade were the Ovimbundu, whose main centre was Bihé, to the south of Luanda, in Benguela. The members of this tribe obtained, in addition to slaves, wax and ivory from the Chokwe, who dwelt further to the east. They too extended their operations into Central Africa, where they came into contact with the Imbangela. They remained important slave traders until well into the 19th century, their caravans travelling early in the second half of the 19th century as far as Tete on the lower Zambezi.

iv) *The economic consequences of the slave trade*
A recent estimate of the movement of enslaved persons from Africa puts the total throughout the entire period of the Atlantic slave trade within the range of eight to ten and a half million, though an estimate of the total losses through this enforced emigration would also have to take into account deaths suffered through, among other things, slave raids and deaths at sea (reckoned at an average of 15 per cent of those embarked). The

> eighteenth century was a kind of plateau in the history of the trade – the period when the trade reached its height, but also a period of slackening growth and beginning decline. The period 1741–1810 marks the summit of the plateau, when the long-term annual average rates of delivery hung just above 60 000 a year.

TRADE 167

The edge of the plateau was reached, however, just after the Peace of Utrecht in 1713, when the annual deliveries began regularly to exceed 40 000 a year, and the permenent drop below 40 000 a year did not come again until after the 1840s. Thus about 60 per cent. of all slaves delivered to the New World were transported during the century 1721–1820. Eighty per cent. of the total were landed during the century and a half, 1701–1850.[6]

Almost all the slaves were destined for the Americas, overwhelmingly for South America and the West Indies. Rather more than half of the slaves despatched across the Atlantic came from West Africa, in particular the area between the Gold Coast and the Cameroons, the rest from the Congo, Angola and Mozambique. Little is known about the precise districts from which the slaves were drawn, but they seem to have come from both densely and sparsely populated places, from the coastal region and the interior. The major, but not the only, factor appears to have been the extent to which some people had the will and the strength to become predators, and others the ability to defend themselves. It is imprudent to dogmatise about the demographic consequences. Not enough is known about the population loss of particular societies in specific periods. Generally speaking, although depopulation was characteristic of some areas, the African population as a whole displayed a remarkable capacity for recovery. The Ibos, for example, remained a numerous people despite the drain of the slave trade. It might be argued that qualitatively Africa was deprived of the best of its youth; equally that those who were sold into slavery were incapable of preserving even their own independence.

Some Slave Trade Statistics

VOLUME OF SLAVE TRADE BY NATIONAL CARRIER, 1761–1810

Carrier	Exported		Imported
Britain	1 535 622	(1 385 300)	1 428 701
13 Colonies/USA	294 900	(166 900)	265 410
Portugal	1 055 700	(1 010 400)	950 130
France	595 881	(545 300)	539 379
Netherlands	116 416	(173 600)	102 097
Denmark	59 896	(56 800)	53 906
Total	3 658 415	(3 338 300)	3 339 623

Source: Roger Anstey, 'The slave trade of the continental powers, 1760–1810' (*Economic History Review*, 2nd ser, XXX, 1977, p. 259–68), p. 267 P. D. Curtin's estimates in brackets. (See Note 6.)

INFERRED EMBARKATION OF SLAVES; AFRICAN REGION OF EMBARKATION BY INTENDED AMERICAN REGION OF IMPORTATION, SELECTED YEARS, 1821–1843

	Western Guinea	Bight of Benin	Bight of Biafra	Congo North	Angola	Southeast Africa	Total
Cuba							
1821–25	3 773	3 629	6 140	—	—	—	13 542
1826–30	7 255	4 355	9 210	—	—	—	20 820
1831–35	5 804	5 806	14 326	2 033	3 025	—	31 004
1836–40	21 475	18 145	16 373	4 878	2 601	11 130	74 602
1841–43	3 773	3 992	341	2 439	—	557	11 102
1821–43	42 080	35 927	46 390	9 350	5 636	11 687	151 070
Brazil North							
1821–28	2 223	1 289	1 721	1 344	3 203	557	10 337
1831–38	317	644	—	—	10 677	—	11 638
1839–43	635	322	—	1 008	249	3 339	7 795
Bahia State							
1821–28	—	1 933	—	2 015	—	—	3 948
1826	—	1 933	—	2 687	712	—	5 332
1827	794	4 511	334	2 687	1 068	—	9 396
1831–43	794	14 499	334	—	1 068	—	16 695
Brazil South							
1831–35	—	—	334	407	4 077	557	6 038
1836	—	—	668	—	15 610	3 336	19 614
1839	—	336	—	10 163	22 113	14 469	47 081
1840	264	—	337	6 098	9 973	7 791	24 463

Source: David Eltis, 'The export of slaves from Africa, 1821–1843' (*Journal of Economic History*, XXXVII, 1977, p. 409–33), p. 419.

NUMBER OF SLAVES SHIPPED FROM LUANDA, 1723–1771

Year	No. of Ships	No. of Adults	Total Slaves (Adults & Children)
1723	18	6 704	—
1724	17	6 108	—
1725	22	6 726	—
1726	22	8 321	8 440
1727	20	7 539	7 633
1728	21	8 418	8 532
1731	16	5 715	5 808
1734	25	8 713	10 109
1738	19	7 623	8 810
1740	22	8 075	8 484
1741	23	8 268	9 158
1742	24	10 207	10 591
1744	20	8 256	8 848
1747	25	8 328	9 869
1748	30	10 815	11 810
1749	25	8 895	9 776
1758	24	9 799	9 938
1762	22	8 268	8 415
1763	21	7 525	7 634
1764	18	7 500	7 648
1765	27	10 394	10 672
1766	25	9 237	9 420
1767	26	9 228	9 318
1769	17	5 651	5 733
1771	21	7 591	—
TOTALS	550	203 904	186 646 *
Average slaves per ship		371	396
Standard Deviation		109	111

*The total number of ships for adult and children slaves was 471.

Source: Herbert S. Klein, *The Middle Passage, Comparative Studies in the Atlantic Slave Trade* (Princeton, N.J., 1978), p. 28.

The economic consequences of the trade have been a matter of some dispute. Its cruelty is beyond doubt. Mungo Park described slaves on the Gambia.

> Most of these unfortunate victims are brought to the coast in periodical cara-
> vans; many of them from very remote inland countries . . . On their arrival at
> the coast, if no immediate opportunity offers of selling them to advantage, they
> are distributed among the neighbouring villages, until a slave-ship arrives, or
> until they can be sold to black traders, who sometimes purchase on spec. In the
> meanwhile, the poor wretches are kept constantly fettered, two and two of them
> being chained together, and employed in the labours of the field; and, I am sorry
> to add, are very scantily fed, as well as harshly treated.[7]

This, of course, was only a preliminary to the savagery of their treatment at
the hands of the European merchants, beginning with their branding. 'This
is done,' wrote the Dutchman, William Bosman, describing arrangements
at the Gold Coast at the beginning of the 18th century,

> that we may distinguish them from the slaves of the *English, French* or others;
> (which are also marked with their Mark) and to prevent the *Negroes* exchanging
> them for worst; at which they have a good hand.[8]

Hitherto, because of the inhumanity of the trade, any debate upon its possible economic advantages, in the form of the development of trade routes
and of African entrepreneurship and capital accumulation, has been obscured
by a cloud of moral indignation, and it is only recently that it has been
thought proper to suggest the existence of economic gains. The trade was
carried on very much on terms decided by the African middleman. 'The
English at Annamabo', wrote William Bosman,

> are horribly plagued by the *Fantynean Negroes*, that they are sometimes even con-
> fined to their Fort, not being permitted to stir out. And if the *Negroes* dislike the
> Governour of the Fort they usually send him in a *Canoa* in contempt to *Cabocars;*
> nor are the *English* able to oppose or prevent it, but are obliged to make their Peace
> by a Present . . . Besides that this Land is so populous, it is very rich in Gold, Slaves
> and all sorts of Necessities of Life; but more especially Corn, which they sell in
> large Quantities to the *English* Ships: This great Opulency has rendered them so
> Arrogant and Haughty, that an *European* who would traffick with 'em is obliged
> to stand bare to them . . . The *Negroes* of *Fantyn* drive a very great Trade with
> all sorts of Interlopers, and that freely and boldly in the sight of both Nations;
> I mean the *English* and *Dutch*, neither of them daring to hinder it: For if they
> should attempt it, 'twould ruin them there, we not having the least Power over
> this Nation . . .
> From what I have said you may be informed what places the *English* and we
> possess in *Fantyn*, both of us having an equal Power, that is, none at all. For when
> these villanous People are enclined to it, they shut up all the Passes so close that

not one Merchant can possibly come from the In-land Country to trade with
us, and sometimes not content wi' this, they prevent the bringing Provisions to
us, till we have made Peace with them . . .[9]

The disadvantages of the slave trade are more obvious than its alleged advantages. They include internecine warfare that wasted resources and ingenuity and discouraged agriculture. The majority of slaves were war captives and slaving was a perennial source of fighting. Direct capture was supplemented by tribute, itself a consequence of the strong imposing their will
upon the weak, and by the punishment of offenders. Ancient customs and
sanctions, it has been argued, were abused in order to manufacture criminals
for sale as slaves, and the more innocent indigenous kind of slavery was
transformed into a degraded enslavement for export. Indeed, it has even
been argued that, far from being grafted on to an existing system of slavery
and internal slave trade, the external slave trade created indigenous slavery
in coastal society. There was an unholy alliance between European slavers
and a small African clique which, with a high marginal propensity to import
luxuries, used the profits of the slave trade to purchase the horses and weapons
that secured its position of superiority, as well as undesirable commodities
such as alcohol. Even innocuous imports such as textiles competed damag-
ingly with local products, with the result that the technological gap between
Africa and Europe, confined in the 15th century to shipping and firearms,
widened to such an extent that African technology failed to progress. Instead of having beneficial effects on the economy as a whole, foreign trade
warped internal development. The local economy was subordinated to the
interests of Europe.

The indictment of Europe comprises three charges: African societies were
demoralized by the appetite for slaves; local trade was often taken over or
even destroyed by European middlemen, particularly the coastal trade; and,
most important, in the commercial relationship established between Africans
– with their restricted knowledge of the outside world – and Europeans –
with their monopoly of transport overseas and their superior information
about world markets – the former were the victims of an 'unequal exchange'.
This, on the one hand, furnished Europe with capital for industrialization and,
on the other, led to the 'underdevelopment' of the African continent. There
is a celebrated passage in Marx powerfully summarising this point of view.

The discoveries of gold and silver in America; the extirpation of the indigens
in some instance, their enslavement or their entombment in the mines in others;
the beginnings of the conquest and looting of the East Indies; the transformation
of Africa into a precinct for the supply of the negroes who were the raw material
of the slave trade – these were the incidents that characterised the rosy dawn of
the era of capitalist production. These were the idyllic processes that formed the
chief factors of primary accumulation.[10]

According to one explanation of underdevelopment, which sees the relationship between the more industrialized nations and their trading partners as a
nexus between centre and periphery, with the periphery being the helpless
captive drained of its resources for the benefit of the core, Africa was merely
the periphery of a periphery, the latter, the plantation economy of America,
being itself subordinate to mercantilist Europe. Africa exported wasting
assets – gold, ivory and human beings – while Europe accumulated capital,
industrialized and flooded Africa with manufactured goods. As soon as it
ceased to serve their purpose, the dominant economic interests in Europe,
giving way gracefully to humanitarian sentiment, agreed to the abolition
of the slave trade.

Perhaps the disadvantages of the slave trade for Africa have been unduly
stressed. It did not kill off the existing interior trade and may even have been
of marginal significance to it. 18th-century Kumasi, capital of the Asante
confederation, though dealing with Europeans on the coast, arguably had
more important trading contacts with the cities of the upper and middle
Niger and Hausaland. In some measure foreign slavers on the coast
and slave caravans in the interior provided a market for agricultural
produce, while locally produced textiles became a significant item in
trade in which Europeans participated. Traditional industries, such as
weaving and iron working, maintained their importance until well into
the 19th century and even later. The alleged unfortunate impact of European
contact upon African technology seems therefore somewhat questionable.
Indeed, the proposition often made that the gap between European and
African technology was narrow is difficult to accept even for the 15th century. The science and technology embodied in a European ship of that
period represented a superiority that can scarcely be confined merely to
shipbuilding. To some, though perhaps meagre, extent the slave trade helped
to reduce the technological gap. Africans were trained in European skills
for service in the European forts, and no doubt these skills were passed on.

The fact of unequal exchange can hardly be doubted. Ignorant people did
part with their goods sometimes for a paltry return. It was not, however,
Europeans dealing with shrewd merchants on the coast who benefited.
Major Dixon Denham accompanied an Arab caravan (kafila) to Lake Chad
in 1823.

> About two in the afternoon we arrived at Lari, ten miles distant from Mitti-
> mee. On ascending the rising ground on which the town stands, the distressing
> sight presented itself of all the female, and most of the male inhabitants, with
> their families, flying across the plain in all directions, alarmed at the strength of
> our kafila . . . It was long before Boo-Khaloom's best endeavours could restore
> confidence: the inhabitants had been plundered by the Tauricks only the year be-
> fore, and four hundred of their people butchered; and but a few days before, a

party of the same nation had again pillaged them, though partially. When, at length, these people were satisfied that no harm was intended them, the women came in numbers with baskets of gussub, gafooly, fowls, and honey, which were purchased by small pieces of coral and amber of the coarsest kind, and coloured beads. One merchant bought a fine lamb for two pieces of amber, worth, I should think, about twopence each in Europe; two needles purchased a fowl; and a handful of salt four or five good sized fish from the lake.[11]

Such evidence as there is seems to suggest that Europeans engaged in the slave trade made but a modest profit, scarcely of the magnitude to make a significant contribution to the capital requirements of industry, even assuming that money made in trading slaves found its way to the industrial entrepreneurs of the 18th century.

NOTES

1. Howard, C. (ed.): *West African Explorers* (London, 1951), p. 50
2. *Travels in Asia and Africa 1325–1354* (London, 1929), p. 335–6
3. Quoted Skinner, Elliott P.: 'West African economic systems' (Herskovits, Melville J. and Harwitz, Mitchell eds.: *Economic Transition in Africa*, Chicago, 1964), p. 86
4. *Travels* (London, 2nd edn. 1954), p. 18
5. Howard, C.: Op. cit., p. 42
6. Curtin, P. D.: *The Atlantic Slave Trade, a Census* (Madison, Wisconsin, 1969), p. 265
7. *Travels*, p. 18
8. Howard, C.: Op. cit., p. 71
9. Ibid, p. 56–8
10. *Capital* I (Everyman edn., London, 1930), p. 832
11. Howard, C.: Op. cit., p. 176–7

Further reading

Amin, Samir: *Accumulation on a World Scale, a Critique of the Theory of Underdevelopment* (New York and London, 1974), 2 volumes
Amin, Samir: 'Underdevelopment and dependence in black Africa – origins and contemporary forms' (*Journal of Modern African Studies*, X, 1972, p. 503–524)
Anstey, Roger: *The Atlantic Slave Trade and British Abolition, 1760–1810* (London and Basingstoke, 1975)
Anstey, Roger & Hair, P. E. H. (eds.): *Liverpool, the African Slave Trade, and Abolition. Essays to Illustrate Current Knowledge and Research* (Historical Society of Lancashire and Cheshire Occasional Series Volume 2, 1976)
Birmingham, David: *Trade and Conflict in Angola 1483–1790* (Oxford, 1966)
Blake, John William: *European Beginnings in West Africa, 1454–1578* (London, 1937)
Boxer, C. R.: *The Portuguese Seaborne Empire, 1415–1825* (Harmondsworth, 1973)
Craton, Michael: *Sinews of Empire; a Short History of British Slavery* (London, 1974)
Curtin, P. D.: *The Atlantic Slave Trade; a Census* (Madison, 1969)
Davies, K. G.: *The North Atlantic World in the Seventeenth Century* (Minneapolis, 1974)

Davies, K. G.: *The Royal African Company* (London, 1957)
De Gregori, T. R.: Op. cit. (see p. 83)
Donnan, Elizabeth: *Documents Illustrative of the Slave Trade to America*, 4 volumes (Washington, 1930–1935)
Duffy, J. E.: *Portuguese Africa* (Cambridge, Mass., 1959)
Dunn, Richard S.: 'Quantifying slavery and the slave trade' (*Journal of International History*, IX, 1978, p. 147–150)
Fage, J. D.: *A History of West Africa, an Introductory Survey* (Cambridge, 1969)
Frank, Andre Gunder: *World Accumulation 1492–1789* (London and Basingstoke, 1978)
Klein, Herbert S.: *The Middle Passage, Comparative Studies in the Atlantic Slave Trade* (Princeton, N. J., 1978)
Latham, A. J. H.: *Old Calabar, 1600–1891: the Impact of the International Economy upon a Traditional Society* (Oxford, 1973)
Levtzion, N.: Op. cit. (see p. 153, note 6)
Magalhães-Godinho, Vitorino: *L'économie de l'empire portugais aux XVe et XVIe siècles* (Paris, 1969)
Martin, P. M.: *The External Trade of the Loango Coast 1576–1870* (Oxford, 1972)
Martin, P. M.: 'The trade of Loango in the seventeenth and eighteenth centuries' (Gray, R. and Birmingham, D.: Op. cit. – see p. 131)
Oliver, Roland (ed.): *The Cambridge History of Africa*, Volume 3, *c.1050–c.1600* (Cambridge, 1977)
Rodney, Walter: 'Africa in Europe and the Americas' (Chapter 9, Gray, R.: *The Cambridge History of Africa*, Volume 4 – see p. 153)
Rodney, W.: 'African slavery and other forms of social oppression on the Upper Guinea coast in the context of the Atlantic slave trade' (*Journal of African History*, VII, 1966, p. 431–443)
Rodney, W.: 'The Guinea coast' (Chapter 4, Gray, R.: *The Cambridge History of Africa*, Volume 4 – see p. 153)
Rodney, W.: *A History of the Upper Guinea Coast 1545–1800* (Oxford, 1970)
Rodney, W.: *How Europe Underdeveloped Africa* (London and Dar es Salaam, 1972)
Vansina, Jan: *Kingdoms of the Savanna* (Madison, 1966)
Vansina, Jan: 'Long-distance trade-routes in Central Africa' (Collins, R. O.: Op. cit. – see p. 153)
Williams, Eric: *Capitalism and Slavery* (London, 2nd edn. 1964)
Wyndham, H. A.: *The Atlantic and Slavery* (London, 1935)

4. EASTERN AND SOUTHERN AFRICA

i) *The medieval trade of East Africa*

Egypt seems to have had no trading interests in the East African coast beyond Zeila. Further south the survivors of the emporia described in the *Periplus* and by Ptolemy, adopted Islam, and before A.D. 1000 new settlements were founded that were either Muslim from the beginning or subsequently became so. The Cushitic-speaking Somali – known to the Arabs as black Berbers – inhabiting the African shore of the Gulf of Aden and the Benadir coast (the Horn of Africa south of Cape Guardafui) remained in close commercial contact with Arabia and the Persian Gulf and probably adopted

Islam from as early as the 8th century. Arabian and Persian merchants settled in towns like Zeila, Berbera, Mogadishu, Merca and Brava. Mogadishu, indeed, may have owed its origin to immigrants from the Persian Gulf in the 10th century, and there appear to have been further migrations from Yemen and the Persian Gulf later on. At all events, it seems to have had a heterogeneous population and to have led the way in developing the gold trade with Sofala, near modern Beira. In the 13th century it became the centre of a sultanate.

South of the River Juba the littoral is more inviting than the Benadir coast. It attracted immigrants from the harsher lands of South Arabia and the Persian Gulf, or at least settlers of Yemeni and of Persian – so-called Shirazi – origin from the Benadir coast, people engaged in the gold trade. Settlers also colonised the Comoro Islands and north-west Madagascar. After the loss of contact between Roman Egypt and East Africa, the Bantuspeaking people had moved into the coastal region and for the most part absorbed its inhabitants. For Arab geographers the East African coast, at least as far south as Pemba, was the land of Zanj, the land of the black people. Arab travellers and 16th-century Portuguese intruders unite in describing the inhabitants of the trading towns – other than recent arrivals and visiting merchants – as black, so that the Arab and Persian or Shirazi immigrants, who no doubt gave ruling dynasties to many of them, must have been absorbed into the Bantu-speaking population. Nonetheless, close cultural and commerical ties persisted between even the most southerly of the East African towns and Arabia. Their lingua franca was Swahili, a Bantu tongue modified by Arabic, and Arabic was the official language in documents and remained so until the 16th century.

By the 13th century, the settlements, by then wholly Muslim and numbering between thirty and forty, were spread out between Kilwa in the south and Mogadishu in the north, more numerous on the Somali coast, and further south frequently situated for the sake of convenience or possibly defence on larger (for example, Zanzibar) or smaller (for example, Kilwa) islands. They enjoyed a considerable prosperity founded on trade, chiefly with Yemen and the Persian Gulf, but also directly or indirectly with Egypt, India, Indonesia and China and with one another. Finds of Chinese coins and porcelain and Chinese documentary evidence testify to a sporadic direct trade carried on by Chinese vessels, and certainly to more regular indirect links. Indian merchants took up residence and exerted a profound influence. Conversely, merchants from the East African coast are known to have frequented Malacca at the beginning of the 16th century, and it is possible that there were sailings, as there had been in ancient times, directly from Java to East Africa. There is evidence of trade between Madagascar and East Africa and between Madagascar and the Gulf of Aden.

The chief exports from the Horn of Africa were frankincense and myrrh and from further south, ivory, which was prized in India and China, and gold, a large part of which came from the empire of Mwene Mutapa via the coast around Sofala. Slaves from more notherly latitudes are known to have been sent from the 12th century as far as China, and other exports included mangrove wood from the Rufiji river and further north, ambergris, rhinoceros horn, tortoise shell and skins, that is, unprocessed primary products, but also copper from Sofala, iron smelted in Mombasa (and probably Malindi and perhaps elsewhere), cotton cloth manufactured in Mogadishu, which found a market in Egypt, and silk made at Pate. Cloth for interior trade was made at Kilwa. Cloth, glassware, porcelain, perfume, beads and pottery of various qualities were imported from Egypt, Arabia, Persia, India, China and elsewhere at different periods, and such imports, especially cloth and beads, spread far back from the coast. The beads, including at first beads made on the coast from sea shells, may well have been used as money in the intra-African trade. Kilwa seems to have been a rice exporter to Aden, or possibly re-exported rice from Madagascar.

Not all the East African settlements had direct relations with Arabia, the Persian Gulf and India. Some centres – particularly Kilwa and Mombasa – were entrepôts serving the others through coastal trade. One reason for this was the uncertainty of the monsoon, which restricted traders to the shortest journeys and precluded visits to the more remote parts. The southern part of the East African coast was dominated between the early 14th century, when it displaced Mogadishu in the Sofalan gold trade, and the late 15th century by Kilwa, the authority of which at its height ran as far as Mafia Island in the north and Sofala in the south. South of Sofala, traders operated as far down as Pondoland. The prosperity of Kilwa – indeed, of the entire coast – was based largely upon access to the ivory and gold of the interior.

To the north of Mafia Island there was a series of small rulers, the most important of whom was, perhaps, by the end of the 15th century, the sultan of Mombasa, a port well-placed for both ocean-going and coastal trade. According to Portuguese estimates of the 15th century Mombasa had a population of 10 000, compared with Kilwa's 4 000, though the latter figure may have been very much higher. Malindi, rather more than a hundred kilometres north of Mombasa, was its chief rival in the northern part of the coast. These mainland settlements were compelled to import grain from along the coast to supplement a diet of locally produced bananas and fish. The bigger off-shore islands – Pemba, Zanzibar and Mafia – were by contrast largely agricultural, producing rice and coconuts, but were on the whole less wealthy than the trading towns of the mainland.

Trade between the coast and the interior and between different points in the interior was very ancient, though undoubtedly to begin with it was indirect, with goods passed from hand to hand and on a small scale. In northern Tanzania, five hundred kilometres from the coast, marine shells have been found in Stone Age burial sites dating from before the birth of Christ. Early Iron Age sites of the later 1st millennium A.D. have yielded small numbers of shells, shell beads and glass beads of exotic manufacture, for example, Mabveni in modern Zimbabwe, Kumadzulo near Victoria Falls, Sanga on Lake Kisale in Shaba. Ivory and perhaps gold were reaching the coast by the 10th century A.D. Most early trade between coast and hinterland seems to have been confined to the region between the Zambezi and the Limpopo.

The staples of internal trade were salt, copper and gold. Salt was the basis of trade at Ingombe Ilede, an iron-using agricultural settlement near the confluence of the Zambezi and Kafue rivers, occupied during the last two or three centuries of the 1st millennium A.D. and reoccupied, according to archaeological evidence, in the 14th and 15th centuries. It commanded large salt deposits. Another salt-trading centre was Ivuna, near Lake Rukwe in modern Tanzania. Artifacts of copper, gold and iron excavated at Ingombe Ilede and Sanga indicate the existence of a trade in these materials, since there were no local sources. The various-sized cross-shaped ingots, bars and standardized lengths of wire, all of copper, that have been found at these sites and at others further south may have served a quasi-monetary purpose. Great Zimbabwe, the centre of political power between the Zambezi and the Limpopo, was in its heyday a considerable importer of luxury goods of both local and overseas origin.

There was a great expansion of trade between the interior and the coast in the 14th century. By then, possibly earlier, Muslim traders were going up the Zambezi to Tete and beyond, purchasing gold with silk and cotton cloth, carpets, ceramics and glassware, mostly for the use of a political élite. The export of gold reached a peak in the late 14th and early 15th century. After that, not so very long before the Portuguese arrival in East Africa, it suffered a severe blow through the disintegration of the Mwene Mutapa's empire.

ii) *The Portuguese*
The arrival of the Portuguese on the East African coast at the end of the 15th century had a catastrophic effect upon the prosperous Muslim towns. Though economically advanced, they were politically divided, and the Portuguese were able to take advantage of differences among their Arab rulers. In 1498 Vasco da Gama was able to establish friendly relations with Malindi, which was at odds with Mombasa, and in 1502 he installed his own nominee as sultan of Kilwa. Violence and intimidation were freely employed. Kilwa, Mombasa and Brava were devastated at various times for failing to pay

tribute. Fortresses were built at Sofala and on the island of Mozambique, the latter intended as a trade centre and refreshment station for ships going to India and also as a local base for blockading the coast against Muslim traders. The Portuguese hoped to take over the valuable Sofala-Mozambique trade and use its profits for the purchase of oriental spices, but their intervention served only to disrupt it through the suppression of the Muslim middlemen. Preferring force to commerce, the Portuguese did not have the numbers to sustain a policy of effective coercion, despite the military superiority which usually enabled them to gain the upper hand in any trial of strength.

The northern Portuguese headquarters was fixed first at Malindi, but because of the inadequacy of its harbour during the north-east monsoon, the encroachment of the sea upon the land and the general decline of the town's prosperity, the Portuguese moved to Mombasa in 1593, which had two good harbours and an off-shore island that was fertile, comparatively salubrious and defensible. North of this the Portuguese had some influence over the Bajun islands, especially Pate, but they exercised no real authority over the Arab towns situated on the shores of Somalia. South of Mombasa they had a varying degree of control of the off-shore islands, such as Mafia, Zanzibar and Pemba, and their most southerly place of interest was Kilwa, where they had a fort at first and to which they afterwards occasionally sent a factor in search of trade, but the town was mostly in ruins after its sacking by the Portuguese and the loss of the Sofalan gold trade. Sofala was the furthest southern permanent settlement on the coast. Its authority extended no more than a few kilometres from the fortress.

The plight of the Arabs was parlous after the arrival of the Portuguese. Although they could survive only by means of trade, the gold trade was no longer open to them. Dhows had to furnish themselves with passports before putting to sea in the north-western Indian Ocean and, although it was often inconvenient or impossible to obtain them, any ship without one ran the risk of seizure by a Portuguese vessel, confiscation of its cargo and the imprisonment or enslavement of its crew. Such measures greatly reduced the volume of traffic between the Persian Gulf, India and East Africa. The requirement that all imports be taken to Mombasa to pay customs duties was regarded as an injustice, forcing up prices of goods and postponing the arrival of goods at towns north of Mombasa. The competition of Portuguese factors reduced Arab trade still further. The Africans of the coast, on the whole, preferred the Arabs to the Portuguese. They had built up commerical relations with them and many found Islam an acceptable religion, though others took to Catholicism just as readily. There was a general decline in the economic well-being of the coastal towns in the 16th century, with some exceptions, such as Pate. Although this deteriorating situation has been attributed entirely to

Portuguese depredations, other factors had some influence, notably the
turbulence of the interior and possibly a fall in the level of the watertable,
which posed difficulties.

The chief Portuguese trading interest was gold, to a lesser extent ivory.
Slaves were obtained, but there was no great demand for them. There was
also some traffic in amber, coral, copper, pearls, rhinoceros horn and hooves,
and hippopotamus teeth and hooves. To pay for these goods the Portuguese
principally imported Indian manufactures, notably cloth and beads.

In the interior the Portuguese took over, in an effort to secure control
of the gold trade, the Muslim posts at Sena and Tete in the Zambezi valley.
Trade in the 16th century was conducted on the terms dictated by the Mwene
Mutapa and by the rulers of Uteve and Manyika, who controlled the area
around Sofala. The conditions of trade towards the end of the 16th century
were described by Father João dos Santos.

Sena is a Fort of Lime and Stone, furnished with Artillery; the Captayne is
placed by the Captayne of Mosambique. There were in my time eight hundred
Christians, of which, fiftie Portugalls. Seven or eight leagues from hence on the
other side of the River, is the high Hill Chiri, which may be seene twentie leagues
off, the Hill and Valleys exceeding fertile. To this Factory of Sena, they come
from Tete to buy Merchandize with their Gold.

Tete is a stone Fort sixtie leagues further up the River in the Kingdome of
Inhabaze, under the Manamotapa, the Captayne is placed by the Captayne of
Mosambique. In this place were in my time sixe hundred Christians, of them for-
tie Portugalls. These one hundred and twentie leagues the Portugalls goe up the
River, and from thence goe by Land with their Merchandize. The Countrey is
very fertile, and Portugall wares are here sold at great prizes. From Tete they goe
with their wares thorow a great part of Manamotapa to three marts, Massapa,
Luanze, Manzovo, in which the Inhabitants of Sena, and Tete have houses and
Factories, thence to store all the Countrey.

Massapa is the chiefe, where resides a Portugall Captayne, presented by the
Portugalls, and confirmed by the Manamotapa, which cals him his Great Wife,
a name of honour, as before is observed. This Captayne holds jurisdiction over
all the Cafres without Appeale, as also over the Portugalls in that Kingdome,
granted by the Vice-Royes, as all other Captaynes of those parts have. This Captayne of Massapa treats all businesse with the Manamotapa, whose Customer he
is also, taking one cloth of twentie, in which respect the Countrey is free to them.
But beyond Massapa, neerer the Manamotapa, (no) one may goe without license
from the King or the Captayne . . . The Captayne of Mosambique payes at his
entrance to the Manamotapa, three thousand Cruzados in goods for the three
yeares of his Captayne-ship, for free Trade in his Countreyes, which they may
travell securely laden with Gold; it beeing never known that Theeves assaile
them, or any without the Kings authoritie . . .

Neere to Massapa is a great high Hill, called Fura, whence may bee discerned
a great part of the Kingdome of Manamotapa: for which cause he will not suffer
the Portugalls to goe thither, that they should not covet his great Countrey and
hidden Mines . . .[1]

The 'Portugall Captayne' at Massapa was called the 'captain of the gates' by the Portuguese and one of his functions, as Father dos Santos explains, was to act as the 'Customer' of the Mwene Mutapa, that is to collect the customs duties – one cloth in twenty – from Portuguese traders on his behalf.

Subsequently the Portuguese took advantage of succession disputes and tribal rivalries to intervene more effectively in the interior. By supporting one or another African leader, they obtained mineral rights in the territories of the Mwene Mutapa in 1607, and in 1633 they reduced him to vassalage. Their trading posts were extended as far as the upper Sanyati river. Plans were made for introducing settlers from Portugal, peasants and artisans, but they amounted to little in the event, and there was not much settlement other than the substantial estates of the prazo-holders.

Portuguese rights in the far interior tended to be somewhat illusory and, in any case, with the decline of the power of the Mwene Mutapa and the rise of the Rozwi, they lost their position. Consequently, they sought gold north of the Zambezi. In 1714 they set up a market at Zumbo, at the confluence of the Zambezi and Luangwa rivers, and in 1732 another post called simply the Fair – Feira – across the latter river. Gold was obtained from south of the Zambezi and locally, and, in the course of time, copper and ivory were brought in too from increasingly further afield. These commodities were exchanged chiefly for cloth and beads (mostly Indian in each case). The trade shrank in the later 18th century and finally petered out in the early 19th.

On the coast, as early as the 1580s, the Portuguese had to contend with revolts, Turkish raids and the attacks of fierce interior peoples. Turkish intervention and local revolt in the northern part of the coast led the Portuguese to construct the great fort of Mombasa, begun in 1593. At about the same time, the cannibalistic Zimba, who were as hostile to Muslim as to Christian, after overrunning Sena and Tete and attacking Kilwa, moved up the coast to Mombasa, then attacked Malindi, where they were themselves attacked by the Segeju. In the 17th century the Portuguese situation deteriorated further. In 1650 the Omani captured Muscat, their stronghold on the Persian Gulf, and proceeded to build up a modern navy that was a match for Portuguese ships. Within the next half century they captured Mombasa (1698) and asserted their sway over the whole coast north of Cape Delgado, though their suzerainty was somewhat ephemeral. The Portuguese were unable to reassert their position except briefly in 1728–1729.

iii) *The slave trade*

From the middle of the 18th century the East African slave trade, though very ancient, gained a new importance. Demand came from the sugar planters of the French islands of the Ile de France (Mauritius) and Bourbon (Réunion) – the Mascarenes – in the Indian Ocean. The first source of slaves

for this destination was Madagascar, where the expansion of the kingdom
of the Imerinas in the late 18th century and early 19th and the disintegration
of the kingdom of Betsimisarakas provided plenty of war captives. This
supply was supplemented from La Bourdonnais' governorship of the Mascarenes (1735) with supplies from the Mozambique coast, the trade being
extended in the 1770s to the north. Kilwa and Zanzibar became the most
important supply centres north of Cape Delgado, where Omani rule became more effective from the middle of the 18th century. To the south of
this cape the important markets were Mozambique Island, Ibo in the Ke-
rimba Islands and subsequently Quelimane. The French were active in both
the Portuguese and the Omani spheres of the coast, more particularly at Mozambique. They were taking slaves from Mozambique to the new world from
the 1770s, Brazilian slavers joining in towards the end of the 18th century.
North of Cape Delgado, Arab and Swahili slavers predominated. By the
1770s a thousand or fifteen hundred slaves were entering the French islands
annually from Mozambique Island alone. After the French Revolution the
authorities in Mauritius prohibited the trade, and this ban was reimposed
after the British conquest in 1811, but imports into Bourbon, temporarily
occupied by Britain, resumed after its return to France and continued at
least until the French abolition of the slave trade.

The Zanzibar slave trade, with an annual sale that increased according to
some estimates from 10 000 slaves in the early 19th century to between
40 000 and 45 000 in the mid-19th century, was at its height during the rule
of Sayyid Said (1804-1856 – born 1794), sultan of Muscat and Oman, who
transferred his court to Zanzibar in 1840.

Loosely linked with slaving was trading in ivory. This, too, was an ancient activity, but it acquired additional importance as growing demand in
Europe and the United States, where it found new uses in the manufacture
of piano keys and billiard balls, sent up its price from the 1820s. East Africa
became the world's most important source of ivory. As the elephant herds
were slaughtered in greater and greater numbers, new areas were exploited,
for example the Lake Rudolf region by the 1880s. In exchange for ivory
and slaves European and Indian manufactures were available, especially firearms, mostly of an obsolete pattern, and gunpowder, calico and other cloth
and beads, as well as local produce, especially salt. Need for salt was often
the primary stimulus for trade. Firearms played an important part in both
hunting (in which they predominated by the mid-19th century) and slaving.

East African trade was a partnership on varying terms of inland African
peoples with Portuguese, Arab, Indian and Swahili merchants on the coast.
In the area south-west of Kilwa, as far as Lake Malawi, the chiefs of the Yao
people were dominant by the late 19th century. In search of salt, they had
opened a trade route to Kilwa in the 17th century, shifting its terminus to

Mozambique Island after the Omani capture of Kilwa in 1698, then a century later back to Kilwa. Trading at first their tobacco, hoes and skins, which they exchanged for cloth and beads as well as salt, the Yao turned increasingly to ivory at the end of the 16th century, and it was only in the 18th century that the emphasis shifted to slaves. At first they obtained their ivory or slaves by hunting and raiding, but in the course of time they became primarily traders. Caravans set out in both directions, Yao to the coast, Arab to the interior, the latter to do business with the Africans, not as a rule to undertake slaving directly. A Yao trading trip to the coast might well take several months to complete.

The Yao also had dealings with the Bisa, situated east of Lake Bengweula, who provided the chief eastern trade outlet for the Lunda kingdoms of the Mweta Yamvo and Kasembe. The Bisa did not always trade with the coast indirectly via the Yao. They ran their own caravans of copper, ivory and slaves to Tete and Sena on the Zambezi and down to the coast. Other considerable ivory hunters and traders were the neighbours of the Yao to the south-east, the Makua and the Maravi (Malawi), settled to the south-west of Lake Malawi from the 14th century. In the 17th century the paramount chief of the Maravi, the Kalonga, controlled territory as far as the mouth of the Zambezi and evidently conducted an ivory trade with the Portuguese at Mozambique. His power waned in the later years of the century and Maravi trade was eclipsed by the more northerly trade of the Yao. The Makua-Lomwe people, athwart the Yao and Maravi trade routes to the coast, sought to obtain some share of the trade.

Further to the north, in what is now central Tanzania, the Arabs had a regular trade route into the interior with permanent trading posts. Beginning on the coast opposite Zanzibar, the principal route proceeded to Tabora and continued to Ujiji on the shores of Lake Tanganyika. Just as in their dealings with the Yao, the Arabs were merchants rather than slavers, purchasing their slaves and ivory. They dealt with the Nyamwezi, enterprising traders who opened trade routes in the 18th and 19th centuries both to the coast and into the interior as far as Katanga and the interlacustrine kingdoms of Buganda. From the 1870s, after a Buganda blockade had been circumvented, they also dealt with Bunyoro, where slaves were available as a by-product, as it were, of warfare carried on for other purposes.

In the Lake Victoria area the coastal Arabs came into contact with slave traders operating from the north, from Egypt and the Sudan. Egypt, still nominally part of the Ottoman empire, sought control of the Sudan in 1821 in order to ensure a supply of slaves for the army and for domestic purposes. Under pressure from Europe the Egyptian government expressed the wish to bring the trade to an end and made gestures to placate European opinion. In 1838 the pasha (viceroy) of Egypt, on a visit to the Sudan, announced the

abolition of slavery and measures to stop slaving, a declaration repeated by
his successor in 1856, but in fact the government itself continued to demand
slaves and the trade in them increased in volume after 1860. It was conducted by Arab, Sudanese and European private entrepreneurs, based
in Khartoum. Attracted first of all by ivory, they became increasingly interested in slaves. In the early years of the century slaving was carried out
mainly in Kordofan and the southern Gezira. It shifted to the upper White
Nile as the use of firearms overcame the resistance of the Shilluk people
and the introduction of steam river boats facilitated the penetration of the
Sudd swamps. Private traders so far south were beyond the government's
control. The greatest of them, with their slave soldiers and their local al-
liances, became effective rulers of considerable territories. In the 1870s,
however, Ismail, the khedive of Egypt (as he was now called), appointed
British governors to his Equatorial Province in the southern Sudan, Samuel
Baker and, after him, Charles Gordon and, particularly under the latter,
a determined effort was made to stamp out slaving.

In modern north-eastern Tanzania Arab and Swahili traders from Tanga
collaborated with chiefs of the Shambaa, Pare and Chagga. Still further
to the north they came into contact with the Kamba, who, like most others,
were initially primarily interested in ivory, but were drawn into the slave
trade. They built up a trading network reaching the coast at Mombasa and
Lamu, a trade which reached its most flourishing in the middle of the 19th
century. Thereafter it was adversely affected by disputes with the Kikuyu
and other enemies, by the shooting out of the elephant herds and by the
competition offered by the Swahili and the Arabs, who took over the more
active rôle. North of Lamu Swahili traders operated along the coast, up the
Juba river and into the interior as far as Lake Rudolf.

A proportion of the slaves obtained by Zanzibari Arabs was retained on
the coast to work in clove and coconut plantations, producing, apart from
cloves and coconuts, copal, copra and coconut oil for export. The main
external demand for slaves came from India in particular and from Turkey
and Persia. However, there was some surviving European interest in the
traffic from 1845 to 1864, viz the euphemistically named Free Labour Emigration Scheme, which furnished the French sugar island of Réunion and
subsequently French settlements in Madagascar and the Comoro Islands
with slaves purchased from Arab dealers in Mozambique, nominally freed
and 'invited' to undertake a five-year contract. The scruples of the sultan of
Zanzibar (who felt that his sovereignty was being violated) and the Portuguese authorities, were overcome by the threatening attitude of the French
government. The scheme was brought to an end after the French labour
problem was solved by the granting in 1861 of permission to recruit contract workers in British India.

African peoples who acquired slaves did not do so exclusively for their disposal in the export trade. Some slaves were needed for hunting and cultivating. The Kamba, for example, purchased slaves in the later 19th century from Arab and Swahili dealers who needed new markets to make good, loss of sales on the coast as the result of increasingly effective anti-slaving measures. British pressure upon Zanzibar to bring the slave trade to an end culminated in the closure of the Zanzibar slave market in 1873, though it still took many years of unremitting effort to terminate the trade completely.

Enslaving and slave trading in East Africa were peculiarly savage in a traffic notable for its barbarity. Villages were burnt, the unfit villagers massacred. The enslaved were yoked together, several hundreds in a caravan, and on their journey to the coast, which could be as long as 1280 kilometres, as the ivory and slave trades became integrated, slaves were used to carry the ivory on their march. At Tanga, Pangani, Bunga, Saadani, Bagamoyo, Mboamaji and Kilwa, the termini on the coast, they were either sold or crammed into dhows for the voyage to Zanzibar. It is estimated that only one in five of those captured in the interior reached Zanzibar. The slave trade seems to have been more catastrophic in East Africa than in West Africa. Throughout the 19th century slave raiding was endemic, disrupting agriculture and destroying villages, a disruption exacerbated by the Ngoni migrations. There was intense rivalry among and within African peoples for control of trade. Traditional and usurping leaders amongst the Yao and the Nyamwezi struggled for dominance. Trade was not without its beneficial aspects, encouraging the production of foodstuffs for caravans, which could be several hundred people strong, and of hoes and other artifacts and salt as supplementary trade goods. Critics, however, argue that the benefits accrued chiefly to European exporters and European import-export firms who established themselves in the East African ports during the 19th century, chiefly to purchase ivory.

ESTIMATED ANNUAL SLAVE EXPORTS FROM EAST AFRICA

Period	East African Coast	Sudan and Coast North of the Horn
1820s	20–30 000	5–6 000
Mid-century	30 000	40 000
1870s	20 000	40 000
1880s	4–7 000	
Total exports in the 19th century at least 2 million.		

Source: R. W. Beachey, *The Slave Trade of Eastern Africa* (London, 1976), p. 260–2.

iv) *Southern Africa*

The African peoples of the southern part of the continent traded among themselves both before and after the advent of European settlement, sometimes apparently over considerable distances. Some were more active traders than others, the Tsonga, for example, a coastal people living between Kosi Bay and the Save (Sabi) River. They were accustomed to travelling hundreds of kilometres by canoe on the Limpopo. However, the most northerly part of the Limpopo valley seems to have been in contact with the north rather than the south or south-east. This is evidently so in the case of the later Iron Age settlement of Mapungubwe, where glass beads and ornaments of copper and gold dated to the 14th and 15th centuries have been dug up. Trade appears to have been far less developed in Southern than in Central Africa, and certainly West Africa. A basic requirement like iron was in acutely short supply in some areas, among the Nguni, for example, until the 19th century. These people were less involved in trade than most.

To an extent there was trade in foodstuffs and cattle. Some, engaged primarily in hunting or pastoral farming, bartered skins for grain. There is evidence of regular bartering of metalware for cattle. Trade in metal was the consequence of the dispersal of ore deposits and of the skills needed to work them.

> Fifteen Marootze passed in the morning on their way to a mine of iron stone . . . From the iron thus procured, they were said to manufacture assagais, knives, beads, etc. which they exchange for other articles with the neighbouring nations. Most of the men had nets to carry the ore in, made of grass or rushes.[2]

Another local specialization that gave rise to trade was the making of karosses.

> During the time I was in the Bechuana country between twenty and thirty thousand skins were made up into karosses: part of them worn by the inhabitants and part sold to traders: many, I believe, find their way to China. The Bakwains bought tobacco from the eastern tribes, then purchased skins from it from the Bakalahari, tanned them, and sewed them into karosses, then went south to purchase heifer-calves with them . . .[3]

While that quotation illustrates the volume of trade, its variety is shown by the following.

> The Blip come each year to the tribes living along this river to trade, bring with them tobacco, ivory spoons, bracelets, copper and iron beads, glass beads, copper earrings and bracelets, knives, barbed assagais and also smooth axes and awls. This is the way they trade: for a heifer they give eight assagais, an axe and an awl, a small bag of tobacco and a small bag of dagga, and for a bull or an ox, five assagais plus all the other things as for a heifer. They also bring soft, well tanned skins of hartebeest with the grain removed . . .[4]

A distinctive feature of Southern African trade was the absence of a trade in slaves, and there was little desire to start one.

Wooden bowls, spoons, and ornaments in abundance, were brought to exchange for commodities which we possessed; among others, two elderly men came and presented their children for sale; a sheep was expected for one, and a quantity of beads for the other. I embraced the opportunity of pointing out to them, and to all present, how unnatural such conduct was, and the direful consequences which must arise from such a course... They walked off, evidently disappointed, while those around, who were listening to what I said, professed their fullest conviction of the horrors to which such a system, if connived at, would lead. It is proper, at the same time, to remark, that slavery, in the general sense of the term, does not exist among the Bechuanas.[5]

European settlers had either to use local forced labour or to import slaves from overseas for their labour requirements.

Trade greatly expanded under the influence of European settlement. Though primarily fulfilling the purpose of protecting and succouring the eastern trade, the Dutch colony at the Cape produced as well an exportable quantity of wine, hides and grain, supplemented by ivory and skins. But external markets were remote and Cape grain was expensive. European farms remained highly dependent upon sales of meat and other foodstuffs to the Company for its ships and garrison and to such foreign vessels as called at Cape Town. St. Helena, where there was a considerable British garrison during Napoleon's exile there, set up a certain demand for Cape produce, but a diminishing one. Trade with the Khoikhoi did not develop after some promising early contacts. Despite the temptations of copper, beads, tobacco and spirits, they parted with their cattle, sheep and goats only reluctantly and, in any case, were decreasingly able to trade as they lost stock and land or, at best, escaped with their beasts into the interior. Those who did thus retreat sometimes combined hunting with cattle breeding and traded ivory for gunpowder and wagons.

From the beginning of the 18th century cattle were being obtained from the Xhosa on both sides of the Great Fish River by the Company and its Cape Town contractors and, illegally, by frontier settlers and professional itinerant traders, in exchange for beads, metals, cloth, knives and tobacco. As the white frontier moved inland, more distant peoples were brought into this commercial network – in the early years of the 19th century the Griquas and the Tswana across the Orange River. Firearms and gunpowder became the most sought-after trade goods. Although there was mutual attraction, black-white relations were abrasive, and malpractices on both sides – plundering and forcible trade on the part of the colonists, stealing by the Africans – were responsible for recurrent warfare which impeded trade. The official policy of the Company, continued at first by the British, was to discourage contact between the races, or at least to reduce tension between them. In 1817, the British authorities established a fair at Grahamstown to regulate interracial trade.

Increasingly, meat was supplied to both Cape Town and visiting ships by white pastoralists. The demands of this market were an inducement to settlers to move further into the interior. Apart from meat, various products of farm, home industry and hunting found a sale in Cape Town – butter, tallow (the fat of the tail of the indigenous sheep), ostrich feathers, ivory, skins, hides, leather and draught oxen. An important frontier industry until it encountered a factory-produced competitor in the 19th century, was the manufacture of soap for the market, made from the fat of the fat-tailed sheep and alkali obtained from a commonly found plant. The cattle could transport themselves to market, while the other commodities were not overburdened by transport costs. During the course of the 19th century, particularly from the 1820s, when there was a substantial settlement of British immigrants in the Eastern Province of the Cape, coastal trading between Cape Town and Algoa Bay and Port Elizabeth, conveniently near the frontier of settlement, became important. Trade was subsequently extended to Port Natal and Delagoa Bay. With the proceeds of their sales the farmers of the interior bought their firearms and gunpowder, a certain amount of clothing and utensils, iron, wagons, salt, tea, coffee, sugar and brandy.

An occasional trade that took place between the Cape and the Herero territory to the north-west of the colony in what is now the northeast of Namibia, viz the export from the latter of cattle, ivory and ostrich feathers, either overland or by sea from Walvis Bay in exchange for European manufactured goods, grew more regular and of greater volume – up to twenty thousand head of cattle and nine hundred kilograms of ivory every year – as the 19th century progressed. In the 1840s exports from this region were greatly enhanced in value by the addition of guano from the off-shore islands and by sporadic supplies of copper from Namaqualand (in the north-western Cape). Guano exports reached a peak of some hundreds of thousands of tons by the mid-1840s. This modestly profitable trade, however, was disrupted by frequent outbreaks of tribal fighting. A similar traffic developed during the 19th century in southern and south-eastern Angola, European textiles and wine being exchanged for hides, cattle, wax, honey and wild rubber. At first carried on by itinerant European merchants, it became more regular and extensive, leading to the establishment of small trading towns.

NOTES

1. Axelson, E. (ed.): *South African Explorers* (London, 1954), p. 42–3, 44
2. Ibid, p. 163
3. Quoted Wilson, Monica & Thompson, Leonard (eds.): *The Oxford History of South Africa*, Volume I (Oxford, 1969), p. 148
4. Ibid, p. 149
5. Axelson, E.: Op. cit., p. 201–2

Further reading

Ali, Abbas I. M.: *The British, the Slave Trade and Slavery in the Sudan 1820–1881* (Khartoum, 1972)
Alpers, E. A.: *Ivory and Slaves in East Central Africa* (London, 1975)
Arkin, Marcus: *Storm in a Teacup, the Cape Colonists and the English East India Company* (Cape Town, 1973)
Axelson, Eric: *Portuguese in South-East Africa 1488–1600* (Cape Town, 1973)
Axelson, E.: *Portuguese in South-East Africa 1600–1700* (Johannesburg, 1960)
Axelson, E.: *South-East Africa 1488–1530* (London, 1940)
Baer, G.: Op. cit. (see p. 65)
Beachey, R. W.: *The Slave Trade of Eastern Africa* (London, 1976)
Beachey, R. W.: *The Slave Trade of Eastern Africa, a Collection of Documents* (London, 1976)
Boxer, C. R.: Op. cit. (see p. 173)
Cooper, Frederick: *Plantation Slavery on the East Coast of Africa* (New Haven and London, 1977)
Coupland, Sir Reginald: *The British Anti-Slavery Movement* (London, 1933)
Duffy, J. E.: Op. cit. (see p. 174)
Duffy, J. E.: *A Question of Slavery* (Cambridge, Mass., 1967)
Duyvendak, J. L.: *China's Discovery of Africa* (London, 1949)
Filesi, T.: *China and Africa in the Middle Ages* (London, 1972)
Freeman-Grenville, G. S. P.: *The East African Coast, Select Documents* (Oxford, 1962)
Freeman-Grenville, G. S. P.: *The Medieval History of the Coast of Tanganyika* (Berlin, 1962)
Gray, R. (ed.): *The Cambridge History of Africa*, Volume 4 (see p. 153)
Hourani, G. F.: *Arab Seafaring in the Indian Ocean in Ancient and Medieval Times* (Beirut, 1963)
Lancaster, C. S. & Pohorilenko, A.: 'Ingombe Ilede and the Zimbabwe culture' (*International Journal of African Historical Studies*, X, 1977, p. 1–30)
Mollat, M.: Op. cit. (see p. 154)
Neumark, D. S.: Op. cit. (see p. 131)
Nicholls, C. S.: *The Swahili Coast, Politics, Diplomacy and Trade on the East African Littoral 1798–1856* (London, 1971)
Ogot, B. A.: *Zamani, a Survey of East African History* (Nairobi, 2nd edn. 1973)
Oliver, R. (ed.): *The Cambridge History of Africa*, Volume 3 (see p. 174)
Oliver, R. & Mathew, G. (eds.): *History of East Africa*, Volume I (Oxford, 1963)
Posnansky, Merrick (ed.): *Prelude to East African History* (London, 1966)
Roberts, Andrew: *A History of Zambia* (London, 1976)
Strandes, Julius: *The Portuguese Period in East Africa* (Nairobi, 1961)
Walker, Eric A.: *A History of Southern Africa* (London and Harlow, 3rd edn. 1957)

CHAPTER IV

ECONOMIC SYSTEMS OF ANCIENT AND PRE-PARTITION AFRICA

1. ANCIENT MEDITERRANEAN AFRICA

i) *Ancient and Hellenistic Egypt*

Social differentiation came as early as the 4th millennium B.C. in the history of Egypt. The agricultural surplus made possible a ruling class of priests and lay officials, and the administration of the irrigation system required one. Already in the pre-dynastic period, writing was practised, an esoteric art which contributed to the development of an élite and rendered the administration more effective. Already in the archaic period, Egypt was an absolutism. It remained so, at least in theory. The divine pharaoh was the state, the laws his will, the officials his servants and the land his property. Having the products of his kingdom and the activities of his people at his disposal, he devoted them largely to what would now be considered unproductive ends. Resources were diverted to the construction and maintenance of temples in the belief that only offerings to the gods would conserve the divine energy necessary for continued national prosperity. In practice, the product of temple lands was consumed by a mostly parasitic class of functionaries. Further resources went to the construction and furnishing of tombs because of the importance attached to life after death and the precautions necessary to ensure a safe journey into eternity.

Social mobility was slight, though not wholly absent, and the mass of the population was composed of peasants and agricultural labourers, subject to the harsh control of pharaoh and his district governors (nomarchs). The Egyptian peasant – the tenant on the royal, state or temple estate – and the landless man, paid the price for the blessings of the Nile in burdensome, if intermittent, toil, at the beck and call of estate owner or manager, bound by both religious duty and physical coercion to the corvée and to a state treasury that requisitioned, often with great brutality, the lion's share of their crop. Frequently too, they were victims of the capriciousness of nature, floods and droughts and plagues of locusts and other pests.

State enterprise was of significance in all sectors of the economy – mining, quarrying, construction, shipping, trading and manufacturing. It would perhaps be more accurate to suggest that the needs of the state had a prior claim upon all economic activity. Foreign trade was a state monopoly and the merchants engaged in it occupied a semi-official position. Entirely private merchants found no scope for their energies other than petty local trade, mostly dealing in such agricultural produce as was left over after the demands of the state had been met. External trade was conducted in pursuance of state interests, to acquire, for example, strategic materials such as timber and metals, and was therefore virtually a branch of foreign policy. The strict control of internal distribution served a double purpose: not only the advantage of the state and the payment of its officials, but also the interests of society at large, whose supplies were safe-guarded. The state share of crops was stored in state granaries at many points throughout the country for distribution to officials and those engaged in public works and as a safeguard against famine in time of harvest failure. Nor was it only foodstuffs that were affected by this pervasive state paternalism. Other necessities were similarly stored. This rigid control of distribution was, however, possible only because of the ubiquitousness of water transport in the populated area, the absence of which elsewhere in Africa precluded such intervention.

Despite the immense property and powers of the pharaoh, there were disintegrating forces at work within Egyptian society and administration, apart from the tendency for Upper and Lower Egypt to separate. Royal estates were sometimes entrusted on life-tenure to the management of officials, who were then remunerated from the estate revenues. When central authority weakened, the danger existed of the permanent appropriation of these estates, for example by the establishment of perpetual endowments for the cult of the dead, and in times of rural exodus the crown was only too pleased to grant land to prominent men to ensure its continued cultivation. There were too, other opportunities for building up private fortunes, through royal gifts and the salaries of hereditary offices, secular and religious, sometimes several in the hands of a single person. Private estates were a feature of Egyptian landowning from the earliest times, some through the reclamation of wasteland. Powerful nobles, such as monarchs, could keep numerous retainers and there were periods when central authority broke down altogether (the Intermediate Periods). During such times a type of government analagous to feudalism emerged, and it is suggested that this was associated with Upper Egypt, where a nobility with hunting proclivities predominated; while in Lower Egypt a bourgeoisie of merchants and shipowners is supposed to have exercised an influence that was felt throughout the entire country during times of prosperity. Few, however, now accept that there is sufficient evidence to support the notion of a class struggle between a feudal aristocracy and a free bourgeoisie, or, indeed, of the existence of a bourgeois class at all in a society where officialdom was so influential and state service the road to privilege. There was an immense gulf between the ruling class and the mass of the population, with no true middle class, urban or rural, in between. Apart from the cultivators of the soil, almost all Egyptians, including priests and artisans, were higher or lower officials or were in the service of great men.

When the central authority was unimpaired, Egypt, according to Max Weber's typology, was a 'patrimonial régime', where the state is run like an immense private estate and where there is no distinction between sovereignty and property because all political authority and all property are formally vested in the ruler. On the other hand, Karl Wittfogel has applied to Egypt, Marx's concept of an 'Asiatic mode of production', though Marx himself had India chiefly in mind. Its characteristics are political despotism, an absence of private property (and hence of classes) and a village self-sufficient in agriculture and manufacturing. The state organises public works, particularly aqueducts, and extracts the surplus product in the form of tribute (that is, rent in kind) and communal labour. Such production and exchange of commodities as take place are to serve the needs of the despot and his principal officers. The essence of this mode of production is fundamental changelessness in spite of constant dynastic changes. 'The structure of the economic elements of the society remains unaffected by the storms in the political weather.'[1] Whereas in other pre-capitalist economic formations change is possible, for example through warfare or conquest, the 'Asiatic form necessarily hangs on more tenaciously and for the longest time'.[2]

Although the Asiatic mode of production was conceived by Marx, his followers, from Lenin onwards, saw that Russia showed too many of its alleged features for comfort. Early Marxists professed to see in Tsarist Russia an incipient capitalist mode of production; later Marxists preferred not to see the close parallels between Stalinist, or, indeed, post-Stalinist, Russia and oriental despotism. It was Wittfogel who revived interest in the concept, making the essence of this mode of production the control of water resources. Egypt was thus a conspicuous example of the 'hydraulic society'. His arguments, however, have been criticized by both Marxist and non-Marxists. Among the former, there are theoretical objections to the idea of the existence of a state without classes, since the state exists, so some say, only as an expression of the class struggle. Not all non-Marxist critics accept that Egypt had no private property. State ownership of all land was to a considerable degree a legal fiction. It is also arguable that communal dependence on public works, including irrigation, could just as well foster democracy as despotism, as was the case, for example, in the drainage of the Dutch polders in medieval Europe. While it is true that the administration of the irrigation system tended to deteriorate when political authority weakened, it had a certain momentum of its own that enabled it to continue functioning even in the absence of a strong central government.

The despotic régime of the pharaohs was maintained by the Ptolemies after the fall of the Egyptian kingdom and, indeed, became even harsher and more inquisitorial as the paternalistic elements gave ground to naked exploitation. Ptolemaic Egypt has with justice been called 'one of the most perfect examples of a totalitarian state that the world has ever seen'.[3] Like his Egyptian predecessors the Hellenistic ruler laid claim to divine honours and to the ownership of all the land. In effect, Egypt under the Ptolemies was a more efficient, or more thorough-going, 'patrimonial régime'. Estates were in fact granted to privileged individuals in return for a quit-rent and leases were sold by competitive auction as a way of raising revenue. There was, however, no hereditary nobility with rights and privileges that the king had to respect, and the bureaucracy, though powerful, was not permitted to become hereditary. Although there was a social hierarchy, there was no structure of classes determined by relationship to the means of production.

Royal ownership of the land was common to the entire Hellenistic world, but only the king of Egypt had a bureaucracy capable of exercising a tight control over cultivation. This control, going far beyond the super-vision of the irrigation system, extended to the determination of the crops sown and the area of cultivation for each, a monopoly of the supply of seed, the appropriation of a share of the harvest as tax and compulsory sale to contractors of certain crops, such as plants from which oil was extracted. The contractors who bid for the exclusive right to purchase this oleaginous grain were compelled to use factories and labour furnished by the state and to retail the final product at officially determined prices. Such carefully regulated monopolies, exercised by private entrepreneurs who tendered for them, were characteristic of the Ptolemaic economy, extending to al-most every article of common use. The state retained the monopoly of retailing imported spices, and it supplemented its income and protected home industries, particularly oil and wine, by the imposition of very heavy internal and frontier tolls. Internal dues were payable on goods moving between one region of the country and another, and from one nome to another. Boats arriving at the river port of Memphis, for example, were searched at the customs-post. These imposts were retained by the Romans, who also re-tained, or perhaps themselves introduced, an export tax.

ii) *Carthage and Rome*
To the west of Egypt, in North Africa, despite the relatively favourable conditions for agriculture in areas of good rainfall, no state structure de-veloped before the arrival of the Phoenicians from Lebanon and Syria during the 2nd millennium B.C.. Communications were poor and the lack of readily accessible minerals hindered the development of metallurgy, with its civilis-ing effects. Before the Phoenicians arrived the inhabitants were still largely at a Stone Age level of technology, though in the eastern part of North Africa the Libyans had long been familiar with copper and bronze. Some

had adopted a sedentary life, especially in what is now Tunisia, but the majority were still semi-nomadic pastoralists living in small clans or tribes. Among the poor and backward people of Spain and North Africa, the Phoenicians founded their trading posts and refreshment stations. These were largely autonomous and they established close links with the native inhabitants. Intermarriage was common. Carthage, with a good harbour and situated on an easily defended peninsula, commanding the narrows of the Mediterranean, was the most important of the Phoenician settlements.

Like Rome, Carthage was a city state which came to be the head of a highly centralized empire. There was, however, a profound difference between Rome, where the landed interest was dominant, and Carthage, where merchants were in command. Carthage was founded from Tyre, where, as Isaiah said, the 'merchants were princes'. As Tyre weakened under Assyrian pressure, Carthage overbore the other Phoenician colonies of the western Mediterranean, and she founded her own on the Mediterranean islands and along the African coast. In the struggle with the Greeks in the 6th century B.C. the city was ruled by a dynasty of kings, the Magonids, who were both warriors and merchants. When defeat was suffered in Sicily in 480 B.C., these were replaced by an aristocracy of birth and wealth derived from trade, industry and, later, land. The government was composed of a self-perpetuating oligarchy, with an executive of two annually appointed officials – not unlike the consuls of Rome – known as suffetes, who had to be men of property. Provision was made however for popular referenda.

The oligarchy split into factions that sometimes sought popular support against rivals in their struggle for control of the legislature and the magistracy. After the severe economic and military setbacks of the First Punic War against Rome, (263–241 B.C.) the Barcid faction (which included Hannibal) asserted a predominant position, partly through appeal to the people, partly through the creation of a power base in Spain. Vilfredo Pareto in his typology of political régimes classified Carthage as a mixed type of government, one relying chiefly on physical force and on religious and similar sentiments, with an admixture of demagogy for exploiting the interests and feelings of the governed. As a state of that sort, permitting considerable social mobility and therefore rejuvenation of the governing élite, Carthage was capable of great prosperity. However, as the demagogic component became more pronounced and the rôle of force decreased, the state lost its ability to withstand Roman hostility. There was no economic failure, but a loss of will.

To begin with, Carthage, perched on its promontory, was entirely seaward-looking. After the defeat of 480, however, she sought compensation by territorial expansion into the hinterland, which continued into the 3rd century B.C.. Carthaginian nobles acquired estates, but there is no evidence of a division of interests within the ruling group. Although they lived on their estates, these were modest in extent and situated in the *chora*, in the area immediately adjacent to the city. There is no sign of the existence of a class of landowners hostile to the merchants. The latter diversified their interests by obtaining land and producing olives and fruit and raising livestock. The city, with its estimated population of 100 000, dominated the conquered territory. The division within Carthage was rather between citizens and non-citizens, who were only grudgingly admitted to citizenship. There were no genuine working or peasant classes within the dominant race. Most non-aristocratic Carthaginians were attached in some way to the powerful. Aristocratic families built up a following of slaves (domestic and estate), employees and clients, who were impoverished citizens whom they maintained. Despite their close contact with each other and the absence of barriers to intermarriage, Carthaginians and Berbers remained sharply separated, and there were marked social tensions. In the late 4th century B.C. there was a rebellion of the free but harshly exploited Berbers and the rural slaves; then after the First Punic War, another of mercenaries, supported by a heterogeneous mass of discontented rural slaves, Berbers and even the inhabitants of towns subject to Carthage. Carthaginian citizens had no military obligation and their wars were fought by mercenaries and the conscripts of subject peoples. But in the face of such threats they closed ranks, setting aside factional and economic differences. Carthage tended to be ruthless and xenophobic. Although at different times Etruscan, Greek and other foreign merchants were allowed to take up residence, the commerce of foreign states was excluded as far as possible from the western Mediterranean and the ignorance of primitive trading partners was exploited.

After the destruction of Carthage in 146 B.C. the Romans were obliged to establish themselves in Africa in order to prevent a Carthaginian resurgence. A century later the whole of the Mediterranean littoral was drawn into civil wars between Pompey and Caesar and between Octavius and Antony and Cleopatra. In 30 B.C., on the defeat of Antony and the death of Cleopatra, Egypt was incorporated into the Roman empire. This change in the status of the country coincided with the reorganization of the empire by Octavius, now Augustus. The decadent Roman Republic was replaced by the Principate, more commonly referred to as the Empire. Augustus did not admit to terminating the Republic and he retained republican forms of government. Nonetheless, he put an end to rule by an aristocratic clique and instituted an autocracy in which it became the practice to accord the emperor divine honours.

Despite the real concentration of power that underlay the superficial retention of republican government, Rome was not, before its economic troubles of the 3rd century A.D., prone to interfere unduly in economic processes. An infrastructure appropriate to the era – roads, harbour installations and water supply – and law and order were furnished by the state, but the government was no monolith. There was a large measure of administrative decentralization and little intervention as a rule in the economic decisions of the individual. Private property, trade and manufacture were normal, and a wide latitude was permitted in the realm of thought and beliefs. Even in Egypt, for all its traditions of state control, there was some relaxation of state intrusion, though it remained far from negligible. The situation of the Egyptian tiller of the soil remained fundamentally unaltered and the emperor, as king of Egypt, took over crown land. The state, in fact, preserved the Ptolemaic claim to the ownership of all land, mines and quarries, and perhaps flocks, but in practice restricted itself to exacting a tax in kind or a quit-rent, and was not opposed to a free market in land, favouring the establishment of a class of small landowners among Greek and Roman settlers. Leases of crown land were auctioned as under the Ptolemies, but the Roman administration adopted as a policy what had been rarely resorted to by its predecessors, namely the compulsory leasing of land by villages or private landowners wherever lessees were not forthcoming at the rent demanded.

The Ptolemaic monopolies were apparently retained only in some products and some districts, for example in the production and sale of salt, beer, alum, metals, precious and semi-precious stones and building stone. They were exercised by a mixture of state and private enterprise, but were abandoned altogether wherever they were unprofitable. The government found it more useful in many instances to impose on producers or traders a tax in kind or a sales tax or to institute a licensing system. The oil monopoly disappeared in most areas and state intervention in commerce was given up, with the important exception of the shipment of grain to Italy.

The annexation of Egypt probably benefited the country to begin with, substituting a more efficient and less corrupt government than that of the later Ptolemies. The best gift of Augustus was to make the *pax Romana* a reality. With the end of the civil wars of the last century of the Republic it became possible for merchants to sail the Mediterranean without let or hindrance, and other conditions necessary for economic activity were provided – security of contract, a network of communications, a stable and universally accepted currency and a wide and, as population and living standards rose, expanding market. Such advantages did not go unpaid for. At first, taxation was not excessive: customs duties at 20 per cent. on goods imported into the empire and much lower internal tolls; a poll-tax, payable in Egypt by males between the ages of 14 and 65; and a land tax, which was a percentage of the estimated value of the land according to its use, e.g. arable or pasture. The chief drawback of the land tax was its inflexibility, fixed irrespective of the size of the harvest or the quality of the land, and the rate was the same irrespective of the size of the holding. Taxes were farmed out, as they had been in the Ptolemaic period.

In prosperous times Egypt and North Africa were able to meet the costs of the Roman occupation without suffering exhaustion. Egypt in particular had a favourable balance of commodity trade with Italy and was able to recoup herself to some extent through the profits of the eastern trade, transport charges, income from tourists and students and government expenditure upon administration, public works and the military establishment. But the burden of the Roman connection became heavier, especially in times of political disturbance. Roman citizenship was granted ever more freely, until, in A.D. 212, Caracalla granted it to all free men within the empire. Its extension devalued it, and it is likely that the grant was primarily actuated by fiscal considerations.

In the 3rd century the empire suffered from severe inflation and, as taxation remained fixed, revenue fell in real terms. To offset this the state resorted to requisitions of produce to feed armies and officials. In the reforms of the emperor Diocletian (A.D. 284–305) these requisitions were regularized. Taxation (the *annona*) was assessed on the basis of land and people. Until the end of the 5th century it continued to be collected in kind and even after that Constantinople and Alexandria went on being fed with levies of that sort. The collection by canal and river of the *annona* of wheat and other foodstuffs (supplemented by purchases) for the feeding of Rome and the other major cities, and the organization of the annual fleet that carried it across the Mediterranean, were closely supervised by government officials. In other ways, too, state intervention in economic processes became more intrusive. Control of industry became as strict as it had been in Ptolemaic times, especially of industry thought to be of importance to the state. Diocletian's reforms also included the regulation of prices and measures to ensure the adequate provision of essential public services. But state interference stopped short of permeating and directing all economic activity; nor did it destroy proprietary rights. More far-reaching aims were within the scope of neither the aspirations nor the competence of the later Roman empire. This is not to say, however, that the behaviour of the Roman state could not have severe economic repercussions.

Taxation fell most heavily upon agriculture and, particularly, the small farmers; nor did that exhaust their obligations. Those who were tenants shouldered a heavier and heavier burden of rent. Many lived in desperate poverty. Even in the 2nd century Egyptian peasants were deserting the countryside owing to the difficulty of trying to survive on the slender proportion of the harvest not seized by the state, and they were taking their chance in Alexandria and other industrial cities. In the 3rd century Caracalla tried to deport these immigrants as Alexandria went through a depression that may have been partly due to famine and plague. Growing distress was not confined to the country-dwellers, but affected all classes of society except the very rich and powerful. From the burdens of the 'liturgical system' few escaped. The liturgies – originally public responsibilities accepted as an honour, but transformed into an incubus – and *munera* ranged from manual labour on the irrigation system to the performance of administrative functions, including the collection of taxes. As candidates for election to the magistracy ceased to come forward because of the expenses of municipal office and the subsequent requirement that shortfalls in revenue, the expectation of which was set unrealistically high, be met from the pocket of officials, compulsory appointments were made. Civic service ceased to be a sought-after honour but a tiresome and costly duty, and this was as much true of North Africa as of Egypt.

Despairing peasants resorted to flight and banditry and more and more land was absorbed by the big estates. Sometimes private landowners were made responsible for the rent of unwanted land. The powers of the central government slipped away and private armies, prisons, postal services and even money became common. Smallholders found themselves increasingly in the power of their wealthy neighbours. The rule of Byzantium saw the culmination of the tendencies inherent in the later Roman empire. By the 6th century taxation amounted to about a third of the crop, rents accounting for another half. A long-suffering and apathetic population was in no mood to resist the onslaught of Islam in the 7th century. The relatively brief interlude of Vandal occupation in the 5th and 6th centuries in North Africa did not alter the system there, but merely imposed a new, relatively small ruling class (comprising not more than five per cent. of the total population).

iii) *The ancient city and capitalism*
For Marx the cradle of capitalism was the European medieval city, and he repudiated any suggestion of its existence in classical antiquity. Certainly he recognised that there were forms of capital that existed before the evolution of a capitalist socio-economic formation, viz. merchant or commercial capital and usurer's, or financial, capital, and indeed that their existence at a certain level was a necessary, though not the only, condition for that evolution, because they stimulated the production of goods for the market, a prerequisite of a capitalist mode of production. True capitalism, however, presupposes the separation of the producers from the means of production, that is, the existence of wage labour, and the appropriation of their surplus labour in the form of money. Marx regarded the primitive Roman Republic as a community of 'free and equal private proprietors' that disintegrated because of its warlike character, the introduction of slavery, the concentration of property owning and the development of commerce and the use of

money. By Marxist criteria, then, the Roman empire was either a 'slave mode of production' where, as a consequence of the development of commerce, slave labour was the chief source of surplus value; or possibly an 'ancient mode of production', characterized by the exploitation of non-citizens by citizens through war and taxation together with the exploitation of poorer citizens by richer citizens – senators and knights – who dominated the state and exercised power through the control of clients and debtors.

If a broader definition of capitalism is accepted, signifying not the Marxist 'socio-economic formation', but simply the presence in a society of capitalist institutions that co-exist with other institutions without eclipsing them, then evidence for capitalism in the Egyptian and North African cities of classical antiquity is not difficult to find – the private ownership of the means of production, production for the market, the pursuit of profit, the rational conduct of business, monopoly and oligopoly, company organization, and so forth. Trade in ancient times fostered the division of labour by its demand for exchange commodities; contrasted the individual with the community; created new needs; circulated money; and presented opportunities for its accumulation. If acquisitiveness is the hall-mark of a capitalist society, then there was genuine capitalism. Speaking of Alexandria, a writer of the 2nd century A.D. said,

> The people are most factious, vain and unruly; the city is rich, wealthy, and prosperous . . . They have only one god – money. Christians, Jews, everyone worship this divinity.[4]

There was, too, a well-articulated class structure and there were hints of class warfare. The class of bankers, financiers, wholesale merchants, retail traders and well-to-do artisans may, without devaluing the term, be designated bourgeois, and from the 2nd century A.D. Alexandria had an urban proletariat – or lumpenproletariat – of rural immigrants whose standard of living, always low, was further eroded by the rising prices of the 3rd century. How far their discontent was directed at the affluent and how far at an all-pervasive government that more and more ground down both classes, is a matter of conjecture.

Max Weber discerned capitalism in antiquity, but a sort of robber capitalism derived from opportunities to exploit the weak and defenceless. In so far as this related to 'spoils, taxes, the pickings of office or official usury, and finally to tribute and actual need', it was irrational. If 'organized with a view to market opportunities', even though dependent upon opportunities opened by the state ('the leasing of the *ager publicus* or conquered land, and of domain land or to tax farming and the financing of political adventures and of wars'), it was rational. Such political capitalism succumbed with the freedom of the cities after the establishment of 'a bureaucratically organized world empire'.[5] Weber identified the Roman knightly class, the *equites*, as the capitalist class, exercising the real power in the state, for all their inferior social position compared with the senatorial patricians. In the extreme statement of this identification, the knights propelled Rome, despite feeble protests from the senators, into the prosecution of a series of wars in Italy, against Carthage, Macedonia and Egypt, to obtain commercial supremacy and to extort tribute, both to equestrian advantage; while the senators, who constituted the façade of the Roman Republic, though ostensibly aloof from and contemptuous of the profits of usury, speculation and public contracts and loans and legally precluded from financial dealings, ground down the wretched provincials through financial extortion.

Michael Rostovtseff, like Weber, viewed the establishment of the Augustan principate, the Empire, as a watershed, but one that saw the florescence of capitalism, not its demise. He lumped together the senators and the equites as 'half-feudal landowners and business men who owed their material prosperity to the resources of the state and their political power to their wealth'.[6] His bourgeoisie was composed of those who lived

from the investment of their accumulated capital in some branch of economic activity. In the field of agriculture the *bourgeois* of the Greek cities were landowners whose land was tilled by tenants, hired hands, and slaves, or who were themselves tenants employing labour of the latter classes. In the field of industry they were owners of workshops, supervising and directing their employees, slaves or free men. In the field of commerce they were owners or tenants of shops in the retail trade, or of ships and storehouses for trade between cities or states. Many of them were money-lenders of one kind or another, who lent their accumulated capital mostly on mortgage to those who needed it. Some may have been professional *trapezitai* (bankers) . . . Many were slave-owners and derived their income from their slaves, hiring them out to owners of mines, shops, or ships, or permitting them to conduct a business of their own on condition of paying a regular fee. In many cases their investments were diversified and they were interested in a variety of enterprises.

The main and characteristic feature of the *bourgeoisie* from an ecomonic standpoint was, however, not their manner of investing their capital, but the fact that they were not professionals, craftsmen of one kind or another, salaried employees, or the like, but investors of accumulated capital and employers of labour.[7]

The bourgeoisie constituted the ruling class in the Hellenistic cities and the Roman cities of the west, the holders of municipal office who were responsible for the performance of services, including the payment of taxes, to the central government. Egypt, with its 'elaborately planned and state-controlled economy', was the exception in the Hellenistic world. There the bourgeoisie was composed of members of the Greek bureaucracy, who ruled the country as the private estate of the Ptolemaic kings. Into this state-controlled economy the Romans introduced a liberalizing force. Capitalism burgeoned, only to be blighted in the 3rd century A.D. by renewed intrusion on the part of the state, which, in trying to solve its economic problems, imposed 'state capitalism'. This deadening effect was reinforced by the tendency of the urban bourgeoisie (the *honestiores*) to invest in land rather than trade and industry and to seek a social exclusiveness that antagonised the lower strata of society (the *humiliores*).

The Rostovtseffian model of a Hellenistic decline arrested by Roman intervention and a subsequent degeneration of the Roman empire has not commanded universal support amongst scholars. Indeed, Ulrich Kahrstedt took quite the opposite position, attributing the fall of Hellenism to the ruin wrought by the Romans, who destroyed an incipient industrial capitalism. Clearly, whether one accepts Kahrstedt's Hellenistic capitalism destroyed from without or Rostovtseff's Roman capitalism wrecked from within, one cannot escape the fact that the rôle of the state varied, even in Egypt, where the weight of the past was so heavy. There was, as has been argued by Karl Polanyi, a co-existence of capitalism – or rather, in his terms, a market and exchange type of economy – and a planned, marketless economy, with now one, now the other, dominant, the marketless type reaching its fullest expression in Ptolemaic Egypt and post-Diocletian Rome.

Polanyi is perhaps wise in his caution. The use of terms like 'capitalism' gives a false impression and tends to misjudge the basic elements of ancient society. Although Greek and Roman society was distinguished from other ancient civilizations by the existence of the city composed of free men, and the Roman empire was itself a federation of cities and territories that recognized the pre-eminent position of the city of Rome, and although the Greek and Roman cities continued to the end of the empire to go through the motions of self-government, the real source of power lay during the Republic with the landowners, who monopolised administration, major political decisions and high rank in the army, and during the Empire with the bureaucracy, which was antipathetic to the 'business ethic'. Basically the city was economically parasitic. 'I do not remember,' wrote David Hume,

> a passage in any ancient author, where the growth of a city is ascribed to the establishment of a manufacture. The commerce, which is said to flourish, is chiefly the exchange of those commodities for which different soils and climates were suited.[8]

For all its luxury industries and even its mass production of commodities to suit the taste of the moderately wealthy, the ancient city was primarily a centre of administration, military power and cultural influence, either dominated by the countryside or irrelevant to it, a foreign body like Alexandria, 'in Egypt but not of it'.[9] Industrial production was largely for a restricted market.

In the Roman empire commerce, industry and finance were not fields in which the ambitions of the dominant landowning senatorial *ordo* could be satisfied, and, indeed, its members were effectively debarred from participation in foreign trade by law (the *lex Claudia* of 218 B.C.) and in trade, industry and tax collecting by convention. 'Commerce,' wrote Cicero,

> if it is on a small scale, is to be considered mean; but if it is large-scale and extensive, importing much from all over and distributing to many without misrepresentation, is not to be greatly censured. Indeed, it even seems to deserve the highest respect if those who are engaged in it, satiated, or rather, I should say, content with their profits, make their way from the harbour to a landed estate, as they have often made it from the sea to a harbour. But of all things from which one may acquire, none is better than agriculture, none more fruitful, none sweeter, none more fitting for a free man.[10]

There appears to be little evidence to support either the view of the *equites* as a business class or of the senators hypocritically flouting a class code to which they paid lip-service. Most knights were in fact landowners and there was a property qualification for membership of their *ordo*. They were not typically industrialists or merchants and cannot be represented as a class according to Marxist criteria. Tax farmers (publicans) and big money lenders constituted an influential but exceptional sub-group. The extent to which members of the senatorial class dabbled in business was governed largely by political tactics, by the need to build up a following or otherwise gain influence. The necessity of distributing largess made large-scale borrowing by candidates for public office unavoidable. These people could look forward to recovering their expenditure at the expense of the wretched provincials of Africa and elsewhere, whom they bought the right to govern. But with the establishment of the Empire by Augustus, the power of both publicans and aristocratic governors to grind down the provinces diminished, as the state abandoned tax farming and replaced the republican system of annual magistrates at all levels of the administration with a permanent civil service. The tax farming inherited from the Hellenistic administration, that continued in Egypt, was subject to strict state control.

Because of the relatively humble status accorded to commerce the great cities of the classical Mediterranean differed profoundly from the cities which revived or were established in medieval Europe.

> The difference was not in the professional composition of the town dwellers ... When we compare the medieval town with the towns of other areas and other times we find a broad similarity both in the professional composition of the population as well as in urban functions. Yet there was an essential difference.
> In the towns of the classical world ... the merchant, the craftsman, the doctor, and the notary never acquired a socially prominent position. Even when they

acquired wealth, they acquiesced in an inferior social position: they passively accepted a low position on the social ladder and, at the same time, the prevalence of the cultural values of the ruling groups. The rural ideas of the upper classes permeated the whole society, and as the landed gentry dominated both the countryside and the towns socially, politically, and culturally, powerful elements of cohesion obliterated the differences between the urban and the rural world. The town was not an organism in itself, but rather an organ within the broader context of an urban-rural continuum . . .

The medieval city was dominated politically, socially, and culturally by the merchants and the moneychangers . . . and also by the pharmacists, the notaries, the lawyers, the judges, the doctors, and the like. It was this composite social group that from the beginning had been the driving force of the emergence of towns as independent bodies . . .[11]

Even Carthage, a city dedicated to trade and dominated by merchants, was remote in spirit from medieval Florence and Bruges, still more from 17th-century Amsterdam or London. The capitalism of the Carthaginian merchants one might say was an 'adventure capitalism'. They made large profits by exploiting 'unequal exchange' with barbarians and they allied trade to smuggling and piracy. Perhaps their reputation among the Romans for dishonesty and deceit was not entirely unjustified. They made little progress in commercial techniques or in money and banking. Indeed, one must be careful not to exaggerate the rôle of trade and money in the whole of ancient history. Domestic self-sufficiency and isolated local markets were typical, and there was little productive investment.

Egypt was always *sui generis* in the ancient world because of the ease with which its central government could impose its will. Alexandria was the greatest city in Africa, and yet urban autonomy was unknown in Egypt and devolution of authority came only in the later Roman period through the enfeeblement of central administration. Alexandria and the other Egyptian cities received a degree of self-government at the very end of the 2nd century A.D. The purpose of the concession was, it is suggested, primarily to ensure a supply of state officials by giving the city councils powers of appointment, and to secure the existence of institutions that could be held responsible for the good behaviour of those officials. The cities became the partner of the state in administration.

The presence of the gild in both ancient and medieval cities gives them a certain superficial resemblance to each other, but the ancient *collegium* was essentially different from the medieval gild. While the spontaneity of its origins cannot be doubted, the *collegium* came to be incorporated into the machinery of the state and even to be imposed by the government. Primarily devoted to the religious rather than the economic interests of merchants and craftsmen, it was regarded at the start with suspicion, but found to be useful for the collection of taxes, the requisition of goods and services and the imposition of discipline upon individuals. Trades essential for feeding and defending the empire were especially subject to state intervention. There was a tendency to compel sons to follow the calling of their fathers to punish desertion and to regulate marriage and inheritance. No gild was so important or so closely supervised as that of the *navicularii*, the shippers responsible for getting the African *annona* to Italy. The gilds of the classical world were never the vehicle of bourgeois self-assertion.

NOTES

1. Marx, Karl: *Capital* I (London, Everyman edition, 1930), p. 379
2. Marx, K.: *Grundisse, Foundations of the Critique of Political Economy* (Harmondsworth, 1973), p. 486
3. Jones, A. H. M.: 'Egypt and Rome' (Glanville, S. R. K. ed.: *The Legacy of Egypt*, Oxford, 1942), p. 289
4. Quoted Johnson, A. C.: *Roman Egypt to the Reign of Diocletian* (Patterson, N. J., 1938), p. 335–6
5. Weber, Max: *General Economic History* (London, n.d.), p. 334–5
6. Rostovtseff, Michael: *The Social and Economic History of the Roman Empire* (Oxford, 2nd edn. 1957), Volume I, p. xii
7. Rostovtseff, M.: *The Social and Economic History of the Hellenistic World* (Oxford, 1941), p. 1116
8. Quoted Finley, M. I.: *The Ancient Economy* (London, 1973), p. 22
9. Jones, A. H. M.: Loc. cit., p. 283
10. Quoted Finley, M. I.: Op. cit., p. 42
11. Cipolla, Carlo M.: *The Fontana Economic History of Europe*, Volume I (London, 1972), p. 17–8

Further reading

Carney, T. F.: *The Economics of Antiquity: Controls, Gifts and Trade* (Lawrence, Kansas, 1973)
Charles-Picard, Gilbert & Colette: Op. cit. (see p. 46)
Charles-Picard, Gilbert & Colette: *The Life and Death of Carthage* (London, 1968)
Decret, François: *Carthage ou l'empire de la mer* (Paris, 1977)
Eisenstadt, S. N.: *The Decline of Empires* (Englewood Cliffs, N. J., 1967)
Emery, W. B.: Op. cit. (see above, p. 104)
Finley, M. I.: Op. cit. (see above, note 8)
Fraser, P. M.: Op. cit. (see p. 130)
Gsell, Stéphane: *Histoire ancienne de l'Afrique du nord*, Volume II (Reprinted Osnabrück, 1972)
Harris, J. R.: Op. cit. (see p. 83)
Heichelheim, Fritz M.: *An Ancient Economic History*, 3 volumes (Leiden, 1958–1970)
Hindess, Barry & Hirst, Paul Q.: *Pre-capitalist Modes of Production* (London and Boston, 1975)

Johnson, A. C. & West, L. C.: Op. cit. (see p. 47)
Johnson, A. C.: Op. cit. (see p. 47)
Jones, A. H. M.: *The Cities of the Eastern Roman Provinces* (Oxford, 1937)
Jones, A. H. M.: *The Roman Economy; Studies in Economic and Administrative History* (Oxford, 1974)
Krader, L.: *The Asiatic Mode of Production* (Vangorcum, 1975)
Marx, Karl: *Pre-capitalist Economic Formations* (London, 1964)
Montet, P.: Op. cit. (see p. 66)
Polanyi, Karl: *The Livelihood of Man* (New York, San Francisco and London, 1977)
Rostovtseff, Michael: *The Social and Economic History of the Hellenistic World* (Oxford, 1941)
Rostovtseff, Michael: *The Social and Economic History of the Roman Empire* (Oxford, 2nd edn. 1957)
Stevens, Courtenay Edward: 'Agriculture and rural life in the Roman Empire' (Chapter II, Postan, M. M. ed.: *The Cambridge Economic History of Europe*, Volume I, Cambridge, 2nd edn. 1966)
Walbank, Frank William: 'Trade and industry under the later Roman Empire in the west' (Chapter II, Postan, M. M. ed.: *The Cambridge Economic History of Europe*, Volume I, Cambridge, 2nd edn. 1966)
Weber, Max: *General Economic History* (London, n.d.)

2. MUSLIM AFRICA

i) *Muslim feudalism*

The Arabs, having no tradition of highly centralized government, took charge of the existing administrative manchinery, Persian or Byzantine, in the territories they overran. In Egypt certain changes were made in the fiscal system. Some cities undertook to pay an agreed annual lump sum, while big estates which had previously been responsible for their own taxation lost their independence. Non-Muslims had to pay the *Jizyah*, a poll-tax which may have been roughly graduated, and Muslims the less onerous *Zakāt*, an income-cum-capital tax. The land revenue (*Kharāj*) was maintained in much the same form as it had always had and was as burdensome as ever. There were also taxes payable by traders, heavier for non-Muslims.

The Arab empire did not have a strong central government. Both ideology and tradition condemned it to disintegration. The conquerors formed a military élite which did not interfere with the internal arrangements of the vanquished communities, and the victor in each territory that was overrun expected to be left largely to his own devices. Although the pre-Muslim state structure was accepted, it was regarded with the deepest suspicion by the pious, who considered the legitimate rôle of the state was confined to the protection of the community of believers and who were unwilling to entrust much power to their rulers. Fissiparous tendencies were reinforced by internal dissension expressed in tribal and doctrinal terms, by the difficulty of meeting the costs of maintaining professional armies and by the deterioration, already apparent before conquest, in the quality of the inherited bureaucracies. Divided Islam gave way to absolutist successor states, and the constitutional theory of the orthodox, Sunni, jurists developed to the point that an incumbent sovereign, irrespective of how he obtained power, was upheld as the legitimate authority in the state, entitled to obedience, however unjust and immoral his rule. Where mere success legitimated the seizure of government and as effective administration weakened, power was prone to fitful and arbitrary exercise, particularly in remote areas.

With the decline of their ability to maintain an efficient administrative structure, Arab authorities were compelled to resort to tax farming. The tax farm, initially leased to the wealthy and influential for a varying period, tended to become hereditary and to yield a decreasing revenue to the state. In Egypt the Fātimids were able to dispense with it in their first vigour and restore some efficiency to the administration. For their armies they relied upon mamluks, slaves trained as soldiers and set free, Turks for cavalry, Sudanese for infantry. In the course of the 11th and 12th centuries, however, the slave soldiers became unmanageable and the Fātimid caliphs became puppets in the hands of military adventurers. The tax farm reappeared to raise sufficient revenue to pay the troops and maintain a luxurious court.

In the latter part of the 12th century the tax farm gave way, under the Ayyubids, to the iqṭāʿ, in imitation of Seljuk practice. This was the right to collect taxes in a specified district, other than those on trade, and its purpose was the support of the sultan himself, military officers, high officials and members of the sultan's family in lieu of a state salary. It differed from tax farming in that all the money collected went to the grantee. The iqṭāʿ system persisted under the Mamluk sultanate, though towards the end of its rule, in the 15th century, there was a shrinkage of iqṭāʿ land and a tendency to an increase in both state land and private estates that originated in the conversion of the iqṭāʿ by one device or another. Since much allodial (freehold) land was legally or illegally free of taxation, the trend had an adverse effect upon state income and resulted in all those revenue-raising expedients – especially debasement and monopoly – that had disastrous consequences for the Egyptian economy. Land ceased to be the chief source of state revenue.

Although the iqṭāʿ system is reminiscent of the feudalism of medieval Europe, especially in the obligation of the high military officer to maintain a force of retainers, it differed in a number of ways. For one thing, it did not involve conditional land tenure, which was characteristic of European feudalism. Although it may have tended to be assimilated to land ownership and, like a fief, its granting was conditional upon the performance of services, yet the iqṭāʿ was not a grant of land, but a grant of revenue collecting rights. European feudalism was associated with fragmentation of sovereignty.

Egypt, though disintegrating tendencies became apparent under the Mamluks, remained a centralized state with a bureaucracy that had a special department for the supervision of the *iqṭāʿs*. The *iqṭāʿ* was a benefice rather
than a fief. Although it did tend to become hereditary, it was, at least to
begin with, revocable, and it was subject to periodic, if infrequent, realloca-
tion. It was not a seigneurie or manse; it was not run as an estate and the
grantee exercised no rights of jurisdiction or administration; and it did not
turn the peasant into a legal serf. Unfreedom that stopped short of chattel
slavery had existed from time immemorial in Egypt and the *iqṭāʿ* made little
difference to the situation of the Egyptian cultivator. He remained part of a
village community that paid taxes to an *iqṭāʿ* holder instead of a state official.
Frequently the *iqṭāʿ*, which could vary in size from a share in a village to many
villages, was composed of separate fragments and the grantee lived in town,
not on the land whose revenue he appropriated. Personal vassalage was not
unknown, but it was not necessarily associated with the *iqṭāʿ*, as in Europe
it was with the fief, and it was largely confined to the towns. In Marxist
terms, the *iqṭāʿ* made no difference to the method of surplus value appropriation. Serfdom was not the dominant mode of production, and Muslim feudalism was only a superstructural phenomenon.

    In the two and a half centuries of their rule, after the overthrow of the
Ayyubids, the Mamluks ruled Egypt and their possessions in Syria under a
sultan who was himself the nominal representative of the ʿAbbāsid caliph.
In practice they constituted an alien oligarchy that kept up its numbers by
the purchase of slaves, but it was an oligarchy subject to severe internal dissensions. The centralized state remained intact, but the senior members of the
caste, the amirs, each with his slave retainers and local centre of power, sometimes defied, and often contended for, the sultanate. In the earlier, Turkish,
period of Mamluk rule the crown sometimes passed from father to son, but
there was always scope for the adventurer able to build up a following,
while polygamy and the absence of primogeniture led to succession disputes.
In the later, Circassian, period, from the late 14th century, the hereditary
principle received scant respect.

    The *iqṭāʿ* was also a feature of administration in the Maghrib, where the
beneficiary was commonly the tribal chief, Berber or Arab. Although it required payment for privileges in the form of military service by tribal levies,
its resemblance to the fief was superficial. Since in practice the tribe retained
its communal rights in the land – legally vested in the state – and was sufficiently resilient to curb chiefly power, the possibility of seigniorial powers
did not exist. It is doubtful whether feudalism can ever truly emerge when
tribalism is powerful. Nomadic pastoralism, characteristic of desert and
steppe, was conducive to tribal cohesion, and the ubiquity of the martial
arts where every man was potentially a mounted soldier meant that no one

stood in need of protection by professional warriors who extorted seigniorial privileges in payment. The disintegrative forces were there, but promoting disintegration into tribes, not intoarbitrarily determined territorial fragments as in medieval Europe.

After the break-up of the Arab empire the Berber states of North Africa were subject to tension between centrifugal and centripetal forces. Themselves tribally based, the Berber dynasties (Fāṭimids, Hafsids, Zirids, Marinids, etc.) had difficulty in imposing their will upon rival tribes. In attempting to do so they were sometimes able to exploit tribal differences and divisions and they were helped by the profits of trade, which could be used for a paid bureaucracy and for servile or mercenary troops, by the support of the towns and settled agriculture and by the moral strength that Islam could give. This centralizing reinforcement, however, was not entirely to be relied upon. The trading towns of the northern fringe of the desert – Sijilmasa, Wargla and Ghadames – resisted a control that tended to be intermittent, little more than suzerainty or even occasional bullying. Trade itself was subject to disruption; mercenary troops were sometimes ill-disciplined; and religious legitimacy was not readily available to dynasties that had to no claim to caliphal authority or were not legitimated by identification with doctrinal reform. This situation was not profoundly disturbed by the imposition of Ottoman rule, which, in any case, was restricted to the eastern Maghrib.

The Ottomans annexed an Egypt suffering from inflation and economic depression. Such was the state of industry that Egyptian textiles were being undercut on the home market by European imports. The chief economic problem they faced was to restore the economy, and the chief administrative problem, to destroy the power of the Mamluks. An attempt was therefore made to transform the *iqṭāʿs* simply into administrative units run by officials who collected the revenue on behalf of the state. The Ottoman empire was itself familiar with the practice of making a grant of land (*timar*) in exchange for military service. This was very similar to the European fief. Though legally not heritable, it did in fact normally pass to the holder's heir. The grantee himself held land in the locality and he came to exercise seigniorial rights. However, at the time of the conquest of Egypt, the 'fief' was falling out of use in the Ottoman dominions as the government was increasingly able to govern and collect taxes and furnish itself with a professional fighting force, the Janissaries. Yet in Egypt, in spite of the fact that *iqṭāʿ* system was already in a state of decline owing to the fall in the value of the income from it, the Ottomans experienced the utmost difficulty in finding a substitute and in excluding the Mamluks from power. Competent salaried officials were hard to come by; those installed tended to be corrupt and lax; and there were limits to the extent to which the sultan in Constantinople could enforce his will in his outlying provinces. The shortage of officials (*emins*) led to the amalgamation of *iqtā's* (increasingly called *muqāṭa'as*) into units too large for supervision by a single man, and the outcome was the readmission into the administrative apparatus of the Mamluks, to whom the *emins* assigned tax farms (*iltazām*). Little as they liked the resurgence of the Mamluks, the government of the Porte acquiesced in an arrangement which guaranteed a regular, though small, share of the taxes collected and which ensured the supply of Egyptian grain to the metropolitan area.

The tax farm typical of Ottoman administration in Egypt did not constitute private landed property, though there was a small amount of land in private ownership exempted from taxation. It was mostly run as a business enterprise by a syndicate of partners who each held shares in more than one. At first all sorts of people, apart from Mamluks, participated, including state officials, bedouin chiefs and members of the imperial family. More and more it fell into the hands of the great Mamluk families who succeeded in eliminating their rivals and eventually it became hereditary (as the *malikāne*) and virtually private property that could be bought and sold subject only to the payment of a transfer fee to the state. The revenue transferred to Constantinople, though not declining in absolute terms, represented a decreasing share of the total revenue actually collected in Egypt. The burden of taxation became heavier as population growth induced pressure upon the land. Locked in a perpetual struggle for power that prevented united defiance of the Porte, the Mamluks pushed their demands beyond all reason. Tax collection became an annual plundering expedition conducted by soldiery. The population growth was halted and reversed. This was the situation found by the invading French at the end of the 18th century.

By the end of the 18th century Ottoman power in Africa was reduced to an ill-defined suzerainty. Other Muslim states in Africa, too, were held together somewhat loosely because of the difficulties of direct rule. The 19th century Omani dominion of East Africa was in practice a confederation of local rulers acknowledging the suzerainty of the sultan at Zanzibar. They collected the taxes on trade and paid a fixed sum at regular intervals. The eastern Maghrib, nominally part of the Ottoman empire, was split up into tributary states of no great power. As early as the middle of the 17th century the Ottoman ruler of Algeria was a mere figurehead and real power was the prize of a contest between the military (Janissaries) and corsairs. Piracy, with its rewards in the form of ransom for captives or the proceeds of their sale into slavery and of export of booty, provided Algiers with economic support until the latter part of the 17th century, and with its decline, the city itself was impoverished. From the end of the 17th century the ruler of Algeria was the dey, originally the creature of the corsairs. His power, however, was limited and precarious. Each of the three provinces of the state had a bey and each was virtually independent, recognising the suzerainty of the dey by the payment of tribute. The beys in turn had to show a certain deference to the tribal leaders. The situation was not much different in Morocco, where the state's ability to impose its will on the tribes was no better than it had been in the Middle Ages. The *qāid*, tribal governor, nominally appointed by the sultan, owed his position to his tribal authority and appropriated his due share of the taxes that he collected. Punitive expeditions against recalcitrant tribes were at best temporary in their effect.

Frederick Horneman's description of Fezzan at the end of the 18th century illustrates the relationship between its ruler and his suzerain in Tripoli, the instability of the state due to the absence of well-defined rules of succession, the important part played by slaves in the administration, the significance of trade as a source of revenue and the alienation of revenue sources for the support of princes and officials.

Fezzan is governed by a sultan, descendant from the family of the Shereefs. The tradition is, that the ancestors of the reigning prince, coming from western Africa, invaded and conquered Fezzan about 500 years past. The sultan reigns over his dominions with unlimited power, but he holds them tributary to the Bashaw of Tripoly: the amount of tribute was formerly 6 000 dollars, it is now reduced to 4 000; and an officer of the bashaw comes annually to Mourzouk, to receive this sum, or its value in gold, senna, or slaves. This officer, whilst in commission, is called *Bey-el-nobe*. On his departure from Tripoly, which is every year in November, he takes all travelling merchants under his protection . . .

The throne of Fezzan is hereditary: the crown, however, descends not in all cases, directly from father to son: it is the eldest prince of the royal family, who succeeds; and such may be a nephew, in preference to a son who is younger. This custom frequently occasions bloodshed: the son of the deceased sultan may be of sufficient age to govern, though younger than the collateral heir; and having interest and adherents formed by his past high connections and situation, will often be ready to controvert the law of succession, as inapplicable in principle to the case of himself and competitor, equally arrived at the age of manhood and discretion: the question of right is then decided by the sword . . .

The sultan's court or official attendants are, the *kaledyma*, or first minister; the *keijumma*, or second minister and the general of his forces; a number of black slaves, and a few white slaves, who are by the Mahometans termed Mamelukes. The *kaledyma* and *keijumma* must both be free-born men; whatever their nominal rank, they at present have but little influence. All the interest and power rests with the Mamelukes, who are mostly Europeans, Greeks, Genoese, or their immediate descendants. The black slaves, are purchased whilst yet boys, and are educated for the court according to their dispositions and talents; some of these too have gained great ascendancy with the sultan . . .

The revenues of the sultan are produced from certain assessments of tax on all gardens and cultivated lands, and from arbitrary fines and requisitions. The slaves employed in collecting these imposts, are most exorbitant and oppressive, if not bribed. The sultan derives further income from duties on foreign trade, paid by several caravans. That from Cairo pays from six to eight dollars for each camel load. The caravans from Bornou and Soudan pay two *matkals*, for each slave on sale. He further possesses a territorial revenue, collected from domains of the crown; from salt-pools; from the natron lakes; and from the royal gardens and woods. The present sultan has made great addition to his treasures by predatory expeditions, which he occasionally directs against the Tibboes of the tribe of Burgu.

The public expenditure consists chiefly in maintenance of the sultan, his court, and palace. The cadi and department of justice, those of the religious order, and the great officers of government, are severally supported from the produce of datetree woods and gardens, granted as *usufruct* to those holding the respective offices. The princes of the royal family are supported from the proceeds of appropriate territory, and by certain proportions of corn delivered weekly from the sultan's stores, and from occasional exactions on the people, levied by their personal authority, and by means of their slaves. Such oppression is a natural result of the powers of collection, and means of enforcement, and adjudication of right, being vested in each occasional lord of the domain.[1]

ii) *Muslim merchants and states*
The Arab empire, united for a time by political authority and for much longer by shared religion and law, embraced so many geographical regions and civilizations that there was ample scope for regional specialization and exchange. The Arabs were a trading people, accustomed to urban life and long established as the middlemen of the transit trade of the Middle East and the Indian Ocean. Exaggeration must be avoided. The great Arabian peninsula was given up largely to subsistence pastoralism, and production for the market was minute. Yet trade brought profit to merchants and to organisers of transport and, no doubt, to the tribal leaders in a position to exact tolls from passing caravans. Indeed, it has been suggested that the rise of Islam itself was related to rivalry between Mecca (whence Muhammad fled) and Medina (which received him) over control of the Yemen-Syria trade route, and to social tensions within Mecca, where Muhammad espoused the cause of the poor. Even in the context of social and economic explanations of the phenomenon of Islam, it is scarcely possible to draw attention exclusively to the significance of overpopulation among an unsophisticated pastoral people. Although the rank and file of the Arab armies that overthrew the ancient empires of the Middle East may well have been uncouth bedouin, Mecca, the birthplace of Islam, was a trading city, where money was lent for interest, trading companies were active and merchants were influential. In the lush days of conquest profits were made more easily in administering – or simply battening upon – the newly-won empire, but Arab merchants continued to trade and were in a position to become prosperous from ministering to the needs of their co-religionists grown fat on the proceeds of conquest. As conversion became common and arabization proceeded, the class of Muslim merchants changed in ethnic composition and grew ever larger.

Islam, by virtue of its egalitarian and cosmopolitan nature and its impact upon the existing social order, did something to promote the social mobility that was conducive to trade and was in turn reinforced by the expansion of trade. It produced some distinguished geographers and made an important contribution to cartography and navigation, while the debt of African historiography to such indefatigable and discriminating travellers as Ibn Baṭṭūṭa can scarcely be exaggerated. Nor was the habit of travel confined to the select few. For the honour and prestige accorded to pilgrimage were not without their effects on trade. Mecca and Medina were the principal destinations, but Cairo was the place where a great annual caravan assembled, drawing the faithful from all over northern Africa for the journey to the holy cities; and trade was carried on throughout the pilgrimage.

Much more so than Christianity, Islam, without priests and hierarchy, was the religion of a book, the Koran, held by the faithful to be the word of God as vouchsafed to Muḥammad. The Koran was a manual of ritual, morals and law, and it brought together under a common moral code and, therefore, in mutual trust, merchants over the whole Islamic world. The development of Dyula and Hausa trade in West Africa owed much to shared religion. The Sufi brotherhoods, although primarily serving a religious purpose, did much to foster trade by providing accommodation for merchants and their goods, facilitating communications, creating a climate of trust favourable to the granting of credit, providing the means of settling disputes and even themselves engaging in trade. Yet it would be rash to suggest that a common religion sweeps away all commercial barriers or that it is the only tie that can draw together widely separated merchants in a trading network. It is necessary to weigh in the balance the disruptive effects of revivalist movements, like those that swept the western Sudan in the 19th century or the reform movement of Muḥammad Ahmad, the Mahdi of the eastern Sudan, which evinced a desire not only to purge doctrine of heretical accretions, but above all, to return to the supposed integrity, social equality and economic justice of primitive Islam. The outcome was often the formation of states of which the raison d'être was the prosecution of Muslim holy war, with its concomitants of plunder and slavery.

Muslim state policy tended to have varying effects upon the prosperity of commerce. The states of Egypt and North Africa took a keen interest in its conduct, partly because of its contribution to their treasuries, partly because of its importance as a source of strategic imports – firearms in the 17th and 18th centuries in Morocco, military slaves in Mamluk Egypt, tin from Cornwall in the Ottoman empire. State interest was on the one hand beneficial and constructive, on the other hand regulatory to the point of suffocation. Wells were dug along the desert routes, inns established along the more populous ones. Merchants frequenting the Red Sea were obliged by the

Mamluk sultans to possess a passport, the issue of which was a source of income for the state, but which was a guarantee of protection for the private merchant. Throughout the Muslim states, as a rule, private traders were free to carry on trade subject to taxation. Not all of them were Muslims. Jews were very active everywhere, and some Egyptian merchants were Christian Copts. Jews were also prominent in banking and administration. Foreigners, though highly taxed, were provided with *funduqs*, allowed their own consuls and given the protection of the law for themselves and their goods. As an English observer reported towards the end of the 16th century, when Egypt was ruled by the Ottomans,

> It is certaine, that this haven of Alexandria is one of the chiefest havens in the world: for hither come to traffique people of every Nation, and all sorts of vessels which goe round about the citie. It is more inhabited by strangers, merchants, and Christians, then by men of the countrey which are but few in number. Within the citie are five Fontechi, that is to say, one of the Frenchmen, where the consul is resident, & this is the fairest and most commodious of all the rest. Of the other foure, two belong to the Venetians, one to the Ragusans, and the fourth to the Genoueses. And all strangers which come to traffique there, except the Venetians, are under the French Consull. It is also to be understood, that all the Christians dwell within their Fontechi, and every evening at the going downe of the sunne, they which are appointed for that office goe about and shut up all the gates of the saide Fontechi outward, and the Christians shut the same within: and so likewise they doe on the Friday (which is the Moores and the Turkes Sabboth) till their devotions be expired. And by this meanes all parties are secure and voide of feare: for in so doing the Christians may sleepe quietly and not feare robbing, and the Moores nede not doubt whiles they sleepe or pray, that the Christians should make any tumult, as in times past hath happened.[2]

The fondachi were, however, a mixed blessing. While they did ensure protection to European merchants, residence in them was compulsory and therefore, like the compulsory sale of goods to the state or at least conformity to regulations governing sales, they interfered with the free conduct of business.

Officials and rulers were themselves actively engaged in trade, participating in private caravans or organising their own and operating their own merchant vessels, warehouses and shops. The Fāṭimid caliphs of Egypt, in addition to trading, owned and rented out all or most of the shops and brick houses of Cairo. Rulers were, however, frequently tempted to look beyond the modest income that came from steady trade and indulge in forays for booty or extort the gains of monopoly and enforced sale. In 734 the Umayyad governors of the Maghrib despatched a raiding expedition into the western Sudan, which seized and brought back large quantities of gold and many slaves. The Fāṭimids assumed pre-emptive rights in the case of imported iron and timber. The Almoravids destroyed the capital of Ghana in 1086 and the

Moroccans overthrew Songhai at the end of the 16th century. The Zirid rulers of Ifriqiya took to piracy in the 11th century, the Hafsid rulers of Tunisia in the 14th, and the Algerian deys and the Moroccan sultans in the 17th. State monopolies were imposed in 15th- and 16th-century Egypt and Morocco, and the insolvent Mamluk sultans of Egypt also manipulated the currency in a variety of ways to their own immediate advantage and looked around for rich merchants to mulct. The farming of numerous taxes on trade was practised from earliest Muslim times. Debts were settled by the assignation of specific taxes, and the recipient exploited his farm to the limit, inflicting great damage in the process. Intermittent government fiscal reforms were as superficial as they were ephemeral.

The Barbary rulers of the Ottoman empire were especially rapacious. The following was the experience of a French factor, Romane Sonnings, aboard an English vessel trading at Tripoli in 1584.

The commodities of that place are sweete oiles: the king there is a merchant, and the rather (willing to preferre himself before his commons) requested our said factors to traffique with him, and promised them that if they would take his oiles at his owne price, they should pay no manner of custome, and they tooke of him certaine tunnes of oile: and afterwards perceiving that they might have farre better cheape notwithstanding the custome free, they desired the king to licence them to take the oiles at the pleasure of his commons, for that his price did exceede theirs: whereunto the king would not agree, but was rather contented to abate his price, insomuch that the factors bought all their oyles of the king custome free, and so laded the same aboord . . .

Then went wee to warpe out the shippe, and presently the king sent a boate aboord of us, with three men in her, commaunding the saide Sonnings to come a shoare: at whose comming, the king demaunded of his custome for the oyles: Sonnings answered him that his highnesse had promised to deliver them custome free. But notwithstanding the king weighed not his said promise, and as an infidell that hath not the feare of God before his eyes, nor regarde of his worde, albeit hee was a king, hee caused the sayde Sonnings to pay custome to the uttermost penie.[3]

Sonnings was subsequently hanged for trying to smuggle out a Christian debtor, and the ship was impounded.

State industrial enterprise and regulation of private manufacturers were common in the Muslim world, particularly in Egypt with its strong tradition of étatisme. Intervention was not only in such obvious spheres as coinage, armaments, shipbuilding and ship-repairing, but also in the manufacture of paper and fine fabrics.

iii) *Capitalism in Islam*
Islam, the community of the faithful, each of the same value in the eyes of God, gave rise to egalitarian ideas that were a recurring inspiration to puri-

tanical sects which sought to convince themselves that, at some earlier period, there had been a golden age of social justice. All the evidence, however, seems to point to the existence of economic and social differentiation from earliest times. Merchant and financial capital both existed in the Muslim world as they had done in the classical world. While the Koran appears to condemn it (though its meaning is a subject of dispute) and the Sunnah (a collection of traditions concerning Muhammad's deeds and words, but lacking the authority of the Koran) prohibits it more explicitly, lending at interest – even lending at usurious rates – was nonetheless widely practised, and its practice exercised the ingenuity of Muslim lawyers in providing justification for it. Abu Ishāk in the 11th century argued that it was admissible for the borrower to pay back more than he had borrowed on condition that he was not under constraint and made no written promise. Where there were sizable non-Muslim communities, it was often the case that usury became the speciality of Christians or Jews who had no doubts about the legitimacy of interest and did not have to go to the trouble of camouflaging what they were doing, but it is evident that Muslims too were far from averse to usurious practices, even when willing non-believers were available. In the trading centres of the East African coast in the 19th century Indian Muslims were the money lenders, advancing both money and trade goods to Arabs running caravans into the interior.

Apart from its disputed prohibition of usury there is nothing in the Koran incompatible with the values of capitalism. In wealth, to be sure, lay the source of possible spiritual danger, and it was, *sub specie aeternitatis*, futile, unless accompanied by the fulfilment of all the obligations of dispensing charity. Yet the Book condemns neither property nor the pursuit of profit; nor is wage labour frowned upon. The Sunnah goes so far as to speak highly of merchants – 'God's faithful trustees on earth' – and of honestly performed trade. The trading profession attracted more social prestige than that of the farmer and artisan, especially trading in cloth. The only suspect commercial activities were money-changing (because of its association with usury), and trading in grain. The latter was thought discreditable because of the opportunities it offered for speculation in foodstuffs. Muslim lawyers condemned any interference in the free play of supply and demand, some even condemning price-fixing by public authorities. Free enterprise was favoured, and generally the constraints upon the Muslim merchant were not irksome. If Ibn Khaldūn is to be believed, such obligations as religion did impose, were treated with little respect, and, he suggested, no merchant permitted himself to be hampered by the demands of morality or even civilised behaviour, in an occupation 'in which one necessarily has to make use of cunning, quibbling, tricks, quarrelsomeness, tactless insistence'.[4]

In medieval Islam the partnership was developed as a means of mobilising

scarce capital for both legitimate trade and corsairing, and it has been suggested that the European *commenda* was modelled on the Muslim *qirād*. Muslim Africa had many great merchants, to be found equally in the Maghrib,
where they participated in trade across the Sahara and across the Mediterranean, and in Egypt, one of the areas where the Kārīmī merchants conducted a trade which extended on a large scale throughout the Middle and
Far East and the Horn of Africa. Although the risks they ran were great,
their profits were commensurate, and some were extremely wealthy. A 10th-
century Arab traveller saw at Audaghost in the western Sudan a cheque for
42 000 dinārs drawn by a merchant from Sijilmasa. When merchants invested in land, as they sometimes did, it was an exercise in prudence, insurance against crippling loss, rather than because landed wealth enjoyed
greater prestige, or trade was thought degrading. There were partnerships
and firms, mostly family firms, conducting business over a wide area, for
instance the Maqqarī brothers in the 13th century, who carried on trade
not only within North Africa, but also with Europe and the Sudan, and had
representatives in Tlemcen (Algeria), Sijilmasa (Morocco) and Walata
(western Sudan); or Abu'l- Abbās al-Hijāz⁻ and his seven sons, trading
through eastern Islam and beyond its boundaries to China. Such a vigorous
trade was an indisputable stimulus to the production of goods for the market
and, therefore, to the development of production capital. Much Islamic
trade was undoubtedly of a transit character, but there was also a good deal
of local and regional specialization in craft and agricultural production, and
at least some industrial production was carried on in enterprises that may
with justice be considered typical of a capitalist mode of production. The
element of rational calculation stressed by Max Weber as a characteristic of
capitalism was by no means absent.

However, despite these indications of incipient capitalism there was no
sign, even in Egypt, economically the most precocious region of Muslim
Africa, of the emergence of a cohesive and self-confident bourgeoisie. The
rôle of the state and of nobles, whose revenue was drawn primarily from the
land, penetrated trade and industry too deeply. There was no chance of
merchants, craftsmen and professional people dominating the towns and
challenging the military ruling class. The Muslim city did not differ fundamentally from the classical city.

> The town, the uncontested basis of Islam, was in the first instance a citadel of
> the faith, the seat of the governor, and the centre of an administrative area.[5]

In medieval Europe, the bourgeoisie, frequently asserting its will through
merchants' gilds, secured a share or control of municipal government.
In the Islamic world, even the great Kārīmī merchants with their vast for-

tunes, their extensive organization and their trading fleets were unable to withstand the exactions of the Mamluk government in its increasingly desperate search for revenue. Their wealth and power declined after the 14th century. In the later Middle Ages, Europe overtook Islam in the development of business organization and methods.

The economic practice of medieval Islam furnished in many respects as propitious a climate for the blossoming of capitalism as did Europe in the Middle Ages, but capitalist institutions and the capitalist mentality failed to achieve a dominant position. The city had no independent existence recognised by Islamic law and was subject, if not always to the central government, then to a feudal (if the term is appropriate) magnate, who normally resided in the city rather than on an estate, unlike his European counterpart (except in Italy, where he identified himself with the economic forces released by the cities, if he could not contain them). The conquerors of Egypt and North Africa took over the existing cities, leaving them to function in much the same way as before. The new cities they built, notably Cairo, were modelled on the old, but soon became chaotic as private interest prevailed in the absence of any sense of civic solidarity. The contrast between the bourgeois-dominated city states of the northern shores of the Mediterranean, especially Italy, and the Muslim cities of its southern shores was marked. Although Muslim rulers certainly had an interest in trade and, in some instances, privateering, they were not essentially merchants themselves or the representatives of the merchant community, dedicated to commerce and profit maximization. After the 11th century European merchants were far more dynamic and aggressive, adequately supported by the force and diplomacy of governments they themselves controlled, not thwarted by states with interests which did not always coincide with mercantile ones. Venice and Genoa and the other Christian trading states invested their resources in ships, having mercenaries to protect their territorial interests (though it is true that these grew). Egypt, governed by mercenaries, certainly did invest sporadically in ships for the protection of commerce, but preferred in the end to protect their commercial revenue by bullying the merchants. The Ottomans, with considerable success in the eastern Mediterranean, sought command of the sea, but they were checked by Venice and Spain at Lepanto in 1571, and even in the eastern Mediterranean they were unable to sustain their position.

Perhaps the trading towns of the northern fringe of the Sahara and of the East African coast came nearest to providing the conditions that favoured capitalism in the Muslim world, ruled as they were by merchant prince or commercial oligarchy and dedicated to trade and the pursuit of profit. They had the advantage of being remote from the ambitions of the rulers of large territorial states and had environs that were either too empty, in the case of the Sahara, or too alien, in the case of East Africa, to fire the ambition of local rulers to turn from commerce to conquest. But these towns were tiny compared with those of the Mediterranean basin, crude provincial imitations of the Muslim cities of the Middle East and India. Their geographical remoteness was a source of weakness as well as strength. The self-assertion of the Italian cities had a primarily political explanation, the collapse of the power of territorial states, rather than a geographical one. The East African and Saharan towns suffered from a dependence upon a trade that was almost exclusively in luxury commodities, a weakness that afflicted all Muslim cities and mercantile communities except the very biggest, which necessarily had a considerable trade in foodstuffs and industrial raw materials.

Rural life in the Muslim world did not quicken in response to urban development. On the contrary, the city was ruralized, in the sense that it was dominated by a parasitical class living at the expense of the countryside. Urban values did not permeate rural society. Although the conquered peoples had found little incentive to resist the Arab onslaught on behalf of rulers who were grasping and oppressive, their situation remained unimproved, apart from the relief of Christian heretics and schismatics from Byzantine persecution. Their economic position remained the same, thus inhibiting the growth of a capitalist organization of society. In Italy the countryside was subordinated to genuine urban interests, while elsewhere in Europe either landowners lived on their estates and sought to increase their income through agricultural improvement or they became courtiers and a money-using peasantry developed. The Muslim cultivator was usually the inert victim of the exploitation of a ruler or a ruling class. Moreover, he came to be cut off from his rulers by language and sometimes by religious differences. The Arab or the arabized Egyptian peasant, despised by his Turkish-speaking masters, Seljuk, Mamluk, Ottoman, took refuge in quietism and mysticism. It was only where tribal organization remained strong that the countryside escaped the domination of a city-dwelling élite that drew its income from agriculture.

Throughout the Muslim world, such was the disparity of wealth and such the poverty of the overwhelming majority that no mass market existed. Islamic society typically displayed a stark contrast of grinding poverty suffered by the majority and unbridled luxury indulged in by a small ruling group that, to a greater or smaller extent, mitigated the sufferings of the many by the fulfilment of the duties of charity demanded by religion. Most people were shackled to a rural life of unending and ill-rewarded toil, against which they from time to time rebelled by supporting puritanical religious movements such as those that periodically swept the Maghrib. The same remedy was the only one available to the urban poor, too. Because they were, however, concentrated near the centres of power, their needs attracted more sympathy from their rulers, who at least saw to it that they were fed.

Even if one can reasonably talk of a Muslim bourgeoisie comprising merchants and those entrepreneurs engaged in comparatively large-scale manufacture, it cannot but be acknowledged that it was a tiny class because of the risks attendant upon commerce and industry and of a shortage of the requisite capital and skills. Marxists would deny that they constituted a true bourgeoisie, controlling as they did only a small portion of the means of production and disposing of only a small share of the total product. Land, the chief means of production, was owned either by the state or, in Egypt, to an extent by great landowners, and little agricultural production was destined for the market, even that of private estates. The rôle of the state, moreover, extended beyond mere landownership. In Egypt it exercised a monopoly of production in some industries and appropriated an important share even of those goods produced outside its direct control.

Medieval Islam experienced no class struggle. The merchants were not in conflict with a feudal class. In the early Middle Ages they formed part of a composite multifunctional ruling class in a state of constant flux, founded on wealth rather than on birth, on military prowess or on land, and deriving an income from land and, either through taxation or direct participation, from trade. The continuity of trade and the circulation of money were never disrupted in the Arab countries to the extent that they were in Europe in the early Middle Ages, so that landowning never became virtually the sole source of power and the sole means of remuneration, and merchants did not reappear after an interval as suspect intruders, but retained an honourable and even influential position in society. They had close ties with the state, to their mutual advantage. Tax farming was common and a means to capital formation, and loans to rulers, though hazardous, were profitable. Individuals from the mercantile community acquired high positions in the service of the state, yet no independent power. In Egypt their prestige and influence suffered from the policy of the Mamluks, who arrogated to themselves an increasing rôle in commerce. Merchants had neither the will nor the power to impose their interests or Kārimī them. Nowhere was this better seen than in the fate of the wealthy protect merchants in 15th-century Egypt.

It was perhaps above all the 'spirit of capitalism' that was missing. Ibn Khaldūn's view of mercantile behaviour notwithstanding, society was essentially conformist, subservient to authority and to the accepted social code, and according status to the individual only as a member of an acceptable group or institution. Order, stability and continuity were valued, not innovation and enterprise. There was a profound belief that the human predicament was beyond remedy. Yet it would be difficult to argue that fatalism was the necessary consequence of Islam. The Protestant ethic, said to have fostered western capitalism, was a no more significant aspect of Calvinism than a belief that could easily lead to fatalism, the belief in an unalterable predestination to spiritual salvation or damnation. The Muslim usurer was adept at evading the restrictions imposed by religion, which were therefore no insuperable barrier to the emergence of capitalism. The argument from religion is ambiguous to say the least.

NOTES

1. Howard, C. (ed.): *West African Explorers* (London, 1951), p. 164–7
2. Hakluyt, Richard: *Voyages* (London, Everyman edn. 1907), Volume III, p. 169
3. Ibid, p. 140, 142
4. Quoted Rodinson, M.: *Islam and Capitalism* (London, 1974), p. 31
5. Labib, Subhi: 'Egyptian commercial policy in the Middle Ages' (Cook, M. A. ed.: *Studies in the Economic History of the Middle East*, London, 1970), p. 76

Further reading

Abun-Nasr, J. M.: Op. cit. (see p. 46)
Ahmad, K. J.: *Heritage of Islam* (Lahore, 1956)
Burke, Edmund III: *Prelude to Protectorate in Morocco, Precolonial Protest and Resistance, 1860–1912* (Chicago and London, 1976)
Cahen, C.: 'L'évolution de l'*iqta*' du IXe au XIIIe siècle: contributions à une histoire comparée des sociétés mediévales' (*Annales: Economies, Sociétés, Civilisations*, VIII, 1953, p. 25–52)
Cook, M. A.: Op. cit. (see above, note 5)
Evans-Pritchard, E. E.: *The Sanusi of Cyrenaica* (Oxford, 1949)
Gallissot, René: 'Precolonial Algeria' (*Economy and Society*, IV, 1975, p. 418–45)
Goitein, S. D.: 'The rise of the Middle Eastern bourgeoisie in early Islamic times' (*Journal of World History*, III, 1957, p. 583–604)
Gray, R.: Op. cit. (see p. 153)
Holt, P. M., Lambton, A. K. S. & Lewis, B.: Op. cit. (see p. 84)
Hrbek, I.: Loc. cit. (see p. 115)
Hussey, J. M. (ed.): *The Cambridge Medieval History*, Volume IV, Part I (Cambridge, 1966)
Inalcik, Halil: 'Capital formation in the Ottoman empire' (*Journal of Economic History*, XXIX, 1969, p. 97–140)
Johnson, Marion: 'The economic foundations of an Islamic theocracy – the case of Masina' (*Journal of African History*, XVII, 1976, p. 481–95)
Julien, Charles-André: *Histoire de l'Algérie contemporaine*, Volume I, *La conquête et les débuts de la colonisation (1827–1871)* (Paris, 1964)
Julien, Charles-André: *History of North Africa; Tunisia, Algeria, Morocco from the Arab Conquest to 1830* (London, 1970)
Labib, Subhi Y.: 'Capitalism in medieval Islam' (*Journal of Economic History*, XXIX, 1969, p. 79–96)
Lacoste, Yves: 'General characteristics and fundamental structures of medieval North African society' (*Economy and Society*, III, 1974, p. 1–17)

Lewis, A. R.: Op. cit. (see p. 154)
Lewis, Bernard: 'The Arabs in eclipse' (Section 4, Cipolla, C. M. ed.: *The Economic Decline of Empires*, London, 1970)
Lopez, R. S.: Loc. cit. (see p. 131)
Ra'ana, Irfan Mahmud: *Economic System under 'Umar the Great, a Treatise on Muslim Economy in Early Seventh Century* (Lahore, 1970)
Rodinson, M.: Op. cit. (see p. 115)
Schacht, J.: Op. cit. (see p. 84)
Shaban, M. A.: *Islamic History: a New Interpretation*, Volume I, A.D. 632–750 (A.H. 132) (Cambridge, 1971)
Shaw, S. J.: Loc. cit. (see p. 66)
Von Grunebaum, G. E.: *Islam: Essays on the Nature and Growth of a Cultural Tradition* (London, 1955)
Vucinich, Wagner S.: *The Ottoman Empire: its Record and Legacy* (Princeton, N. J., 1965)

3. SUB-SAHARAN AFRICA

i) *The economic basis of sub-Saharan states*

Where subsistence required a great deal of space, as it frequently did throughout the history of a large part of Africa, and the habits of permanent settlement were not entrenched, highly articulated state organization enjoying authority over an extensive territorial area and capable of decisive intervention in economic processes were not to be found. The more precarious the economic base of a society, the more thinly spread was the population, the smaller the social unit and the greater the degree of consensus in arriving at economic decisions. In a hunting-collecting economy such as that of the San the largest social unit was the small band, of two dozen or so members, which moved in conformity with a seasonal pattern determined by the availability of game and wild fruits. Its day-to-day plans were the outcome of common discussion and its chief merely made the necessary arrangements for their implementation.

Although the existence of a particular mode of livelihood did not determine the nature of political organization, the practice of agriculture, or at least pastoralism, linked in some way with cultivation, and the development of adequate storage technology, were the normal prerequisites for the emergence of a state, that is an authority capable of imposing its will upon a territorial area by means of an administrative apparatus and settling disputes by means of its juridical institutions. Agriculture had to be sufficiently rewarding to produce a surplus necessary for the support of a ruling class. A surplus, moreover, made possible a division of labour not only between rulers and ruled, but also between agricultural and non-agricultural pursuits, viz. craft production and trade. The greater the surplus, the larger was the population and the greater the economic complexity of society, while a growing population brought pressure to bear on the land supply and enhanced the rôle and power of the ruling class. There are many examples of the significance of agriculture for state formation in Africa. Among the savanna kingdoms, medieval Mali was able to produce abundant quantities of rice and other crops on the upper Niger. In Nubia, the kingdom of Kush was based upon livestock, millet and probably cotton in the fertile 'island' enclosed by the Nile and the Atbara. It is not impossible that its decline was connected with the erosion of the soil. Its rival, Axum, also owed its prosperity at least partly to its agriculture. In the early modern period the introduction of exotic crops seems to have had something to do with state formation. The continuous cultivation of the banana, for instance, provided the economic basis for the kingdom of Buganda, founded in the 17th century, while the spread of American crops may have influenced the growth of the Luba and Lunda states of Central Africa. On Madagascar, the Imerina kingdom of the Merina plateau owed its well-being to irrigated rice cultivation.

State organization was likely to be stimulated where fertility depended upon renewed deposits of alluvial mud and agriculture called for a high degree of co-ordination of effort. Thus, in the 19th century, the Lozi kingdom of Barotseland (in modern Zambia) developed in order to organize the common exploitation of the upper Zambezi valley after the flood waters had receded. Yet settlement on a flood plain did not necessarily lead to state formation. The Nuer of the southern Sudan, though dwelling along the White Nile and the Bahr el Ghazal on land subject to seasonal flooding, remained stateless. They undertook no co-operation beyond a village level, perhaps because their primary mode of livelihood was stockbreeding, for which their territory was much more suitable in spite of the annual flood. Those societies engaged in alluvial farming which did evolve into states, paid for whatever advantages came from that evolution in greater dependence upon the continuation of effective government, the breakdown of which could shatter a fragile prosperity. Dry-farming regions, less dependent upon complex organization and supervision, could recover relatively quickly from devastation inflicted by man and nature.

Mere density of population did not of itself lead to large and advanced states. Physical barriers to communication, or at least the absence of the technical ability to overcome them, hampered state building. On the slopes of Mount Kilimanjaro in East Africa, although a generous rainfall and fertile volcanic soil fostered a dense population of great cultural homogeneity, the ravines that scored the mountain sides hindered the formation of extensive territorial states. Similarly, in the tropical forest of West Africa the big state was an exception. Powerful and prosperous states like Asante and Benin were not typical. Settlements tended to be small, isolated, egalitarian, largely self-sufficient and self-regulating. Authority was vested in the head of the family, who accepted strict limits upon its exercise.

Stateless – acephalous, or 'headless' – societies of cultivators were found throughout Africa, made up of small autonomous groups that settled differences by negotiation and compromise or, at worst, by inter-group violence according to mutually accepted rules, rather than by submission to a superior authority. Irreconcilable feuds tended to widen the gulf between communities and, although such peoples as the Nuer, the Dinka of the upper Nile, the Tallensi of northern Ghana and the Ibo of eastern Nigeria, who knew no chiefs or only those with limited and specialized functions, retained to a considerable degree a common identity, they were ethnic groups rather than political communities, and the effective unit was the village or kin group. Even when a common authority was recognized, its power might be ephemeral and tenuous. Confederations of related ethnic groups were not uncommon (for example the confederation of the Makua chiefs of East Africa) but were likely to be unstable, with little control by the paramount chief over his sub-chiefs, who perhaps selected themselves. Secession, though resorted to with reluctance, was, in the event of abuse of power or succession or leadership disputes, relatively easy when land was abundant. This was as true of white South Africa as of black Africa.

Where there was no advanced agriculture it was possible for effective states to evolve on the proceeds of plunder, often in the form of slaves or cattle. Plunder was the economic foundation of the polity of the Zulus of South Africa. Their highly efficient military state emerged in the late 18th and early 19th century through the genius of Dingiswayo (died c.1818) and Shaka (1787–1828), who emphasized the territorial basis of his kingdom at the expense of kinship and subordinate chiefs, by insisting that men of different districts and different clans fight side by side in age-based regiments which were under the king's own eye and authority. Cattle were the spoils of victory.

He went out and seized the cattle of Faku in Pondoland;
he seized those of Gambushe in Pondoland;
he took those of the Basuto, the blanketed ones,
and those of the Baca who wear fringed hair . . .
Tshaka is not to be spat out, nor is he like water.[1]

The result was not only conquest, but also the absorption of defeated groups. The rise of the Zulu state has, however, been attributed to a change in the ratio of population to land: population grew and the need for expansion, restricted by the Drakensberg escarpment, the sea and the encroachment of the Boers, encouraged centralizing tendencies and led to conquests that had repercussions throughout South and Central Africa.

Resistance to force could be just as powerful a stimulant to state formation as aggression. People living in security dwelt in independent homesteads; those under threat in nucleated villages, which tended to lend emphasis to territory at the expense of kinship, and territorial authority at the expense of the claims of lineage. Possibly Ife in modern Nigeria developed as a state in the 12th century in response to slave raiding, and Ghana in the second half of the 1st millennium A.D. in response to nomadic attacks from the north. Indeed, the use of force by the Zulus gave birth to the Sotho kingdom of Basutoland in the Drakensberg, founded by Moshesh.

Frequently, plunder merged into tribute and tribute into taxation, depending upon the continuity of contact between conquerer and conquered and the distance of the victim from the exploiter's power centre. This was so in the complex relationships amongst the petty, unstable and loosely organized states in and around the Sahara. Sometimes plunder was combined with and almost indistinguishable from trade. In the heyday of the Atlantic and Arab slave trades many a state – Asante, Dahomey, the Yoruba states, Buganda, Lunda and others – had an economic basis dependent to some extent upon the enslavement of weaker neighbours, though slaving was not the sole or even the most important explanation for their emergence as states, or, indeed, for the decline of states whose subjects were preyed upon. An element of plunder was found in most trade. Trading states were usually small, sometimes little more than towns – the Hausa states (e.g. Kano), sometimes competing, sometimes collaborating, united by the Fulani in the 19th century with their capital at Sokoto; the Akan states, welded together in the 18th century by Asante; Benin; the Niger delta states; the Muslim sultanates of the Gulf of Aden; and the Muslim towns of the East African coast. But even large territorial states with a population overwhelmingly engaged in agriculture or pastoralism, such as the kingdoms of the western Sudan (Ghana, Mali, Songhai), Kanem-Bornu, Oyo and medieval Ethiopia could derive benefit from long-distance trade. To them there accrued gains in money or kind and often administrative advantages through services rendered by both native and foreign merchants. Christian Ethiopia, for example, in the 15th century learnt through its trading links with Muslim Egypt something of up-to-date weapons and administration. Income was drawn sometimes from direct participation in trade, sometimes from taxes on trade and sometimes from both.

The Sudanese kingdoms of the Middle Ages did well from their export and import taxes on salt, copper and luxury commodities and, above all, from their control of the gold trade. Access to gold, either through mining or through trade, could be of vital importance. It is not without significance that the decline of Ghana and the rise of Mali in the 13th century coincided with the exhaustion of the goldfields of Bambuk, of which Ghana was a beneficiary, and the opening up of the Bure goldfields, which was to the advantage of Mali. Just as Mali, though failing to secure control of the mines themselves, grew in power at least partly through the trade in gold, the subsequent emergence of the Akan state of Bono owed much to its production. Similarly gold in Nubia was an important element in the rise of the kingdom of Kush, just as it was in the development of the kingdom of the Mwene Mutapa and the successor Rozwi state in modern Zimbabwe. On the coast of East Africa the sultans of Kilwa and Mombasa and other rulers, in addition to engaging in trade themselves, seem to have exacted very heavy taxes on the gold exported from Sofala and on the cloth and other goods used to purchase it. Salt and copper could also be of great importance. It is suggested that the kingdom of Ndongo owed the power it enjoyed to its control of the rock-salt mined at Kasama; and the Luba states to their control of the Katanga (Shaba) copper trade.

Revenue was not the only gain from trade, which could also assure supplies of superior weapons, slaves, horses and scarce metals. Horses made armies more mobile and formidable and slaves were extensively employed as soldiers. In Dahomey slaves were acquired for sacrifice in the annual ceremony that demonstrated the king's power and prestige. Describing a not unusual situation, Mungo Park wrote in 1795,

> From the central position of Bondou, between the Gambia and Senegal rivers, it is become a place of great resort . . . The customs, or duties on travellers, are very heavy; in almost every town an ass load pays a bar of European merchandize, and at Fatteconda, the residence of the king, one Indian baft, or a musket, and six bottles of gunpowder, are exacted as a common tribute. By means of these duties, the King of Bondou is well supplied with arms and ammunition; a circumstance which makes him formidable to the neighbouring states.[2]

The superiority of the weapons depended upon time and place. The armies of Ghana, with their swords and spears, had an immense advantage over their enemies; those of the successor state of Songhai were defeated at the end of the 16th century by a relatively small Moroccan army using firearms for the first time in the western Sudan.

The trouble with trade as an economic base was its precariousness. A shift in trade routes could easily terminate a fragile prosperity. The decline of Ife has been attributed to the severance of trading links with the north, possibly as a result of the rise of Old Oyo, and the decline of the kingdom of Kongo also to its loss of control of long-distance trade, what with the intervention of the Portuguese and the rise of coastal trading states, such as Loango. The decline of Great Zimbabwe, the shift of the capital to the Zambezi valley and the inability of the Mwene Mutapa to control his southern provinces were perhaps an accumulation of effects from the Swahili development of the Zambezi trade route at the expense of one that had supplied Great Zimbabwe via the Sabi valley. However, few states were ever exclusively dependent upon one source of income. This was true even of those small states where trade was especially important. Most states worthy of the name were founded upon a mixed economy, largely agricultural, but in addition drawing some strength from trade. Hausaland, for example, was particularly favoured with fertile soil and adequate rainfall for agriculture, pasture for cattle and transport animals and incentives and opportunities for craft manufacture and trade.

Development of trade did not necessarily give rise to state organization, either because it was not rich enough to support one, or because it could be conducted without one. Trade in minerals of high intrinsic value was much more likely to facilitate and encourage or even require powerful state organization, than trade in other commodities. The Nyamwezi, the Bisa, the Kamba and the Chokwe were all trading peoples who did not evolve a complex political structure. On the other hand, among the Yao, another trading people of East Africa, rudimentary states did emerge, territorial chiefdoms that fell short of full statehood in the absence of any formal system of administration. East Africa, developing later than West Africa, was overtaken by events in the shape of Europe intervention.

ii) *The African state and the economy*
With the foundation of states an element of command was introduced and the rôle of consensus diminished. A ruler exacted tribute from his subjects in the form of cash, grain, cattle, precious and base metals, ivory or slaves, and that tribute could be arbitrary and onerous. Labour services were required. Tribute and services were needed for the maintenance of the ruler's household, his administrative machinery, such as it was, and his judicial institutions. The introduction of agriculture and trade rendered his functions more complex and specialized and of great economic importance – the maintenance of internal peace, the propitiation of natural forces, for example the performance of a rain-making ritual, the organization of defence, the distribution of land, the protection and regulation of trade and the institution of public works. Trade and a centralized administration stimulated the growth of towns, and their administration and defence posed problems and created opportunities. The construction of town walls, for prestige as much as for defence, made heavy demands on resources, but facilitated population control and furnished a source of revenue in the form of octrois on incoming products. A certain amount of town planning was imposed, markets were regulated and law and order maintained, but little was done by way of the provision of sanitation, education, care of the sick and other amenities.

Frequently only the ruler had the means for assembling trade goods, such

as ivory, rubber or slaves. Slave trading most particularly lent itself to state
participation, since the source of slaves was normally either warfare or
tribute or a by-product of judicial processes. 'The first business of one of our
Factors when he comes to Fida,' wrote William Bosman of trade on the
Slave Coast at the beginning of the 18th century,

> is to satisfie the Customs of the King and the great Men, which amount to about
> 100 Pounds in *Guinea* value, as the Goods must yield there. After which we have
> free Licence to Trade, which is published throughout the whole Land by the
> Cryer.
>   But yet before we can deal with any Person, we are obliged to buy the King's
> whole stock of Slaves at a set price; which is commonly one third or one fourth
> higher than ordinary: After which we obtain free leave to deal with all his Sub-
> jects of what Rank soever.[3]

Thus trade was sometimes an official or semi-official enterprise. This was
true of Dahomey, Asante and the Mossi states. Sometimes trade was channelled through a single port, such as Whydah in Dahomey, where it was
administered by the state in its own interest; or the production of staples,
such as gold, ivory or kola nuts (in the case of Asante), was reserved by the
state. In the medieval states of the western Sudan, the authorities, with the
object of expanding trade and thus increasing their revenue from customs
duties and other taxes, sought to foster trade by safeguarding merchants and
their property (though their ability to do so was limited), and by improving
the roads. Their monarchs also created and protected markets, appropriated
(or at least the king of Ghana did) gold nuggets to maintain the value of the
metal, and regulated the use and provision of cowrie shells, not only as an
instrument of taxation, but also as small change for the distribution of food.
    Royal and chiefly monopolies over exports and privileged access to
imports were common even in areas where trade was relatively backward.
Slave trading in medieval Nubia, which provided Egypt with slaves, was
probably a state enterprise for the most part. In the kingdom of the Mwene
Mutapa the production of and trade in gold was a royal monopoly, and this
practice was continued by the Changamire after the collapse of the Mwene
Mutapa's power. In the East African kingdom of Bunyoro there were royal
markets and the right to purchase firearms was confined to the ruling class.
Ivory hunting was restricted to a privileged group, a feature of a number of
other societies. In the much more backward region of South-East Africa
in the late 18th century Dingiswayo encouraged trade.

> In the first year of his chieftainship he opened a trade with Delagoa Bay, by send-
> ing 100 oxen and a quantity of elephants tusks to exchange for beads and blankets.
> Prior to this a small supply of these articles had been brought to that country
> from Delagoa Bay by the natives. The trade thus opened by Dingiswayo was

afterwards carried on, on an extensive scale, though the Portuguese never in person entered his country. The encouragement held out to ingenuity brought numbers around him, liberal rewards being given to any of his followers who devised things new and ornamental. His mechanical ingenuity was displayed in the carving of wood. He taught this art to several of his people.

Milk dishes, pillows, ladles of cane or wood, and snuff spoons were also produced . . . A kaross manufactory was also established, a hundred men being generally employed in that work.[4]

State-run trade was aimed primarily at the acquisition of commoditie^s required, in some instances, for the direct support of the state – weapons fo^r defence and offence, luxury goods for display – and, in others, for the indirec^t support gained through the prestige of liberal distribution of largess. It was a long-distance trade carried on in a different way from local trade, with export prices fixed by the state rather than by supply and demand and currency exchange rates kept stable at least partly through state regulation of the use and supply of cowrie shells. The behaviour of kings and chiefs, however, was not always beneficent. It is arguable that the far-reaching regulation of economic life in Dahomey discouraged production and cramped trade. Interference by a plethora of political authorities, each eager to assert its interest or secure its share of the profits, must have had similar restraining effects. Such interference was not always designed simply to secure profit. It was sometimes actuated by a desire to cut the trading links of rival states. The Baganda were successful for a large part of the 19th century in preventing Arabs from trading with Bunyoro. In some instances states dedicated to warfare blighted a process of development which they themselves had initiated by their economic requirements. The 19th-century state of Ibadan in Yorubaland, modern Nigeria, was a case in point.

A major factor inhibiting state intervention in economic processes was an absence of effective government machinery. For a bureaucracy to function, or an economic institution of any complexity, the skills of writing, measuring and keeping accounts were indispensable, and their absence was as much an obstacle to economic and political advance in Africa as was the lack of a progressive technology. Africa lacked an efficient and universally recognized medium of exchange, making the cost-benefit analysis that is a prerequisite for economic decisions, impossible. There was no written language outside Egypt and the area, such as Nubia and Axum-Ethiopia, under Egyptian or Arab influence; North Africa, where the first was that of the Phoenicians; and those areas that were drawn into Islam or at least – like 19th-century Asante – benefited from the immigration of Muslims literate in Arabic. Dahomey had a method, using pebbles, of recording population size and classifying it by age, sex and district, but there has been some doubt cast on its effectiveness. The system served both a fiscal and a military purpose.

Strong centralized government was exceptional in sub-Saharan Africa. Poverty of communications made it difficult to prevent states from breaking up, and it is no accident that some of the most stable and enduring ones had navigable rivers, notably the kingdoms of the western Sudan, served by the middle Niger. Secondly, even relatively wealthy rulers, like the Mwene Mutapa, could not maintain a professional army of any size to enforce commands. Executive weakness and bad communications, together with total or general illiteracy, necessitated a devolution of powers of administration, either to appointed officials or to subordinate rulers, and in the absence of currency those exercising such powers had to be paid in kind. This meant in effect that they had either to be granted the right of appropriating a share of locally collected tribute or taxes (such as market dues and tolls) or to be given non-heritable cattle or, if it was coveted and not freely available for the taking, land. Delegation of privileges typically included rights over tribute and labour, balanced by simple duties – the settlement of local disputes and the collection of tribute and the organization of labour on behalf of the central authority. In Bunyoro subordinate chiefs were allowed to distribute land, conscript labour and collect tribute, part of which had to be passed on to the king. The provincial governors of the Kongo kingdom had to collect taxes on behalf of the king, once he had fought his way to the throne in the succession contest that generally followed the previous king's death. Similarly, among the Nguni authority was divided among subordinate chiefs. Their dependence took the form of payment to the king of a portion of the death duties and fines they collected, attendance upon him to give counsel or assistance in war and perhaps the stationing of a representative at the king's court. In the western Sudanese empires taxes payable in kind by those engaged in agriculture, fishing and cattle-raising were levied by local rulers who passed on a share of the proceeds to the central government as tribute.

Parallel performance of similar functions by local and central authorities could be a stage of state building, an advance upon the 'segmentary lineage system', where power was dispersed among family descent-lines and the autonomous village community the rule. This process might or might not be the result of conquest. In the case of the Alur people in modern Uganda and Zaïre it evidently was not. Where there was conquest, division of authority was not so much a question of delegating power as of integrating conquered chiefs into the administration and curtailing their freedom of action. Personal dependence transcended ties of kinship. This is what happened in the case of the empire of the Lunda, south of the River Kasai, established in the 17th century. Here subordinate chiefs were kept under the surveillance of officials appointed by the king, the Mwata Yamvo. A somewhat similar arrangement was adopted in the contemporary state of Oyo and the Hausa state of Zaria. In 16th-century Benin the king felt strong enough effectively to replace hereditary with appointed officials. The trend, often promoted by the influence of Islam, was towards greater power at the centre, which took the form, not merely of closer control over official positions, but also of an extended use of forced and slave labour and the establishment of servile standing armies, as in the Hausa states in the 15th century and Asante in the 18th and 19th. Such empires, however, could fall apart as suddenly as they were built up, as did Oyo in the first half of the 19th century and Akwamu on the Gold Coast in the 18th. Neither had a literate bureaucracy. Even Asante, with its rudimentary and partially literate bureaucracy, was subject to internal tensions and never obtained complete control over some of its constituent parts.

In African states, as in medieval Europe, appointed officials tended to become hereditary, and hereditary subordinate rulers to become less zealous in carrying out the wishes of the paramount ruler. Control became more nominal and less real, the more remote the centre was. Dispersal of taxing rights invites – indeed, constitutes – fragmentation of sovereignty: land (or cattle) set aside for the support of public officials (in theory non-heritable) is likely in practice to become hereditary and likewise to cause loss of power and even collapse at the centre. It was perhaps to avoid the danger of un-controllable officials that sometimes members of the royal family were given administrative – or, at least, tax-collecting – posts, the practice on occasion in the Ovimbundu states of the Benguela highlands in the 19th century, the Hausa state of Nupe, the empire of the Mwene Mutapa and the sultanate of Fez in Morocco. Recourse was sometimes made, as in medieval Ghana, to the services of slave officials for collecting tribute, each with his own administrative staff; or to eunuchs, as in 18th-and 19th-century Asante; or to slave generals as in the Hausa state of Zaria. Such was the functional mobility of slaves that it was not impossible for exceptionally able ones to establish their own states, like the celebrated Ja-Ja of Opobo in the latter part of the 19th century.

Some of the large territorial states – Funj is an example, the kingdom of the Mwene Mutapa another – were virtually confederations of autono-mous areas. Poor communications, together with local particularism and dynastic intrigue, made it frequently difficult for a central government to assert its will. This was to be seen even in Ethiopia, a region subject to the unifying force of religion and faced with threats from both Muslim pastoral-ists, chiefly Galla and Somali, and Muslim sheikdoms, which, however, were themselves constantly at odds with one another despite the bond of Islam. Much more vulnerable was Songhai at the end of the 16th century, where external pressures exacerbated internal divisions, between Muslim and pagan, town and country, district and district.

iii) *The 'African mode of production' and feudalism*

Since, it appears, they no longer adhere to a unilinear progression through a fixed series of modes of production, Marxists have more room for man-oeuvre than they seem to have had formerly in dealing with non-European societies. It must be recognised, however, that Marx's writings on pre-capitalist economic formations are not very helpful for analyzing African societies or for showing how they develop. Although some of the character-istics of his Asiatic mode of production – village self-sufficiency, communal property and reluctance to accept change – seem to fit the African situation, he was thinking rather of the so-called hydraulic societies, of which Egypt was an obvious example, where the state enforced corvées for the construct-ion and maintenance of public works. Public works, including irrigation, were never elsewhere prosecuted on anything like the same scale or with the same degree of discipline and organization. However, Karl Wittfogel, distinguishing four main categories of hydraulic society, depending on its 'hydraulic density', which varies firstly according to the degree of economic hegemony of hydraulic agriculture and secondly, in the absence of such hegemony, according to whether it is sufficiently important to 'assure its leaders absolute organizational and political hegemony', places in his 'Loose 1' group, the Chagga in East Africa, and in the 'Loose 2' group, the Suk, also of East Africa. The 'L1' category is distinguished from the 'L2' by a society's possession 'among its installations' of 'large units which are com-pact within their immediate locale or which go beyond the borders of a single region'. Egypt falls into his 'Compact 1' category.[5] It is not necessary to go so far as to accept Wittfogel's complicated and contrived schema to recognize instances in sub-Saharan African history of that technologically primitive, relatively egalitarian and autarkic society, without private owner-ship of the means of production but with an aristocracy able to appropriate a surplus, which to Marx exemplified the Asiatic mode of production.

Although 'orthodox' Marxists abandoned the Asiatic mode of production, it was subsequently revived by those who played down the importance of public works and attached significance chiefly to the extraction by an élite of a surplus from a society composed of patriarchal villages, primarily through its control of trade. Confronted with the major difficulty of using the term in the absence of a thorough-going despotism and mass forced labour, others have described a distinctive African mode of production, a society devoted primarily to self-subsistence, without private appropriation of land, and made up of social units based on kinship, yet involved in both local and long-distance trade and supporting a territorial state-building bureaucracy in alliance with king against chiefs or nobles and possibly a ruling class drawing its privileges from birth or capital accumulated in trade and perhaps aiming at territorial authority. There was no direct interference with production. The surplus for the support of the élite came from trade and perhaps plunder or some form of unequal exhange. Such agricultural surplus as was extracted in the form of tribute was not used or needed for the support of the political authorities or of forced labour engaged in public works, but was distributed as largess. Such a pre-capitalist economic formation lay outside European experience and cannot be forced into the Asiatic category, nor was slave cultivation on behalf of the ruling class on a scale that would justify the description 'slave mode of production'. The African mode of production, it is argued, was an economic cul-de-sac in most cases. There was no real production for the market and the state organized to extract a surplus from trade could not usually survive the collapse of that trade, especially the slave trade. One of the few that did in the 19th century was Dahomey, which turned from slaving to slave-produced palm fruit.

If the societies of the African past cannot be comprehended under the Asiatic rubric and the African mode of production is equally inapplicable, hunter-gatherer societies would qualify, in the Marxist typology, as primitive (classless) societies and agricultural societies as feudal. Given the lack of guidance from Marx himself, it is hardly surprising that economic anthropologists claiming to derive their inspiration from this source have devoted much energy and ingenuity to the analysis of the primitive communist mode of production, and in doing so have disagreed profoundly with one another. There is indeed even some doubt whether relations of production (that is, the relations between classes) determine or are determined by the forces of production (that is, the manner in which men wrest a living from nature) or whether they influence each other, the 'orthodox' view evidently being that the latter is correct. One argument is that there are many modes of production as there are forms of co-operation, though these seem to amount to nothing more than the common-sense distinction between agriculture on the one hand and hunting and gathering on the other. Yet, it has also been suggested that it is not appropriate to talk of a mode of production at all in a classless society. There can only be class when there is appropriation of surplus value, and there can be no surplus value if there is no commodity production, that is production for the market. The labour theory of value is inoperative where there is production only for use and not for exchange.

Because of their practice of devolving power and of their centrifugal tendencies, African states seem to bear a striking, if superficial, resemblance to medieval Europe. In other respects, too, different parts of Africa at some time or other displayed characteristics that may perhaps be called feudal. 19th-century observers freely used the term to describe African political systems. Thus Africanus Horton:

The political constitution of the interior tribes on the Gold Coast is of a very primitive order, and their social organization resembles most closely the feudal system of Europe in the middle ages. A king is acknowledged, who in former years exercised the most unbounded authority as feudal lord, retaining paramount right or *dominicum directum* over the life and property of all the wealthiest nobles or caboceers of his kingdom. Under the kings are powerful chiefs (barons) and princes of the blood, who exercise considerable authority over their vassals, levy taxes, command a division (cohort) of the army, undertake distant expeditions, receiving under their protection inferior chiefs or free families who are wealthy, but do not possess sufficient number of vassals to protect themselves from the influences of neighbouring powerful caboceers or chiefs. These families consent to hold their property and estate as their feudatories, and may be regarded as the *inferior nobility* of the ancient feudal states. Then come the free inhabitants, who, although not wealthy, have considerable influence in the country; these people are dependent on or claim vassalage to powerful feudal caboceers for protection. Then come the real vassals or serfs (*villicus*), who cultivate the land, and who are generally slaves received into the inheritance of a feudal caboceer (baron) or their vassals.

Before the English became influential on the Gold Coast this feudal system was carried on to a very high degree. The feudal kingdoms were conglomerations of many heterogeneous states, who acknowledged a king as their feudal lord, and he, on his part, was to a considerable extent a vassal of the powerful King of Ashantee.[6]

Apparent feudal characteristics evolved from local conditions and needs. Even in the eastern Sudan, in the Keira sultanate of Darfur, the granting of an estate in lieu of salary, though called an *iqṭā'* in land charters, was an indigenous practice. Similarly Egypt and the Maghrib had little influence upon the western Sudanic states, which in other respects were significantly affected by Muslim culture. The very widespread institution of clientship was an entirely spontaneous development. It bore a resemblance to feudal vassalage, especially where it was a question of dependence by sub-chief or client chief upon paramount chief or king, and involved military obligation on the part of the client. At a lower level, like the feudal retainer, the ordinary client was living testimony to the position of his patron in society. Thus, the Hima, who constituted an inferior caste in the kingdom of Bunyoro, made over to the king periodic gifts of beasts and were required to support him in war, in exchange for which they received protection and aid in times of danger and distress. But clientship could be mobilised against central authority as well as on its behalf. In the East African interlacustrine kingdoms of Ankole and Bunyoro it was not uncommon for an 'over-mighty subject' to build up his personal following of clients, attempt to establish himself as an independent ruler and pit his clients against those of his king, a situation familiar to students of European medieval history. However, feudalism in Europe was the outcome of a breakdown of central authority, which was certainly not the case of sub-Saharan African situations that have sometimes been designated feudal. In Africa it was rather a question of state building than of state disintegration, taking place where there were important centripetal forces. In Bunyoro, for example, the king, the Mukama, among various other powers that endowed him with political authority, had the right to appoint and dismiss chiefs, the putative equivalent of tenants-in-chief, and these did not succeed in establishing hereditary succession.

Feudalism is associated with heavily armed mounted knights. Such warriors were to be found in Africa, too, like the cavalry of the sultan of Sokoto described, in 1824, by Captain Hugh Clapperton, who himself used feudal terms.

The cry of 'Shields to the wall' was constantly heard from the several chiefs to their troops; but they disregarded the call, and neither chiefs nor vassals moved from the spot. At length the men in quilted armour went up 'per order'. They certainly cut not a bad figure at a distance, as their helmets were ornamented with black and white ostrich feathers, and the sides of the helmets with pieces of tin, which glittered in the sun, their long quilted cloaks of gaudy colours reaching over part of the horses' tails, and hanging over the flanks. On the neck, even the horse's armour was notched, or vandyked, to look like a mane; on his forehead and over his nose was a brass or tin plate, as also a semicircular piece on each side. The rider was armed with a large spear; and he had to be assisted to mount his horse, as his quilted cloak was too heavy; it required two men to lift him on; and there were six of them belonging to each governor, and six to the sultan.[7]

Quilted armour and iron helmets were introduced into the western Sudan in the late Middle Ages from Mamluk Egypt. But the influence of Egypt upon institutions was no more profound than the introduction of a rather ineffective mode of combat.

The horse was known early in African history north of the West African forest and the Nile Sudd, as was the stirrup, the use of which made heavy cavalry possible; and the horse was the symbol and privilege of the ruling class, which alone had the means and the leisure to become skilled horsemen. In fact state building in the Sudan and Hausaland and the area to the south of Hausaland has been attributed partly to the influence of mounted nomads armed with iron weapons who introduced the horse into the region. Although such a view is now treated with some scepticism, the association of horse-owning with status is valid. A similar situation obtained in the Sahara, where Tuareg society tended to bifurcate into a class of nobles who controlled the ownership and use of camels, and their vassals, who had only goats. The camels of the desert, however, and much of the cavalry of North Africa and the savanna (such as among the Gonja of northern Ghana, the Wolof of Senegambia and the Yoruba of Oyo) were but lightly armed and armoured, engaged rather in slave raiding and plunder than in combat, and were supported primarily on the proceeds of depredation, not from the agricultural surplus of serf-cultivated estates.

The granting of land, cultivated by dependants of one sort or another in return for services, was a dominant feature of European feudalism. In the empires of the western Sudan, Buganda, Barotseland and Ethiopia officials were supported in this way, and there were cases of land grants in return for payments in kind or service, in the kingdoms of Ruanda and Burundi. There remain, however, essential differences between the African political system and European feudalism. In Europe, in legal theory all land belonged to the crown, which made grants to its vassals and these in turn made available land to the actual cultivators, either directly or through a chain of vassalage. In Africa, though a claim to the ownership of all land on the part of the king was common, access to land usually remained a right inherent in membership of the community. It was exceptional to find in Africa a clear division between a land-owning class and a dependent peasant class. There was no sharp cleavage in society expressed by marked differences in standards of living or way of life. The social equivalent of the European serf was the African slave rather than the African commoner, but the resemblance is only superficial.

The applicability of the term feudalism to Africa depends much upon the definition given it. The more imprecise it is, the wider its application. The penalty of vagueness is loss of analytical value. The closest parallel with the medieval European situation existed in pre-revolutionary Ethiopia. Here there was a class of officials, lay and ecclesiastical, military and civil, many of them not residing in the districts of which they appropriated the surplus, supported either by the proceeds of the taxes of a specific piece of land (*gult*) allocated by the crown or from the rent of land granted in return for a specific service. Land granted for service was in theory temporary, but in practice heritable. Although typically land granted in this way was in the form of large estates in exchange for administrative and military functions, small plots in return for humbler services, such as woodcutting, were also allocated by both the sovereign and large landowners, in the latter case giving a rough equivalent of European sub-infeudation. As in medieval Europe the emperor contended with princes and princes with nobles. Succession disputes were common after the decline of the monarchy in the 18th century. The restoration of the monarchy in the 19th did not change the system, but simply ensured that it worked for the benefit of the emperor.

After his conquests in the south in the late 19th century, Menelik II seized between two-thirds and three-quarters of all the conquered land from its Galla, Sidamo and Guragi owners and distributed it among local tribal leaders and nobles, officers and officials from the north, with the object of establishing an administration and, at the same time, a contented and powerful class of supporters. The crown, however, remained a considerable direct owner. Its estates were let out to tenants, usually on temporary tenure to produce food for the imperial palace. The Ethiopian peasant, whether on crown, ecclesiastical or private land, was in wretched circumstances. His farm was mostly smaller than a hectare and he relinquished between a third and a half of his crops. His resemblance to the medieval serf was close. On the other hand, there was no enforced cultivation of a demesne which was such an important feature of the European manorial system.

Karl Polanyi escaped from such Eurocentric preoccupations, preferring to classify what he called primitive societies differently. He distinguished four different but not mutually exclusive 'principles of integration' actuating societies – reciprocity, redistribution, market exchange and householding. The characteristics of householding he saw as group self-sufficiency (for example, the 'Central African kraal') and the absence of production for the market. Reciprocity was the exchange of rights and duties between equals, such as pairs of clans; redistribution, the payment of tribute and other dues to political authorities who undertook certain obligations in return, including the maintenance of public services and public order. With reciprocity and redistribution, which could co-exist in a single society, social relations were paramount, economic considerations of secondary significance. It was only in Europe with its industrial revolution that economic factors came to dominate, when market exchange with its money price flexibility and profit motive became the integrating principle and appropriate economic theory developed. Markets existed in primitive societies, but were of marginal importance. Polanyi criticized Marxism on the ground that it attached excessive significance to the status of labour in its classification of economic systems; he in turn was criticized because he was concerned largely with the circulation of goods, not with their production. For the Marxist, the mode of production is at the heart of every society.

iv) *Class and caste*

Marxist anthropologists have been preoccupied by the question of how class divisions appear in the absence of the private ownership of the means of production. Some appear to accord primacy to social relations rather than to relations of production in the allocation of the means of production and the distribution of the social product. One view associates the origins of class with age differences in primitive agricultural society. Where hunting predominates, the economic formation will be egalitarian and unstable because hunting expeditions are short and the division of the product simple and final, a matter of mutual agreement, involving no further obligations. Where agriculture predominates, class formation occurs, not because of private control of the means of production, but through the obligation imposed upon the younger ones by the older, who have provided in the past the means of current consumption. An ideology results that puts a value upon kinship, age, ancestors and reproduction, all of which stress continuity. The relations of production are between 'seniors' and 'juniors', with the former predominant because of their control over the means of reproduction, that is, the distribution of food, marriage, the disposal of children and the acceptance of outsiders, in order to preserve the continuation of a society with a proper balance of sexes and ages. These relations of production, originally merely a question of age, harden, as production for self-subsistence gives way to production for the market or as some exogenous influence is brought to bear, into class relations, with one group asserting its seniority, exacting tribute and eventually controlling the means of production, though with the development of trade it might become possible for juniors to challenge the authority of their seniors. However, this tracing of class origins to age groups has been disputed on the grounds that societies divided in that way may be stateless and, since it is the state that provides the coercion for the appropriation of the social product necessary for a class structure, such a society must be classless.

One does not need to be a Marxist to appreciate that, with an increase in wealth and the development of states, following from improved agriculture and the growth of trade, especially when accompanied by the spread of a money economy, social and economic differentiation becomes more marked, dividing society into rulers and ruled, into better-off and worse-off. Sedentary life increased the scope for the accumulation of property, which tended to lose its collective character. Land acquired a new value and the surplus available for exchange increased. When land was in short supply and where communal ownership tended to give way to individual ownership, the road was opened to the aggregation of plots into estates and the emergence of a class system based upon economic differences. Such a situation was most likely to arise where the soil was fertile and, as a consequence, population was dense. Trade, too, raised the standard of living and both encouraged and facilitated the accumulation of slaves and possessions. This class structure – such as it was, for the gap between the top and the bottom of society in material condition was rarely wide – often took the form of a caste system based upon distinction of culture. Many societies were economically heterogeneous as a result of ethnic intermingling. It was in conquest that the power of the ruling class frequently originated. It would be less convincing to argue that class was the result of a differential relationship to the means of production than that that relationship was determined by individual or collective physical prowess or by birth. Marx and Engels themselves attached significance to conquest as a factor in the emergence of classes.

While no doubt in some instances conquest was attributable to superiority of weapons and therefore to access to a more advanced technology as a result of economic power, military superiority was not always the result of better weapons. It was not access to superior technology that gave victory to the Zulus; rather, it was the adoption of better designed, not better made, weapons and the imposition of strict military discipline. Dependence on firearms had severe disadvantages. Europeans did not export their best and most up-to-date, and there was an acute shortage of the skills of the gun-smith. Gunpowder was made in parts of Africa – Mungo Park saw it being made at the town of Sampaka in the western Sudan in 1796, though with imported sulphur – but there was never enough of that or of shot.

Class or caste was frequently the outcome of the continuing struggle of agriculturalists with pastoralists, who, mobile and accustomed to defending themselves and their animals against wild beasts, were able to impose their will upon their sedentary neighbours. Thus in Ruanda the Nilotic Tutsi ruled over, but adopted the language of, the Bantu-speaking Hutu and in Uganda a cattle-owning aristocracy lorded it over a dependent agricultural class in the kingdom of Ankole, where Hima ruled Iru. In South-West Africa the Herero herders moved into the lands of the Berg-Damara in the 18th century and exacted tribute in the form of goods and slaves. In West Africa, by contrast, those Berber nomads of the Sahara who succeeded in vanquish-ing the Sudanese of the Sahel bowed to the cultural superiority of the culti-vators, and the Sudanese states that were the outcome, owed more to the conquered than to the conquerors.

In acephalous societies social influence flowed from a number of sources – birth, wealth, wisdom, courage and skill in war, access to esoteric knowledge (such as rain-making) and age – none of them alone sufficient to institutionalize political authority. With the development of the state, however, what count-ed more than anything else was birth and kinship. The king was the repre-sentative of the original lineage group that was the nucleus of the state.

> The authority of the tribal chief rests mainly on the fact that he is the descendant of the first leader of the group. He is the representative of the ancestors, the custod-ian of their law and their magic powers, and thus symbolizes the unity and pride of the tribe. In honouring the chief, the tribe honours itself and its own past.[8]

Within the state wealth tended to gravitate to political power, rather than political power to wealth. The king used his position to appropriate the agricultural surplus, and he demonstrated his power and status by the num-ber of wives, cattle, slaves and clients he had. Where land was too abundant to have much store set by it, political authority meant control of people rather than of territory.

The king, it is true, was not the only one who could acquire slaves and clients. Any man rich in cattle could support a large number of followers.

Among cattle-owning peoples a typical client arrangement was for a poor man to borrow some of the cattle of a patron who had more than he could look after and more milk than he could consume himself, and, in exchange for the right to milk the cows and keep some of the calves, to pledge his service in work and war. From the point of view of the client the arrangement had the obvious advantage of aiding his fortunes and therefore promoting his social advance; and the patron gained from the spreading of risk through the dispersal of his cattle. Sometimes there was a reciprocal dependence without suggestion of a patron-client relationship. That was when herders – Fulani, for example, and Turkana – exchanged livestock with one another. A more specialized type of dependence was that of hunters upon pastoralists or agriculturalists (for example San upon Khoikhoi stock-farmers or upon Bantu-speaking cultivators), often the outcome of restrictions placed upon hunting by encroachments upon game land. Sometimes they were provided with dogs in return for a share of the meat and skins acquired in hunting expeditions. Such a relationship might well be an uneasy one, with fundamental antipathy on each side.

Clientship was one of the means by which chiefs or kings maintained their authority. It also presented the possibility of challenging that authority. Trade opened yet another avenue to the accumulation of wealth and therefore to the acquisition of support, provided by clients and slaves, widening the opportunity for political leadership, which was often in dispute in African societies because there was commonly uncertainty about succession. In West Africa there were instances of traders rising from obscure or even servile conditions to political power, such as John Kabes in the Gold Coast in the late 17th and early 18th centuries and Ja-Ja in the Niger delta in the 19th. However, there was no simple link between wealth and political power. Wealth, if not derived from the exercise of political power, depended in the last analysis upon physical prowess and the deployment of force. But as a rule, it was the king, traditionally the recipient and distributor of gifts, who was best placed to control, and acquire the profits of trade.

Wealth in the form of trade goods, cattle and crops, despite the prestige it conferred and the popularity it could earn through the display of generosity, generally had limited value in the purchase of support and was unlikely to give rise to deep class divisions, because there were so many social obligations to fulfil and because it could so easily be lost. There were few opportunities for productive investment. Cattle provided one opportunity, but wealth in cattle was insecure, subject to the ravages of disease and cattle raiding. A far surer road to social advancement, hence a source of intense rivalry, was service of chief or king, from whom, in case of loss, the cattle owner could seek restitution, illustrating the ultimate dependence in most cases of wealth upon status. Of much greater importance than wealth of this primitive character were the economic privileges which were the concomitant of political power, namely the right to distribute land (where there was competition for the best available) and to exact tribute and the right to demand labour services and, which, conversely, were far more effective means for preserving political power than any possible private accumulation of wealth was for securing it. There was little else that could be done with such economic privileges except use them for maintaining political power. Where the level of technology was low and trade marginal it was difficult, though not wholly impossible – given the rights claimed by most chiefs and kings over certain rare natural products, such as gold, ivory and fine animal skins, and given the possibility of constructing more elaborate dwellings – to achieve a standard of consumption superior to that enjoyed by the rest of society. In any case, privileges were accompanied by inescapable economic obligations such as those of hospitality or relief in times of famine and the liberal reward of services rendered. The ruling group was not immeasurably wealthier than the ruled because the constant dispersal of wealth prevented its concentration at the top. The complexity of the relationship between the ownership of the means of production and status and power in pre-capitalist society and the difficulty of interpreting conflict over power and authority in terms of a class struggle throws doubt upon the value of the class concept in the analysis of African economic systems.

v) *The capacity for change*
In all but a few societies the rôle of custom in allocating resources was powerful, restricting the scope for state command, individual decision and capital accumulation. Although it was not incompatible with the conduct of a brisk trade, deep-rooted custom was capable of a high degree of resistance to the changes that it threatened. Economic specialization was discouraged and market forces neutralized by the use of traditional distributive mechanism. Prices, insulated against the effects of supply and demand, were arbitrarily determined. Custom prescribed various reciprocal obligations and other arrangements for the distribution of goods. The ruler was entitled to tribute and services, but he was obliged to provide hospitality and distribute largess. For example, the Mwene Mutapa collected livestock and foodstuffs as tribute and distributed cloth and other imported goods. At Duala in the Cameroons, the chiefs who received the 'comey', or tax or trade licence fee, from European merchants, were compelled to share their gains with their people or run the risk of rebellion or defections. In such societies many of the characteristics of an 'economy' in its conventional modern meaning were absent. Karl Polanyi, however, argued that there is a confusion in the modern use of the very term 'economic' and that the narrow interpretation current among economists, confined to the 'economizing'

or scarcity implication of the word, is appropriate only to the market economy. Their 'formal' definition fastens upon an abstract relationship between scarce means and an infinite array of ends. There is, however, a broader 'substantive' definition comprehending the whole of man's relationship with the environment that provides him with the means of fulfilling his wants, and this is appropriate to every type of society. In African society the formalist concepts of 'economy' and 'economic policy' were alien, and 'economic' interests were frequently assigned a low priority in the allocation and use of resources. Economic decisions were frequently made not on their 'economic' merits, but as part of a process that involved much wider issues. In Polanyi's phrase, the economy of the non-market society was 'embedded in social relations'. The unit of production was not autonomous, but coincided with, or was derived from, other social groups which used their time and resources in accordance with motives and objectives that were not necessarily of an 'economic' nature. To such groups the individual was subordinated, and they were rigidly stratified and inimical to social mobility. In a society where collective controls based upon time-honoured rules were unquestioned, acquisitiveness inhibited and the weight of social obligation heavy, the scope of government and the initiative of the individual were severely restricted.

Marx, too, recognized the limitations upon freedom of choice in pre-capitalist societies. 'Economic man', who made untramelled decisions in accordance with economic rationality was, he argued, the product of capitalist society, where relationships were contractual, not fixed at birth or determined by physical coercion. The formalist school of economic anthropologists, however, differing as much from the Marxists as from the non-Marxist substantivists, do not accept that men in pre-capitalist societies are so imprisoned by custom and so absorbed by non-economic preoccupations that their response to economic questions is wholly different from that of men in modern society. They argue that the laws of economics, formulated in modern society, are of universal application. Economics is about allocating scarce resources. There has always been scarcity and it has always been necessary for men to make rational choices among a range of possibilities. The dispute is not necessarily about rationality, but about objectives. The formalist emphasizes the individual and his pursuit of personal satisfaction; the substantivist, the community and its pursuit of survival.

Certainly it would be false to see Africans trapped by custom, locked in inescapable egalitarianism and unwilling to take risks. They were not uniformly free of acquisitiveness and competitiveness. There is a large body of evidence to show that families, individuals and peoples sought their own advantage in varying degrees. There was a keen sense of ownership of moveable property, shown by the attention paid by custom in many societies to rights of inheritance. Nevertheless, competition among individuals for material possessions was not the common driving force. No doubt this was largely because they were not readily available. Primitive societies were naturally preoccupied with food. The satisfaction of immediate needs and the leisure earned through their satisfaction, security and the spreading of risks that came of collaboration were all more highly valued than pursuit of elusive or unimagined gains. If in a sense the African was the prisoner of traditional social organization and sometimes resented it, he in turn valued it because of the security it offered. Clan, lineage and family protected the individual from the adverse effects of illness and incapacity and provided him with moral and material support at critical times. The premium of social insurance was subordination to the collective, but it was one thought worth paying.

There are two issues involved: the extent of freedom of choice and the influence of entirely economic (in its formal meaning) considerations in the making of decisions. The intrusion of non-economic motivation is to be seen in the attitude to cattle typical of large parts of Africa. Clearly, cattle did serve an economic purpose. Besides their more obvious function of providing subsistence, they performed somewhat crudely the function of money, not only as a measure of value and a store of wealth, but also as a medium of exchange, frequently used for the payment of bride-price and fines. They represented one of the few forms of capital investment available, paying an interest in the form of off-spring. While there was a pronounced reluctance to part with beasts in trade or to slaughter them except on ceremonial occasions that had a religious significance, that may be explained up to a point by the priority given to their milk and the blood that in many cases was regularly drawn for consumption. Meat and hides could be obtained through hunting (a pastime, however, that appealed far more to the cultivator than the pastoralist). Nevertheless, cattle were kept without regard for the carrying capacity of the grazing land available. What was once economically rational ceased to be so. Prestige and safety were thought to lie in numbers, so that quantity not quality was the criterion, leading to the over-grazing that occurred whenever access to pasture diminished, and which in turn caused soil erosion and low milk yields. Similar overstocking was found among the Boers of South Africa.

In most African societies ambition was directed to prestige and status, derived chiefly from control of people, and to security, not to the accumulation of possessions. These ends were served by customs that tended, through the mechanism of redistribution, to disperse rather than concentrate resources. Wealth was less likely to be invested than paraded for display and used for winning support by means of lavish generosity. There was a curious inconsistency. On the one hand, there was an improvident consumption of surplus, combined with a fatalistic and apathetic attitude to events; on the other, there was calculated risk exemplified by the adoption of new crops and a careful spreading of risks exemplified by the accumulation of cattle and the acceptance of reciprocal rights and obligations. Bride-price and reciprocal gifts of cattle, even tribute, were all a form of insurance, or the equivalent of social welfare. There were outlays, but there was also income. The aim was not growth but security, fair distribution at the expense of expanded production. Clientship and generosity might convey status, but they also had their redistributive and egalitarian aspect. Individual ownership in the sense of largely unrestricted power to dispose of land and goods by the individual was inconceivable, and economic activity aimed merely at the satisfaction of immediate needs or at the performance of services to kin and community. In the absence of any incentive to more efficient production, division of labour, itself a condition for progress towards still greater efficiency, was rudimentary.

Division of labour in sub-Saharan Africa was pushed furthest in West Africa, where, with some exceptions – for example Iboland – there was considerable urban development. Towns were numerous, but the population of a typical town of the western Sudan and the West African forest was not very big before the 19th century and was in no way comparable with the great cities of ancient, classical and Muslim Egypt and North Africa. In the early Middle Ages Kumbi-Saleh, the largest of the Sudanese towns of the time, had probably fewer than 20 000 people; Timbuktu in the 15th century some 25 000; Kumasi, the capital of Asante, between 12 and 15 thousand in the early part of the 19th century; Gao, at its most populous in the late 16th century, had 75 000; and the river port of Segu on the Niger bend had at the end of the 18th century a population put at 30 000 by Mungo Park. By then, however, the Hausa town of Katsina had an estimated population of some 100 000. The population of Ibadan grew in the 19th century to about a quarter of a million and that of Salagu, a centre of the important kola nut trade, is said to have been 400 000 by 1824. But even the largest towns were before recent times scarcely differentiated from their rural environment.

Towns were mainly residences of rulers and had the characteristics of agglomerations of villages. A considerable proportion of their population engaged in agriculture. They were organized in villages in which members of the same ethnic group congregated, with their own organization, chiefs, councils of elders, and mosques, and following their distinctive customs. Consequently they lacked all municipal feeling and disappeared without leaving a trace.[9]

Much of the long-distance trade of the western Sudan in medieval times was in foreign hands, controlled by Muslim Arabs and Berbers from the

Sahara and the Maghrib. In Kumbi-Saleh these foreigners settled as an alien community under a non-Muslim king. There, as also in Gao, they had their own town, separated from the king's town. Typically, division of labour had an ethnic basis and the merchant community was an alien element. Although in time the foreign traders did influence society, as they married local women and as Islam attracted converts, they were impotent to effect an embourgeoisement of society. They never defied the political authorities and their only protest was to transfer their business elsewhere. Their situation remained precarious, subject to the hostility of pagan neighbours, like the Soso, who forced them to move from Kumbi-Saleh, to Walata in the 13th Century. In the kingdom of Mali they enjoyed the patronage of the ruler and they lived in a capital (Niani) that was Muslim, but they remained foreigners, living in their own part of the town. The patronage of kings was never, moreover, assured. Witness, for example, the harsh treatment meted out to the Muslim community of Timbuktu by the 15th-century Songhai emperor, Sunni Ali, when he suspected treachery. Although his successor, Askia Muhammad Turay, took them once again under his protection, the urban Muslims were merely the passive beneficiaries of a policy that could well change once more. In the rivalry between town and country, religious as much as economic and social, the former was far from strong enough to impose its will upon the other. It was not until the 18th century that Islam became a popular, non-urban religion in the western Sudan. At best town lent support to the ruler in his efforts to strike a balance between town and country; at worst it looked for Berber support against the local ruler, as did Timbuktu – at least to begin with – during the Moroccan invasion of Songhai in 1596. Even the class of indigenous merchants that grew up, the Wangara, though extremely influential in some towns, particularly Jenne, also tended, outside Mali, to be a group set apart either by their Muslim religion or by their language or by both. The same might be said of the Hausa and Nupe merchants.

For all its participation in long-distance trade, its manufacturing, and its craft specialization, not even the city of the western Sudan gave birth to capitalism. The commercial stimulus to manufacture was not sharp enough, nor did commerce play the dominant rôle in the economy. The cultivator of the countryside was largely uninvolved, not only as a producer for the market, but also as a consumer. The rural population was too sparse and too poor to provide much of a market, and there was a high proportion of slaves among the urban population, perhaps acting as a discouragement to technical innovation. Wealth in money was rare, and if the spending spree in Cairo of Mansa Musa, the emperor of Mali, when on his way to Mecca in the 14th century, is any guide, what there was was squandered on consumption.

The West African coast, furnishing slaves and primary products for luxury goods, where trade was a function of the state, its agents or its hangers-on or was subject to arbitrary exactions and where the surplus was consumed by the state apparatus, was likewise not an area in which incipient capitalism was likely to be found. Dahomey's trading relationship with Europe, for example,differed little from that of Carolingian Europe with Islam and Byzantium, while the following excerpt from Mungo Park's journal could be the description of any feudal magnate in medieval Europe who had the fortune to have an estate astride a trade route. It refers to the Gambia trade at the end of the 18th century.

> The number of canoes and people constantly employed in this trade makes the king of Barra more formidable to Europeans than any other chieftain on the river; and this circumstance probably encouraged him to establish those exorbitant duties which traders of all nations are obliged to pay at entry, amounting to near-ly £20 on every vessel great and small. These duties, or customs, are generally collected in person by the Alkaid, or governor of Jillifree, and he is attended on these occasions by a numerous train of dependants, among whom are found many who, by their frequent intercourse with the English, have acquired a smat-tering of our language: but they are commonly very noisy and very trouble-some – begging for everything they fancy with such earnestness and importunity, that traders, in order to get quit of them, are frequently obliged to grant their requests.[10]

The nearest resemblance in Africa to the European city that gave birth to capitalism was the so-called city state of the Slave Coast and the Oil Rivers, such as Old Calabar. Max Weber argued that in its fully matured form the city had the following functions:

> 1. a fortification; 2. a market; 3. a court of its own and at least partially auto-nomous law; 4. a related form of association; and 5. at least partial autonomy and autocephaly.[11]

By a 'related form of association' he meant a 'privileged citizen estate', a bourgeoisie. The West African city states certainly were garrisons, markets and centres of self-government. It would, however, be difficult to recognise in their oligarchies of slavers or their parvenu rulers a class of burghers acquiring corporate status and forming a true bourgeoisie. It has been sug-gested that the growth of capitalism in Africa was inhibited by Africa's more knowledgeable trading partners, who imposed upon West Africa the rôle of provider of slaves and primary products. If, however, the balance of advantage tilted in favour of European traders in the 19th century, it was the Europeans who had to accommodate themselves in the 18th and indeed well into the 19th, as the above quotation from Mungo Park shows. They had to accept indigenous methods, to make use of the services of African middlemen and to seek the protection of African princes. The long-term advantage lay with Europe because of its very capacity to adapt readily to changing circumstances, as it did in the 18th century.

In the 18th century world trade was entering a critical phase. Since the 15th century it had continually expanded because of the discoveries of Europeans, but by the 18th century new trading opportunities were no longer presenting themselves. Europe responded by diversifying and vastly increasing its own exports. Africa lacked the technology and habits of productive investment to make a comparable adjustment. Primitive capital accumulation was sacrificed to conspicuous consumption and the maintenance of large and unproductive households for the sake of prestige. Too often the African response to opportunity was to do more of the same thing – to supply more slaves, to exploit more relentlessly wasting assets, such as ivory. Africa was a market for European manufactures, but there is no evidence that it was the importation of cheap factory-made commodities that killed off an African handicraft industry which could have given birth to a native capitalism. The introduction of power-driven machinery which put Europe in the position of flooding Africa with mass-produced goods came only after centuries of contact between Europe and West Africa, and even after European exports to Africa became mass-produced goods, African handicraft industry proved to be very resilient.

As late as the 19th century the merchant of the West African interior had an archaic look about him, reminiscent of the peripatetic trader of the early Middle Ages in Europe. He too travelled in armed caravans, made up of as many as two thousand people, in transit for months on end, making their snail-like way hundreds of miles along well-defined routes. In the heyday of the gold, salt and slave trade of the Sahara Wangara merchants were dealing in very large sums of money, but they remained itinerant traders doing their accounts in their heads. A European observer of the 16th century, impressed by the volume of their business and by their integrity, incidentally drew attention to the backwardness of their methods.

> The traders who take the journey to the goldmines make considerable business. Some of them carry out a trade of over sixty thousand *mithqals;* even those who only bring the salt to Jenne do business worth ten thousands of *mithqals.*
> They trust each other without receipts, written agreements or witnesses. The credit that they are given extends until a certain date in the year . . . They are so honest that if one of them died before the payment was due, his son or his heir would hastily repay the debt exactly . . .
> They travel with their merchandise very far into the interior, farther than any other people of that region . . .[12]

Richard Jobson, another European writing in the 17th century, speaking of the Diakhanke, commented upon their prestige, learning, experience and prosperity, but noted their alien and peripatetic existence. Two centuries later Gordon Laing testified to the shrewdness of the merchants of Ghadames in Libya. Yet, despite their use of bills of exchange, they were still relying chiefly upon their memories in the conduct of their business. There were, it is true, even in the early days of the trade of the desert and savanna, firms operating, owing to the large amount of capital required and the slow turn-over. These, based at first in North Africa and mostly family firms, had their branches, sedentary agents and travelling representatives. Dubois, visiting Jenne at the end of the 19th-century, observed the

> 'business firms' in the European sense of the word, which were provided with a routine and staff similar to our own. They established representatives in import-ant centres and opened branches at Timbuktu. They sent out travelling agents who were, in fact, none other than 'commercial travellers'. The staff was com-posed of relatives and slaves, or free men who were obliged to earn their living.[11]

There was, too, a degree of functional specialization in the so-called land-lords (who furnished warehousing and accommodation for man and beast) and the brokers (who acted as commission agents and interpreters) of the major trading centres that, strung along the Sahel and along the frontier between savanna and forest, were the termini of the caravan routes. But the firms tended to be under-capitalized because they were thrown largely upon family resources for their capital needs, and the typical trader, such as the Dyula or Hausa merchant, was a small man dealing in every kind of mer-chandise. Some traders combined trade with farming or the practice of a craft. Firms 'in the European sense of the word' were in fact rare even in the trading organization of West Africa. Trade gilds in Yorubaland and Asante; 'canoe houses' in Bonny and Kalabari (New Calabar), which evolved from communities of lineage-related fishermen and specialized in slaving; and 'secret societies', such as ekpe at Old Calabar; all these displayed some of the functions of a business corporation, but, in some respects like the European chartered company, they were multi-functional organizations, social, political and military as well as commercial.

In Central and East Africa business organization was less developed. Al-though the boldness and resourcefulness of such trading peoples as the Kam-ba, Nyamwezi, Yao, Bisa, Chokwe and Thonga cannot be disputed, their organization and methods were primitive. Such merchants were also peri-patetic, travelling in groups, frequently dependent upon force, and often combining trade with slaving or elephant-hunting. If it is possible to talk of business organization, it was confined to collaboration among kinsmen in the fitting out of a caravan.

NOTES

1. Zulu traditional song in Cope, J. & Krige, U. (eds.): *The Penguin Book of South African Verse* (Harmondsworth, 1968), p. 290
2. Howard, C. (ed.): *West African Explorers* (London, 1951), p. 94
3. Ibid, p. 70
4. Fynn, H. F. quoted Wilson, M. & Thompson, L. (eds.): *The Oxford History of South Africa*, Volume I (Oxford, 1969) p. 115
5. Wittfogel, K. A.: *Oriental Despotism, a Comparative Study of Total Power* (New Haven, 1957), p. 166
6. Nicol, D. (ed.): *Africanus Horton, the Dawn of Nationalism in Modern Africa* (London and Harlow, 1969), p. 54–5
7. Howard, C.: Op. cit., p. 272–3
8. Westermann, D.: *The African Today and Tomorrow* (London, 2nd edn. 1939), p. 164
9. Trimingham, J. S.: *Islam in West Africa* (Oxford, 1959), p. 191
10. Park, M.: *Travels* (London, 2nd Everyman edn., 1954), p. 3
11. Weber, Max: *The City* (New York, Collier Books edn., 1962), p. 88
12. Fernandes, V., quoted Levtzion, N.: *Ancient Ghana and Mali* (London, 1973), p. 165–6
13. Quoted Skinner, Elliott P.: 'West African economic systems' (Chapter 4, Herskovits, M. J. and Harwitz, M. eds.: *Economic Transition in Africa*, Chicago, 1964), p. 95

Further reading

Beattie, J. H. M.: 'Bunyoro: an African feudality?' (*Journal of African History*, V, 1964, p. 25–36)
Bloch, Maurice (ed.): *Marxist Analyses and Social Anthropology* (London, 1975)
Coquery-Vidrovitch, Catherine: 'Research on an African mode of production' (Gutkind, P. C. W. & Waterman, P. eds.: *African Social Studies, a Radical Reader*, London, 1977)
Dalton, George (ed.): *Economic Development and Social Change* (New York, 1971)
Dalton, George (ed.): *Tribal and Peasant Economies, Readings in Economic Anthropology* (New York, 1967)
Firth, Raymond (ed.): *Themes in Economic Anthropology* (London, 1967)
Forde, C. Daryll & Kaberry, P. M. (eds.): *West African Kingdoms in the 19th Century* (London, 1967)
Forde, C. Daryll (ed.): *Efik Traders of Old Calabar* (Oxford, 1956)
Fortes, M. & Evans-Pritchard, E. E. (eds.): *African Political Systems* (London, 1940)
Fried, Morton H.: *Readings in Anthropology*, Volume II (New York, 2nd edn. 1968)
Godelier, Maurice: *Rationality and Irrationality in Economics* (London, 1972)
Goody, Jack: *Technology, Tradition and the State in Africa* (London, 1971)
Herskovits, M. J.: *Dahomey, an Ancient West African Kingdom*, 2 volumes (New York, 1938)
Hindess, B. & Hirst, P. Q.: Op. cit. (see p. 203)
Keenan, Jeremy: 'The concept of the mode of production in hunter-gatherer societies' (*African Studies*, XXXVI, 1977, p. 57–69)
Law, Robin: 'In search of a Marxist perspective on pre-colonial tropical Africa' (*Journal of African History*, XIX, 1978, p. 441–52)
Law, Robin: 'Royal monopoly and private enterprise in the Atlantic trade: the case of Dahomey' (*Journal of African History*, XVIII, 1977, p. 555–77)

Leclair, Edward E. & Schneider, Harold K. (eds.): *Economic Anthropology, Readings in Theory and Analysis* (New York, 1968)

Meillassoux, Claude: 'From reproduction to production, a Marxist approach to economic anthropology' (*Economy and Society*, I, 1972, p. 93–105)

O'Fahey, R. S. & Spaulding, J. L.: *Kingdoms of the Sudan* (London, 1974)

Polanyi, K.: Op. cit. (see p. 115 and 204)

Sahlins, Marshall D.: 'On the sociology of primitive exchange' (*The Relevance of Models for Social Anthropology, A. S. A. Monographs* 1, London, 1965, p. 139–236)

Sahlins, M. D.: *Stone Age Economics* (London, 1974)

Seddon, David (ed.): *Relations of Production: Marxist Approaches to Economic Anthropology* (London, 1978)

Southall, Aidan W.: *Alur Society, a Study in Processes and Types of Domination* (Cambridge, 1953)

Stevenson, R. F.: *Population and Political Systems in Tropical Africa* (New York and London, 1968)

Terray, Emmanuel: *Marxism and 'Primitive' Societies* (New York and London, 1972)

Tuden, Arthur & Plotnicov, Leonard (eds.): *Social Stratification in Africa* (New York and London, 1970)

Wilson, M. & Thompson, L.: Op. cit. (see note 4)

4. EUROPE IN AFRICA

i) *The Portuguese*

Portugal's African possessions and trading posts were only one part of her world-wide interests, extending from Brazil to Japan. Yet the country that established such an enormous maritime empire was, by the European standards of the 15th and 16th centuries, 'less developed'. Population was under a million when the voyages of discovery began, and the only town of any great size was Lisbon with some 40 000 people. Most Portuguese lived on the land. The merchant was a despised member of society and status was accorded rather to landowning and soldiering, though trading in gold and slaves was not thought incompatible with the latter. However, Portugal was not geographically homogeneous or socially static. There was a marked contrast between the coast, where salt making and fishing were important industries and where a vigorous, though relatively modest, overseas trade was conducted, and the agricultural and pastoral interior; and there were some sharp social divisions giving rise to conflicting class interests. The urban bourgeoisie was by no means lacking in influence, particularly after the civil wars of the 14th century, and to a considerable extent Portuguese discovery, trade and colonization can be interpreted as an extension of social tension at home, the nobility favouring territorial conquest, the bourgeoisie commercial expansion. The initiative in the spread of Portuguese influence in Africa was taken by the crown, but there were other powerful sectional interests that stood to gain a great deal of economic benefit from that expansion.

The crown arrogated to itself the monopoly of trade, and this monopoly it either exercised itself or disposed of to those willing to pay for the privilege. John II (1481–1495) excluded most private interests, but his strict policy was subsequently modified, though the crown continued to regulate the trade very closely through, firstly, its Casa de Guiné, later the Casa da Mina, both situated in Lisbon. The usual practice was the farming out of specific areas, for example São Thomé or a section of the Guinea coast, though this did not preclude the licensing of particular voyages to Africa by private traders. Farms, valid for up to five years, were put up for auction, but sub-contracting was common, for example in the slave trade. The licensee or contractor (who could be non-Portuguese) undertook to send a certain number of vessels to Africa, to abstain from trade in certain commodities (weapons and spirits, though not wine) and, in the case of West Africa, to call for customs clearance at Santiago in the Cape Verde Islands. The drawback to the system was lack of continuity and restraint. Each licensee aimed at making what he could as soon as he could without thought for the long-term interests of the trade.

In the 18th century two chartered companies, similar to those common in the northern European states, were established by the virtual ruler of Portugal between 1755 and 1777, best known as the Marquis of Pombal. Although these were given the monopoly of the Amazon and Brazil trade, their activities concerned Africa too. They collected slaves on the Upper Guinea coast and elsewhere in West Africa and sold them at cost price on long-term credit to Brazilian planters, to their great advantage. However, they did not long survive Pombal's fall from power.

In East Africa the three fortresses of Mozambique, Sofala and Mombasa received their orders from Goa, with which communications were convenient only at certain times of the year, according to the monsoon. At the same time they were very far from Europe. Local officials were therefore left to their own devices for long periods. There was one captain for Mozambique and Sofala and another for Mombasa. These positions were normally sold to the highest bidder for a three-year period, and the proceeds were used for the support of the garrison, while the purchaser recouped himself by exploiting the trade monopoly and, no doubt, the prerogatives of his office too. Thus there was a conflict of loyalties, loyalty to private profits and loyalty to the policy of the crown. The captain did very well, but the administration and the interests of the crown suffered. Lesser officials were also dishonest and corrupt. Not surprisingly, the East Coast settlements were run at a loss to the crown. It is estimated that there was a deficit of 40 per cent. of expenditure over revenue. However, the crown was not above selling a colonial post to a whole succession of purchasers. It was not impossible for a claimant to be in a queue of a dozen or so others with a prior claim. Such a reversion of office could be bequeathed or sold.

Monopolies were most unpopular, though not all contractors made their fortunes. A good deal of illicit trade was carried on and even tolerated in the absence of effective means of stopping it. To compensate for their very poor wages and to encourage people to take up posts in distant and unhealthy places, soldiers, sailors and officials were allowed to carry on a private trade, officially very limited, in practice pursued as far as its beneficiaries dared. Officials abused their positions by promoting the interests of private enterprises and by money lending, sometimes even using official funds. A decree of 1720 forbidding private trade by officials was ineffective, despite an increase of salaries to reduce temptation. There was considerable smuggling. too, and infringement of crown rights, particularly by the Cape Verde islanders. Corruption and gross acquisitiveness were the curse of Portuguese administration everywhere. To them was added an ineptitude that was often the result of nepotism and the precedence given to persons of high birth in appointments to public office.

The Portuguese displayed little interest in settlement. Trade was their overriding preoccupation, and the African coast seemed insalubrious and unattractive compared with Brazil. Apart from trading posts and factories, such as El Mina, the only settlement was made on the off-shore islands, the Cape Verde Islands, Fernando Po and São Thomé. The quasi-feudal grant (donatária), imposing the obligation to promote settlement and secure defence in return for taxing (but not trading) privileges, was found both in the islands and in Angola, but in every case eventually reverted to the crown. TheGuinea islands – two large (São Thomé and Fernando Po) and two small (O Principe and Annonbon) – were settled at the end of the 15th century, São Thomé from 1485, Fernando Po from 1493. The first settlers were a mixture of convicts, adventurers and enforced exiles, including deported Jews. In Portuguese colonial society, especially in unhealthy places like São Thomé and the Zambezi valley, convicts (degredados) were always a conspicuous element, though, of course, the harsh penal code of the 16th, 17th and 18th centuries swept into the convicted criminal class many minor offenders, even those whose only offence was poverty or political disaffection. Occasionally they did well for themselves in their place of enforced exile. Since white women were as scarce as male criminals were abundant, miscegenation was usual, and there was a pronounced tendency towards Africanization.

The Guinea islands turned out to be suitable for sugar cultivation and the settlers had little interest in the mainland except as a source of slaves. These were obtained from as far north as Benin and as far south as the Congo. The islands enjoyed great prosperity until about 1570, when they began to be troubled by slave revolts and internal dissensions that persisted throughout the 17th and 18th centuries. After 1600 they became less important as sugar producers than as assembly points for slaves awaiting shipment to Brazil.

At the mouth of the River Congo (or Zaïre), the Portuguese came into contact with the kingdom of the Kongo, ruled by the Manicongo, who, like most African kings, was not the head of a centralized unitary state, but the suzerain or paramount chief of a confederation of tribal groups in an area bounded by the rivers Congo, Loje and Kwango, and who also claimed a vague authority over the kingdom of Ndongo, named Angola by the Portuguese after the title of its king (Ngola). The official Portuguese policy in the Congo, at least the policy of John II, was as disinterested as it could be in the circumstances. Missionaries and artisans were despatched, and there were hopes of converting the Manicongo to Christianity and forming an alliance with him. Hopes of economic advantage there were, but apparently not dominant. The Congo seemed to have little to offer. There was no gold and to begin with there was no strong demand for slaves. There was not even any pepper.

The Manicongo became a Christian and his capital, Mbanza, was renamed São Salvador, but the Congo experiment was not markedly successful. Christianity did not penetrate very far down the social scale. Economic demands began to intrude, to some extent from the crown. When Afonso, the Christian Manicongo, requested help, especially in spreading Christianity, Portugal was sympathetic, but her resources were over-stretched and she wanted some return in the form of slaves, copper and ivory to defray expenses. At first slaves were obtained beyond the borders of the kingdom, but before long the king's own subjects were being enslaved for the plantations of São Thomé, and the Portuguese authorities were unable to control their own nationals. There were about two hundred Portuguese in the Congo by the 1530s, quarrelsome, devious and intervening in local politics. Intermarriage resulted in a class of restless mulattoes. Portuguese officials repeatedly warned their government to give support to the Manicongo, but its intervention was spasmodic and ineffectual. The Portuguese came to put a higher value upon São Thomé. Afonso died in 1543 and his kingdom was weakened by a series of disputes fomented by the Portuguese expatriates, then overrun by the Jaga. By 1615 the white population of São Salvador had disappeared and there were few remains of Christianity, and by the end of the century it was in ruins and deserted.

The neighbouring kingdom of Ndongo was bounded by the rivers Dande in the north and Kwanza in the south and extended into the interior possibly as far as the River Kwango. Slaves were the primary interest of the Portuguese, but there was some belief in the existence of deposits of silver, for which there was an acute need in Portugal, and several expeditions were organized to search for them. There was no direct government by the Portuguese until the 1570s. In 1571 a large area south of the River Kwanza was granted as a donatária to Paulo Dias de Novais, who in turn made grants of land to his followers. He undertook certain obligations, the most important of which was the promise to explore the coast as far as the Cape of Good Hope and to settle a hundred families in the colony within six years. He arrived in 1575 and the city of Luanda was founded in 1576, but not much progress was made during his donatária, as he became involved in local wars and failed to bring in any settlers. In 1592 the grant reverted to the crown. Some effort was then made by Lisbon to protect the African people from the exactions of Portuguese landowners, but in fact they continued to be subject to the burdens imposed by both landowners and governors. During the rule of Pombal some attempt was made to broaden the economic base of the colony. Francisco Inocencio de Sousa Coutinho, during his governorship of the colony (1764–1772), started various industrial and agricultural enterprises and established a chamber of commerce at Luanda. His policy was not maintained after his departure. In a mercantilist age colonial manufacturing displeased too many vested interests.

Mozambique was administered from Goa until the 18th century. Mozambique Island was intended as a stopping place for vessels proceeding to and from India, but it was very unhealthy with a high loss of life among visiting seamen. Portuguese influence on the mainland, largely in the Zambezi valley, was attributable chiefly to a body of local estate owners. Grants of land were made in return for military and fiscal services, the *prazos*, and a few were made to religious orders. In practice the secular holders were very independent of the crown, disregarding their obligations and maintaining private armies in pursuit of their feuds.

> The Portuguese lords of the lands have in their hands that same power and juris-diction as had the Kaffir chiefs from whom they were taken, because the terms of the quit-rent were made on that condition. For this reason, they are like German potentates, since they can lay down the law in everything, put people to death, declare war and levy taxes. Perhaps they sometimes commit great barbarities in all this: but they would not be respected as they should be by their vassals if they did not enjoy the same powers as the chiefs whom they succeeded.[1]

Government measures to secure periodic reversion to the crown to ensure that the *prazos* were kept in European hands and to keep them to a reasonable size, were ineffective. They became very large and their holders were more interested in dealing in gold, ivory and slaves than in the cultivation which the authorities felt was desirable. Lack of will, capital and transport facilities rendered any hope of plantation-type agriculture unrealistic, though a small amount of sugar cultivation and processing was carried on. The *prazos* fell increasingly to mulattoes and Goans and in the long run the holders were thoroughly Africanized. Portugal was never able to make an effective presence felt throughout the vast territories under her influence because of the paucity of troops and settlers. At places like Tete or the islands only a handful of Portuguese resided. The small population of Portugal could not sustain a considerable emigration both to Brazil and to her African and Asian possessions.

ii) *Other European nations in West Africa*
Those European states that followed the Portuguese to Africa were economically more advanced than Portugal, having a more developed industry and a larger, more respected and more influential commercial class. However, between the 16th and 18th centuries the prevailing economic theory (or perhaps 'collection of economic presuppositions' would be a more apt description of a body of economic doctrine that was somewhat amorphous) was mercantilism. The rôle of the state was considered important and its intervention in economic processes welcomed for the pursuit of opulence and national power. The degree and nature of state action varied. As in Portugal, though less so, in France the initiative came to a considerable extent from the crown owing to the comparative weakness of the commercial class and the reluctance of the noble and wealthy to invest capital and talent in trade and industry. In England the state played an important part, but the government had closer ties with, and was more susceptible to, the influence of merchants (particularly after the temporary fall of the monarchy in 1649), and from them came a demand for state support against foreign, especially Dutch, competition. Both England and France used state power primarily to emulate the economic performance of Holland, dominant in sea transport, international trade and many branches of manufacturing. By the standards of the period two lesser developed countries were endeavouring to catch up with the most developed. Dutch merchants, with their superior efficiency, did not need the support of the state, but nonetheless conducted their operations outside Europe in a warlike manner. In their case, they were neither subject to pressure from the state, as was the case in France, nor bringing pressure to bear upon it, as was the case in England. For they virtually controlled the state, or at least administration and commerce were run by the same or similar people.

The necessity or desirability of monopoly was accepted by these European countries. Companies, chartered by various governments and given political powers and trading monopolies as far as their own nationals were concerned, were much favoured. They alone could afford to construct and maintain the necessary trading forts for the storage of goods and the custody of slaves awaiting transport and for defence against European competitors. They were more likely to attract the necessary capital from investors unwilling to take the grave risks characteristic of free competition. In exchange for the privileges they received from the state, the companies were compelled to undertake obligations that were difficult to fulfil, such as the provision of a specific annual supply of slaves, and they incurred the jealousy and hostility of all those opposed to monopoly either in principle or because of their own exclusion. Often incompetently run and short of capital in a trade where returns were slow and hazardous and infrastructure expensive; flouted by interlopers; burdened with bad debts among the planters in the West Indies; cheated by their own servants, who were difficult to control at a distance; and in conflict with foreign rivals; for all these reasons they were not as a rule very profitable and had to be propped up by state subsidy.

The first of the great chartered companies operating in West Africa was the Dutch West Indies Company. The first incorporated English company was the Guinea Company of 1618, which survived until 1660, when it was succeeded by the Royal Adventurers into Africa. Slaving was specifically mentioned in a new charter granted to it in 1663. The company lasted only twelve years. It was followed by the Royal African Company (1672). As for the French, they had their West Indies Company, which was chartered in 1664, not their first company for the Atlantic trade, but their first effective one. Others followed, the Senegal Company (1673) and the Guinea Company (1684). In 1682, Brandenburg chartered a company, which, from 1686, supplied the Danish West Indies with slaves. This was an early casualty of the difficulties that beset such enterprises. In 1717 the company sold off its forts on the Gold Coast to the Dutch. The Danes themselves experienced trials with their own West Indies Company because of the tendency of trade to divide on national lines. Their possessions in the West Indies provided too narrow a market and, after participating in it between 1697 and 1733, the Company abandoned the slave trade.

The tenets of mercantilism – state regulation of national commerce and the exclusion of foreigners – were not seriously questioned or challenged until late in the 18th century, chiefly by Adam Smith in Britain and the Physiocrats in France. The aspect of the commercial system that was first attacked with success was monopoly, at least in Britain. Chartered companies no longer seemed so necessary for the mobilization and protection of capital. Although the greatest of them, the East India Company, was not touched because it was recognzied as a special case, the Royal African Company lost its monopoly in 1698, retaining responsibility for the upkeep of the West African forts, to which, however, private traders had to contribute. In 1752 it was wound up, and a much looser organization came into being, the Company of Merchants Trading to Africa, which was in effect an association of merchants who traded independently and collaborated in maintaining, with the help of a government subsidy, the infrastructure for the conduct of trade. The fact that it was actually prohibited from corporate trading is an indication of the decline of commercial monopoly.

In France, too, monopoly was subject to criticism and in 1716 the African trade was thrown open to all. In 1720, as part of the schemes of John Law, the financier, a new Compagnie des Indes was formed. Plagued by the old weaknesses, it surrendered its African forts to the crown (1763, with the exception of Whydah, 1767). It proved impossible to dispense with chartered company operation and monopoly in the Senegal area, where the trade in slaves was less important than that in gold and gum and where hostility with Britain recurred and forts had to be maintained, sometimes at a loss. The Senegal Company operated on the Senegal river and as far south as Cape Verde, beyond which, however, the rule was private trade subsidized by the crown and supported with royal forts and a naval presence. Although state-backed monopoly went out of fashion in Europe, the nature of the West African trade, with its high risks and long-term investment, brought with it a trend towards oligopoly. Large companies were formed, such as the French Angola Company and the Dutch Middelburg Company.

The Dutch, French and English displayed little interest in settlement, beyond the establishment of forts and trading posts. The biggest of the European West African settlements was the French foundation of St. Louis, situated on an island in the Senegal river. It had a population of several hundred Europeans and a rather more numerous group of mulattoes and Africans, many of whom were artisans or engaged in local or long-distance trade. It was here that a European power, apart from Portugal, came nearest to forming a colony. In the early part of the 18th century the attempt by a French governor, André Brue, to gain control of the sources of gold failed in the face of African opposition and suspicion. Similar British ambitions of penetrating up the Gambia in search of gold were futile. During a period when they had expelled the French (1758–1779), the British joined their Senegal and Gambia territories to form the colony of Senegambia, but during its relatively brief existence it was not a great success.

A more significant development was the British foundation of Sierra Leone settlement in 1787. This was intended from the start to be a colony of settlement, though for freeborn and emancipated blacks. Territory was acquired from the local ruler. After an initial and precarious start under the aegis of private philanthropy, though with substantial state assistance, it became in 1791, the responsibility of a chartered company, which ran the the settlement through a board of directors in London. Like many of the colonizing ventures in North America, Sierra Leone sought a secular means to a spiritual end. Trading profits were aimed at, but for the support of the colony, and they were subordinate to the provision of a home for released slaves. When hopes of promoting the production of export crops were thwarted by capital shortage and unpropitious growing conditions, trade became the main support for the settlers. The Company, attempting to raise some revenue through an unpopular quit-rent imposed on the settlers' holdings, found its position deteriorating from the effects of the French Revolutionary Wars and the continuation of the slave trade, and so the colony was taken over by the government in 1808.

The foundation of Sierra Leone was the result of the need to find a solution to the problem of dealing with an embarrassing group of blacks in America and England, cut free from their existing place in society by the American War of Independence and the Mansfield judgment outlawing slavery in England. However, it was in keeping with new attitudes towards West Africa that were developing in Europe. There were vague, mostly utopian, ideas of European settlement for the production of crops and the promotion of exports of raw materials. While such ideas pre-dated by decades the ending of the slave trade, anti-slavery sentiments gave them a new vigour. The Sierra Leone experiment, though it too went through grave trials, was the best supported and really the only successful implementation of these ideas before the end of the 18th century. A British attempt in 1792 to start sugar, cotton and indigo plantations on Bulama Island, employing free black labour, was a disaster.

Similar settlements for free or freed blacks were established under French auspices at Libreville on the north of the estuary of the River Gabon and under American auspices at Cape Mesurado on the Grain Coast. The latter, at first composed of a number of separate establishments, blossomed in 1847 into the Republic of Liberia, with its capital Monrovia. It was the creation of the American Colonization Society, which was founded in 1816 to solve an American social problem rather than an African one, just as Sierra Leone had been, at least partly, designed to solve a British one. Resentment and hostility were encountered among both the native Africans and European merchants. The colonists laid claim to an extensive part of the interior, but their effective control was confined to the coast.

Libreville had a very different origin. It was the outcome of a somewhat inconsistent and ambivalent new phase of French imperialism after 1815. In Senegambia they reoccupied St. Louis and Goree, which had been under British control during the Napoleonic Wars, and, after unsuccessful attempts at plantation agriculture, endeavoured to rebuild their trade. This they did with great success along both the Senegal and the upper Gambia, though the lower part of the Gambia was abandoned to the British in exchange for the latter's withdrawal from the Goree area. In the 1830s government policy became much more vigorous, its most conspicuous feature being the conquest of Algeria, which began in 1830. Another aspect was the setting up of 'points d'appui et de relâche' along the west coast of Africa as well as in the Pacific and Indian Oceans. These were to perform both commercial and strategic functions. Between 1840 and 1842, treaties which included the sale of land, were signed with African chiefs at Garroway, on the coast of modern Liberia, at Grand Bassam and Assini on the Ivory Coast and at Gabon, the site of present-day Libreville, all places at river mouths, already frequented by European merchants and facilitating future penetration of the interior. Garroway came to nothing, and subsequent protectorates along the Slave Coast were short-lived. But after the establishment of the Second Empire a commission representing government, parliament and commerce recommended the retention of Grand Bassam, Assini and Gabon, despite the meagre commercial success of the last two. It was after the establishment of the Second Empire, too, that territorial conquest became the policy in Senegal, especially during the governorship of Louis Faideherbe (1854–1865). Dakar was occupied in 1857.

iii) *The Dutch and the British at the Cape*

The Cape Colony was founded by the Dutch East India Company as a refreshment station and to forestall occupation by England at a time when relations between England and Holland were on the point of open conflict. That Company was an amalgamation of previously existing companies which, based upon Amsterdam and five other Dutcht owns, continued as separate chambers, sending delegates to a co-ordinating committee known as the Seventeen. The Seventeen was a powerful body, drawn from the leading families of the participating towns and closely connected with government circles. It was able in its initial period to draw upon very large capital funds and to resist any attempts by individual shareholders to influence policy. At the same time, meeting infrequently, lacking executive powers and constantly changing in membership, it had difficulty in imposing its will upon the distant Governor-General and Council of the Indies in the Far East (to whom the Cape settlement was subject) and its ability to control events and follow a consistent policy was limited.

In the Cape Colony the Company required the local production of foodstuffs for visiting ships and for the support of the garrison. Finding the unwilling, part-time services of its garrison unsatisfactory, it reconciled itself, though with some misgiving and against the advice of the Council of the Indies, to dependence upon what were called 'free burghers', though these were begrudged more than a modicum of control over their own livelihood. Intensive agriculture in the immediate vicinity of Cape Town met with only limited success. Methods and implements were rudimentary; land clearing, ploughing (with a heavy wooden plough) and sowing, rough and ready; and manuring little practised. Wheat was the principal crop, alternating with oats and interrupted by a prolonged period of fallow. To the production of meat and wheat, wine of varying but generally indifferent quality, and brandy, were added. Fishing off the coast, especially from Saldanha Bay, was very rewarding, as well as whaling and sealing. Wool, olives, silk, indigo, flax, rice and tobacco were all tried in vain. High transport costs made even moderately profitable arable farming impossible more than eighty kilometres from Cape Town. Cereal production was highly competitive and, because of the small size of the local market and the difficulty of competing successfully on external markets, often plagued by over-production.In the 18th century the situation worsened as the size of the complement of the Company's eastern fleets decreased.

Settlement so far from Europe presented few attractions to immigrants, but those who settled there, Dutch, German and French Huguenot, proved to be extraordinarily fecund and absorptive. Unable to make a living from cultivation and subject to the parsimonious regulation of the Company, they spread rapidly into the interior, where they modified the agricultural methods of Europe under the influence of an environment characterized by abundant land and long distances and, for the most part, by uncertain or irregular rainfall and poorish soil. Short of capital and skill and to a considerable degree cut off, in the absence of transport, from the outisde world, they developed a hunting, pastoral and barter economy not unlike that of the people they first encountered. In the 18th century it was an economy based chiefly upon the local breed of sheep and goats, which were able to thrive in areas of low rainfall and yielded better meat than the cattle did.

The Dutch East India Company was on the horns of a dilemma, anxious on the one hand to secure the regular supply of meat that, contrary to its hopes, was not forthcoming from the Khoikhoi, unwilling on the other hand to see cultivation neglected and a dispersal of the colonists that would strain the meagre administrative services it was willing to provide and that was all too likely to lead to conflict with the Khoisan and later the Bantu-speakers. In the last two decades of the 17th century efforts were made by Governor Simon van der Stel, though he was by no means averse to the enlargement of the colony by close settlement, to prevent trekking into the interior, but in the 18th century the Company gave in to what it could hardly regulate, let alone control, and comforted itself with the rents demanded of those who occupied what it claimed as Company land. The policy became one of cheap and easy access to grazing land. Despite repeated attempts by the government to proclaim a boundary that would be respected by the pioneers, the frontier of settlement moved rapidly northwards along the west coast and eastwards along the south coast, brushing aside in its progress whatever claims to land the Khoikhoi had. Such resistance as the latter were capable of offering was gravely weakened by smallpox and other epidemics that assaulted both man and beast in the second decade of the 18th century.

To begin with the Dutch stock owners combined permanent residence in the older agricultural areas with utilization of distant pastures, but, as the frontier moved on, there was a growing community of white herders, cultivating just enough to meet their own needs, shifting their herds to different pasture as the seasons dictated or moving on from exhausted land to new, and trading their surplus beasts for the simple requirements of frontier life. By the last quarter of the 18th century the trekboers, deterred in the north by the barrenness of Namaqualand and the Great Karoo, were in the north-east in contact, and sometimes in conflict, with the San and, on the Orange and Great Fish Rivers, the Bantu-speaking Xhosa, themselves in search of new land.

The Company's administration was rudimentary. The governor was responsible to the Seventeen, and was assisted by an official known as the Fiscal and by a Council of Policy. As new settlements were established – Stellenbosch, Swellendam, Graaff-Reinet and so on – local affairs were entrusted to a *landdrost* and *heemraden*.

The development of local industries that would compete with those in the metropolitan country was prevented.

> During the period of the Company's rule there was hardly any manufacturing industry at the Cape, with the exception of (a) a few subsidiary industrial esta-blishments, such as flour mills and saw mills (driven by water or wind), wagon-makers' workshops, tanneries, bakeries, and a brewery, and (b) a few minor handi-crafts, such as carpentry, cabinet-making, ropemaking, brick-laying, plastering, and iron-forging. These were conducted on a relatively small scale and mostly by means of primitive methods.
>
> The Company had consistently opposed all branches of industry involving special processes in preparing the raw material or in manufacturing the finished article. Not even the roughest fabrics were permitted to be made at the Cape from the raw wool obtainable. The Fiscals had always been most strongly opposed to any suggestion for the establishment of manufacturing institutions and the admission of the more important handicrafts, on the ground that it would be detrimental to the Company's factories in Holland.[2]

Even at the end of the 18th century the white population did not exceed twenty thousand and was very widely dispersed. Its poverty and sparseness did not offer any stimulation to modern industry. Industrially, European settlement was important not for what it achieved in its first two centuries, but for what it promised whenever the necessary stimulus should be applied.

The Company had at its disposal all the land available for settlement, was the major customer for local produce, exercised a monopoly in external trade and controlled the issue of licences for retail trade. Although in practice its control over trade and land was evaded up to a point, the grievances of the 'free burghers' against the Company and its officials remained manifold. They came to the surface as early as the last decade of the 17th century, when

Simon van der Stel was governor, but were especially bitter in the later 18th century, when the Company was nearing bankruptcy and making sporadic attempts at financial retrenchment. Farmers wanted access to other markets, an ambition difficult to satisfy given the remoteness of the colony (as van der Stel and other energetic governors found), and better prices for their products, though in fact prices were more than usually volatile, even for farm products, for reasons quite beyond the Company's control. The chance visit of ships for victualling or changes in the size of the garrison in accordance with the international political situation would bring about a sudden expansion or contraction of demand that had little to do with local Company policy. Perhaps more resentment was directed against the Company's servants or ex-servants who abused their official connections, using their influence when contracts for the supply of the Company with local produce and retailing licences were granted. Rebellious settlers simply took themselves off into the interior, where the Company's control was tenuous, and led a frontier life characterised by a high degree of self-sufficiency but punctuated by occasional visits to town for essential manufactured goods. Sometimes licence fees for 'loanplaces' fell into arrears, tithe payments disregarded and land occupied without licence.

The British interest in the Cape derived solely from its strategic position on the route to India, where Great Britain did have an important economic stake. Within the Colony the imperial government was concerned only with maintaining the peace and, partly for the promotion of peace, partly for their own sake, imposing

> liberal, Christian standards upon the Boer colonists in their relations with the coloured and Bantu population. The slaves were freed. Masters were restrained. Servants were given liberty of contract and equality in the courts, the tribes protected in possession of their lands, and the principle of political equality was laid down.[3]

The Cape Colony became British at a time when the metropolitan country was making a hesitant start with dismantling the old colonial system, the foundations of which had been laid in the 17th century, and with introducing free trade; when slavery had become odious; when colonial land settlements were in vogue; when the 'spirited landlord' was transforming English agriculture; and when there was a groping towards the principle of autonomy for colonies of settlement. During the first British occupation (1795–1803) the imperial government honoured a promise to free internal overland and coastal trade. The removal of restraints upon external trade came more slowly. In the sphere of external trade, the policy of preventing all foreign contact with the colonies gave way to one of imperial preference. Accordingly, in 1797 the ships and goods of friendly foreign countries were admitted to Cape ports, subject to duties that British vessels escaped. Restrictions on foreign ships were reimposed in 1811, after the second occupation (1806), remaining in force until 1820, the British East India Company retaining privileges until 1833. By the time complete freedom was granted in 1832 to foreign ships to participate in Cape trade (with the exception of a heavier duty on foreign goods), British maritime dominance was so well established that the foreign share of that trade was quite small. The system of imperial preference lasted until 1854, when all colonial duties differentiating in favour of Britain were swept away. During the period of imperial preference Cape grain and wine farmers received protection in their own market and Cape wine received preferential treatment on the British market. The latter became less advantageous in 1831, when the duty on Cape wine was raised. Preference was finally abolished in 1860.

The 50th Ordinance of 1828 (which was meant to free the Khoikhoi from forced labour) and the abolition of slavery in 1833 contributed to the decision by many Boer settlers to forsake the Cape Colony and undertake the exodus known as the Great Trek. These measures, however, were only one of a number of pressures that in some cases stemmed from government policy and, in others, were more or less fortuitous. Land hunger and persistent drought were undoubtedly incentives to move to areas where there appeared to be plenty of better land for the taking. Frontier families were large and such land as was incorporated into the colony after the annexation of Zuurveld in 1812 relieved the Boer pressure upon the land only slightly. Discontent, moreover, was the result not merely of diminishing access to land, but also of resentment at British land administration. After a vain attempt to establish a republic in Natal, which was annexed by Britian in 1843, the trekkers set up small frontier democracies on the other side of the Orange and Vaal Rivers, republics so small and poor that they were scarcely able to evolve and support the apparatus of a modern state. They were dedicated, at least at first, to the proposition that the burgher had an inalienable right to a farm of adequate size and to the forced labour of the native inhabitants. Like the Dutch East India Company before it, the British government tried to restrict penetration into the interior and experienced an equal lack of success. As the trekkers moved inland they were pursued by British rule in order to maintain control of the coast and prevent the possibility of Boer collaboration with other European powers. Hence the annexation of Natal. As the Boer republics across the Orange and Vaal Rivers posed no threat, their independence was recognised by the Bloemfontein and Sand River Conventions of 1852 and 1854 respectively, but it was a severely circumscribed independence given their deliberate exclusion from the outside world.

NOTES

1. Fr. Manuel Barreto, S. J., quoted Boxer, C. R.: *The Portuguese Seaborne Empire 1415–1825* (London, 1969), p. 139
2. De Kock, M. H.: *Selected Subjects in the Economic History of South Africa* (Cape Town and Johannesburg, 1924), p. 282
3. Robinson, R. & Gallagher, J.: *Africa and the Victorians: the Official Mind of Imperialism* (London and Basingstoke, 1961), p. 53

Further reading

Axelson, E.: Op. cit. (see p. 188)
Blake, J. W.: Op. cit. (see p. 173)
Boxer, C. R.: Op. cit. (see above, note 1)
Davies, K. G.: Op. cit. (see 173–174)
De Kiewiet, C. W.: *A History of South Africa, Social and Economic* (Oxford, 1941)
De Lannoy, Charles & Van der Linden, Herman: *Histoire de l'expansion des peuples euro-péens, Portugal et Espagne (jusqu'au début du XIXe siècle)* (Brussels and Paris, 1907)
Diffie, Bailey W. & Winius, George D.: *Foundations of the Portuguese Empire, 1415–1580* (Minneapolis, 1977)
Duffy, J. E.: *Portuguese Africa* (Cambridge, Mass., 1959)
Fage, J. D.: Op. cit. (see p. 174)
Fyfe, Christopher: *A History of Sierra Leone* (London, 1962)
Gallacher, J.: 'Economic relations in Africa' (Chapter XXIV, 1. Lindsay, J. O. ed.: *The New Cambridge Modern History*, Volume VII, Cambridge, 1957)
Gray, R.: Op. cit. (see p. 153)
Hancock, Sir Keith: 'Trek' (*Economic History Review*, 2nd ser. X, 1958, p. 331–9)
Isaacman, A. F.: *Mozambique: the Africanization of a European Institution, the Zambezi Prazos, 1750–1902* (Madison, Wis., 1972)
Lawrence, A. W.: *Trade Castles and Forts of West Africa* (London, 1963)
Magalhães-Godinho, V.: Op. cit. (see p. 174)
Newitt, M. D. D.: *Portuguese Settlement on the Zambezi, Exploration, Land Tenure and Colonial Rule in East Africa* (London, 1973)
Parry, J. H.: 'Transport and trade routes' (Chapter III, Rich, E. E. and Wilson, C. H. eds.: *The Cambridge Economic History of Europe*, Volume IV, Cambridge, 1967)
Robertson, H. M.: 'The politico-economic background of Jan van Riebeeck's settle-ment' and 'Jan van Riebeeck and his settlement' (*South African Journal of Economics*, XX, 1952, p. 205–19, 309–30)
Schnapper, Bernard: *La politique et le commerce français dans le Golfe de Guinée de 1838 à 1871* (Paris and The Hague, 1961)
Scott, William Robert: *The Constitution and Finance of English, Scottish and Irish Joint-Stock Companies to 1720*, Volume II (Cambridge, 1910)
Strandes, Julius: Op. cit. (see p. 188)
Verlinden, Charles: *The Beginnings of Modern Colonization* (Ithaca and London, 1970)
Walker, Eric A.: *The Great Trek* (London, 1934)
Walker, E. A. (ed.): *The Cambridge History of the British Empire*, Volume VIII, *South Africa, Rhodesia and the High Commission Territories* (Cambridge, 1963)
Wilson, M. & Thompson, L.: Op. cit. (see p. 66)

CHAPTER V

THE INTEGRATION OF AFRICA INTO THE INTERNATIONAL ECONOMY

1. AFRICAN ATTEMPTS AT ADJUSTMENT

i) *Mediterranean Africa*

In an effort to close the alarming technological and military gap between themselves and the West, various states in Africa made attempts to modernize. Such modernizing efforts began in Egypt, where Muḥammad 'Alī, an Albanian mercenary who became the Turkish sultan's viceroy, destroyed the rule of the Mamluks between 1807 and 1811. He took action against the great estates and laid the basis for the development of private land ownership, reformed the bureaucracy and created a national army. The *multazim*, the lessees of the right to collect taxes, constituted a profitless social stratum between the state and the fellahin, whose labour and surplus were needed by the state for its own purposes.

The development programme included the encouragement of cotton growing, the extension of irrigation, especially in Upper Egypt, through dam construction and the introduction of thousands of waterwheels, the establishment of factories for the manufacture of military equipment, cotton cloth and sugar and the recruitment of foreign experts, the training of young Egyptians abroad and the opening of new-style schools. State control was far-reaching. Manufacturing was declared a state monopoly, entailing, apart from the establishment of publicly-owned modern industries, state assumption of responsibility for providing the craft industries with their raw materials, imposing upon them standards of quality and marketing their products. A similar state intervention characterized agriculture, including the trade in agricultural products, especially those destined for export. Direction of manpower – chiefly to public works (the age-old corvées) but also to military or even industrial service – was undertaken by the authorities. This policy was arguably one of modernization. It bore, too, many reminiscences of a past going back to the pharaohs. State control of the Egyptian economy had a very long history.

The new régime was not outstandingly successful in achieving its objectives. The attempts at industrialization were not very rewarding and the burden of taxation to pay for development projects and for the maintenance of a powerful army that was used in expensive adventures (including the conquest in 1820 of the eastern Sudan from the decaying Funj sultanate), added to the resentment of peasants already hostile to the cultivation of cash crops

which the government was requiring of them, and to government interference in the use of their surpluses. They resorted to the age-old expedient
of the fellahin in the face of intolerable pressure, namely flight from the land.
The big estates, under the guise of 'uhdas, i.e., once again, tax collecting
rights, revived in order to bring the land back into cultivation. Muḥammad
Ali's own family included great landowners.

The programme of reform was severely curtailed by Muḥammad's
successor, Abbas I (1849–1853), only to be resuscitated on a more ambitious
scale by subsequent rulers, notably Said (1853–1863) and Ismail Pasha
(1863–1879), granted the rank of khedive by Constantinople in 1869. Said
Pasha is best remembered for initiating the construction of the Suez Canal,
but this was only the most ambitious project of a programme of development
and reform. An attempt was made to strengthen the authority of the central
government at the expense of village headmen and district governors.
Village taxation, apportioned and collected by village headmen and paid
in kind, gave way to individual taxation collected by government tax
collectors in money, a change that conformed to the current change from
communal to individual landownership and the wider use of money. Private
ownership was recognized and facilitated by legislation concerning land
transfer and registration. At the same time the influence of contemporary
European ideas of economic freedom led to the removal of internal customs
barriers, the abolition of octroi duties and the annulment of monopoly
privileges. Development projects included the construction of a railway from
Cairo (by then linked to Alexandria) to Suez and of a graving dock at the
latter.

The Suez Canal was begun very much under French influence and in the
face of Turkish protests. The concession for its construction was won by
Ferdinand de Lesseps, the former French consul in Egypt and Said's tutor.
The Compagnie Universelle du Canal Maritime de Suez was constituted in
1858. It was the recipient of generous privileges, including a rent-free ninety-
nine-year lease on the necessary land and the provision of the labour required.
The government was to receive 15 per cent. of the net profit earned by the
company, together with interest on its shares. More than half the shares were
taken up in France, which meant that the company was in effect French-run.
The bulk of the remaining shares went to the viceroy, who was induced by
de Lesseps to subscribe for more than he had at first intended and who had to
borrow heavily from French bankers to do so. Critics of European imperialism have argued that most of the profits and advantages of the canal
went to the French investors and the British government, which in 1875
purchased the viceroy's shares. There can be little doubt that in the long term
the French shareholders did well, though not outrageously well, out of their
investment, drawing interest even during the first years of the company's

existence, when there was substantial expenditure and little return, though they incurred considerable risk in subscribing to an enterprise for which it was difficult to attract sufficient private capital. The British government's investment was also remunerative, and with little risk because the chief obstacles to success had been overcome by 1875. The Egyptian government gained little directly from its investment, chiefly because it had had to borrow freely at high interest rates in order to invest. Egypt, however, gained considerable imponderable benefits. It is difficult to see how the canal could have been built at all on any other terms given the shortage of capital available for such investment in Egypt at the time.

The debts that Said left to his successor in 1863 were recklessly swollen by Ismail's extravagance. His projects included the extension of irrigation and a huge railway building programme. By 1875 a hundred thousand Europeans were in his employment. Added to this was a forward policy abroad, including an unsuccessful expedition against Ethiopia; nor was the administration of Egypt and the Sudan noted for its purity and integrity. By 1876, despite crippling taxation and the British government's purchase of the canal shares (for a mere £4 000 000), revenue was insufficient to meet the interest charges on the public debt, which stood at £98 000 000. The European powers intervened and a Caisse de la Dette Publique, with control of certain taxes and other sources of revenue, was imposed upon the Egyptian government. Clearly this debt commission represented a considerable derogation from the sovereignty of the country, but in fact foreign intrusion went further. A Dual Control by the principal creditors, France and Britain, offered advice that the khedive was in no position to disregard. Then in 1882, following a nationalist rising, Britain sent in an army of occupation and thenceforth Egypt was virtually ruled by a British High Commissioner, subject only to the influence that could be exercised by other European states through the Caisse. After 1890 the relative importance of the sources of revenue controlled by the Caisse diminished and the power of that body to obstruct the British administration disappeared in 1904, when France, who had resented the British occupation in the first place, left Britain in peace in Egypt in exchange for British support for French ambitions in Morocco. In the meantime, in 1885, the Sudanese Muslims, in revolt against heavy taxation, corruption and the campaign that the British General Gordon waged against the slave trade, threw off the Egyptian yoke and was governed by a popular and incorruptible theocracy until 1898, when Britain and Egypt established the Anglo-Egyptian condominium.

British rule in Egypt was not the first European intervention in Mediterranean Africa. There was a similar course of events in Tunisia. Here in 1859 a modernizing government gave a French company the concession to build a railway from Tunis to Goletta. Subsequently Muḥammad es Sadeh got into debt and, as in Egypt, the outcome was the establishment of an international commission, composed of Britain, Italy and France, to ensure that Tunisia's financial obligations were fulfilled.

In Morocco a policy of modernization, the first hesitant steps of which, in the form of administrative reforms and the encouragement of agriculture and industry, were taken by Muhammad b. 'Abd al-Rahmān, who ruled from 1859 to 1873, was prosecuted with greater vigour by his successor Mawlāy al-Hasan (1873–1894), who sought principally to bring his army up to date, with modern arms and instructors, drawn on purpose from several European countries to avoid undue influence by any one. He also reformed the currency in 1881 and embarked on a number of administrative reforms, with the aim of increasing the authority of the central government, and some industrial and agricultural projects. Hopes for the success of the considerable expenditure on reform were blighted partly by conservatism, especially religious conservatism, which retained its grip upon education and distrusted innovations that came from Europe, and partly by the extent of foreign intervention that had already taken place. The heavy burden of taxation, inflation and the ubiquity of corruption were not calculated to win the sultan popular support. Reformist ideas penetrated Morocco from the Near East, but those susceptible to such ideas were compromised by their connections with both the existing order and European commercial interests. The reign of Mawlāy 'Abd al-'Azīz (1894–1908), the son of Mawlāy al-Hasan, was the analogue of Ismail's in Egypt. Actuated though he was by a sincere desire for modernization, his improvidence and impetuousness increased his dependence upon France, one of the several European powers with interests in Morocco, and aroused the active hostility of his own people. Postponed by the international conference of Algeciras in 1906, which met at the demand of Germany, a French protectorate was imposed in 1912, though this marked only the beginning of effective French rule.

The modernization of Egypt and North Africa and their integration into the world economy, tentatively begun by native rulers, were continued by foreign masters. Egypt became linked to the industrialized world through its export of raw cotton. There cotton growing by smallholders was reluctantly undertaken under government pressure. Production grew very rapidly over the last ten or fifteen years of the 19th century, and rather more slowly, though still substantially, during the years immediately preceding the First World War. The diminishing rate of growth was probably due to decreasing water supply at the margin. The area devoted to cotton cultivation continued to expand, but yields declined. The price of cotton rose steeply from 1895 to 1913, furnishing the incentive for a shift to its cultivation. The value of exports of cotton and cotton seed grew very quickly. Cultivation was also taken up with much success by smallholders in the Anglo-Egyptian

Sudan after the First World War. By contrast, in French North Africa the exports came from European enterprise, from the mining of iron and phosphates and the production of wine. In Algeria there was serious overproduction of wine, leading to the elimination of small proprietors and the concentration of vineyard ownership in the hands of big producers.

EGYPT

VALUE OF EXPORTS IN EGYPTIAN POUNDS

Five Year Averages

		Cotton	Cottonseed	Cereals	Other	Total
1885–9	£E	7 548 000	1 352 000	964 000	1 455 000	11 319 000
1890–4		8 561 000	1 629 000	1 524 000	1 366 000	13 080 000
1895–9		9 683 000	1 421 000	947 000	1 460 000	13 511 000
1900–4		14 228 000	1 766 000	794 000	1 807 000	18 595 000
1905–		19 700 000	2 271 000	760 000	1 799 000	24 530 000
1910–14		23 788 000	2 299 000	1 745 000	2 205 000	30 037 000

Source: Russell Stone 'Egypt', (Chapter 8 of W. Arthur Lewis, ed., *Tropical Development 1880–1913, Studies in Economic Progress* (London, 1970), p. 209)

ii) *West Africa*

The abolition of the British slave trade, it has been said, brought about radical, even revolutionary, economic change, with social and political repercussions. Yet the process of adjustment to new external demands was facilitated by the long-established trade in 'legitimate commodities' and the continuation of slave exports. Slaves were still a major item of export at several points along the West Coast until the 1860s, especially at Whydah and Lagos, and from the Portuguese territories. The volume of slave exports did not diminish very sharply as a result of British withdrawal from the trade, which in fact recovered perceptibly in the 1820s, perhaps because of the need to satisfy demand pent up during the war period. The sugar planters of Cuba, then the coffee planters of Brazil, clamoured for more slaves and it was not until the 1850s that there was a marked decline, when Brazil ceased to import. More and more nations, often under diplomatic pressure from Britain, forbade their citizens to take part in slaving and abolished slavery in their territories. Slave-trading conditions became more and more hazardous and inconvenient, what with the unremitting pressure of the British anti-slavery squadron which operated from bases on the West Coast, the closing of slave markets and the increasing difficulty of getting trade goods.

Its African beneficiaries, not unnaturally, did not take kindly to the abolition of the slave trade. This was appreciated by the English merchants trading in West Africa.

> Can the wildest theorist expect that a mere act of the British legislature should in a moment inspire . . . natives of the vast continent of Africa and persuade them, nay more, make them practically believe and feel that it is for their interest to contribute to and even acquiesce in, the destruction of a trade . . . by which alone they have been hitherto accustomed to acquire wealth and purchase all the foreign luxuries and conveniences of life?[1]

As a British trader collecting and exporting wild rubber as late as the 1880s observed, slave trading had decided advantages for African middlemen.

> I think it will be readily understood that the natives found business of this nature more attractive from every point of view than that of spending long periods in the forest on the production of rubber, and one will not fail to realise the difficulty we were faced with in establishing a legitimate export trade in this produce.
> It was found utterly impossible to get them to take any interest in it without first giving them credit and afterwards harassing them in every possible way for its settlement.[2]

The notion that West Africa could be a source of raw cotton was one that arose early in Europe and persisted late. In 1808, the Committee of the African Institution, a private body, reported the purchase of Georgian and Brazilian cotton for distribution in Sierra Leone. Cotton, it continued,

> is an article the growth of which in Africa will occasion less of competition with our own Colonies than almost any other article of tropical produce which could be named: and that it is important to be preparing sources from which a supply of cotton may be drawn, should circumstances arise to interrupt our commercial relations with America, or with the other places which now furnish it. But independently of these considerations it may be presumed, that in proportion as the natives of Africa supply us with the raw material, they will be capable of paying for a larger quantity of the manufactured article .[3]

In the 1820s the French set up an experimental farm in Senegal that undertook, though with little success, the growing of cotton, as well as indigo, and they made further attempts to promote its cultivation there during the cotton famine that resulted from the American Civil War. In 1841 the British government, under pressure from the humanitarians, founded a model farm at Lokoja, at the confluence of the Niger and Benue rivers. Captain L. D. Trotter, head of the British Commission charged with carrying out the expedition, explained its purpose to a local ruler.

Her Majesty the Queen of Great Britain had sent him and the three other gentle-men composing the Commission, to endeavour to enter into treaties with African Chiefs for the abolition of the trade in human beings, which Her Majesty and all the British nation held to be an injustice to their fellow-creatures, and repugnant to the laws of God; that the vessels which he saw were not trading ships, but be-longing to our Queen, and were sent, at great expense, expressly to convey the Commissioners appointed by Her Majesty, for the purpose of carrying out Her benevolent intentions, for the benefit of Africa. Captain Trotter therefore re-quested the King to give a patient hearing to what the Commissioners had to say to him on the subject.

The Commissioners then explained that the principal object in inviting him to a conference was, to point out the injurious effects to himself and to his people of the practice of selling their slaves, thus depriving themselves of their services for ever, for a trifling sum; whereas, if these slaves were kept at home, and em-ployed in the cultivation of the land, in collecting palm-oil, or other productions of the country for commerce, they would prove a permanent source of re-venue . . .[4]

The attitude of the British government, which had been lukewarm over the Lokoja project, became more decisive when Palmerston became Foreign Secretary in 1846. It was he who appointed a consul for the coasts of Benin and Biafra in 1849 and instructed him in 1850 to visit Dahomey and Abeo-kuta, the chief city of the Egba people, with a view to fostering legitimate commerce and discouraging the slave trade. In this policy the efforts of the British government were aided by commercial interests in the guise of the Manchester Cotton Supply Association, a non-profit making, but obviously not wholly altruistic, society for the promotion of cotton cultivation, and by the Church Missionary Society and other mission bodies. Seed and gins were given to West Africans who were interested in, or whom it was hoped to interest in, cotton growing. In 1857 the British consul at Lagos wrote to the Foreign Secretary, Lord Clarendon,

The Reverend Samuel Crowther, the highly intelligent native Clergyman at-tached to the Church Missionary Society's Establishment at this station, through whose instrumentality the Chiefs and others at Abeokuta have extended their cultivation of the cotton plant as a commercial export . . . is of the opinion that in the present state it would not be advisable to distribute the seeds of a foreign and more valuable description of Cotton to the Chiefs and others at Abeokuta: the native cotton now grown by them is of that description of which the greatest quantity is used, and is known at Manchester, 'good ordinary', and fetches to the cultivators a remunerating price; but, Mr. Crowther is of the opinion that seed of a higher priced description of Cotton would be advantageously placed in the hands of the Native Converts to Christianity many of whom are planters, be-cause they would readily submit to any Instructions and directions as to the mode and manner of cultivating the new seed . . .

The great drawback hitherto experienced has been the want of good machines for separating the Cotton from the seed. Those hitherto used are the description called the Saw Gin, but as they deteriorate the Cotton a halfpenny and more the lb., in consequence of the tearing of the fibre, another description called the roller Gin was sent out, but this machine being unadapted for the cotton cultivated in this part of Africa, not cleaning five lbs of Cotton per day when the Saw Gin cleaned upwards of 30 lbs., the natives refused them even as a gift; another great drawback also has been the want of a press.[5]

Clearly, British help was somewhat fumbling and uninformed, and cotton never caught on except in a modest way in the Lagos area, where exports were worth £60 000 annually in the aftermath of the American Civil War. As American production was restored and prices fell, production declined. West Africans turned much more spontaneously to the production of palm oil. According to a report compiled in 1841 by Dr Robert Madden, who investigated slavery and slaving on the Gold Coast on behalf of the British government, the oil trade was carried on chiefly at the Bonny River in the Niger delta, though it was beginning to have some importance on the Gold Coast.

The average import of palm oil into Liverpool for some years past has been about 12 000 tons a year, value about £400 000 sterling. Three-fourths of this quantity are exported from the Bonny, and the other outlets of the Niger, and gives employment to 12 000 or 15 000 tons of shipping in the year . . . Captain Brown of the 'Mary', who has made 11 voyages to the coast . . . states that the oil is brought down from the interior, a distance of about 150 miles, and sold to the Bonny traders in small quantities. It is purchased from them by the English trader . . .

It is a very singular circumstance, and one deserving of serious consideration, that nearly the whole of this trade has sprung up within the last 30 years, in a place where we have no government agents, ports or settlement. That without any protection or a single British merchant or mercantile agent residing at the place where this great trade is carried on, namely, the River Bonny, that trade has originated, grown up, and steadily augmented up to the year 1834 . . .

If we compare the trade of the Bonny with that of any one of our settlements on the coast of Africa, where we have large and costly establishments, we find the trade of the latter, with all the protection afforded them, fall far short of that of the Bonny, that has no aid or support of any kind from Government . . .[6]

The production of and commerce in palm oil were stimulated by demand from Europe, where it was required for the expanding manufacture of soap, lubricants and candles. Production encountered relatively few technical problems. The oil palm grew wild and its fruit already featured in the common diet. It was merely a question of harvesting wild fruit or the simple transition from collecting it to deliberate planting and tending of trees in plantations. There was no shortage of land and, in so far as it displaced slaving, oil production could call upon adequate labour. Africans who would hitherto have been shipped to the Americas remained behind, either as slaves or freemen, to harvest palm fruit on behalf of their masters or themselves.

Naturally, there were difficulties. Warfare, a legacy to some extent of the slave trade, was endemic; transport costs were prohibitive for producers at any distance from coast or river; and traders were vexed by the tendency of the quality of the product to vary. In the second half of the 19th century the demand for palm-oil decreased owing to the competition of mineral and other vegetable oils, but this was compensated for by an increased use of palm-kernels, which, though having no local value, unlike the fruit, could yield oil for margarine, leaving a residue for cattle feed. Before the First World War Africa, especially Nigeria, was furnishing virtually the whole of the world's supply of palm-oil.

What the oil-palm was to Nigeria, the groundnut was to Senegambia. The European demand sprang initially from its use in France for making soap and cooking oil, and subsequently for its use in the production of margarine. The Gambia region began exporting in 1834, the Senegal region in 1840. With the elimination of warfare and the construction of railways from the 1880s, cultivation spread into the interior. Railway construction also permitted the introduction of cultivation into northern Nigeria, to some extent through the influence of Hausa traders anxious to supplement their traditional trading goods, which in some instances were decreasing in significance as tastes changed.

The introduction and spread of cocoa exemplified much more strikingly the enterprise shown by Africans in adapting to world trade. It was not a familiar crop and it was not a food crop. It required, moreover, considerable resolution and foresight to invest money and labour in a project that gave a reward only after several years of waiting while the trees matured. It was first grown in Africa as a plantation crop on the islands of Fernando Po and São Thomé. In the 1860s the Basel Missionary Society experimented at Akropong on the Gold Coast in cocoa cultivation and also in coffee cultivation, an earlier and evidently more promising crop. Coffee growing was taken up by Africans partly through this missionary influence, partly on the initiative of African merchants, but it was cocoa that outstripped coffee and owed its spread largely to African enterprise. Cultivation on a considerable scale seems to have originated in the Akwapim Ridge area north of Accra at a time of falling palm-oil prices. In the 1890s the Akwapim farmers migrated thence in search of more space and purchased forest land from the Akim people. On the Ivory Coast, too, before 1914, immigrants from the savanna, some of them Dyula traders with capital to invest, went in for cocoa on their own or rented land.

Exports of Palm Oil From Principal Producing Countries in Metric Tons and as Percentages of Total World Palm Oil Exports

	Nigeria	Ex-Fr. West Africa	Congo (Zaire)	Other
1909–13	81 900 (67,7%)	19 200 (15,9%)	2 100 (1,7%)	17 800 (14,7%)
1924–28	128 100 (59,5%)	24 100 (11,2%)	19 200 (8,9%)	17 300 (8,1%)
1934–38	137 000 (29,7%)	21 200 (4,6%)	60 300 (13,1%)	25 000 (5,4%)
1962	120 600 (22,3%)	10 400 (1,9%)	151 100 (27,9%)	21 200 (3,9%)

Exports of Palm Oil From the Whole of Africa in Metric Tons and as Percentage of Total World Palm Oil Exports

1909–13	121 000	100 %
1924–28	188 700	87,7%
1934–38	243 500	52,8%
1962	303 300	56,1%

Source: R. J. Harrison Church, *West Africa, A Study of the Environment and of Man's Use of it*, (London, 5th edn. 1966) p. 108

Exports of Groundnuts in Metric Tons

	1837	1851	1853	1870	1881	1885	1894
Gambia	671	12 000	...	...	...	...	...
Senegal	...	...	3 000	9 000	34 000	45 000	65 000

Source: J. S. Hogendorn, 'Economic initiative and African cash farming, pre-colonial origins and early colonial developments' (Chapter 8, P. Duignan and L. H. Gann, eds., *Colonialism in Africa 1870–1960*, Volume 4, Cambridge, 1975), p. 292

Exports of Cocoa Beans in Metric Tons

	1898	1908	1918	1928	1938	1962
Ghana	188	12 946	67 404	223 339	261 557	427 970
Nigeria	35	1 388	10 383	49 950	97 542	197 770
Ivory Coast	–	3	420	14 515	52 719	101 010
Togo	–	84	1 576	6 317	7 628	11 070
São Thomé & Principe	9 945	28 560	17 332	14 638	12 729	10 610
Fernando Po and Rio Muni	800	2 267	4 220	8 664	12 212	29 360
Cameroon and the rest of Africa	311	3 181	3 699	8 478	24 965	76 270
Africa	11 279	48 429	105 034	325 901	469 352	854 060
Central & S. America and West Indies	72 070	138 600	162 792	181 264	229 450	160 380
Asia & Pacific	3 451	5 468	6 374	7 234	8 094	19 310
Grand Total	86 800	192 497	274 200	514 399	706 896	1 043 000

Percentages of Total Cocoa Exports

	1898	1908	1918	1928	1938	1962
Ghana	0,2	6,7	24,6	43,5	37,0	41,0
Nigeria	0,0	0,7	3,8	9,7	13,8	19,0
Ivory Coast	–	0,0	0,2	2,8	7,5	9,7
Togo	–	0,0	0,6	1,2	1,0	1,1
São Thomé & Principe	11,5	14,8	6,3	2,9	1,8	1,0
Fernando Po and Rio Muni	0,9	1,2	1,6	1,7	1,7	2,8
Cameroon and the rest of Africa	0,4	1,7	1,2	1,4	3,6	7,3
Africa	13,0	25,1	38,3	63,2	66,4	81,9
Central and S. America and West Indies	83,2	72,1	59,4	35,4	32,5	15,4
Asia and Pacific	3,8	2,8	2,3	1,4	1,1	1,8
Grand Total	100	100	100	100	100	100

Source: R. J. Harrison Church, *West Africa, A Study of the Environment and of Man's Use of it*, (London, 5th edn., 1966), p. 111

Africans could participate in the world economy not only by the cultivation of cash crops, but also by collecting and hunting. This was by no
means new, and to some extent there was no rigid distinction between cultivation and collection, for instance in oil-palm harvesting. A product newly
in demand, whose collection was encouraged and often imposed by European
merchants, was wild rubber. It was never much of a success as a means of
livelihood for small men, though there were periods when it was carried on
spontaneously and with some persistence. On the Gold Coast, when palm-
oil prices fell, the tapping and processing of rubber seemed an attractive
alternative, requiring, it appeared, no great skill or expensive equipment.
With an export of 1,5 million kg. valued at £231 282, in 1890, the Gold
Coast became the third biggest rubber producer in the world, under the
stimulation of a steady rise in rubber prices, until the end of the 19th
century. In fact, however, more skill was required than seemed necessary
at first sight, or at least more restraint than was shown. Trees and vines were
recklessly tapped and thus destroyed. After 1900 cocoa cultivation was a
more rewarding activity. Rubber exports were at their greatest in 1899 (at
2,5 million kg.). A similar train of events occurred in Nigeria, where exports
from Lagos Colony and the Protectorate of Southern Nigeria reached a peak
of 3,0 million kg. in 1896 and 1,0 million kg. in 1904 respectively, thereafter
declining for the same reason. One problem was poor quality, though this
disadvantage was offset by the low price of what was offered. Competition
of plantation-produced rubber from Malaya and the East Indies proved too
much for the wild variety. With encouragement from the colonial authorities, some plantations, indigenous as well as expatriate, were established in
Nigeria, but cultivated rubber did not become a major export.

During the long period of adjustment to 'legitimate trade', before the
matter was taken out of African hands by European colonization, attempts
were made to set up European-style governments, not only in the states
specially founded for liberated slaves, but also amongst peoples brought into
close contact with European officials and merchants. James Africanus Horton
described two such ventures.

The spirit of self-government seems to be taking a healthy hold on the inhabitants of the metropolis of Aku – viz., Abeokuta; the savage old native government is now undergoing a very decided change for the better, and it is modelled
according to civilised constitutions, which shows the happy influence which
British civilization has upon minds otherwise disposed to improvement. It is true
that in Abeokuta, liberated slaves (and their descendants) of the country, who had
been instructed and educated at school at Sierra Leone, had returned and made
it their permanent abode and rendered the existing native government great service; but it was not until there was established in Lagos a European Christian
power that we saw the march of improvement rapidly advancing.

At present, there is established at Abeokuta a board of management for the express purpose of directing the native government, of forwarding civilization, and promoting the spread of Christianity, as well as of protecting the property of European merchants and British subjects. The Secretary and Director of this Board, which is styled the Egba United Board of Management, is an educated native of Sierra Leone. The first ordinance enacted related to the imposing of customs duties, which is necessary for the development of the government.

The Fantee Confederation . . . sprung (sic) into existence soon after the exchange of territory between the English and Dutch Governments, and its main object is to advance the interests of the whole of the Fantee nation, and to combine for offence and defence in time of war; the tentative manner in which it has been carried on for nearly two years, and the influence and power which it had over the kings in the interior . . . is a sufficient guarantee that it is the most needful and necessary constitution to advance the civilisation of the interior tribes . . .[7]

The former experiment received little sympathy from the king of Dahomey. The latter was quashed by British officials on the coast. 'This dangerous conspiracy must now be destroyed for good, or the country will become altogether unmanageable.'[8]

A different response to contact with Europe came from the city-states of what is now Nigeria. The chiefs who moved with the times were those who turned their backs on the slave trade, seized the new export opportunities and tried to keep in with the intrusive European. Old Calabar was turning to palm-oil as early as the end of the 18th century, and in 1828 Captain W. F. W. Owen, then Superintendent of the British settlement on Fernando Po, drew attention to the unsuccessful request of the chiefs for instruction in sugar making and for the necessary machinery, a request repeated in 1842. In Bonny, on the Niger Delta, William Dappa Pepple, secured in his position as king by British warships in 1837, saw that his future lay with legitimate trade and propitiating the British. He found, however, his relationship soured by the non-fulfilment of promises of compensation for his undertaking to end the slave trade.

'One white man come,' he said, 'and make book (treaty) and another white man come tomorrow and break it; white man be fool, but treaty is in my head'.[9]

The British engineered his exile to Fernando Po in 1854.

In 1869–70 Ja-Ja, an ex-slave who had become head of one of the 'houses' at Bonny and then quarrelled with the king, founded Opobo. An astute and ruthless business man, he absorbed other houses through loans and foreclosures and, with the assistance of sympathetic European traders, undermined the trade of Bonny from Opobo. He too clashed with the British and in 1887 was exiled to the West Indies, having retaliated against the restrictive practices of the locally based British merchants by shipping

produce directly to England. Action against Ja-Ja was taken by Harry
Johnston, then a young man, and the sentence imposed was subsequently
revoked, though Ja-Ja died on his way home.

Such attempts at modernization in West Africa, however, were both restricted in scope and comparatively rare. The response of Asante and Dahomey was at first stubborn adhesion to the slave trade and military resistance but even they eventually adjusted to changed circumstances. Dahomey combined the production of palm-oil with slaving and King Ghezo
sent two of his sons to school in Marseilles. Ghezo and Gulele, who succeeded
him in 1858, kept up friendly relations with the French, though the only
value he attached to the French connection was as a means of countering
British encroachment. In Asante European-educated officials entered the
government service, notably John Owusu Ansa and his sons, who from the
middle of the century were chiefly employed in representing the state in
negotiations with Europeans. These modernizers favoured the construction
of railways and the development of the country's agricultural and mineral
resources by Europeans. In 1895 they granted a concession to a British subject, George Reckless, and his associates.

> for the purpose of giving mineral rights and other rights to the said Company,
> for the purposes also of railway construction and other public works, to employ
> skilled and other labour, to build manufactories, lay out townships, construct
> waterworks, and waterways, to appoint and maintain a resident agent or agents;
> to organise a constabulary, to erect a mint and issue coinage, establish factories
> for trading and other purposes, to establish banks, to grant licences for trading,
> mining, and other purposes, to impose such duties as may be deemed expedient
> on goods imported into the country, to lay out and cultivate plantations for all
> kinds of vegetable and other products, to establish schools for elementary, tech-
> nical, and scientific education, to publish newspapers, to aid in the organisation
> of the military forces of the Kingdom, to assist the King in his Government, in-
> cluding the administration of justice and the codification of laws . . .[10]

It came too late to forestall conquest.

African rulers whose revenue had depended upon the slave trade were
often unable or, because of the political repercussions, unwilling to shift to a
trade in goods now deemed more respectable by the former European slave
trading states. The Lunda Empire, for example, was unable to survive the
end of the slave trade, and the new ivory trade fell into other hands. But some
of the entrepreneurs – king and chiefs in Dahomey and some of the Yoruba
states – saw in the production of oil a solution to their problems, and they
used slave labour to harvest palm trees and cultivate groundnuts and transport the produce to market, with the result that slavery became more entrenched than ever in West African society. On the marketing side, too, the
slave-trading wholesalers were frequently able to adjust to their changed

circumstances by dealing in cash crops. Some of the old slave entrepôts, such as Whydah, Lagos, Bonny, Old Calabar and Kaolack, were able to switch from slaves to palm-oil or groundnuts, and their rulers continued to tax visiting ships. Others, for example in southern Dahomey, supplemented their old trade in slaves with a new one in the newer exports. Nonetheless, the position of the West African states was weakened by the change to staple crop export. It was not only they who could engage in the production of palm-oil or in its collection or in the distribution of the manufactured goods that were imported in exchange. Since the capital required was negligible, small men could enter both trade and production, and at the same time private merchants who had operated the old slave trade within the limits permitted by the state, or new men, were quick to take advantage of new conditions. There were new forces in society that to some extent challenged established authority.

Yet another response to 19th-century changes in the economic and political climate in West Africa was Muslim revivalism and the jihad. The small states of Senegambia, for example, were in a ferment from the 1820s until the situation was transformed by European imperialism.

iii) *East Africa*
In Ethiopia some attempt at modernization and centralization was made from the second half of the 19th century onwards by a series of innovating emperors – Theodore II, Yohannes IV, Menelik II and Haile Selassie I. Theodore and Yohannes did not enjoy much success; their two successors, rather more. The territorial integrity of the country was constantly threatened by powerful regionalism. Some of the provinces, such as Tigre and Shoa, were virtually independent states during periods of central government weakness. The government was also menaced during the early 19th century by bandit gangs. In fact, Theodore II was himself a bandit leader who became powerful enough to seize the throne in 1855. He was the first of the Ethiopian rulers to try and replace local rulers with a permanent, centralized administration, but he could make no headway against the aristocracy, and he also fell foul of the Church through his confiscations of ecclesiastical land. He welcomed Europeans to his capital, Magdala, in the hope of establishing an armaments industry and he proposed to conclude a treaty of commerce and friendship with Britain to open his country to the outside world. This policy failed, too, however. The emperor incarcerated his European guests and the British sent a punitive expedition to rescue them (1867).

In 1871 a Tigrean ras (prince) fought his way to power as Yohannes IV. He resumed Theodore's policy of modernization, but encountered the same problem of regional particularism. In addition he had to deal with European, especially Italian, encroachment on his territory and attacks from the Muslim

Mahdists of the Sudan. His successor, Menelik, King of Shoa, came to the throne with the support of the Italians. However, when the latter attempted to impose a protectorate on Ethiopia, they were soundly defeated at the Battle of Adowa in 1896. Menelik also greatly extended the boundaries of his country, especially towards the south. He then proceeded to introduce reforms much more effectively than his predecessors, employing European advisers to modernize his army, to introduce a modern transport system, to bring the administration up-to-date and to found a public school system. A concession was granted for the construction of railway and telegraph lines from Djibouti (occupied by the French) to Addis Ababa, the new capital.

In 1913 Menelik died, but even before his death the old forces of disintegration had begun to operate again. In 1916 Ras Tafari became regent and in 1930 emperor with the title Haile Selassie I. The programme of reform was resumed. In 1923 Ethiopia joined the League of Nations and in 1924 Haile Selassie travelled to Europe. More European experts were imported and in 1931 Ethiopia was given a nominal constitution. Reforming attempts, however, were cut short by the Italian invasion and conquest of 1935-1936, and the total achievement of the reforming emperors did not amount to much. Little was done by way of fostering industry. In particular Ethiopia remained heavily dependent upon imported arms to maintain its constantly threatened independence. Nothing was done to solve the land problem and the appropriation of the profits of agriculture by a parasitic ruling class.

To the south of Ethiopia there were few comparable attempts at modernization. Mutesa I sought to strengthen the military and commercial power of Buganda, and in Zanzibar in the 1830s, the sultan, Sayyid Said ibn Saif, sought entry into the international economy through the production of cloves, introduced into both Zanzibar and Pemba from the Mascarenes. Arab immigrants acquired land on both islands, though in Pemba some of the planters were indigenous. Labour was provided by slaves, brought in from the mainland in large numbers. The sultanate became the world's chief source of supply, but attempts to refine sugar of sufficient quality for export, with the assistance of foreign experts, failed. The sultan's administration remained rudimentary, the collection of customs farmed out to an Indian merchant; his authority on the mainland was largely dependent upon his capacity to disrupt the commerce of the subordinate rulers. Under Sultan Barghash ibn Said, Zanzibar acquired a modern army and its capital new facilities, including a piped water supply. Negotiations took place with British and French interests between 1876 and 1880 for the development of the sultan's mainland territories. These, however, proved abortive and, in any case, the sultan was moved less by desire for development than by concern to increase his revenue with the minimum of trouble. By this time he was so much under British influence that he was no longer a free agent.

Elsewhere in East Africa the search for export staples occurred largely after the partition of Africa and was bound up with colonial attempts to increase revenue and, in the case of Kenya and Uganda, to find traffic for the railway that was built into Uganda. Exports of skins and hides helped to fill the commercial vacuum created by the abrupt abolition of the trade in slaves, slave-transported ivory and slave-produced copra and grain, and the construction of the Uganda railway permitted the export of beeswax and ivory, as well as hides and skins, but these exports were not sufficient to rehabilitate the region and, in the event, after colonization, the solution was sought in planting, mixed farming and ranching, carried on to a considerable extent, though not exclusively, by European settlers, especially in Kenya. Pioneering attempts in Kenya to produce wheat, wool, meat and dairy products were not conspicuously successful, and, in the years before the First World War, some settlers turned to coffee planting, encouraged both by the colonial authorities and by the high price it commanded on world markets. Although in 1914 it still represented only 4 per cent. of Kenyan exports, by 1925 it was up to 30 per cent, and the most valuable of all exports. In German East Africa settlers introduced and successfully experimented with sisal growing, a crop requiring considerable investment and a high level of expert knowledge. Exports rose from 641 tons in 1905 to 1059 tons in 1913.

African smallholders were willing to switch from food crops to export crops only if it were possible to do so without endangering the production of the former. There were two possibilities, namely, cultivation of additional land or intercropping, both open to West Africans. In East Africa, however, settlers did not like African commercial agriculture because it competed with them for land and labour, and they were influential enough to sway colonial government policy. The mere presence of European farming, furthermore, discouraged African production for the market. Up to a point wage labour was an easier, certainly more secure, way of acquiring what money was needed for taxation and for satisfying undemanding tastes for consumer goods. Besides, it should be borne in mind that East Africans lacked the advantage enjoyed by West Africans of having cash crops ready at hand, one – palm-oil – that could be collected virtually without special cultivation, another – groundnuts – long familiar as a food crop. From these it was a relatively short step to the cultivation of crops for the market. The banana, so important in the East African diet, did not lend itself to production for export by small farmers. Its market value was low in relation to its weight; it was difficult to store; and it was awkward to transport. The best producing areas lay far from the coast. Then again, there were incentives operating in West Africa, with its long history of commercial contact with Europe and its familiarity with and taste for European goods, that exerted scarcely any influence in East and Central Africa. It has been suggested, too, that the nature of the social system was of significance. The fact that peasant cultivation of cash crops – primarily cotton – did catch on in Uganda much more than in Kenya, may have had something to do with the presence in Buganda of a vigorous ruling class and the predominance in Kenya of the acephalous society.

Africans in Uganda were urged to take up cotton growing by the colonial authorities, the British Cotton Growing Association (founded in 1902), the Uganda Company (founded in 1903) and T.F.V. Buxton of the Anti-Slavery and Aboriginal Protection Society. Egyptian and American cotton was distributed from 1904 and hand-gins were sold cheaply or given away, though these proved to be unsuitable. On the whole, the chiefs were enthusiastic, but were in any event susceptible to government pressure, and in time their enthusiasm was caught by their people. Early production was concentrated in Buganda, but other areas came into increasing production with the improvement of communications. In Tanganyika before the First World War the Germans attempted to dragoon Africans into cotton production, thereby arousing great hostility and resentment.

Official and expatriate encouragement of cotton growing does not seem to have been any less in Kenya than in Uganda, but it enjoyed less success. On the other hand, there can be little doubt that official support in Kenya for the settlers had much to do with the absence of peasant production of coffee and maize. The Kavirondo farmers of the Lake Victoria basin, who were unenthusiastic about cotton, went in for maize for the internal market, and they grew simsim, an important crop before the First World War. But the export of simsim waned and maize for the market became primarily a settler crop. Robusta coffee cultivation, which required less skill than the growing of arabica, was taken up in the 1920s with much success by African farmers in Uganda and Tanganyika with the support of the colonial authorities.

UGANDA: COTTON EXPORTS BY VOLUME AND VALUE

1904–05	£256	(0,39% of all exports)	54 bales (of 177 kg)
1907–08	£51 800	(35%)	3 973
1910–11	£168 000	(55%)	13 378
1914–15	£369 300	(71%)	27 568 (1913–14)

Source: W. Arthur Lewis (ed.), *Tropical Development 1880–1913, Studies in Economic Progress* (London, 1910), p. 191

Exports of Cloves from Zanzibar, 1852–1868

Year	Volume (Frasilas)	Amount (M.T. Dollars)	Price ($/fra)
1839–40	9 000		
1852–53	128 000		
1853–54	140 000		
1856	142 857		2–3
1859	138 860	250 000	=1,8
	200 000	382 000	=1,9
1859–60		210 000	
1860*	200 000		
1861–62		175 000	
		201 840	
1862*	200 000	400 000	=2,0
1862–63		275 000	
		343 000	
		232 087	
1863–64	137 220	155 000	=1,5
		179 498	
		214 000	
		206 498	
1864–65		469 400	
		227 000	
		335 000	
1865*	100–342 000		
1865–66		304 000	
1866–67		237 000	
1867–68		273 000	
		300 000	
		125 644	
pre-1872*			1—1,5

*Estimate of average at this time   =Calculated from Volume—Amount data
M.T. Dollars = Maria Theresa Dollars   Frasila = approx. 16 kg.

Source: Frederick Cooper, *Plantation Slavery on the East Coast of Africa* (New Haven and London, 1977), p. 61

East Africa Protectorate Coffee Exports

Year	Tons	£ Value
1907–08	–	69
1908–09	–	235
1909	8,5	236
1910	31,5	1 086
1911	61,0	2 995
1912	104,5	5 765
1913	151,5	11 071
1914	275,0	18 502
1920	5 329,0	392 507
1925	7 363,0	823 901
1930	15 504,0	1 426 869

Source: R. D. Wolff, *The Economics of Colonialism: Britain and Kenya, 1870–1930* (New Haven and London, 1974), p. 79

iv) *South Africa*

Adjustment to the changing conditions of the world economy was essayed by both white settlers and indigenous blacks. Among Africans were those who trusted in the uplifting power of European education – for example Kgama III (c. 1837–1923), chief of the Ngwato in what is now Botswana – while others were quick to seize the economic opportunities that were offered. Fugitives known as the Fengu (Fingoes), rendered homeless by the Difaqane, who began entering the Cape Colony early in the 19th century and were given land by the British authorities in the wake of the frontier wars that broke out in 1834, 1846 and 1850, 'by a combination of regular work, parsimony, and acquiring fresh concessions through making themselves agreeable to their protectors, soon became the chief economic power among the Bantu tribes'.[11] Accustomed to cattle-raising, they went in for the production of wool, too, and when the British withdrew from the Transkei in 1864 and ceded land there to the Fengu, among others, this enterprising people introduced into the territory not only sheep rearing, but also methods and crops borrowed from the Europeans. It is estimated that African-produced cattle and cattle products, tobacco, grain and, above all, wool marketed in the Eastern Province in 1875, were worth three-quarters of a million pounds sterling.

The earliest settler export staple was wine. Although its production went back to the 17th century, it was not an export of much consequence before the beginning of the 19th century. The British authorities took measures to improve quality and, after 1813, admitted Cape wine to the British market at a preferential tariff. The industry declined after the reduction and then abolition of imperial preference, and it was the expansion of the internal market, in the latter part of the 19th century, that arrested the decline, though even then the industry was beset with difficulties – phylloxora in the 1880s and crises of overproduction. Wool replaced wine and grain as the South African staple.

VALUE OF WINE AND WOOL EXPORTS FROM THE CAPE (IN £)

Year	Wine	Wool
1826	98 000	545
1842	43 000	72 000
1861	34 000	1 460 000

Source: N. C. Pollock and S. Agnew, *Historical Geography of South Africa* (London, 1963), p. 103

The wool industry was a 19th-century development. Although the Dutch settlers had kept hairy sheep, it was the British who, with some government encouragement, first went in for raising merino sheep in the semi-arid regions of the Eastern Cape and the Karoo. Other staples of some importance were mohair and ostrich feathers in the Cape. The production of mohair began with the importation of Angora goats from Asia Minor from the late 1830s. Although there were no exports before 1857, within thirty years South Africa surpassed Turkey as the world's chief source. The demand for this fibre was very dependent upon fashion, and it was this, too, but even more so, that dictated the price of ostrich feathers. In the earlier history of the Cape Colony wild ostriches were hunted for their feathers, but the availability of feathers increased markedly after the introduction of ostrich farming in the 1860s. A steep rise in feather prices in the 1870s, reaching a peak in 1880, encouraged a rapid expansion of the industry that could not be sustained, though another boom, supported by greatly improved farming and breeding methods, followed in the more immediate pre-war years.

VALUE OF WOOL, MOHAIR AND OSTRICH FEATHER EXPORTS (IN £)

Year	Wool	Mohair	Ostrich Feathers
1842	72 000		
1849	199 432		
1857		10	
1862	1 315 000		
1865			66 000
1869	1 708 072		
1875			305 000
1877		116 000	
1882	2 544 000		1 094 000
1891			468 000
1897		677 000	
1902	2 177 000		
1904			1 059 000
1907		966 000	
1912		967 000	
1913	5 719 000		2 954 000

Source: M. H. de Kock, *Selected Subjects in the Economic History of South Africa* (Cape Town and Johannesburg, 1924), p. 223, 227, 236; G. C. W. Schumann, *Structural Changes and Business Cycles in South Africa* (London, 1938), p. 75

Sugar planting in Natal likewise felt the effects of fluctuations in demand, though these were less capricious than those experienced by mohair and ostrich farming, more the result of the competition of other sources of supply, for example German sugar beet after the turn of the century. The industry began in the middle of the century and its development was assisted by the

introduction of steam-powered mills and indentured Indian labour. Sugar
was not an export staple before the First World War, however, owing its
growth to the expansion of the internal market due to the increase of population and the construction of the railways.

    The 1850s were prosperous years in South Africa, but for most of the 1860s
the economy was depressed. A boom in the early 1850s, of a speculative
nature and associated with the first exploitation of the Namaqualand copper
mines, burst without markedly adverse effects upon an economy chiefly
based upon agriculture. The depression of the 1860s, from 1862 and more
particularly from 1865, was caused partly by severe drought in the early
1860s, partly by a financial crisis at the end of a period of very easy credit, and
partly by a depression in Britain, South Africa's chief customer, an indication of the country's integration into the world economy. It was the discovery and exploitation of diamonds and gold that rescued South Africa from
depression and completed, almost violently, her integration into the modern
world. Exports of diamonds and gold very rapidly surpassed in value those of
agricultural and pastoral commodities.

PRINCIPAL EXPORTS OF THE CAPE COLONY (IN £)

Year	Wool	Diamonds	Gold	Hides and Skins	Mohair and Ostrich Feathers
1872	3 275 000	1 618 000	745	378 000	217 000
1878	1 889 000	2 159 000	35 000	295 000	700 000
1892	2 029 000	3 907 000	4 096 000	480 000	891 000
1903	1 818 000	5 473 000	11 980 000	470 000	1 598 000
1909	2 855 000	6 370 000	32 160 000	861 000	2 900 000

Source: M. H. de Kock, op. cit., p. 325. (See previous page.)

ANNUAL OUTPUT OF TRANSVAAL GOLD MINES

Year	Ounces	Value (£)
1887	23 149	81 022
1888	207 660	726 821
1889	369 557	1 300 509
1890	494 817	1 735 491
1891	729 238	2 556 328
1892	1 208 928	4 290 733
1893	1 476 502	5 180 090
1894	2 023 198	6 959 622

Source: D. Hobart Houghton and Jenifer Dagut, *Source Material on the South African Economy*, Volume 1 (Cape Town, 1972), p. 274

With the opening of gold and diamond mining, there was an influx of capital into the country and new opportunities for domestic capital formation were offered. Capital imports were accompanied by an unprecedented influx of European immigrants, many of whom brought new skills. The mining towns – Kimberley and Johannesburg – expanded rapidly, and the ports which served them – Cape Town, East London, Port Elizabeth and Durban, as well as Lourenzo Marques in Mozambique – were also beneficiaries of the quickened economic activity. Kimberley and Johannesburg provided both a motive and an objective for railway construction. The need for mining inputs had other repercussions. Coal mining was developed in the Transvaal and Natal, and there was a certain demand for manufactured inputs, such as dynamite. The new urban concentrations of population set up a demand for foodstuffs. To some degree this demand was met by black smallholders, but that did not continue long. The rôle for which the dominant white population cast Africans was that of an unskilled labour force, not a peasant farming community. Subjected to various pressures to enter the labour market, confined to a relatively exiguous portion of the country and discriminated against in the provision of transport facilities, blacks were unable to compete with white commercial farming.

In the meantime, before they found themselves in possession of a gold mining industry that attracted the covetous eyes of the British government, the Boers who still maintained a precarious independence north of the Vaal River tried industrializing. In 1881, the year of the British withdrawal after the occupation of 1877, the South African Republic imposed high duties on dynamite, liquor, leather, cement, iron, bricks, sugar, woollen yarn, oil, soap, candles and paper for the benefit of concessionaires who undertook to manufacture them. It was not an enormously successful experiment. Concessions tended to fall into the hands of speculators, less interested in promoting manufacture than in selling their privileges at a profit. Such manufacture as took place made extensive use of partially manufactured imports. Amidst mounting criticism, the government abandoned the concession system in 1896 and instead relied entirely upon tariff protection. The new arrangements were soon overtaken by events, in the form of war with Britain.

v) *The consequences of integration*
There was a very considerable expansion of trade between Europe and Africa in the 19th century, particularly, in the case of West Africa, in the second quarter of the 19th century. However, quite startling increases do not mean a great deal when the base is so low. Although British imports of palm-oil multiplied twenty-four times between 1820 and 1850, imports in the earlier year amounted to only 887 637 kg. West African trade in 1850 re-

presented only a tiny fraction of the total trade of West Africa's two chief trading partners. Combined French and British trade with West Africa is estimated at an annual value of £3½ to 4 million in the mid-19th century. In 1850 British foreign trade alone amounted to £186 million.

According to the classical economic theory of international trade, production of cash crops for the overseas market could not fail to benefit the producers because it called surplus productive capacity into activity. But given a high degree of dependence upon the export of a relatively small range of primary products for the purchase of manufactured goods from overseas, the economic well-being of Africa became sensitive to the rise and fall of the demand for these primary products and the movement of industrial prices, over neither of which she had any control. The trade cycle, technological change in the industrialized world and the adventitious appearance of competing sources of supply or competing substances, all had their influence upon African prosperity. In the first half of the 19th century West Africa enjoyed increasingly favourable terms of trade. While imports from Europe declined in price because of improved technology in manufacturing and the fall in marine transport costs, the price of palm-oil, the main West African export, with occasional falls, continued to rise until the late 1850s when it fetched about £45 a ton. Given the increase in total exports as well, the first half of the 19th century was a period of prosperity for West Africa. The boom ended in 1861 and the palm-oil price fell to about £32 a ton. The price recovered in 1866–1867, but the secular trend was downwards. In the years between 1886 and 1890 it stood at £20 a ton and the price of the 1850s was not reached again until 1906. A similar pattern was seen in the price levels of palm kernels and groundnuts as West Africa encountered competition from American mineral oil, Australian tallow and Indian groundnuts, the latter two enjoying the new advantage of a shortened route to Europe after the opening of the Suez Canal. The terms of trade moved against West Africa despite a fall in import prices, the result of lower shipping rates, continuing improvements in industrial techniques, greater competition among traders and, above all, the general fall in prices in the period of the so-called great depression of 1873–1896. The great increase in the volume of West African exports characteristic of the first half of the 19th century was not maintained after the late 1870s and in some instances there was even contraction. The second half of the 19th century was not a period of conspicuous prosperity. Recovery set in after 1900, and until the outbreak of the First World War the terms of trade again moved in West Africa's favour.

In super-Saharan Africa Egypt became highly dependent upon the export of cotton and cotton seed from the closing decade of the 19th century. Since cotton prices began to rise sharply from 1895 and continued to rise until the

First World War, producers did well, despite a deceleration in the growth of output that was due chiefly to a fall in average yields.

Monoculture and continuous cropping brought on soil erosion, and there was increasing neglect of the production of foodstuffs. In Egypt dependence upon imported foodstuffs came as early as the late 19th century. In the years between 1885 and 1889 Egypt had on average a nett export of cereals per annum worth £E194000; and in the years 1905–1909 an average nett import per annum of £E2 501 000. But there was naturally a tendency for fluctuations to occur. Mere pressure of population was probably a more significant factor in food importation than was an excessive shift to cash cropping. Smallholders gave priority to the production of food and animal feed, regarding cotton as a source of extra cash income for the payment of taxes or rent and the purchase of things that had to be bought. Cotton was only one crop of a two- or three-year cycle of some four or five crops. Even on the larger estates it was not permitted to oust other crops.

As Africa's dependence upon imported foodstuffs grew, an increasing proportion of the total output of cash crops came from the bigger producers. In Egypt before the First World War some seventy per cent of all cotton produced was grown on large and medium-sized estates. There can be little doubt that the superior income derived by these estates from cash crop sales was one factor in the ability of the large and medium landowners to maintain to a considerable extent, the integrity of their estates or, perhaps, in the building up of new estates through the absorption of fragments. Although their share of the total cultivated area increased constantly from the end of the 19th century, smallholders on average possessed plots that grew smaller and smaller. On the large estates cotton was sometimes cultivated with hired labour, but the leasing of small plots on the basis of a fixed rent in cash or kind or some form of sharecropping was a very widespread practice. Seasonal work was common. The large number of landless, or owners with plots too small to provide a livelihood, worked for the big owners and sometimes for the small at the busiest times of the year. Wages tended to fluctuate markedly according to market prices and harvests, but were generally at a low level, while rents tended to be high. Working capital was a problem for the small men. Those leasing land from big landlords were supplied with seed and fertilisers, but many had recourse to money-lenders and chronic rural indebtedness became a serious social problem.

By the 1950s, in Nigeria, about ten per cent of cocoa farmers held 41 per cent of all land under cocoa. A similar situation evolved on the Gold Coast before the Second World War and on the Ivory Coast after it. There is evidence, too, to support the view of increasing economic stratification among producers of palm-oil and kernels and groundnuts in West Africa. Wealthier producers frequently advanced money to neighbours and relations. It was not that their holdings were very large (three hectares making a cocoa farmer in Nigeria a substantial producer) and these were normally fragmented; nor was there a considerable rural proletariat, since most of those who worked for others either worked for kinsmen or were supplementing the income derived from their own land. Nonetheless, there was growing individualism of landholding and its virtual conversion to freehold because of the increasing demand for land and, where there were tree crops, a need for stable occupancy. Land for cocoa production was bought in the Gold Coast by families who clubbed together and then divided it up amongst themselves.

A growing stream of migrant labourers found seasonal employment in West Africa with cocoa and groundnut farmers who, though making use primarily of family labour, were compelled to find extra hands. Migration was a very long-established practice. The coastal trading posts had always been attractive places of settlement for a heterogeneous population. Although a good deal of movement was permanent, much was temporary. Seasonal migration was noted by a British Colonial Office report as early as 1848.

> The Sera-Wollies and Telli-Bunkas . . . frequently coming from distances of not less than 500 or 600 miles in the interior, and on paying a small custom to the chief of the country in which they settle, are permitted to cultivate the ground under his protection for one or more years, according to their agreement, and to sell the produce to the European merchant or his trader. The greater proportion of the groundnuts exported is raised in this manner . . .[12]

In fact temporary residence at the coast was even older than that, dating back to the late 18th century. Some farmers from the interior cultivated land near the coast during the wet season and some slave dealers put their slaves to work on rented land pending their sale and export. It was, however, the cultivation of export crops that brought about the enormous expansion of the practice.

Migration undoubtedly became one source of social tension. More important, however, was the conflict that arose between the traditionally valued collective responsibility and a growing competitiveness. Generosity, the traditional source of prestige, was challenged by a new means of obtaining distinction, the possession of more and more varied goods. The sharpness of the conflict, no doubt, should not be unduly stressed, and it raises the entire question of the degree of contrast between market and non-market economies. Certainly some distinguished social anthropologists recognize the presence of stress in societies subject to the economic change initiated by integration into the international economy.

NOTES

1. Quoted Dike, K. O.: *Trade and Politics in the Niger Delta, 1830–1885* (Oxford, 1956), p. 12
2. Davies, P. N. (ed.): *Trading in West Africa 1840–1920* (London, 1976), p. 116
3. Harlow, V. & Madden, F. (eds.): *British Colonial Developments 1774–1834* (Oxford, 1953), p. 389
4. Howard, C. (ed.): *West African Explorers* (London, 1951), p. 466–7
5. Newbury, C. W. (ed.): *British Policy towards West Africa, Select Documents 1786–1874* (Oxford, 1965), p. 115–7
6. Ibid, p. 111–12
7. Nicol, D. (ed.): *Africanus Horton, the Dawn of Nationalism in Modern Africa* (London and Harlow, 1969), p. 51–2, 56
8. Newbury, C. W.: Op. cit., p. 325
9. Quoted Dike, K. O.: Op. cit., p. 85
10. Wilks, I.: *Asante in the Nineteenth Century: the Structure and Evolution of a Political Order* (Cambridge, 1975), p. 651
11. Robertson, H. M.: '150 years of economic contact between black and white' (*South African Journal of Economics*, II, 1935, p. 403–25), p. 411
12. Quoted Newbury, C. W.: 'Prices and profitability in early nineteenth-century West African trade' (Chapter I, Meillassoux, C. ed.: *The Development of Indigenous Trade and Markets in West Africa*, London, 1971), p. 96

Further reading

Baer, Gabriel: *A History of Land Ownership in Modern Egypt, 1800–1950* (London, 1962)
Balandier, Georges: 'Traditional social structures and economic change' (Alexandre, Pierre ed.: *French Perspectives in African Studies*, London, Ibadan and Nairobi, 1973 p. 121–34)
Bennett, Norman R.: *A History of the Arab State of Zanzibar* (London, 1978)
Bundy, Colin: *The Rise and Fall of the South African Peasantry* (London, 1979)
Burke III, E.: Op. cit. (see p. 219)
Crummey, Donald: 'Tēwodros as reformer and modernizer' (*Journal of African History* X, 1969, p. 457–69)
Curtin, Philip D.: *Economic Change in Pre-Colonial Africa: Senegambia in Era of the Slave Trade* (Madison, 1975)
Curtin, P. D.: *Economic Change in Pre-Colonial Africa, Supplementary Evidence* (Madison, 1975)
Davies, Peter (ed.): *Trading in West Africa 1840–1920* (London, 1976)
Dewey, C. & Hopkins, A. G.: *The Imperial Impact* (London, 1978)
Dike, Kenneth O.: *Trade and Politics in the Niger Delta, 1830–1885: an Introduction to the Economic and Social History of Nigeria* (Oxford, 1956)
Hansen, B. & Tourk, K.: 'The profitability of the Suez canal as a private enterprise, 1859–1956' (*Journal of Economic History*, XXXVIII, 1978, p. 938–58)
Harlow, Vincent & Madden, Frederick (eds.): Op. cit. (see note 3 above)
Holt, P. M., Lambton, A. K. S. & Lewis, B.: Op. cit. (see p. 84)
Holt, P. M. (ed.): *Political and Social Change in Modern Egypt* (London, 1968)
Landes, David S.: *Pashas and Bankers; International Finance and Economic Imperialism in Egypt* (London, 1958)

Latham, A. J. H.: Op. cit. (see p. 174)

Law, R.: 'Royal monopoly . . .' (see p. 247)

Lewis, W. Arthur (ed.): *Tropical Development 1880–1913, Studies in Economic Progress* (London, 1970)

Marlowe, John: *Spoiling the Egyptians* (London, 1974)

Meillassoux, Claude (ed.): Op. cit. (see note 12)

Miers, Suzanne: *Britain and the Ending of the Slave Trade* (New York, 1975)

Newbury, C. W. (ed.): Op. cit. (see note 5)

Nicol, D. (ed.): Op. cit. (see note 7)

O'Brien, Patrick: *The Revolution in Egypt's Economic System, from Private Enterprise to Socialism 1952–1965* (London, 1966)

Oliver, R. & Mathew, G. (eds.): Op. cit. (see p. 188)

Pedler, Frederick: *The Lion and the Unicorn in Africa: a History of the United Africa Company, 1787–1931* (London, 1974)

Pim, Alan: *The Financial and Economic History of the African Tropical Territories* (Oxford, 1940)

Reynolds, Edward: *Trade and Economic Change on the Gold Coast 1807–1874* (London, 1974)

Robertson, H. M.: '150 years of economic contact between black and white: a preliminary survey' (*South African Journal of Economics*, II, 1934, p. 403–25 and III, 1935, p. 3–25)

Schnapper, B.: Op. cit. (see p. 262)

Szereszewski, R.: *Structural Changes in the Economy of Ghana, 1891–1911* (London, 1965)

Wilks, Ivor: Op. cit. (see note 10)

Wolff, R. D.: *The Economics of Colonialism: Britain and Kenya, 1870–1930* (New Haven and London, 1974)

2. European Intrusion

i) *The coming of the steamship*

In 1825 a steamship service was inaugurated between Britain and India, calling at Cape Town, and by 1854 there was a regular monthly service from Britain and from India. In 1857 the Union Steamship Company was given a contract by the imperial government to carry mail, which was initially for a period of five years, but was subsequently periodically renewed. It was required to make a monthly voyage of no longer than six weeks' duration. In 1865 the service was extended to Durban. The opening of the Suez Canal in 1869, intended to facilitate trade between Europe and India, had repercussions on both South Africa and East Africa. Because it was so much shorter – and Africa, with limited economic significance, sparse harbours and shortage of coaling facilities, was unattractive – the new route had decided advantages over the Cape route, which therefore suffered at first from the effects of competition. However, the Suez route had its disadvantages too. Navigation of the Canal and the Red Sea was somewhat hazardous and both freight charges and insurance rates were higher. While the new route was better suited to the steamship, the old one remained more advantageous to sailing vessels, including colliers that took coal to eastern coaling stations for bunkering steamships using the Canal. The Cape was particularly favoured by sailing ships carrying cheap bulk commodities which could not bear so well the heavy freight charges of the Canal and where speed was of secondary importance, and the route continued to be used by steamships going to Australia.

The diamond discoveries of 1870 offset the adverse effects of the opening of the Suez Canal. Coastal trade was stimulated and a new service between Britain and Algoa Bay and Port Natal (Durban) was introduced by the Cape and Natal Steam Navigation Company. The Union Company responded to the competition by reducing the passage time to Cape Town and soon forced its rival, which did not enjoy a subsidy, out of business. New competition appeared in the shape of the Castle Line, which ran a service to Calcutta. Attracted by the expansion of Cape exports, it began sending steamships to the Cape in 1872.

In 1872 the Union Company entered into an agreement with the British India Steam Navigation Company for a joint service, subsidised by the British government, to Zanzibar, the former extending its Cape service northwards from Durban and the latter running a monthly service from Aden. The British government's support for the Zanzibar service was associated with its desire to bring the East African slave trade to an end. One effect of its establishment was the weakening of the position of American merchants trading there, to the advantage of the resident Indians.

Steamship services from Britain to West Africa were first provided by Macgregor Laird's African Steamship Company, of London, which was chartered in 1852, and granted a ten-year mail contract and a government subsidy. It promised a round-trip of less than two-and-a-half months, a voyage shorter by more than a half of the time taken by sailing ships. A rival British and African Steam Navigation Company was registered in Edinburgh in 1868, with its office in Glasgow. John Dempster, working for the Liverpool agents of the older company, was induced to transfer his services to the new one, and he was joined by a former colleague, Alexander Elder. This was the beginning of Elder Dempster and Company, the Liverpool agents of the Glasgow firm, and from 1891, of the London firm too. In 1884 it was taken over by Alfred Jones. African Steamship and British and African Steam Navigation competed briefly and then collaborated, bringing down freight rates and chartering extra vessels to force subsequent rivals out of business. Since, however, it proved impossible to overcome the competition of the Hamburg firm, Woermann Line (founded in 1886), an arrangement was made to share business on a geographical basis. In 1891 the British and German lines extended their activities to the Congo, forming the

Compagnie Belge Maritime du Congo (Elder Dempster) and Société Maritime du Congo (Woermann) in 1895, in association with Belgian interests, which guaranteed full cargoes. The French established the steamship line of Fabre-Fraissinet in 1889, and later Chargeurs Réunis, both Marseilles firms.

The introduction of the steamship had an adverse effect upon the old-established European firms in West Africa, because it radically altered the conditions of trade and opened the way for an influx of newcomers. The reduction of freight rates and the speed and greater regularity of service lessened the risk and capital requirements of entry into the trade. Traders no longer needed to supply their own vessels and the old-established trading firms for the most part found it too costly to convert from sail to steam. Shipping and trading became separate. The agent of Messrs. Irvine and Woodward at Bonny for some ten years from 1866 described how the change came about.

> The method of carrying on our trade was to be in some respects different from that of our competitors, as, in order to economise capital, it was our intention to make use of the steamers to keep up our supplies of cargo, which were to be sent out from time to time as opportunity offered, or trade required. . . . We found that our system of working the trade by steamers answered well, as compared with the old-fashioned way followed by other Merchants of sending sailing ships out with full cargoes, and keeping them waiting for months in the River until they were loaded, as in addition to our advantage of sending our Produce home by them, thus getting it to market, and the proceeds converted into the goods two or three times, while the other Merchants had theirs waiting until their ships arrived home, when the same process was again repeated. By this means the trade became revolutionised, and all the Merchants in turn had to dispose of their sailing ships, and adopt the system inaugurated by us. As they were all large ship-owners, making a profit out of their own carrying, this change was not effected without strenuous opposition from them, which culminated in a determined effort on the part of some of the leading Merchants to drive us out of the trade by making prices unprofitable. This policy utterly failed . . .[1]

The steamships kept to regular schedules and limited their ports of call. Dakar, Freetown and Lagos became the major termini of the European intrusion into the interior which completed the transformation of the entire West African commerce. This was facilitated by the use of steam for river transport and by the introduction of quinine as a prophylactic against malaria.

Another change of some importance for the old firms was the decline of barter and the old trading currencies of West Africa. In the second half of the 19th century iron and copper currencies and cowrie shells depreciated as it became cheaper to supply them. They were supplanted by French and British silver coins. The substitution greatly facilitated exchange and emancipated the consumer from the restrictions implicit in barter and payment in kind. Equally, foreign purchasers of West African goods were freed from the necessity of furnishing either the old and complicated currencies or acceptable trade goods in time-honoured assortments, an advantage that may have been viewed without enthusiasm by the old firms but was one that appealed to the newcomer.

The trading situation changed once again, however, in the last two decades of the century, owing to the fiercer competition that prevailed during a period of falling prices and freight rates, though West African trade itself was expanding rapidly. Keener competition had the effect of encouraging merchants to share trade rather than to fight for it and to bring down shipping costs still further by chartering their own vessels or even establishing their own shipping lines, thus reverting to the old position. As early as 1879 British firms trading along the Niger and Benue rivers were brought together as the United African Company (the Royal Niger Company from 1886), though this merger was as much the result of international rivalries and competition with African middlemen as the effect of a scramble for business among British trading firms. More closely related to the economic climate of the end of the century, though also influenced by a conflict of interests with African traders (notably Ja-Ja), was the formation in 1889 of the African Association Limited, which brought together the competing firms of the Niger delta. Ten years later this formed a pool with other firms operating in the Niger basin, including the Royal Niger Company, and in 1905 made a similar pooling arrangement with its competitors on the Gold Coast. Such concentration of trading interests made the shipping companies more susceptible to pressure, and it is understandable why they lobbied energetically in 1886 to prevent the extension to the Niger delta of the virtual monopoly enjoyed by the Royal Niger Company above the delta. Their response to the threat of merchants to use their own shipping was the counter-threat to diversify into trade. Nothing came of either threat.

At the same time as Elder Dempster (which had acquired control of both the British shipping lines operating in West Africa) was alternately negotiating and quarrelling with the trading firms, it was fighting off attempts by other shipping interests to get a share of the carrying trade. The upshot of all the manoeuvring and in-fighting was the withdrawal, with some slight exceptions, of the merchants from shipping in exchange for guaranteed freight rates and the foundation of a shipping conference between Elder Dempster and Woermann to exclude all rivals. Thus from 1895 shipping to West Africa was virtually controlled by an oligopoly. In 1907 it was compelled to take a new member into the ring, namely, the Hamburg-Bremen Africa Line, but the oligopoly was preserved. Moreover, Alfred Jones of Elder Dempster had a wide range of other interests in West Africa, including banking, cotton and minerals. The intricacies of business interests in Africa, overlapping and interlocking, already at the end of the 19th century almost defy unravelling.

FLEETS ENGAGED IN THE WEST AFRICAN SHIPPING TRADE

Year	African Steam Ship Company		British & African S.N. Company	
	Ships	Total	Ships	Total
1874	10	13 605 tons	10	12 760 tons
1875	8	11 305	9	12 597
1876	7	10 051	12	16 782
1877	8	10 236	12	16 782
1878	7	9 218	15	20 728
1879	8	11 175	16	21 259
1880	10	14 298	18	24 298
1881	11	15 550	18	24 298
1882	12	17 250	18	25 069
1883	11	16 069	20	28 669
1884	12	18 284	24	35 245
1885	12	18 299	23	34 956
1886	12	19 830	23	34 956
1887	12	19 830	23	34 956
1888	12	19 831	23	34 956
1889	14	24 468	24	38 615
1890	19	41 181	22	35 260
1891	31	69 087	24	41 889
1892	33	80 526	24	41 889
1893	31	77 544	24	46 466
1894	36	86 593	25	51 340
1895	36	90 862	25	50 194

Source: P. N. Davies, *The Trade Makers: Elder Dempster in West Africa 1852–1972* (London, 1973), p. 82, 89

ii) *Partition*

Explanations for the scramble for Africa, one aspect of a European and American imperialism that was world-wide but did not elsewhere result in such far-reaching direct political control (except in South-East Asia), have been manifold, ingenious and polemical. It has been denied that the late 19th century's imperialism differed, except in methods used, from that of earlier periods, when there was a steady, if unspectacular, expansion of empire. Throughout the 19th century there was a continuity of policy and a reluctance to abandon territory. The recommendation of a Select Committee of the House of Commons in 1865 that Britain withdraw from West Africa with the exception of Sierra Leone, was rejected, and indeed, even before the partition of Africa, her hold on West Africa tightened. Above all, in Britain's case, there was the continuing concern with India, a major outlet for capital and a market for exports, and thus with the security of the Suez Canal, opened in 1869. However, the acceleration of the pace of annexation in the 1880s was revolutionary. Few would question the celebrated dictum of Richard Pares.

> Colonization and empire-building are above all economic acts, undertaken for economic reasons and very seldom for any others.[2]

Yet the evidence seems to suggest that colonies were an economic burden rather than a source of prosperity.

> The historical evidence of the unprofitability of empire to the imperialist is now so clear that it creates two very real puzzles. The first is a puzzle in the history of thought. Why did the view become so widely accepted that imperialism, especially in the nineteenth and twentieth centuries, had any sort of economic base or rationale? . . . The second puzzle is why it seemed to take the rulers and decision-makers of the imperial countries such a long time to find out that from an economic point of view at any rate imperialism was a fraud.[3]

Presumably, the solution to the puzzles is that empire was profitable to sectional interests, and theories of economic imperialism have more to say about such interests than national advantage.

J. A. Hobson, in his book, *Imperialism, a Study*, gave pride of place to 'surplus capital', by which he meant capital in the industrial nations that was unable to find profitable employment at home, not because they were saturated with wealth, but because the mass of the population was deprived, doomed to under-consumption through the inequitable distribution of the profits of industry. European investors, he argued, exported their capital to areas abroad where profits were high but risks great, then used their influence to have their own governments impose political control in order to protect these investments. Hobson was able to demonstrate that British capital exports and earnings from investments overseas had grown *pari passu* with the expansion of British imperial rule. He wrote shortly after the British annexation of the Transvaal, where British investors had interests in gold mining, and also had in mind the British occupation of Egypt, where it was a question of investments in the Suez Canal and in the effete Egyptian government itself.

The surplus capital/ underconsumption theory of Hobson was taken over by Marxists, who sought to explain the apparent discontinuity in the process of domination associated with the scramble for Africa by changes in the nature of the 'imperialist ruling classes', namely a shift from the predominance of 'industrial capital', which was concerned with raw materials and markets, to that of 'finance capital', which was interested rather in the export of capital at a high rate of profit. According to V. I. Lenin, in his essay *Imperialism, the Highest Stage of Capitalism* (1916), the five basic features of imperialism are that

> 1) the concentration of production and capital has developed to such a high stage that it has created monopolies which play a decisive rôle in economic life; 2) the merging of bank capital with industrial capital, and the creation, on the basis of this 'finance capital', of a financial oligarchy; 3) the export of capital as distinguished from the export of commodities acquires exceptional importance; 4) the formation of international monopolist capitalist combines which share the world among themselves, and 5) the territorial division of the whole world among the biggest capitalist powers is completed. Imperialism is capitalism in that stage of development in which the dominance of monopolies and finance capital has established itself; in which the export of capital has acquired pronounced importance; in which the division of the world among the international trusts has begun, in which the division of all territories of the globe among the biggest capitalist powers has been completed.[4]

The suggestion that politicians were the lackeys of investors who clamoured for annexations of overseas territories has not lacked criticism. There is evidence that governments were not easily swayed by the pressure of financiers and merchants. Salisbury in Britain and Bismarck in Germany were unenthusiastic imperialists, and, when he went in for imperialism after all, Bismarck, like Jules Ferry in France and other dedicated imperialists such as he, far from being the instruments of monopoly capitalists, had difficulty in arousing any interest among business men. Moreover, the partition took place with relatively little acrimony among the participants. European powers normally recognized one another's sphere of influence.

The argument that imperialism represented an inevitable stage of capitalist development was rejected by Joseph Schumpeter, who, without denying the validity of an economic explanation, put forward the view in *Imperialism and Social Class* that empire-building was a survival from an earlier age and that capitalism was fundamentally opposed to it, though monopoly capitalism might take advantage of it. More specifically, it has been pointed out that cartelization had not proceeded very far in Britain and France, or even Germany, when the scramble for Africa began. Although capital, it is agreed, was attracted to profitable and dangerous enterprises overseas, such as the Witwatersrand gold mines, most exports of capital went to areas where the rewards and the risks were smaller, that is to areas where there was political stability, particularly to the United States or Europe, and not to high-risk enterprises, but to public authorities and government-supported railway construction. A noticeable tendency was for capital, labour and goods to flow together towards territories of European settlement.

Investment was not always followed by annexation. Though it might lead to 'informal empire', the 'capital export' school of thought sought to explain not that, but political control. There was no keen competition, even after annexation, to off-load in Africa, capital that had, in fact, no lack of profitable outlets at home. Britain had substantial investments in Egypt and the Transvaal, but most of her imperial investments were in the 'old empire'. France invested less than a tenth of her overseas capital in her empire – mostly in Algeria – and Germany's capital exports to Africa were negligible. Investors who did entrust their capital to enterprises in Africa – including those who put it in large companies, such as the British South Africa and the Imperial British East Africa Companies and Huileries du Congo Belge – did not always derive immediate profit or, indeed, any profit at all. Even the South African gold mines taken as a whole gave only a modest return (4,1 per cent. between 1887 and 1932) despite the risk. That, however, may be beside the point: expectations were high.

DISTRIBUTION OF BRITISH FOREIGN INVESTMENT 1865–1914

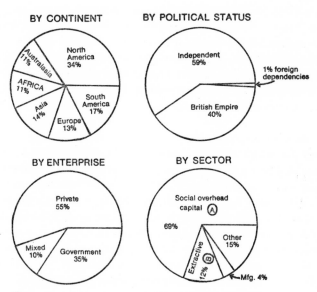

Ⓐ Includes transportation, public utilities and public works

Ⓑ Includes agriculture and mining

Source: Matthew Simon, 'The pattern of new British portfolio foreign investment, 1865-1914' (Chapter I, A. R. Hall, ed., *The Export of Capital from Britain 1870-1914*, London, 1968), p. 23

Scepticism about the rôle of surplus capital does not exclude the significance of investments as a motive for colonization or of investors as a
source of political influence; nor can it be doubted that competition for
markets and sources of foodstuffs and raw materials for growing populations
and expanding industries entered into imperialist calculations. In the last
quarter of the 19th century free trade was becoming discredited and policies
of protection were being pursued by newly industrializing countries. In
such a world colonies would be captive markets to compensate for markets
lost to competitors and would be sources of raw materials for exclusive exploitation. Even to these arguments, however, there are serious objections.
Britain continued to be a free-trading nation until long after the scramble for
Africa and generally tariffs were not so high during the scramble as they were
later to become. In any case partition did not necessarily put to an end free
trade in Africa itself, or annexation lead to the exclusion of foreign interests.

It is indeed questioned whether African colonies were useful either as markets or as sources of raw materials. In 1913, for example, only one half per
cent of Germany's total trade was with her colonies, including those outside
Africa. However, what is more important, perhaps, is that people – rightly
in the long run – thought that Africa was rich in raw materials, especially
minerals. Such a belief was based on the evidence of mineral wealth in
South Africa. There were also hopes of African markets which, if exaggerated,
were not unfounded. Africa was an important market for Manchester textiles
and, to a lesser extent, for Birmingham hardware, and high hopes were
pinned to the construction of railways. Conversely, there were fears that, if
existing markets were not appropriated, they would be lost to foreign
empires. As a rule merchants were not much interested in the flag that flew
as long as the profits were good. In the Gold Coast, for example, Bristol
merchants preferred dealing with African chiefs, who ensured that debts were
paid, than with colonial authorities, whose law courts seemed to favour
debtors. There was, however, the growing fear of foreign intervention.
Britain, though least likely to gain from annexation, since she already dominated African trade, was susceptible to the argument that failure to act might
lead to loss of existing advantage. She was alarmed by the introduction by the
French of discriminatory tariffs in areas under their control, in Senegal in 1877
and the Ivory Coast in 1889, as she had been earlier at the possibility of uni-
lateral French action in Egypt and as she was later at the threat, met at Fashoda
in 1896 by Kitchener, the conqueror of the Sudan, of the establishment of a
belt of French territory right across the continent from Senegal to the Red
Sea; and Rhodes was alarmed at the possibility of Boer pre-emption of
Mashonaland and Matabeleland. Both Britain and France were worried by
growing German interests, which competed strongly with French interests

in Dahomey and with British interests in Nigeria, the Cameroons and East Africa.

Empire-building tended to have a momentum of its own. Defence of existing interests required fresh annexations and these in turn led to still further seizure of territory. Britain's interests in India dictated concern for the route to the east; sensitiveness to the security of the Suez Canal, threatened (it was thought) by the nationalist uprising of Arabi Pasha, contributed to the decision to occupy Egypt in 1882. Defence of interests in Egypt and in the Cape and Natal helps to explain the British intervention in the Sudan and Uganda and in the Boer republics, just as a long-established presence in Algeria and fears of growing Italian commercial activity in North Africa provide a partial explanation for the establishment of a French protectorate over Tunis in 1881. It has been argued, too, that the British occupation of Egypt provoked the French, who withdrew at the last moment from joint action with Britain, into retaliation in West Africa and was thus the catalyst of a chain reaction.

Some explanations of imperialism have stressed the influence of international relations within Europe, domestic European politics and the susceptibility of European governments to lobbies and pressure groups. France may well have been influenced by a desire to compensate in some way – materially or psychologically – for her defeat at the hands of Prussia in 1870 and the loss of Alsace-Lorraine or for her industrial inferiority among the great powers. It has, indeed, been argued that the partition of Africa was simply an extension outside Europe of a power struggle too dangerous to be indulged in within Europe, or that the decision to annex or not to annex was part of the manoeuvres of domestic politics, to win votes or influence parties. All European governments, themselves reluctant to undertake the burden of annexation, were subject to a variety of pressures from, by no means exclusively, monopolistic capitalists, but traders troubled by competitors and vexatious political authority; from soldiers and officials on the spot actuated by personal ambition or conviction that a forward policy was conducive to trade, effective administration and revenue, and from missionaries who saw in trade and European rule, civilizing forces, as well as from special interest groups at home, commercial, industrial, philanthropic, enthusiastic patriotic and romantic imperialist. These pressures were not without effect, though no government danced to any particular tune. Missionary representations were a major factor in dissuading the British government from giving up Uganda in 1893. The churches had a keen interest in the suppression of the slave trade. Merchants, too, wanted the curbing of warlike plundering states whose activities were inimical to trade.

Perhaps general explanations for the partition of Africa are too sweeping and local conditions should be given more weight. In Senegal the spread of groundnut cultivation into the interior by Europeans and gallicized Africans led to a demand for the extension of French administration. The British expedition led by W. B. Baikie in 1854 up the Niger demonstrated the value of steam-driven river boats and of the regular use of quinine to combat malaria and so facilitate European penetration of the interior. The opening of steamship services to the coast brought in new merchants from Europe, trading on a smaller scale than the older ones, and the greater ease of travel permitted the circumvention of African middlemen. Competition became fiercer with the deterioration of the terms of trade on the coast in the late 19th century, when a struggle took place between European firms and African producers and suppliers over prices and the division of profits. British traders invoked the support of their government with some effect. Both sides attempted to gain advantage at the expense of each other, and there were embargoes upon supplies and squabbles about alleged fraud, debt repayments and escaped slaves, creating a situation that invited imperialist intervention.

The influence of personal ambition – or some other psychological imperative – of single-minded men, should not be discounted. Some of these were indeed capitalists – Cecil Rhodes, whose interests included the British South Africa Company, Sir George Goldie of the Royal Niger Company and Sir William Mackinnon of the British India Steam Navigation Company and the Imperial British East African Company – but there is no certainty that they were inspired solely by their thirst for profit, still less that they were in some way representative of the capitalist class or 'finance capital'. If there are doubts about the capitalist credentials of such men as these, what of the soldiers and administrators like Adolf Lüderitz, Louis Faidherbe, Louis Brière de l'Isle, Lord Lugard and J. B. Marchand, men who were not impelled by the pursuit of material gain? Leopold II, whose intervention in the Congo has sometimes been seen as the first move in the partition, though eager for profit, was scarcely a typical capitalist, rather one who had given offence to those capitalists who were excluded from participation in his enterprise.

iii) *Chartered companies and concessions*
The chartered companies of the 19th century, like their predecessors of an earlier age, served a dual purpose, promoting economic activity and advancing political control. With their superior capital resources and political and administrative privileges they were better able than private individuals to open up territory to commerce, agriculture, and mining, and to meet successfully foreign competition. At the same time they were useful screens behind which governments could operate when they were unwilling to commit themselves to the expense and obligations of colonization. Once

their purpose had been served, they ceased to exercise their administrative functions under charter and reverted to simple business enterprises. In Nigeria the Royal Niger Company originated in an attempt to break the monopoly exercised by African trading states and to present a united front of British interests on the Niger against French and subsequently German competition which had political implications. In 1879 these relatively scattered trading interests were persuaded by Sir George Goldie to merge into the United African Company; in 1882 it was enlarged under the name of the National Africa Company; and in 1886 it was incorporated as the Royal Niger Company with the right to make treaties with chiefs along the Niger and Benue rivers and obtain from them trading and territorial concessions. It was also permitted to levy taxes to meet administrative expenses. Theoretically it had no trade monopoly, but in practice it was impossible for individuals to operate in competition with it. At the same time, its political and administrative responsibilities grew. Pacification was a necessary prerequisite to successful trade. Northern Nigeria was affected by slave raiding and tribal warfare, which laid waste substantial areas and reduced the population. Treaties were concluded with African rulers, not only in the interests of peace, but also for the sake of forestalling French and German penetration. The Royal Niger Company was a financial success, but its informal monopoly caused complaints. In 1900 all its treaties, land and mining rights were ceded to the British government and the company retained only its trading assets and warehouses. Part of its area was added to the Niger Coast Protectorate to form the colony of Southern Nigeria, and the rest formed Northern Nigeria.

The pattern followed by the Royal Niger Company was common in Africa. Not all companies were as successful and a number required financial assistance. But all laid foundations for colonization. However reluctant home governments were to take over responsibilities, the outcome was, almost always, an extension of dominion. In East Africa both Britain and Germany worked through chartered companies. The German territory was administered by the German East Africa Company of 1885. Its origin lay in the Society for German Colonization, founded in 1884 by Carl Peters, who immediately proceeded despite official discouragement to conclude a series of treaties with local rulers for the purpose of facilitating the imposition of colonial rule. The company received a charter and recognition of sovereign rights over the areas in which treaties had been made. However, it faced many difficulties, in particular an early outbreak of rebellion. In 1891 it handed over its administrative functions to the imperial government. In practice this made little difference to the administration, which continued to be run by the same people, including Carl Peters, who earned an unsavoury reputation for brutality. In South-West Africa the German South-West African Company, incorporated in 1885, refused to accept a charter, but exercised some administrative functions for a time.

It was the activity of Carl Peters that stimulated the formation of the British East Africa Company, chartered in 1888, under the chairmanship of Sir William Mackinnon. Its overtly colonizing purpose was disliked by the prime minister, Lord Salisbury, who was much more concerned with maintaining good relations with Germany. The sultan of Zanzibar in 1887 assigned to the company (still an 'association' at that time, before it was chartered) the administration of his coastal territories north of the German sphere of influence and agreed to a policy of extending its sovereignty into the interior. So great was the territory that came under the company's control that it could not cope with its responsibilities. In an effort to curtail its commitments, it withdrew from Uganda, which was temporarily taken over by the Foreign Office, and in 1894 it was bought out by the government for £$\frac{1}{4}$ million. From 1905 the whole territory, including Uganda, became a crown colony, under the jurisdiction of the Colonial Office.

In Central Africa the British South Africa Company was chartered for an initial period of 25 years in 1889 and was dominated by Cecil Rhodes, who brought together or acquired the various companies competing for the control of the mineral resources of the Matabele kingdom of Lobengula. The new company was authorized to exploit the so-called Rudd Concession, the exclusive right to prospect for and work minerals, granted by Lobengula in 1888 to C. J. Rudd, one of Rhodes's associates, in exchange for a pension and a supply of modern weapons. Its responsibilities, however, extended far beyond that. Implicit in its charter was the authorization not merely to colonize and administer within the territories of Lobengula, but also to extend control north of the Zambezi river to a geographical limit that was not defined. In 1890 an armed column of settlers founded Salisbury in Mashonaland, over which Lobengula asserted hegemony, and its two hundred pioneers were each given 15 gold claims and almost 1 500 ha. of land. The company's right to assign land was subsequently regularized, or so it was thought, by the purchase of another concession, one that Lobengula was cajoled into granting to E. A. Lippert. In 1893 friction between the settlers and the Matabele led to war, which the company won, thus acquiring sovereignty in Matabeleland. The two territories, Matabeleland and Mashonaland, together made up Southern Rhodesia under B.S.A. Company administration, to which British Bechuanaland was added in 1895. The company also temporarily extended its authority into Nyasaland and from there its influence spread firstly into North-East Rhodesia, then into North-West Rhodesia. Rhodes indirectly obtained a mineral concession in the territories controlled by Lewanika, the ruler of Barotseland, and in 1890 a protectorate over the whole area. In 1911 North-East Rhodesia and

North-West Rhodesia were amalgamated to form Northern Rhodesia.

Economically the Rhodesias were for a long time a disappointment. Administrative and military costs exceeded revenue and the 8 000 original shareholders of the company saw no return on their investment. The original equity capital of a million pounds had to be increased on several occasions and debenture shares issued. With the extension of the railway through Bechuanaland and from Beira, the not inconsiderable inflow of settlers (over 30 000 in Southern Rhodesia and some 2 000 in Northern Rhodesia by 1915), the expansion of gold mining and agriculture, and the quickening of trade, the economy prospered in a modest way, but the shareholders remained dividendless. In 1923, at the end of protracted litigation and sometimes acrimonious negotiation on its landowning claims and on the compensation to be paid for its expenditure on government and development, its administration was wound up in both Northern and Southern Rhodesia, the former reverting to the crown, the latter being granted responsible government. Apart from its cash compensation the company retained its mineral rights in the Rhodesias and substantial land rights in Northern Rhodesia. Its administrative responsibilities shed, the company began to pay dividends, its profits derived partly from its mineral rights, partly from its investment in railways and other enterprises.

In Mozambique Portuguese chartered companies similar to the British ones were given powers over vast tracts of land in the late 19th century. The Nyasa Company retained its privileges until 1929, the Mozambique Company until 1942. They were not, however, either rewarding for the shareholders or very useful to the Portuguese government. One of the obligations they undertook was to promote Portuguese settlement and, in addition, the Nyasa Company was required to construct a railway to Lake Nyasa. Neither of these objectives was fulfilled. The task of developing their territories proved to be beyond their capacity.

In addition to these chartered companies, concessionary companies were granted agricultural or mining rights over huge estates in both Mozambique and Angola. The mining companies of Angola, for example, Diamang and the Lobito Mining Company, gained control over some half million square kilometres each. Such concessions were the rule also in the German, Belgian and French colonies. They were particularly notorious in the Congo Free State, the personal appanage of King Leopold of the Belgians, which was recognized by the Berlin Conference of 1885, its origin lying in hundreds of treaties negotiated by the explorer H. M. Stanley on behalf of the International Association of the Congo. Leopold set up an organization, euphemistically named the Comité d'Études du Haut Congo, for the exploitation of the region under his control and claimed ownership of all vacant land not under African cultivation. The king's share of the profit was secured partly

by the enforced collection of rubber, copal and ivory for delivery to state
agents, partly by the imposition of taxes on private trade and partly by participation in the various concession companies. Millions of hectares of land
were made over to railway companies and mining companies, above all the
Compagnie du Katanga, which, in 1891, received, in addition to mining
rights, one third of the public lands, an arrangement modified in 1900. It
was the scandal aroused by revelations of the barbarity of the methods applied by state and company officials in the collection of forest products that
brought to an end some of the more notorious concessions in 1906 and led to
the transfer of the Congo Free State to Belgium in 1908. Fabulous profits
had been made, however, especially from the export of rubber, which was
collected with such little regard for conservation that, by 1905, the supply
was beginning to fall off. After the transfer concessions continued to be granted, including one in 1911 to Huileries du Congo Belge, a subsidiary of the
British firm of Lever Brothers. But as a result of disquiet about the labour
situation, it was decided at the end of the 1920s to grant no further mining
concessions and to restrict agricultural concessions.

In the French Congo private capital was attracted by the expectation of a
repetition of the large profits being made in the Congo Free State. The
French government, anxious to develop – or exploit – the interior, where
trade was almost non-existent, was much in favour of big concessions. Two
were granted in the 1890s (and a third on the Ivory Coast) and although they
were subsequently annulled – with generous compensation – on account of
the protests of both interested and disinterested parties – thwarted competitors, foreign as well as French, and critics of colonial policy – in 1899
provision was made for a systematic division of the country. Forty concessions were granted in 1899, covering almost seventy per cent. of the total
area of what later became French Equatorial Africa. Their size varied: the
biggest gave rights over 140 000 square kilometres. A concession was valid
for thirty years, at the end of which the concessionaire was to be permitted
to keep in full ownership all the land he had developed. The criterion of what
constituted development was by no means demanding. Although these
concessionary companies differed from chartered companies in having no
rights of sovereignty, in practice they had a more or less free hand in the
territory assigne 1 to them. They obtained exclusive right to the products of
the soil, and they devoted themselves to rubber exploitation and trade.
Foreign traders, mostly British, were forced out.

The methods of the French companies, like those of the Congo Free State,
attracted much adverse criticism, for example from E. D. Morel in 1902.
In 1910–1912 they were induced to disgorge some of the territory they held,
and no new concessions were granted, less because of the outcry than because of the competition of Asian plantation rubber and the economic failure

of the companies. Loss of wider territorial rights was compensated for by grants of land in full ownership. In the meantime the number of concessionary companies had been greatly reduced owing to a process of amalgamation. The original concessions lapsed in 1930. The concessionaires were compensated with land grants and some were able to survive with their position virtually unimpaired.

Two big concessions, one of 72 000 square kilometres, the other of 80 000 square kilometres, were granted by the Germans in their Cameroon protectorate – the Süd-Kamerun and the Nord-Kamerun (1898 and 1899 respectively) Companies. The latter was required to develop communications and plantations; the former was formed for the purpose of collecting rubber. In South-West Africa the South-West Africa Company, founded in 1892, was granted 13 000 square kilometres of land together with the right to exploit minerals and build a railway. This was one of nine concessionary companies which controlled nearly a third of the territory, but it was the only one with sufficient resources to achieve anything. Its subsidiary, the Otavi Mining and Railway Company, mined copper at Tsumeb and constructed a railway, while the parent company promoted settlement and farming.

One feature of the chartered and concessionary companies was their international character. Belgian and French interests had a stake in the French and German concession companies. The Süd-Kamerun Company was largely Belgian and, to begin with, had its head office in Brussels. The British firm of Lever Brothers controlled Huileries du Congo Belge, permitted to lease up to three-quarters of a million hectares of land in the Belgian Congo, and in 1921 took over one of the concessionary companies in French Equatorial Africa. The British South Africa Company had an important share in the German South-West Africa Company. It was prevented from taking over the Portuguese Mozambique Company only by the existence of certain British treaty obligations (incurred in 1898) to Germany. As it was, its territory was largely under the B.S.A. Company's control because of the railway it operated between Beira and Umtali.

iv) *The economic consequences of conquest*
An assessment of the economic effects of the European partition of Africa cannot be anything but a balance sheet of the colonial period and of the years since independence to the extent that they have continued to be influenced by the colonial experience. When the colonialist pebble was tossed into the African pond it created a big splash and a subsequent series of ripples of diminishing strength. All the ripples are part of the story. Here the discussion must be confined to the initial splash.

The effects of conquest varied from region to region. All Africa experienced to some degree the violence and injustice that are the usual concomitant of foreign occupation. In some parts of the continent there was the inexcusable harshness of the phase of *Raubwirtschaft*, like that practised above all by the Congo Free State, a brutality that aroused such a clamour of protest in Europe that its worst excesses were corrected. Seizure of land, sometimes taking the form of calculated dispossession, at other times the result of a genuine belief that the land expropriated was *terra nullius*, was normal. European settlers were more or less deliberately encouraged in Northern, Eastern and Southern Africa. Forced labour of one form or another, accompanied as a rule by a high mortality rate, was to be found everywhere. Yet, even the process of conquest was not without its compensations. Although pacification may have often been a euphemism, it did impose an imperial peace on warring groups and peoples, and did sweep away obstacles to trade and abolish the disincentives to cultivation and other economic endeavours. Above all Europe through its colonial rule did palliate to some extent its own participation in the slave trade by its rooting out of slaving survivals.

It is impossible to believe that the incorporation of Africa into the international economy would not have taken place without the scramble for Africa. That integration had already proceeded far in West Africa before partition occurred, is evident; that formal political domination was not essential, the experience of Liberia demonstrates. On the other hand, vast areas of the continent would have seen their economic contacts with the outside world long postponed if there had not been a conquest that led to the construction of railways, mineral prospecting and the investment of metropolitan capital. The proposition that such intervention was disastrous for Africa, as is passionately argued and only diffidently questioned, cannot be asserted or denied with complete certainty at this chronological perspective, if indeed one view will ever command general support. Even the conquests of the ancient world are still capable of arousing indignation or adulation.

NOTES

1. Davies, P. N. (ed.): *Trading in West Africa 1840–1920* (London, 1976), p. 37–8
2. Pares, Richard: 'The economic factors in the history of the empire' (Section V, Pares, R. *The Historian's Business and Other Essays*, Oxford, 1961), p. 49
3. Boulding, Kenneth E. & Mukerjee, Tapan (eds.): *Economic Imperialism, a Book of Readings* (Ann Arbor: 1972), p. xiii–xiv
4. Lenin, V. I.: *Selected Works* (Moscow, 1960), Volume 1, p. 782

Further reading

Boulding, K. E. & Mukerjee, T.: Op. cit. (see above note 3)
Brown, Michael B.: *The Economics of Imperialism* (Harmondsworth, 1974)

Coupland, Sir Reginald: *The Exploitation of East Africa 1856–1890* (London, 1939)

Davies, P. N.: *The Trade Makers Elder Dempster in West Africa 1852–1972* (London, 1973)

Farnie, D. A.: *East and West of Suez, the Suez Canal in History 1854–1956* (Oxford, 1969)

Fieldhouse, D. K.: *The Theory of Capitalist Imperialism* (London, 1967)

Flint, John: *Cecil Rhodes*, (Boston and Toronto, 1974)

Flint, John: *Sir George Goldie and the Making of Nigeria* (London, 1960)

Galbraith, John S.: *Crown and Charter, the Early Years of the British South Africa Company* (Berkeley, Cal., 1974)

Galbraith, John S.: *Mackinnon and East Africa 1878–1895, a Study in the 'New Imperialism'* (Cambridge, 1972)

Gann, L. H.: *A History of Northern Rhodesia, Early Days to 1953* (London, 1964)

Gann, L. H.: *A History of Southern Rhodesia* (London, 1965)

Gann, L. H. & Duignan, Peter: *The Rulers of Belgian Africa 1884–1914* (Princeton, N. J., 1979)

Gray, J. M.: *History of Zanzibar from the Middle Ages* (London, 1962)

Griffiths, Sir Percival: *A Licence to Trade, a History of the English Chartered Companies* (London and Tonbridge, 1974)

Hailey, Lord: Op. cit. (see p. 47)

Henderson, W. O.: *Studies in German Colonial History* (London, 1962)

Hobson, J. A.: *Imperialism, a Study* (London, 3rd edn. 1938)

Hodgart, Alan: *The Economics of European Imperialism* (London, 1977)

Ingham, Kenneth: *A History of East Africa* (London, 3rd edn. 1965)

Kemp, Tom: *Theories of Imperialism* (London, 1967)

Kiernan, V. G.: *Marxism and Imperialism* (London, 1974)

Koebner, Richard & Schmidt, Helmut Dan: *Imperialism, the Story and Significance of a Political Word, 1840–1960* (Cambridge, 1965)

Landes, David S.: Op. cit. (see p. 289)

Lichtheim, George: *Imperialism* (Harmondsworth, 1971)

Louis, William Roger: *Imperialism: the Robinson and Gallagher Controversy* (London, 1976)

Lugard, Lord: *The Dual Mandate in British Tropical Africa* (London, 5th edn. 1965)

Oliver, R. & Mathew, G.: Op. cit. (see p. 188)

Owen, R. & Sutcliffe, Bob (eds.): *Studies in the Theory of Imperialism* (London, 1972)

Porter, Bernard: *Critics of Empire: British Radical Attitudes to Colonialism in Africa 1895–1914* (London, 1968)

Robinson, R. E. & Gallagher, J.: *Africa and the Victorians: the Official Mind of Imperialism* (London and Basingstoke, 1961)

Shaw, A. G. L. (ed.): *Great Britain and the Colonies 1815–1865* (London, 1970)

Suret-Canale, Jean: *French Colonialism in Tropical Africa* (London, 1971)

Walker, E. A. (ed.): Op. cit. (see p. 262)

Williamson, James A.: *A Short History of British Expansion*, Volume 2 (London, 3rd edn. 1945)

Wright, H. M.: *The 'New' Imperialism, Analyses of Late 19th Century Expansion* (Lexington, Mass., 1961)

MODERN AFRICA – POLITICAL

COUNTRIES OF AFRICA

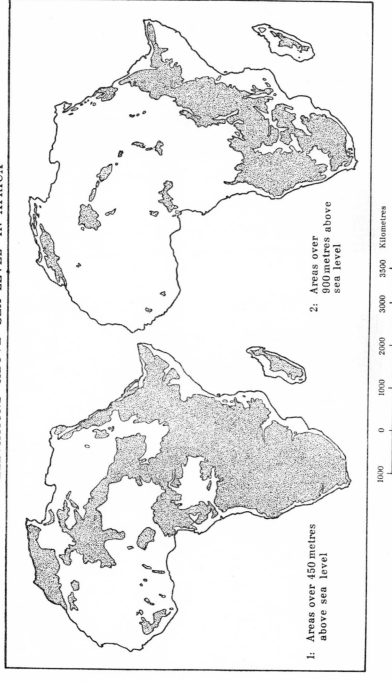

ELEVATIONS ABOVE SEA LEVEL IN AFRICA

1: Areas over 450 metres above sea level

2: Areas over 900 metres above sea level

1000 0 1000 2000 3000 3300 Kilometres

RAINFALL

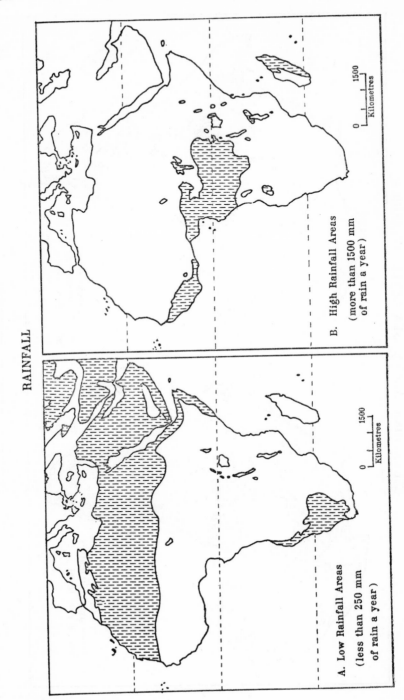

A. Low Rainfall Areas
(less than 250 mm
of rain a year)

B. High Rainfall Areas
(more than 1500 mm
of rain a year)

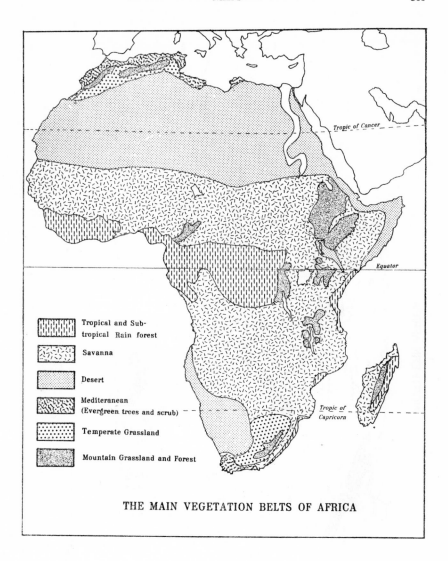

Tropic of Cancer

Equator

Tropical and Sub-
tropical Rain forest

Savanna

Desert

Mediteranean
(Evergreen trees and scrub)

Temperate Grassland

Mountain Grassland and Forest

Tropic of
Capricorn

THE MAIN VEGETATION BELTS OF AFRICA

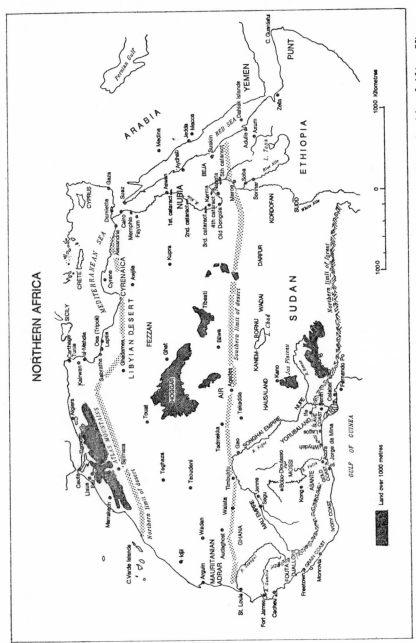

Based on J. D. Fage, *An Atlas of African History*
(Edward Arnold, London, 1958)

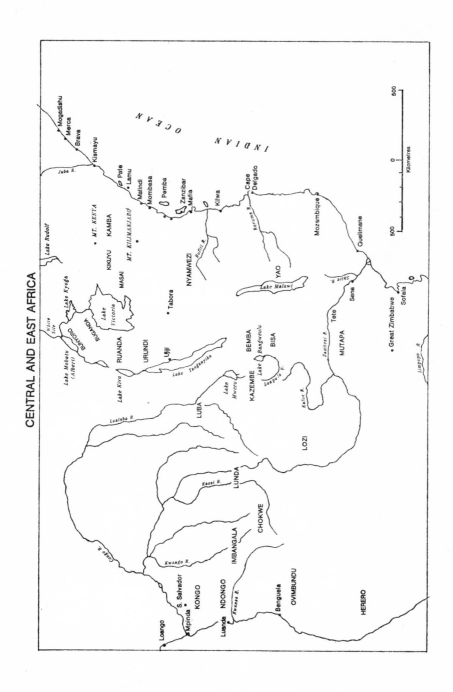

CENTRAL AND EAST AFRICA

INDEX

Abbāsids 10, 11, 59, 88, 122, 206

Agriculture (Egypt) 3, 10, 21–22, 32, 36–38, 39, 40, 49–50, 52, 56, 58–59, 59–60, 131, 136, 189, 190, 192, 195, 196, 263, 286–287; (North Africa) 8–9, 10, 23, 38–40, 50, 56–58, 60, 136, 137, 142, 192, 207, 266; (Nubia) 4, 23–24, 37, 221; (Ethiopia) 4, 23, 24, 25–26, 34, 36, 42, 49, 63, 278; (West Africa) 4, 23, 24–25, 29–30, 34, 35, 36, 41, 42, 43–44, 45, 61–62, 149, 154–155, 171, 172, 228, 242, 243, 246, 255, 256, 269, 274, 276–277, 279, 286, 287–288, 299–300, 305; (Central and East Africa) 24, 25, 26–28, 28–29, 30, 30–31, 34, 35, 35–36, 41–42, 48, 49, 50, 52, 61, 62, 63, 158, 176, 177, 221, 252, 279–281, 304; (South Africa) 26, 28, 30, 36, 45–46, 50–51, 64, 186, 257, 259, 261, 282, 285, 303

Alexandria (Building) 125; (Science) 81, 97; (Industry) 84, 88, 97, 98, 103, 110, 132, 137; (Trade) 117–118, 118, 132, 137, 138, 139, 144, 147, 212, 264; (Banking) 125; (Population) 142, 196, 196–197, 198, 200, 202

Algeria (Muslim) 11, 13, 103, 123, 129, 143, 144, 208, 209, 213; (Colonial) 19, 256, 267, 297, 299

Algiers 13, 103, 123, 129, 143, 144, 208

Almohads 11, 150, 151

Almoravids 11, 150, 212

Alum 98, 142, 144, 146, 152, 195

Angola (Ndongo) 158, 224, 251; (Colonial) 14, 15, 19, 30, 50, 123, 163, 165, 167, 168, 187, 250, 251–252, 303

Animal husbandry (in general) 3, 4, 25, 26, 37, 39, 44, 47, 54, 55, 61, 221, 225; (Domestication and diffusion) 5, 21, 22, 23, 24, 26, 27–28, 34; (Cattle farming) 17, 22, 27, 34, 35, 38, 42, 45, 61, 62, 64, 159, 258–259, 279; (Mixed farming) 39, 42, 279; (Trade, investment and payments in cattle) 116, 121, 125, 131, 133, 145, 154, 185, 186, 187, 222, 225, 226, 228, 229, 232, 237, 238, 241, 242, 282; (Sheep and goats) 22, 23, 24, 28, 30, 33, 38, 39, 42, 100, 154, 186, 187, 258, 282–283; (Draught animals) 128

Ankole 6, 232, 237

Arabia 4, 7, 9, 12, 25–26, 76, 90, 92, 132, 135, 137, 138, 141, 144, 146, 147, 174, 175, 176, 210, 291

Arabs (In general) 14, 23, 33, 118, 119, 137, 150, 156, 172, 215, 217, 223, 227, 242; (Arab Empire) 9–10, 11, 29, 40, 59, 71, 75, 77, 82–83, 88, 91, 96, 97, 98, 99, 100, 102–103, 122, 123, 126, 128, 139–140, 141, 148, 204–205, 207, 210, 218; (Bedouin) 10, 11, 12, 13, 40, 50, 129, 129–130, 145, 151, 152, 206, 208, 210; (East Africa) 7, 15, 29, 63, 114, 126, 138–139, 174, 175, 177, 178, 181, 182, 183, 184, 214, 278; (Omani) 15, 180, 181, 182, 208; (Nubia) 12, 71, 145, 146

Asante 5, 18, 86, 99, 100, 101, 112, 113, 114, 157, 172, 221, 223, 226, 227, 229, 232, 242, 246, 276

Assyria 7, 8, 74, 76, 193

Axum 4, 12, 90, 91, 122, 136, 139, 221, 227

Ayyubids 11, 59–60, 92, 142, 205, 206

Banking and credit 110, 125–127, 160, 197, 198, 199, 201, 202, 210, 211, 212, 214, 215, 219, 246, 250, 268, 275, 276, 284, 287, 294, 296

Bantu migration 5–6, 26–28, 29, 69, 76–77, 175

Basketwork 68, 100, 106, 158

Beads 84, 85, 88, 121, 149, 156, 158, 159, 162, 173, 176, 177, 179, 180, 181, 182, 185, 186, 226

Belgium 19, 292, 297, 303, 304, 305

Benguela 15, 166, 229

Benin 56, 85–86, 87–88, 89, 93, 99, 101–102, 112, 157, 161, 162, 164, 168, 221, 223, 229, 250, 269

Berbers 9, 10, 10–11, 13, 23, 33, 38, 40,

41, 56, 57, 60, 72, 73, 76, 77, 81, 90, 91, 98, 121, 134, 136, 145, 148, 150, 151, 152, 172–173, 194, 206, 207, 210, 213, 233, 237, 242, 243

Boatbuilding 102–103, 114, 127, 129, 132, 171, 172, 213

Boers (In general) 35, 50–51, 64, 93, 222, 241, 258, 259, 260, 261, 298, 299; (Republics) 18, 19–20, 261, 285, 295, 296, 297

Bonny 165, 246, 270, 275, 277, 292

Brandenburg 16, 19, 163, 254

Brass 75, 84, 85–86, 114, 157, 233

Brazil 18, 29, 163, 164, 165, 167, 168, 181, 248, 249, 250, 253, 267, 268

Bronze 7, 73, 75, 85–86, 89, 108, 121, 136, 138, 145, 157, 192

Buganda 6, 55, 93, 118, 182, 221, 223, 227, 234, 278, 280

Building 27, 40, 56, 61, 81, 89–94, 97, 100, 107, 108, 112, 114, 132, 178, 179, 180, 189, 195, 225, 239, 249, 253, 255, 259, Bunyoro 6, 93, 182, 226, 227, 232, 233

Byzantine Empire 9, 39, 40, 50, 58, 59, 98, 103, 122, 139, 140, 197, 204, 217, 244

Cairo 12, 22, 53, 89, 91–92, 110, 111, 118, 119, 129, 144, 147, 151, 209, 211, 212, 216, 243, 264

Camels 97, 101, 128, 129, 130, 145, 148, 149, 150, 152, 155, 156, 157, 209, 233

Cape of Good Hope 14, 18, 20, 30, 32, 33, 35, 36, 45–46, 50–51, 64, 69, 74, 92–93, 96, 114, 117, 126–127, 128, 146, 147, 186, 252, 257–261, 282–283, 290–291

Cape Town 16, 45, 119, 186, 187, 257, 258, 285, 290

Cape Verde Islands 14, 159, 160, 161, 163, 249, 250

Capital (In general) 199, 210, 218, 219, 239, 245; (Agriculture) 42, 43, 45, 46, 238, 241, 252, 255, 258, 271, 277, 279, 287; (Industry) 97, 109–110; (Commerce) 110, 119, 126, 127, 160, 170, 197, 198, 211, 214, 214–215, 230, 238, 246, 253, 254, 257, 275, 277, 292; (Imports) 20, 264, 265, 285, 295, 295–296, 297, 298, 300, 304, 305, 306

Capitalism 171, 197–202, 214–215, 216–

217, 218–219, 240, 243, 244, 245, 296, 299, 300

Chad (Lake) 5, 12, 18, 25, 76, 102, 112, 152, 157, 172

Chartered Companies 15–16, 163, 164, 165, 246, 249, 253–254, 255, 293, 297, 300, 300–305

China 7, 14, 75, 88, 98, 100, 119, 126, 137, 138, 175, 176, 185, 215

Class formation 49, 189, 190, 191, 192, 193, 194, 195, 197, 198, 199, 200, 201, 202, 214, 215–216, 217–218, 220–221, 226, 230, 231, 232, 233, 234, 235–239, 243, 244, 248, 253, 278, 280, 296, 300

Clientship 61, 194, 198, 232, 237, 238, 242

Cloth and clothing (In general) 81, 97, 98, 105, 106, 107, 108, 110, 112, 114, 116, 121, 131, 134, 135, 137, 138, 142, 144, 145, 146, 147, 149, 152, 153, 155, 156, 157, 158, 159, 162, 164, 171, 172, 176, 179, 180, 181, 182, 186, 187, 207, 213, 214, 224, 226, 233, 239, 259; (Bark) 97, 100; (Cotton) 97, 98, 99, 107, 113, 138, 140, 144, 148, 153, 155, 157, 164, 176, 177, 181, 263, 268, 298; (Linen) 22, 74, 97–98, 98, 99, 107, 109, 138, 140, 158; (Palm fibre) 97, 99, 158, 166; (Silk) 97, 98, 99, 101, 110, 138, 140, 155, 156, 159, 176, 177; (Skin) 68, 93, 97, 100; (Woollen) 97, 98, 107, 108, 140, 141, 149, 155, 158, 164

Congo 5, 6, 7, 14, 19, 27, 30, 34, 68, 94, 124, 127, 158, 163, 165, 166, 167, 168, 250, 251, 272, 291–292, 300, 303–305, 305, 306

Constantinople 9, 13, 40, 123, 136, 139, 141, 143, 196, 207, 208,

Copper 72–74, 74, 75, 76, 77, 84, 85, 86, 93, 106, 121, 122, 123, 124, 132, 133, 138, 149, 156, 156–157, 157, 158, 166, 176, 177, 179, 180, 182, 185, 186, 187, 192, 223, 224, 251, 284, 292, 305,

Crops (Domestication) 21, 23, 24–25, 25, 26; (Banana) 29, 31, 42, 96, 176, 221, 279; (Barley) 22, 23, 94, 96; (Cassava-manioc) 29, 30, 31, 149; (Flax) 22, 97, 100, 110, 135, 258; (Cloves) 62, 63, 156, 183, 278, 281; (Cocoa) 271, 273, 274, 287, 288; (Coffee) 96, 147, 187, 267, 271, 279, 280, 281;

(Cotton) 24, 29, 44, 98–99, 149, 159, 221, 256, 263, 266, 267, 268, 269–270, 280, 286–287, 294; (Groundnuts) 29, 30, 149, 272, 276, 277, 279, 286, 287, 288, 300; (Maize) 28, 29, 30, 30–31, 42, 95, 96, 280; (Millet) 24, 25, 27, 28, 31, 42, 43, 44, 51–52, 95, 96, 149, 154, 221; (Rice) 24, 25, 29, 41, 44, 95, 138, 149, 154, 155, 176, 221, 258; (Sorghum) 25, 27, 31, 53; (Sugar) 15, 29, 37, 63, 110, 138, 144, 146, 156, 163, 180, 183, 187, 250, 252, 256, 263, 275, 278, 283, 285; (Tobacco) 30, 95, 149, 163, 164, 182, 185, 186, 258, 282; (Wheat) 16, 22, 23, 25, 37, 38, 39, 41, 44, 51, 64, 94, 95, 96, 116, 125, 129, 132, 134, 135, 136, 138, 140, 141, 142, 143, 144, 149, 157, 186, 195, 196, 203, 214, 257, 258, 261, 267, 279, 282, 287; (Yams) 25, 29, 42, 53, 154
Cushitic-speakers (Galla, Somali, etc.) 6, 24, 26, 27, 33, 34, 93, 100, 136, 174, 229, 234
Cyrenaica 7, 8, 11, 38–39, 135, 152

Dahomey 48, 49, 62, 112, 165, 223, 224, 226, 227, 231, 244, 269, 275, 276, 277, 299
Damietta 98, 103, 110, 142
Darfur 12, 157, 232
Denmark 16, 17, 163, 167, 254
Disease 13, 25, 28, 33, 42, 52, 53–54, 60, 80, 129, 165, 197, 238, 258, 282, 292, 300
Division of labour 21, 60–61, 69, 79, 81, 105, 107, 108, 110, 111, 198, 220, 239, 242, 243, 246
Dutch East India Company 16, 45, 50–51, 64, 126, 186–187, 257–260, 261
Dyes and dyeing 44, 98, 99, 107–108, 108, 110, 134, 136, 142, 144, 149, 155, 159, 256, 258, 268
Dyula 119, 155, 157, 211, 246, 271

East African Lakes 6, 25, 26–27, 29, 32, 36, 42, 67, 76, 77, 87, 97, 102, 117, 177, 181, 182, 183, 232, 280
Egypt (Pharaonic) 3–4, 7, 21–24, 25, 28, 33, 35, 36–37, 49–50, 52, 55, 56, 69, 70, 72, 72–73, 74, 76, 81, 84, 85, 86, 87, 88, 89–90, 94, 96, 97–98, 100, 101, 102, 105–106, 121, 127, 131–133, 189–191; (Hellenistic) 4, 7–8, 32, 37, 49, 81, 84, 88, 91, 97, 98, 102, 106, 107, 108, 121, 125, 134–135, 191–192, 199, 200, 201; (Roman and Byzantine) 4, 8, 9, 32, 50, 58–59, 73, 75, 88, 98, 102, 103, 108, 109, 122, 125–126, 127–128, 135–136, 137–138, 147, 151, 192, 194–197, 198–200, 201, 202; (Arab) 9, 10, 37, 50, 59, 88, 98, 100, 102, 103, 109–110, 117, 117–118, 119, 122, 126, 128, 140, 141, 145, 204, 205, 216, 217; (Fatimid) 10, 11, 53, 59, 82, 91–92, 144, 145, 205, 212, 216; (Seljuk – Ayyubid) 11, 52, 59–60, 82, 92, 142, 144–145, 146, 205, 217; (Mamluk) 11–12, 12, 13, 37, 50, 53, 60, 92, 122, 141, 142, 145, 146–147, 151–152, 157, 176, 205–206, 211–212, 213, 216, 217, 218, 233; (Ottoman) 13, 18, 50, 60, 92, 110, 122, 123, 143, 147, 148, 152, 207–208, 212, 216, 217;, (19th century) 18, 19, 50, 53, 95, 156, 182–183, 263–265, 267, 286–287, 295, 297, 299
Ethiopia 4, 6, 7, 12, 14, 18, 20, 23, 24, 25–26, 33, 34, 36, 42, 49, 63, 70, 72, 76, 90, 102, 120, 129, 137, 146, 147, 148, 152, 223, 227, 229, 234–235, 265, 277–278
European colonisation 17–20, 83, 152, 159, 160, 163, 164, 165–166, 225, 248, 250, 252, 255–257, 257–261, 265, 274, 275, 276, 277, 278, 279, 280, 285, 294 –300, 300–306

Fatimids 10, 11, 53, 59, 82, 88, 92, 140, 142, 144, 145, 205, 207, 212
Fernando Po 63, 118, 163, 165, 250, 271, 273, 275
Feudalism 82, 190, 199, 204–210, 216, 218, 231–235, 244, 250, 251–252, 252
Fezzan 41, 129–130, 134, 136, 149, 150, 151, 152, 209
Fish and fishing 24, 25, 32, 33, 34, 52, 61, 68, 69, 87, 94, 95, 100, 102, 103, 108, 135, 136, 137, 140, 144, 149, 154, 158, 173, 176, 228, 246, 248, 257–258
France 15, 16, 18, 19, 50, 123, 129, 142, 143, 144, 147, 152, 156, 163, 164, 167, 170, 180, 181, 183, 208, 212, 213, 253,

254, 255, 256, 258, 264, 265, 266, 267, 268, 271, 272, 276, 278, 286, 292, 296, 297, 298, 299, 300, 301, 303, 304, 305
Funduq 118, 141, 142, 144, 212
Funj 12, 146, 229, 263
Fustāt 88, 98, 118

Gambia 6, 15, 18, 55, 62, 99, 121, 128, 159, 163, 163–164, 170, 224, 233, 244, 255, 256, 271, 272, 277
Gao 92, 150, 242, 243
Gathering 3, 5, 21, 27, 28, 32, 47, 51, 52, 53, 67, 116, 220, 231, 269, 270, 274
Germany 18, 19, 20, 156, 258, 266, 279, 283, 293, 296, 297, 298, 299, 301, 302, 303, 305
Ghana (Medieval) 4, 11, 41, 71, 92, 148, 150, 151, 212, 223, 223–224, 224, 229, 242, 243
Gilds 109, 111, 112, 113, 117, 124, 202–203, 215, 246
Glass 88, 97, 105, 106, 110, 114, 131, 135–136, 138, 140, 145, 149, 158, 164, 176, 177, 185
Gold (Northern Africa) 70, 84, 86, 108, 110, 121, 123, 129, 132, 133, 134, 136, 138, 142, 143, 158, 209, 212; (Nubia) 70–71, 72, 105, 106–107, 120, 136, 145, 224; (Ethiopia) 70, 72, 120; (West Africa) 4, 5, 14, 15, 71, 85, 86, 101, 117, 119, 120, 123, 124, 124–125, 141, 148, 149, 151, 152, 154, 155, 157, 158, 159, 160–161, 162, 164, 170, 172, 212, 223–224, 245, 255; (East and Central Africa) 70, 71–72, 72, 85, 99, 112, 175, 176, 177, 178, 179, 180, 185, 224, 226, 252, 302, 303; (South Africa) 20, 284, 285, 295, 296, 297
Gold Coast 15, 18, 92, 123, 154–155, 160–161, 162, 163, 164, 167, 170, 229, 232, 238, 250, 254, 270, 271, 273, 274, 287, 288, 293, 298
Great Britain (Empire) 16, 18–20, 181, 183, 265, 266–267, 274, 275–276, 279, 280, 281, 282–285, 286–288, 290–291, 294–300, 301, 302, 303; (Slave trade) 17–18, 64, 163–164, 165, 167, 170, 183, 184, 254, 255–256, 267–268, 274; (West Africa) 15, 18, 19, 163–164, 170,

253, 254, 255–256, 267–270, 274, 275–276, 285–286, 288, 291–294, 294–295, 298, 299, 300, 301, 304; (South Africa) 16, 19–20, 51, 64, 126, 127, 186–187, 257, 260–261, 282–285, 290–291, 295, 297, 298, 299; (Egypt) 18, 19, 143, 144, 183, 211, 212, 213, 264, 265, 295, 297, 298, 299, 300; (East Africa) 181, 184, 277, 279, 280, 281, 291, 297, 299, 300, 301, 302; (Central Africa) 20, 298, 302–303, 305
Great Zimbabwe 6, 55, 87, 93, 177, 224, 225
Greeks 7–8, 8, 9, 37, 38, 39, 74, 75, 76, 81–82, 84, 86, 88, 90, 91, 102, 107, 108–109, 118, 121, 122, 128, 132, 134, 137, 138, 140, 193, 194, 195, 199, 200, 209

Hausaland (Agriculture) 34, 43–44, 62, 225; (Trade) 149, 152, 155, 156, 157, 172; (Merchants) 119, 120, 211, 243, 246, 271; (Industry) 73, 92, 95, 99; (Towns) 55, 56, 155–156, 242; (States) 5, 152, 223, 228–229, 229, 233
Hides and skins 68, 93, 97, 100, 146, 159, 164, 176, 182, 185, 186, 187, 227, 238, 239, 241, 279, 284
Horn of Africa 12, 14, 24, 25, 26, 28, 33, 34, 69, 122, 132, 133, 135, 137, 138, 146, 147, 148, 174–175, 176, 178, 184, 215, 223
Horses 5, 13, 28, 30, 33, 38, 39, 56, 62, 101, 127, 128, 138, 145, 149, 157, 159, 171, 224, 233
Hunting 3, 5, 21, 26, 27, 28, 32, 47, 51, 53, 61, 68, 69, 116, 120, 158, 181, 182, 184, 185, 186, 187, 190, 220, 226, 231, 235, 238, 241, 246, 258, 274
Ibn Battūta 85, 92, 99, 129, 156, 211
Ibn Khaldūn 40, 82, 98, 214, 218
Ife 55, 85, 87–88, 88, 114, 157, 223, 224
India and Indians 7, 14, 15, 18, 64, 75, 82, 92, 99, 126, 135, 137, 138, 139, 144, 146, 147, 164, 175, 176, 178, 180, 181, 183, 191, 214, 217, 224, 249, 252, 260, 278, 284, 290, 291, 295, 299
Indonesia 7, 29, 64, 114, 137, 138, 139, 147, 171, 175, 257, 274
Iqṭāʿ 50, 59, 60, 63, 205–207, 207–208, 232

Iron 4, 5, 26, 27, 72, 73, 74–78, 81, 84, 85, 86, 87, 105, 106, 110, 112, 113, 116, 117, 121, 124, 132, 133, 138, 141, 149, 158, 164, 172, 176, 177, 182, 184, 185, 187, 212, 233, 259, 267, 285, 292

Irrigation 9, 13, 22, 32, 37, 39, 40, 41–42, 49, 56, 59, 75, 189, 191, 192, 197, 221, 230, 263, 265

Italy 18, 19, 20, 91, 99, 116, 123, 127, 135, 136, 141, 142, 143, 144, 147, 152, 156, 196, 199, 209, 212, 216, 217, 266, 277, 278, 299

Ivory 32, 70, 74, 84, 93, 101, 101–102, 120, 133, 134, 135, 136, 137, 138, 141, 144, 145, 146, 148, 149, 153, 154, 155, 157, 158, 159, 162, 164, 166, 172, 176, 177, 178, 180, 181, 182, 183, 184, 185, 186, 187, 225, 226, 239, 245, 246, 251, 252, 276, 279, 304

Ivory Coast 25, 32, 71, 162, 164, 165, 257, 271, 273, 287, 298, 304

Ja-Ja 229, 238, 275–276, 293

Jenne 33, 83, 92, 99, 119, 150, 154, 157, 243, 245, 246

Jewellery 81, 84–85, 86, 88, 93, 105, 133, 138, 149, 185

Jews 82, 84, 110, 119, 126, 139, 141, 142, 198, 212, 214, 250

Kanem-Bornu 5, 12, 99, 101, 118, 120, 151, 152, 155, 159, 209, 223

Kano 55, 56, 95, 99, 149, 152, 155–156, 223

Keira sultanate 12, 232

Kenya 19, 279, 280

Kerma 4, 87, 133

Khoikhoi 5, 16, 27–28, 33, 64, 74, 77, 84, 97, 101, 128, 186, 238, 258, 261

Kikuyu 34, 48, 118, 183

Kilwa 87, 92, 99, 101, 123, 175, 176, 177, 178, 180, 181, 182, 184, 224

Kola nuts 5, 117, 119, 148, 149, 155, 157, 226, 242

Kongo 14, 56, 99, 112, 158, 165–166, 224, 228, 251

Kordofan 12, 183

Kumasi 18, 55, 113, 157, 172, 242

Kush 4, 37, 71, 89, 90, 221, 224

Lagos 162, 267, 269, 270, 274, 277, 292

Land-holding (Ancient Egypt) 49–50, 56, 96, 106, 189, 190, 191; (Carthage) 50, 56–57, 106, 193–194; (Hellenistic Egypt) 125, 192; (Roman Africa) 50, 57–59, 108, 109, 125, 137, 195, 196, 197, 198, 199, 200, 201; (Muslim Africa) 50, 59–60, 62, 63, 126, 204, 205, 206, 207, 208, 210, 215, 217, 218, 232, 263, 264, 278; (Sub-Saharan) 47–49, 61, 63, 120, 221, 222, 225, 228, 229, 230, 232, 234, 235, 236, 237, 239, 242, 270, 271, 276, 277, 278, 288; (Colonial) 16, 51–52, 63, 64, 165, 180, 186, 252, 255, 256, 257, 258, 259, 260, 261, 267, 279, 282, 287–288, 301, 302, 303, 304, 305, 306

Leather 84, 85, 94, 98, 100–101, 105, 110, 137, 142, 148, 149, 156, 187, 259, 285

Legitimate commerce 17, 20, 267, 268, 269, 274, 275, 276, 280

Leopold II 19, 300, 303

Liberia 18, 159, 162, 256, 257, 306

Libya 19, 22, 23, 41, 73, 116, 140, 151, 192, 246

Livingstone, David 30, 79, 80

Loango 158, 166, 224

Luanda 15, 124, 166, 169, 252

Lunda and Luba states 5, 166, 182, 221, 223, 224, 228, 276

Madagascar 7, 29, 41, 64, 175, 181, 183

Mahdi (Muhammad Ahmad) 211

Mahdia 10, 91–92, 140, 142

Mali (Medieval) 5, 85, 92, 118, 119, 124, 148, 150, 151, 152, 221, 223, 223–224, 243

Malindi 14, 176, 177, 178, 180

Markets and fairs 117–119, 120, 121, 124, 136, 141, 148, 157, 158, 179, 180, 181, 187, 202, 225, 226, 228, 235, 244

Marxist views 171, 191, 197–198, 201, 206, 218, 230, 231, 235–236, 240, 295–296

Mascarenes 15, 180–181, 278

Medicine 22, 32, 38, 88, 97, 98, 108, 110, 132, 135, 137, 138, 144, 147, 300

Memphis 3, 84, 89, 192

Menelik II 18, 234, 277, 278

Meroe 4, 12, 35, 41, 71, 76, 85, 87, 90, 135, 139

Mogadishu 99, 123, 175, 176

Mombasa 14, 92, 176, 177, 178, 180, 183, 224, 249

Money 86, 110, 120–125, 155–156, 158, 175, 176, 177, 195, 196, 197, 198, 202, 205, 207, 213, 214, 218, 226, 227, 228, 235, 236, 239, 241, 243, 245, 260, 264, 266, 276, 286, 292, 293

Monsoon 7, 34, 127, 137, 176, 178, 249

Morocco 11, 13, 14, 19, 70, 92, 97, 98, 100, 102, 141, 143, 144, 149, 150, 152, 158, 209, 211, 213, 215, 224, 229, 243, 265, 266

Mozambique 14, 15, 19, 27, 50, 64, 92, 167, 168, 178, 181, 182, 183, 249, 252, 285, 303, 305

Muhammad the Prophet 9, 10, 98, 210, 211, 214

Muhammad ʻAli 18, 50, 263–264

Muscat 14, 180, 181

Mwene-Mutapa 70, 71, 72, 176, 177, 179, 180, 224, 226, 228, 229, 239

Napata 4, 136

Natal 261, 283–284, 285, 290, 291, 299

Naucratis 7, 74, 88, 118, 121, 132

Netherlands 15, 16, 30, 32, 45, 77, 117, 126, 128, 144, 147, 163, 164, 166, 167, 170, 186, 191, 253, 254, 255, 257–260, 275, 282

Nguni 6, 17, 61, 185, 186, 222, 223, 226, 227, 228, 237, 259, 260

Niger 5, 19, 25, 30, 36, 71, 77, 103, 119, 127, 128, 134, 135, 150, 152, 154, 155, 157, 161, 162, 165, 172, 221, 223, 228, 238, 242, 244, 268, 270, 275, 293, 300, 301

Nigeria 18, 271, 272, 273, 274, 287, 288, 301

Nile 3, 4, 7, 8, 10, 12, 13, 21–22, 23, 24, 25, 28, 29, 33, 35, 36–37, 41, 52, 54, 70, 72, 74, 76, 87, 89, 90, 98, 100, 102, 117, 121, 127, 131, 132, 135, 136, 137, 145, 146, 183, 189, 221, 222, 233

Nilotic-speakers (Lwo, Masai, Nuer, etc.) 6, 33, 34, 48, 76, 93, 100, 112, 118, 129, 146, 174, 175, 221, 222, 229, 237

North Africa (Maghrib) (Prehistoric) 69, 100, 133, 192–193; (Greek) 8, 9, 38–39, 90; (Carthage) 8, 9, 32, 39, 50, 56–57, 76, 77, 81, 84, 87, 90–91, 97, 98, 100, 101, 103, 106, 108, 118, 121, 128, 133–134, 148, 193–194, 199, 202, 227; (Roman, Vandal, Byzantine) 8– 9, 38–40, 40, 41, 50, 57–58, 60, 72, 76, 77, 86, 90–91, 91, 103, 106, 108, 116, 121, 122, 125, 127, 129, 135, 136–137, 140, 148, 194, 196, 197, 198, 201; (Muslim) 9, 10, 10–11, 13, 40–41, 50, 59, 60, 70, 71, 84, 88, 91–92, 96, 98, 100, 102, 103, 110, 119, 122, 123, 129, 140, 141, 142–143, 143–144, 148, 149, 150, 151, 152, 154, 155, 156, 158, 206, 207, 208– 210, 211, 212–213, 215, 216, 217, 229, 232, 233, 242–243, 246, 265–266; (Colonial) 19, 152, 256, 266, 267, 297, 299

Nubia 4, 10, 12, 22, 23, 24, 35, 37, 48– 49, 56, 70–71, 72, 90, 91, 92, 102, 105, 108, 122, 132, 133, 135, 136, 145–146, 152, 221, 224, 226, 227,

Nupe 119, 155, 156, 229, 243

Old Calabar 165, 244, 246, 275, 277

Olives 22, 37, 38, 39, 86, 87, 136, 137, 138, 142, 194, 258

Ostrich feathers 133, 134, 145, 148, 149, 153, 157, 187, 233, 283, 284

Ottomans 10, 13, 18, 60, 92, 111, 122, 123, 126, 143, 146, 147, 152, 180, 182, 183, 207–208, 211, 212, 213, 216, 217, 263, 264

Oyo 5, 223, 224, 228, 229, 233

Palm products (Coconut) 29, 62, 97, 103, 176, 183, 279, 304; (Oil palm) 25, 96, 97, 99, 103, 138, 154, 154–155, 157, 158, 166, 231, 269, 270–271, 272, 274, 275, 276, 277, 279, 285, 286, 287, 297, 304

Paper 110, 144, 156, 213, 285

Papyrus 21, 88, 97, 100, 106, 131, 135, 138

Park, Mungo 34, 36, 42, 45, 62, 77, 79, 99, 103, 124, 163–164, 170, 224, 237, 242, 244

Pastoralists (Nomads, Semi-nomads) (In general) 32–34, 51, 53, 55, 93, 94, 97, 112, 116, 129, 185, 206–207, 220, 223, 237, 238, 241; (Arab – Bedouin) 10, 11, 12, 13, 40–41, 50, 60, 129, 129– 130, 145, 146, 151, 152, 206, 208, 210; (Berber) 8, 33, 39, 40–41, 57, 60, 129,

134, 148, 151, 158, 192–193, 194, 206, 233, 237; (Cushitic-speakers) 6, 27, 33, 63, 129, 145, 229; (Dutch) 187, 241, 258–259; (Fulani) 28, 34, 61, 152, 164, 223, 238; (Herero) 237; (Khoikhoi) 33, 34, 238, 258; (Nilotic-speakers) 6, 34, 48, 49, 52, 112, 118, 221, 237

Peasants 10, 13, 39–40, 56, 57–60, 63, 95, 180, 189, 190, 194, 195, 196, 197, 206, 217, 234, 235, 263, 263–264, 266, 279, 280, 285, 287

Pepper 15, 137, 146, 147, 148, 157, 159, 162, 251

Persia 7, 9, 29, 40, 74, 82, 98, 135, 138, 139, 175, 176, 183, 204

Persian Gulf 7, 14, 103, 135, 139, 144, 174, 175, 178, 180

Phoenicians 8, 23, 38, 74, 81, 88, 90, 91, 98, 118, 121, 133, 192, 193, 227

Piracy 129, 134, 135, 140, 142, 142–143, 143–144, 202, 208, 213, 215, 216

Plough 37, 42, 45, 49, 72, 79, 128, 257

Polanyi, Karl 118, 200, 235, 239–240

Population 3, 5, 13, 22, 23, 26, 27, 30, 34, 36, 37, 39, 40, 47–48, 49, 51, 51–56, 56, 58, 60, 61, 64, 68, 126, 128, 137, 154, 158, 164, 166–169, 176, 179, 194, 195, 201, 208, 210, 220, 221, 222, 225, 227, 236, 242, 243, 248, 251, 253, 255, 259, 284, 285, 287, 298, 301

Porcelain 144, 175, 176

Portugal 13–15, 16, 18, 19, 29–30, 30, 49, 50, 71, 72, 92, 96, 97, 103, 123, 124, 143, 146–147, 152, 158–162, 164, 165–166, 167, 175, 176, 177, 177–180, 181, 182, 183, 224, 227, 248–253, 255, 267, 303, 305

Pottery 5, 27, 28, 68, 70, 76, 81, 86–88, 105, 108, 112, 113, 132, 136, 137, 138, 145, 149, 158, 176, 177

Precious stones 19, 136, 138, 144, 179, 195, 284, 285, 291

Pygmies 5, 27

Rainfall 8, 34, 36, 38, 39, 41, 42, 43, 44, 52, 68, 94, 127, 192, 221, 225, 258, 261, 310

Red Sea (Trade) 14, 103, 133, 135, 136, 137, 138, 144, 145, 147, 211, 290; (Ports) 135, 136, 137, 138, 139, 145, 146, 147,

Rhodes, C. J. 20, 298, 300, 302

Rhodesia 20, 72, 298, 302, 303, 305

Rostovtseff, Michael 199–200

Royal African Company 163, 254

Rubber 187, 226, 268, 274, 304, 305

Sahara 4, 7, 8, 10, 11, 19, 22, 23, 24, 26, 29, 33, 35, 38, 41, 42, 73, 76, 87, 97, 123, 126, 128, 129, 134, 141, 142, 148–153, 154, 155, 156, 157, 158, 159, 215, 216, 217, 223, 233, 237, 243, 245, 246

Saladin 11, 59, 82, 92, 144

Salt 86, 87, 94, 95, 96–97, 101, 108, 112, 117, 119, 121, 140, 149, 151, 154, 155, 157, 158, 164, 166, 173, 177, 181, 182, 184, 187, 195, 210, 223, 224, 245, 248

San 5, 16, 27, 32, 77, 220, 238, 258, 259

São Thomé 63, 163, 165, 249, 250, 251, 271, 273

Seljuks 10, 11, 144, 205, 217

Semitic-speakers 25–26, 28

Senegal 5, 15, 85, 89, 119, 127, 128, 158, 159, 163, 164, 224, 233, 254, 255, 256, 257, 268, 271, 272, 277, 298, 299–300

Serfdom 63, 64, 206, 232, 234, 235

Shells 84, 121, 123–124, 149, 155–156, 158, 176, 177, 226, 227, 292

Sicily 7, 8, 9, 10, 98, 108, 134, 140, 141, 142, 193

Sierra Leone 14, 18, 55, 159, 255–256, 268, 274, 275, 294

Sijilmāsa 11, 150, 151, 207, 215

Silver 8, 70, 84, 85, 100, 121, 123, 124, 132, 133, 136, 158, 171, 251

Slave Coast 162, 164, 165, 244, 257

Slave trade (In general) 16, 20, 30, 54, 55, 61, 63, 130, 134, 138, 154, 156, 157, 163, 166–167, 170–173, 184, 186, 223, 226, 244, 245, 248, 249, 253, 271, 276–277, 288; (North Africa) 140, 143, 208, 212; (Nubia) 133, 145, 146, 152, 226; (Sahara) 134, 148, 149, 149–150, 152, 153; (Europe) 11, 13, 141; (Far East) 64; (Upper Guinea) 15, 158, 159, 160, 163, 163–164, 170, 249, 255; (Lower Guinea) 15, 19, 162, 163, 164–165, 167, 168, 170–171,

226, 231, 246, 250, 267, 269, 275, 276, 277; (Congo and Angola) 15, 165–166, 167, 168, 169, 250, 251, 267; (Mozambique) 15, 64, 167, 168, 181, 252; (East Africa) 64, 103, 133, 138, 146, 152, 166, 176, 179, 180–184, 275, 279, 291; (Abolition) 17–18, 64, 153, 165, 182–183, 184, 260, 261, 265, 267–268, 269, 275, 279, 291, 299, 301, 306; (Settlements for ex-slaves) 18, 255–256, 274

Slavery (In general) 61, 63, 81, 108–109, 125, 141, 186, 197, 198, 211, 222, 224, 229, 233, 234, 236, 237, 243, 300; (Agricultural) 38, 43–44, 46, 56–57, 58, 59, 61–62, 63, 64, 134, 149, 162–163, 165, 180, 183, 199, 231, 232, 250, 270, 276, 277, 279, 288; (Industrial) 106–107, 108–109, 109, 110, 114; (Domestic) 33, 59, 182, 194; (Military) 11, 13, 59, 141, 152, 162, 182, 183, 205, 206, 207, 209, 224, 229; (Ostentatious) 62, 162; (Governmental) 209–210, 229, 238, 275; (Porterage and commercial) 119, 128, 162, 184, 276, 279

Sofala 95, 99, 175, 176, 178, 179, 224, 249

Sokoto 43, 44, 55, 62, 152, 223, 233

Songhai 148, 150, 151, 152, 213, 223, 224, 229, 243

Spain 8, 9, 11, 13, 15, 16, 18, 19, 40, 59, 69, 98, 100, 110, 119, 121, 123, 133, 140, 142, 143, 144, 163, 193, 216

Spices 14, 117, 132, 138, 140, 141, 142, 144, 146, 147, 149, 156, 176, 178, 192

Spirits 164, 171, 186, 187, 249, 285

State economic functions and controls (In general) 9, 139, 191–192, 194–195, 196, 197, 198, 199, 200, 201, 205, 225, 227, 230, 235, 240, 253, 260, 263–264, 275, 277–278; (Agriculture) 37, 39, 192, 196, 230, 252, 257, 263, 266, 276, 277, 282–283; (Banks) 125, 276; (Corvées) 56, 61, 128, 197, 230, 239, 263; (Forestry) 109; (Gilds) 109, 111, 112, 202–203; (Industry) 82, 106, 107, 108, 110, 113–114, 145, 195, 196, 227, 252, 259, 263, 266, 275, 276, 277, 278; (Land) 48–

49, 50, 58–59, 63, 192, 195, 218, 225, 234, 235, 250, 252, 258, 259, 260, 282, 304–305; (Money and prices) 121–122, 124, 146, 196, 214, 276; (Public works) 89, 105, 225, 230, 239, 263, 264, 265, 276, 278; (Trade) 97, 118, 120, 129, 133, 135, 137, 146, 150, 159, 160, 161, 165, 166, 179, 189–190, 192, 195, 211–213, 216, 223, 224, 225–227, 230–231, 239, 244, 249, 250, 253, 254, 255, 259, 260–261, 264, 275, 276

Suez Canal 290–291, 295, 299

Swahili 92, 114, 175, 181, 183, 184, 224–225

Syria 8, 56, 74, 88, 102, 132, 138, 140, 142, 144, 192, 206, 210

Taxation and tribute (Pharaonic) 56; (Hellenistic) 192; (Roman) 58, 125, 139, 192, 195, 195–196, 196, 197, 198, 199, 201, 202; (Muslim) 10, 50, 59–60, 111, 143, 145, 204, 205–206, 207–208, 209, 209–210, 212, 213, 218, 263, 264, 265, 266, 278; (Sub-Saharan) 49, 63, 120, 165, 179, 180, 223, 224, 225, 226, 227, 228, 229, 231, 232, 234, 235, 236, 237, 239, 242, 244, 275, 276, 277; (Colonial) 51, 160, 178, 250, 261, 279, 285, 287, 298, 301, 304

Technology (Industrial) 67–83, 86, 89, 90, 93, 99, 101, 102, 103, 107, 108, 118, 127, 171, 172, 192, 211, 216, 220, 227, 233, 237, 239, 243, 245, 259, 263, 276, 284, 286; (Agricultural) 37–38, 42–43, 51, 60, 68, 72, 77, 81, 101, 116, 124, 230, 257

Timber and precious woods 101, 133, 134, 135, 136, 138, 141, 144, 145, 176, 190, 212

Timbuktu 18, 33, 83, 92, 99, 118, 119, 149, 150, 151, 154, 155, 157 242, 243, 246

Tin 73, 88, 133, 136, 138, 159, 211, 233

Trading peoples (Chokwe, Imbangela, Nyamwezi, Yao, etc.) 112, 120, 181–182, 184, 225, 246

Transport and communications 29, 116, 117, 118, 126, 127–130, 133, 140, 148, 160, 162, 183, 186, 187, 190, 196, 210, 221, 225, 226, 228, 229, 249, 252, 253,